Ibero-Asian Creoles

Creole Language Library (CLL)

A book series presenting descriptive and theoretical studies designed to add significantly to the data available on pidgin and creole languages.
All CLL publications are anonymously and internationally refereed.

For an overview of all books published in this series, please see
http://benjamins.com/catalog/cll

Editors

Miriam Meyerhoff
University of Auckland

Umberto Ansaldo
The University of Hong Kong

Editorial Advisory Board

Mervyn C. Alleyne
Kingston, Jamaica

Marlyse Baptista
Ann Arbor, USA

George L. Huttar
Dallas, USA

John Holm
Coimbra, Portugal

Silvia Kouwenberg
Kingston, Jamaica

Susanne Michaelis
Leipzig, Germany

Salikoko S. Mufwene
Chicago, USA

Pieter Muysken
Nijmegen, The Netherlands

Peter Mühlhäusler
Adelaide, Australia

Shobha Satyanath
Delhi, India

John Victor Singler
New York, USA

Norval Smith
Amsterdam, The Netherlands

Sarah G. Thomason
Ann Arbor, USA

Tonjes Veenstra
Berlin, Germany

Volume 46

Ibero-Asian Creoles. Comparative Perspectives
Edited by Hugo C. Cardoso, Alan N. Baxter and Mário Pinharanda Nunes

Ibero-Asian Creoles

Comparative Perspectives

Edited by

Hugo C. Cardoso
Universidade de Coimbra

Alan N. Baxter
Universidade Federal da Bahia

Mário Pinharanda Nunes
Universidade de Macau

John Benjamins Publishing Company
Amsterdam / Philadelphia

The paper used in this publication meets the minimum requirements of the American National Standard for Information Sciences – Permanence of Paper for Printed Library Materials, ANSI z39.48-1984.

Library of Congress Cataloging-in-Publication Data

Ibero-Asian Creoles : comparative perspectives / edited by Hugo C. Cardoso, Alan N.
    Baxter, Mário Pinharanda Nunes.
p.   cm. (Creole Language Library, ISSN 0920-9026 ; v. 46)
Includes bibliographical references and index.
1. Creole dialects--Asia. 2. Creole dialects, Portuguese--Asia. 3. Creole dialects,
    Spanish--Asia. 4. Languages in contact--Asia. 5. Iberian language--Asia.
    6. Comparative linguistics--Asia. I. Cardoso, Hugo C. II. Baxter, Alan N.
    III. Pinharanda Nunes, Mário.
PM7834.A7I23   2012
417'.22095--dc23   2012028999
ISBN 978 90 272 5269 2 (Hb ; alk. paper)
ISBN 978 90 272 7320 8 (Eb)

© 2012 – John Benjamins B.V.
No part of this book may be reproduced in any form, by print, photoprint, microfilm, or any other means, without written permission from the publisher.

John Benjamins Publishing Co. · P.O. Box 36224 · 1020 ME Amsterdam · The Netherlands
John Benjamins North America · P.O. Box 27519 · Philadelphia PA 19118-0519 · USA

Table of contents

Acknowledgements	VII
List of abbreviations	IX
Introduction Hugo C. Cardoso, Alan N. Baxter and Mário Pinharanda Nunes	1
Notes on the phonology and lexicon of some Indo-Portuguese creoles J. Clancy Clements	15
A closer look at the post-nominal genitive in Asian Creole Portuguese Alan N. Baxter and Augusta Bastos	47
Luso-Asian comparatives in comparison Hugo C. Cardoso	81
Measuring substrate influence: Word order features in Ibero-Asian Creoles Ian Smith	125
Indefinite terms in Ibero-Asian Creoles Eeva Sippola	149
Maskin, maski, masque… in the Spanish and Portuguese creoles of Asia: Same particle, same provenance? Nancy Vázquez Veiga and Mauro A. Fernández	181
Nenang, nino, nem não, ni no: Similarities and differences Mauro A. Fernández	205
Bilug in Zamboangueño Chavacano: The genericization of a substrate numeral classifier Carl Rubino	239
Portuguese pidgin and Chinese Pidgin English in the Canton trade Stephen Matthews and Michelle Li	263

Traces of superstrate verb inflection in Makista
and other Asian-Portuguese creoles 289
Mário Pinharanda Nunes

Mindanao Chabacano and other 'mixed creoles':
Sourcing the morphemic components 327
Anthony P. Grant

Language index 365

Location index 369

General index 371

Acknowledgements

The origin of this book lies in an international conference entitled "Ibero-Asian Creoles: Comparative perspectives", held at the University of Macau on the 28th and 29th of October, 2010. This was the first scholarly meeting entirely dedicated to the Portuguese- and Spanish-lexified Creoles of Asia and, while some of the papers presented there are now included in this book, others were added at a later date. We are particularly indebted to the Faculty of Social Sciences and Humanities for its generous support of the 2010 conference, and to all the participants, who turned it into such a stimulating event. A special word of thanks goes to the University of Macau, which funded the research project "Portuguese-based Creole and Semi-Creole languages: typology, grammatical analysis and language endangerment" and thereby enabled both the conference and this book to take shape.

A volume of this nature is truly a collaborative effort. We wish to thank all the authors for their professionalism, dedication, and their understanding when asked to make adjustments in the interest of uniformity. We were also fortunate enough to count on the generosity of a host of colleagues who collaborated as anonymous reviewers or consultants; their comments and suggestions have made this volume much more solid. Finally, we are also very grateful to the editors of the *Creole Language Library* series, Umberto Ansaldo and Miriam Meyerhoff, and all the staff at John Benjamins for their constant support throughout the production of this book.

In addition to the University of Macau, which supported his research activities until 2011, Hugo C. Cardoso also wishes to thank the Fundação Oriente, whose sponsorship allowed him to carry out the final stages of the editorial work.

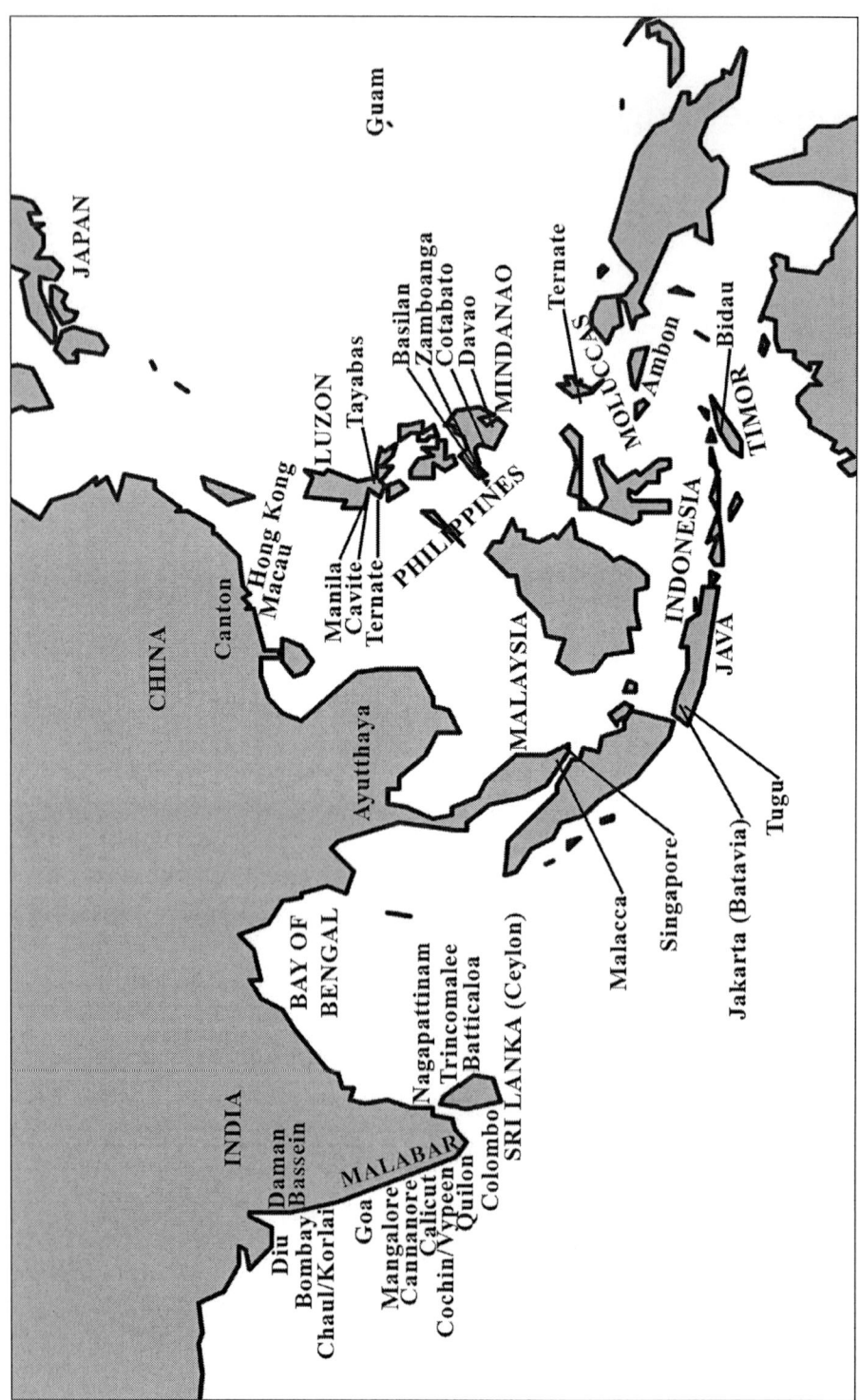

Principal Asian and Pacific locations mentioned in the volume

List of abbreviations

1. Languages

ACP	Asian Creole Portuguese
ANG	Angolar Creole Portuguese
BATT	Batticaloa Creole Portuguese
BER	Berbice Dutch
CANN	Cannanore Creole Portuguese
CHA	Chavacano/Chabacano; Philippine Creole Spanish
COT	Cotabato Creole Spanish; Cotabateño
CPE	Chinese Pidgin English; China Coast Pidgin
DAM	Daman Creole Portuguese
DIU	Diu Creole Portuguese
ENG	English
FR	French
HCE	Hawaii Creole English
HOK	Hokkien
IP	Indo-Portuguese
IPC	Indo-Portuguese Creole
JAV	Javanese
KOR	Korlai Creole Portuguese
MAC	Macau Creole Portuguese; Makista/Maquista
MAL	Malay
MALC	Malacca Creole Portuguese; Papia Kristang
MALM	Malayalam
MIN	Mindanao Creole Spanish
MPP	Macau Pidgin Portuguese
PAP	Papiamentu
PTG	Portuguese
SAR	Saramaccan
SLP	Sri Lanka Creole Portuguese
SP	Spanish
STM	São Tomé Creole Portuguese; Sãotomense
TAG	Tagalog
TUG	Tugu Creole Portuguese
ZAM	Zamboanga Creole Spanish; Zamboangueño

2. Grammatical concepts

1	first person	IMP	imperative
2	second person	INCL	inclusive
3	third person	IND	indicative
ABL	ablative	INDF	indefinite
ACC	accusative	INF	infinitive
ADJ	adjective	INS	instrumental
ADP	adposition	IOBJ	indirect object
ADV	adverb(ial)	IPFV	imperfective
ART	article	IRR	irrealis
AUX	auxiliary	L1	first language
CAUS	causative	L2	second language
CF	counterfactual (particle)	LIG	ligature
CLF	classifier	LOC	locative
CMPR	comparative	LP	linking particle
CNJ	conjunction	M	masculine
COMP	complementizer	MED	medial
CONC	concessive	N	noun
COND	conditional	NCL	numeral classifier
COP	copula	NEG	negation, negative
CORREL	correlative	NL	numeral linker
CTPL	contemplated aspect	NOM	nominative
DAT	dative	NP	noun phrase
DEM	demonstrative	NPCT	non-punctual
DET	determiner	NPM	noun phrase marker
DIM	diminutive	NPST	non-past
DIST	distal	NT	neuter
DP	determiner phrase	OBJ	object
EMPH	emphatic (particle)	OBL	oblique
EXCL	exclusive	OV	object-verb
EXST	existential	PA	personal article
F	feminine	PASS	passive
FIL	filler	PFV	perfective
FOC	focus	PL	plural
FUT	future	PNG	post-nominal genitive
GEN	genitive	POSS	possessive
HAB	habitual	POT	potential
HBL	habilitative	PRED	predicative
HON	honorific	PRF	perfect
HUM	human	PRO	pronoun

PROG	progressive	SBJ	subject
PROX	proximal/proximate	SG	singular
PRS	present	SLA	second language acquisition
PRT	(discourse) particle	SOV	subject-object-verb
PST	past	SUB	subordinator
PTCP	participle	SVO	subject-verb-object
Q	question particle/marker	TAM	tense-aspect-mood
QNT	quantifier	TL	target language
RD	reduplicated	V	verb
RECP	reciprocal	VP	verb phrase
REL	relative	VSO	verb-subject-object

Introduction

Hugo C. Cardoso, Alan N. Baxter and Mário Pinharanda Nunes

1. Introduction

Since 1498, the year European expansionism reached Asian shores, contact between Iberian languages and Asian languages has taken place along a wide coastal stretch of continental and insular Asia, from India in the west to Japan in the East. Accompanying the formation of new communities and identities, this historical process gave rise to a string of contact varieties which attracted the interest of early scholars of language contact such as Hugo Schuchardt, Adolfo Coelho, Sebastião Rodolfo Dalgado, Emilio Teza and Leite de Vasconcelos.

In many ways, current work on Ibero-Asian creoles is the cumulative result not only of these pioneering studies but in particular of research that gathered momentum in the second half of the 20th century. For the Portuguese lexified creoles in East Asia, this work is exemplified by key publications such as Batalha (1953, 1958), Thompson (1960), Morais Barbosa (1968), Ferreira (1978), and Pinharanda Nunes (2011), all on Macau Creole. Key sources focusing on Southeast Asian creoles include Knowlton (1964), Hancock (1969, 1973, 1975) and Baxter (1988) on Malacca, and Wallace (1978) and Maurer (2012) on Batavia/Tugu. Further afield, for South Asia, Theban's (1977) work on Korlai Creole was followed by the book-length studies of Smith (1977) and Jackson (1990) on Sri Lanka Creole, Clements (1996) on Korlai Creole and, more recently, Cardoso (2009) on Diu Creole. In parallel, a series of articles have addressed central issues relating to these varieties, including Smith (1979, 1984), Tomás (1992a), Clements (2000), Clements & Koontz-Garboden (2002), Cardoso (2006, 2010), and Luís (2008). General overviews of the Asian-Portuguese creoles can be found in Holm (1989), Tomás (1992b), Pereira (2006) and Clements (2009).

The trajectory of modern linguistic research on the Spanish-lexified Philippine creoles is similar, although it began earlier (cf. Santos y Gómez 1924). Among many examples here we may point to a chronological sequence of key work as of the 1950s, by McKaughan (1954), Whinnom (1956), Batalha (1960), Riego de Dios (1976), Ing (1968), Llamado (1969), Frake (1971),

Forman (1972) and more recent work by Lipski (1988), Fernández (2001, 2006), Steinkrüger (2008), Romanillos (2006), Sippola (2006, 2011) and Vázquez Veiga & Fernández (2006).

Beyond the study of the Ibero-Asian creoles, there has been of late a renewed focus on the general phenomenon of language contact in Asia. This includes, for example, the publication of the linguistic atlas by Wurm et al. (1996), a dedicated issue of the *Journal of Pidgin and Creole Languages* (Ansaldo 2010) and the inclusion of a significant number of Asian entries in the upcoming *Atlas of Pidgin and Creole Structures* (Michaelis et al., *forthc.*) – see also Ansaldo (2009) for an overview of the phenomenon and references to prior work. Nonetheless, contact languages of Asia and the Pacific remain less prominent than their Atlantic and American counterparts in scholarly publications in the field of Creole Studies; this is particularly true of the Ibero-Asian creoles and, to a lesser extent, the Iberian-lexified creoles in general (see e.g. Arends 2002; Parkvall 2002). As a consequence, evidence from these languages and language communities has been underrepresented in theory building. However, those acquainted with the Ibero-Asian creoles believe that these languages and their specific socio-historical circumstances stand to make an enormous contribution to our understanding of the process of language contact in general, and have the potential to challenge many of the assumptions built largely on Atlantic evidence, much as Western Pacific pidgins and creoles have already challenged mainstream dogma through such works as, among others, Sankoff & Laberge (1973), Mühlhäusler (1980), Siegel (1987), Keesing (1988) and Meyerhoff (2008). On the one hand, the Ibero-Asian creoles resulted from linguistic encounters which were typologically very different from those of the Atlantic sphere, defined by rather different social and demographic patterns. On the other hand, these creoles have typically coexisted with their ancestor languages for very long periods of time, thus posing the question of how to articulate the potential influence of the languages in their ecology (and eventual changes in that ecology) with their diachronic drift.

Many of the Ibero-Asian creoles are now extinct, in particular those lexically-based on Portuguese. However, we do avail of sizeable historical records for a number of them and, in addition, fresh descriptive work has been produced in the recent past for varieties which are still vital. The stage therefore seems set for researchers to embark on in-depth, collaborative comparative work aimed at uncovering similarities and differences between them, historical continuities and discontinuities, and in the process bring to the fore new insights on processes of language contact typical of Asian environments.

With that in mind, specialists on the Ibero-Asian creoles were challenged to produce studies which integrate data from their language(s) of expertise and others, resulting in the contributions to this volume[1]. More often than not, the process involved intense exchanges of primary data and/or analyses, cementing networks of collaboration which are likely to go on producing results in the future. The authors engage in in-depth comparative studies of various issues, contrasting data from their own language(s) of expertise with other Ibero-Asian creoles and beyond, often resorting to recent typological insights and methodology. This type of cross-linguistic analysis allows scholarly progress on many fronts, including the reconstruction of past stages of these languages, the explanation of similarities and differences among them, the identification and consolidation of typological/taxonomic clusters, or the assessment of the linguistic effects of different ecologies.

2. Portuguese, Spanish and Iberian-lexified creoles in Asia

As the precursors of European overseas expansion in the 15th century, the Portuguese were the first to reach the shores of Asia in 1498, after having successfully rounded the Cape of Good Hope. Moving eastwards from their original base at Cochin, in South-western India, they quickly established a cohesive network of trading posts reaching as far as Japan and Insular Asia, supported by a few official strongholds and several more or less unofficial settlements scattered along the Asian coastline. The Portuguese language, carried by traders, missionaries, mercenaries and camp followers, attained wide currency in the region, as attested not only by the numerous loanwords in Asian languages (see Dalgado 1913) but also by several Portuguese and non-Portuguese archival sources (see Lopes 1936), and the wide geographical spread of known Portuguese-based creoles.

The actual makeup of some 16th-/17th-century Portuguese settlements in Asia (such as those in the Moluccas) remains obscure, or is just beginning to attract solid research (such as that of Ayutthaya, in Thailand; see Bernardes de Carvalho 2012). Other cases are better-known. Among these, there were a few large settlements with a considerable European population (such as Goa or Bassein in India) but otherwise, as explained in Baxter (1996: 300), they typically "consisted of a small number of *reinóis* [i.e. Europe-born Portuguese] (usually a *feitor* (the commercial agent of the crown) priests, merchants and possibly soldiers), some of these being *casados* [i.e. settlers], and a larger number of *mestiços* [mixed-race individuals], native Christians and slaves", normally a relative minority among a majority of speakers of the region's dominant languages. Beyond these crown settlements, Portuguese-speaking missionaries and *lançados* (independent traders or mercenaries) operated in an even wider area.

This is the basic socio-historical setting in which Portuguese-lexified creoles formed. In their heyday, they were spoken in many locations of Western and Eastern

India, all the way to the Bay of Bengal, Ceylon (modern-day Sri Lanka), the Strait of Malacca and Singapore, Java, the Moluccas, Timor, and Macau. Portuguese maritime hegemony in Asia was challenged from the mid-17th century chiefly by the incoming Dutch, who seized control of many of the prior Portuguese strongholds. However, by that time Portuguese-creole-speaking communities were firmly established to the extent that they were able to keep their language and customs for a long time under different European rulers (such as in Quilon or Nagapattinam), and even after decolonisation (as in the case of Malacca or Sri Lanka). Currently, Luso-Asian creoles are spoken , with varying degrees of vitality, in Diu, Daman, Korlai and Cannanore [India], Batticaloa and Trincomalee [Sri Lanka], Malacca [Malaysia], Macau [China], and by diasporic groups around the world.

The Spanish presence in the Philippines began after 1521, the year Magellan voyaged west across the Pacific. Although there was an early attempt to establish a presence in the Moluccas in 1526, however, the 1529 treaty of Zaragoza granted those islands as well as the Philippines to Portugal. Later, in 1565, Spain rejected the treaty and took possession of all the Philippine islands. Settlements were established at San Miguel (Cebu) and Manila (Luzón) in 1571, soon followed by many others. Following the unification of Spain and Portugal in 1580, a Spanish colony was established on Ternate in the Moluccas, but it was abandoned in 1663 (Lipski et al. 1996: 272). Spanish colonial rule also extended to the Marianas, and notably to Guam.

While Spain's presence in the Philippines was that of a settlement colony, and resulted in political unification, Spanish never became the native language of any significant proportion of the local population, nor did it become a lingua franca beyond the groups closely associated with the colonial endeavour (Lipski et al. 1996: 272).[2] Undoubtedly, this was owed in many ways to the vast linguistic diversity of the region, and the presence of local *lingue franche*; yet, Philippine languages were strongly influenced by Spanish, as Tagalog and Cebuano testify, both containing approximately 20% Spanish loans (Lipski et al. 1996: 275).

On the other hand, while the nature of Spanish colonization in the Philippines was different from that of the Portuguese enclaves, the settings in which creolisation occurred are not all that dissimilar. The Spanish-lexified creoles (Chabacano) arose in continuous multilingual contexts associated with garrison populations, missionary activities and other aspects of urban contact involving Spanish.[3] For example, according to Lipski (1987: 92) and Lipski et al. (1996: 278) a key factor in the genesis of Zamboagueño Creole Spanish in Mindanao seems to have been the conjugation of Spanish-speaking troops (partly of Mexican origin) with Filipina wives and troops drawn from Tagalog and Visayan-speaking areas, while the genesis of Cotabato Chabacano appears to have been closely connected with missionary endeavours (Lipski et al. 1996: 279–280). According to some researchers, the development of the Chabacano variety of Ternate, on Manila Bay, followed a very different path – see Section 3.

Prior to World War II, there were six varieties of Chabacano reportedly spoken: three in the Manila Bay region – Ternateño, Caviteño and Ermiteño –, and three on Mindanao island – Zamboagueño, Davaueño (an extension of the former) and Cotabato Chabacano.[4] Currently, at least three survive (Lipski et al. 1996; Fernández 2001; Sippola 2011): Zamboagueño, with as many as three hundred thousand speakers in Mindanao (including the varieties of Davao and Cotabato), and Ternateño and Caviteño (in Cavite City), each possibly with around three thousand speakers.

3. Comparative perspectives

While both first-hand data and analyses of archival resources are increasing, a look at the published studies on the Portuguese- and Spanish-lexified creoles of Asia reveals that relatively little attention has been given to wide-ranging comparative work – exceptions include Hancock (1975), the mapping in Wurm & Hattori (1984), Ivens Ferraz (1987), Holm (1989), Bartens (1995), Clements (2000, 2009), Ladhams (2009), and the contributions in Cardoso & Ansaldo (2009). Existing studies largely concentrate either on single varieties or a specific sub-group of these languages (e.g. the Indo-Portuguese varieties, the varieties of Chabacano, the Malacca-Macau and Malacca-Java axes), and yet pose important questions and make concrete proposals with respect to the creoles' interrelationships. One proposal in particular motivates the inclusion of both Portuguese- and Spanish-based creoles within the scope of this book. In the past, scholars have explored to some extent the possibility that the Chabacano varieties – or at least some of them – may have had their origin in a variety of Malayo-Portuguese transported from the Moluccan island of Ternate to the Philippines and then relexified towards Spanish there. The Portuguese and the Spanish were both present in the Moluccas and, in some analyses, the subsequent withdrawal of the Spanish garrison along with some 200 Christian families to New Ternate on Manila Bay may have involved the importation of elements of an earlier Portuguese-based creole (see Lipski 1988; Lipski et al. 1996: 276–277). This hypothesis, advocated particularly forcefully by Whinnom (1956; 1965), reflects the fact that certain similarities can be identified between Chabacano and the Portuguese-based creoles of (South)east Asia, such as those of Malacca and Macau (and also, partially, the English-lexified creoles of the region). Other authors who have commented on this potential link include Taylor (1957), Thompson (1957, 1961) and Batalha (1960), and the debate resurfaces in the contributions to this volume.

Though geographically constrained, then, previous comparative studies have nonetheless unearthed striking patterns of similarity/dissimilarity and opened the door to possible wider links. Several scholars working on the Ibero-Asian creoles feel it is necessary to take a more encompassing look so as to assess these issues and unlock further instances of alignment or divergence among these languages. The diachrony of the Luso-Asian creoles is therefore of primary importance to the studies included in this volume. But they also engage in articulating data from the Ibero-Asian creoles with current debates and theoretical proposals. A highly significant contribution of these articles comes from the fact that several of them include previously unpublished data gathered from fieldwork. In this sense, this volume also adds to our empirical knowledge of the Ibero-Asian creoles and makes it available to all those working in the field of Creole Studies.

The volume opens with three articles dedicated to the study of specific features of the Luso-Asian creoles at large: the one by Clements focuses on the phonology and basic lexicons of the South Asian Creoles; Baxter & Bastos survey the presence and functions of post-nominal genitives across the Luso-Asian creole spectrum; and Cardoso studies the expression of comparatives in all Luso-Asian creoles for which there are sufficient data. The article by Smith is a wide-ranging survey of word order features covering both Portuguese- and Spanish-based creoles of Asia, similar in scope to Sippola's study of the typology of Ibero-Asian indefinite term paradigms. The following two articles discuss the similarities and differences of cognate function words in the Ibero-Asian creoles: Veiga & Fernández describe the distribution and scope of a concessive particle (*maskin, maske, masque,...*) in the Iberian-based creoles of Asia and beyond (e.g. also Chinese Pidgin English), adding detailed historical and dialectal data in search of their source; Fernández's article casts similar light on the origin and development of a widespread particle of negation (*nenang, nino, ni no,...*), proposing a novel etymology. Rubino charts the development of a numeral classifier system in Zamboangueño through the combined effects of borrowing, functional extension and grammaticalisation, and identifies comparable situations in other contact languages of Asia. The article by Matthews & Li offers evidence for the role of a Portuguese-based pidgin/creole in the formation of Chinese Pidgin English, in the form of two structural features typical of Luso-Asian creoles which are also found in Chinese Pidgin English. Pinharanda Nunes compares the Portuguese-derived verbal morphology of the creole of Macau with that of the northern Indo-Portuguese creoles, proposing starkly different developmental paths rooted in the creoles' different sociolinguistic diachrony. Finally, Grant's article compares two mixed-lexifier Ibero-Asian creoles (those with a significant proportion of basic vocabulary derived from a secondary etymological source) with similar creoles and mixed languages around the globe, in search of valid generalisations.

4. Methods and insights

The articles in this book are sequenced by way of thematic considerations and areal clustering. Though all are comparative in nature and grounded in the study of Ibero-Asian creoles, they cover different subsets of these languages, according to their topic and the availability of data. Testifying to the relevance of these studies beyond the strict domain of the Ibero-Asian creoles and their ancestor languages, some authors include other contact languages of Asia and the Pacific (Matthews & Li; Rubino) and even from beyond Asia (Grant).

One issue which cuts across the group of Ibero-Asian creoles is that not only are the available corpora typically less extensive than for e.g. the Atlantic creoles, they also consist of highly heterogeneous sources, in terms of date, length, register or thoroughness. In addition to oral corpora collected in recent times through fieldwork, data analysed in these articles is also gathered from scientific grammatical descriptions, ethnographic surveys, dictionaries, liturgical translations, even phrasebooks and songbooks. Therefore, regardless of their sample, contributors are often faced with significant variation, which poses an initial challenge to valid cross-linguistic comparison. Authors thus try to make sense of such heterogeneity, and often include critical discussions of their sources centred on an assessment of their reliability (e.g. Fernández; Veiga & Fernández; Cardoso) and an understanding of the procedural or ideological roots of much of the observed variation. One recurrent observation is that oral and written corpora often yield rather different data, with Sippola stressing the importance of comparing similar registers (see also Baxter & Bastos). Nonetheless, some authors make the point that the distribution of variants over different registers and sources can also be important evidence of linguistic stratification among some of these speech communities and of diachronic processes of change (see e.g. Smith; Pinharanda Nunes; Matthews & Li). Matthews & Li – with special reference to early accounts of Chinese Pidgin English – also explore an important factor in the study of old written sources, namely the possibility that they may have fed into each other, thus perpetuating certain pieces of evidence or analyses and leaving out potential alternatives.

The studies included in this volume contribute in particular to an understanding of the diachronic development of the Ibero-Asian creoles (and others). An important dimension is that of diffusion, starting with the assessment of the possibility that, in the case of the Portuguese-based creoles, it proceeded in an eastwards direction. In addition to better-known axes of continuity such as the ones linking Malacca to Macau and Malacca to Batavia/Tugu (Pinharanda Nunes; Smith; Cardoso) or the relationship of the various Indo-Portuguese creoles (Clements; Cardoso), some authors explore the influence of South Asian material in the formation of the Southeast and East Asian Portuguese-based creoles

(Baxter & Bastos; Smith). On a different vein, Matthews & Li explore the (partial) continuity between a Portuguese pidgin/creole developed for the early Canton trade and the later formation of Chinese Pidgin English. The relationship between the Portuguese- and Spanish-based creoles of the region is also problematised in various studies. Sippola, for instance, admits that her comparative study originated from observed similarities in the Malacca-Philippines axis, and offers the typological matches between the autochthonous languages that influenced both Malacca Creole and the Chabacano varieties as the potential root of a certain areal clustering. The earlier hypothesis that the Chabacano varieties descend from a Malayo-Portuguese creole also features prominently in the discussion. Veiga & Fernández dedicate their study to debunk the need to resort to a Portuguese (pidgin) past to account for the presence of the concessive particle in Chabacano; and, while Fernández rejects Whinnom's hypothesis of a Malayo-Portuguese-pidgin genesis for all Philippine creoles, he admits it (with reservations) for the Ternateño variety – said by Grant to contain some "aberrant" traits in relation to the other varieties of Chabacano.

The diachronic picture that emerges from many of these studies is one of intense dynamism. Several authors identify developmental paths for certain (function) words, paradigms or structures which involve layers of functional expansion or speciation in response to changes in the language's social and linguistic ecology (e.g. Baxter & Bastos; Veiga & Fernández; Fernández), processes of grammaticalisation (Rubino), metatypy (Grant) and relexification (Matthews & Li). The formative and developmental process of these creoles is also shown to be far from homogeneous, and their reconstruction far from straightforward. With respect to the phonological inventories of the Indo-Portuguese creoles, for instance, Clements identifies the hallmarks of both shift and borrowing in different historical moments; when comparing the retention of Portuguese-like verbal morphology in the Indo-Portuguese creoles and in Macau Creole, Pinharanda Nunes invokes an early process of shift for the former and a later process of decreolisation for the latter; and Grant warns that the layers of linguistic influence on a given creole may be masked by the fact that transfer of fabric and transfer of pattern need not go hand in hand.

The relationship between the Ibero-Asian creoles and their neighbouring languages is also a primary field of inquiry here. Veiga & Fernández hypothesise, with respect to a Spanish-derived function word found in both the creole and its local adstrates, that it may not have been transferred from Spanish to Chabacano directly, but instead mediated by local Philippine languages. This possibility stems from a circumstance which, though not exclusive of the Ibero-Asian creoles, is particularly typical of the Ibero-Asian creoles: the fact that they have coexisted for protracted periods of time with both their main lexifiers and various adstrates (see e.g. Clements and Grant for an exploration of the lexical influence of such adstrates). In most cases, these adstrates were also present in the initial contact situation, and therefore, in the case of the Ibero-Asian creoles, the substrate-adstrate opposition is often untenable.

Virtually all articles describe the essential contribution of such adstrates to the development of the Ibero-Asian creoles (e.g. Baxter & Bastos; Cardoso; Clements; Grant; Rubino; Sippola, Smith; Veiga & Fernández). But these studies also assess the extent to which the various creoles as we know them reflect the input of the Iberian lexifiers (e.g. Clements; Cardoso; Fernández; Smith; Veiga & Fernández). As a matter of fact, given the sociolinguistic histories of the Ibero-Asian creoles, they emerge as particularly suited case-studies of the way lexifiers and adstrates compete to shape the creoles and condition their drift. The issue is here described as a "tug-of war" (Smith) played out by the various contributor languages, a process said to be "dynamic" (Cardoso) in that it responds to changes in the creole's social and linguistic environment. Both Smith and Cardoso devise statistical methods to quantify the relative significance of lexifier and adstrate input to the various creoles and find that differences in the results correlate with external socio-historical variables such as the chronology of colonial domination by speakers of the main lexifier (see also Clements). Sippola weaves similar historical arguments to account for differences between Caviteño and Zamboangueño, and between Malacca or Sri Lanka creoles and the northern Indo-Portuguese creoles. Pinharanda Nunes also points out, for the creole of Macau, the decreolising effects of historically documented changes in the ethnic make-up of the Macanese community and in educational policies. With respect to Zamboangueño Chabacano, Rubino notes that, over time, social alterations have resulted in the addition of English and Tagalog to the pool of lexical donors, in contrast to an earlier situation in which Spanish and Visayan dominated. A more extreme case of lexical competition is that described for the history of Chinese Pidgin English by Matthews & Li, according to whom the shift in economic dominance from the Portuguese to the English in the Canton trade dictated the replacement of one lexifier with another.

The contributions to this volume therefore highlight the explanatory power of such facts as linguistic competition and extralinguistic variables. But this does not exhaust their insights. Other issues which find their way into the discussion include the effects of congruence (Cardoso; Sippola), the frequency of particular features in the input (Clements; Baxter & Bastos; Pinharanda Nunes), linguistic conservatism (Clements) and innovation (Smith; Cardoso). Another aspect in which the contributions in this volume add intricacy to the study of the Ibero-Asian creoles is by recognising – and describing – the complexity of the donor languages. This is particularly obvious in discussions related to the diachrony and dialectal variation of the Iberian lexifiers (e.g. Veiga & Fernández; Clements; Cardoso). In the case of Fernández's article, this preoccupation has led to the exploration of a marginal negative polarity expression in Spanish and Portuguese which is underrepresented in descriptions of either language; this illustrates the ways in which studies of creole languages can and should be integrated with diachronic and dialectal research on their donor languages.

The eleven articles of this volume pose (and answer) a wide array of questions surrounding the contact languages which testify of the spread of Spanish and Portuguese in Asia. Through comparative analyses, they provide a window onto aspects of current research on these languages – including unsettled debates and ways in which the study of Ibero-Asian creoles can contribute to advance several areas of linguistic enquiry. It is our hope that this book will encourage further research on a significant group of languages which, in recent decades, have often been absent in mainstream discussions of language contact and creolisation.

Notes

1. The process began with a scholarly meeting in Macau, in October 2010, supported by the University of Macau. The event brought together a large number of experts on the Ibero-Asian creoles. While some of the contributions to that event have been included in this volume, the body of contributors has been much enlarged.

2. Guam seems to have constituted somewhat of an exception to this, although, while strongly hispanicised, the local population of Guam maintained its own language alongside Spanish (Lipski et al. 1996: 281). The depth of Spanish loans in its lexicon appears to testify to a strong period of bilingualism in its past.

3. Different from the Portuguese settings, maritime trade, although a main activity on the Manila-Acapulco route, does not seem a particularly relevant factor.

4. Recent research by Fernández (2010) suggests that an Ermiteño variety, as such, did not exist, and was in all likelihood merely L2 contact Spanish inaccurately reported.

References

Ansaldo, U. 2009. *Contact Languages. Ecology and Evolution in Asia*. Cambridge: CUP.
Ansaldo, U., ed. 2010. Pidgins and Creoles in Asian contexts. *Journal of Creole and Pidgin Languages* 25 (1) (Special issue).
Arends, J. 2002. The historical study of creoles and the future of creole studies. In *Pidgin and Creole Linguistics in the Twenty-First Century*, ed. G. Gilbert, 48–68. Frankfurt: Peter Lang.

Bartens, A. 1995. *Die Iberoromanisch-Basierten Kreolsprachen: Ansätze der Linguistischen Beschreibung*. Frankfurt: Peter Lang.

Batalha, G. N. 1953. Aspectos do vocabulário macaense. *Mosaico* 5: 195–99.

Batalha, G. N. 1958. Estado actual do dialecto macaense. *Revista Portuguesa de Filologia* 9: 177–213.

Batalha, G. N. 1960. Coincidências com o dialecto de Macau em dialectos espanhóis das Ilhas Filipinas. *Boletim de Filologia* 19: 295–303.

Baxter, A. N. 1988. *A Grammar of Kristang (Malacca Creole Portuguese)*. Canberra: Pacific Linguistics.

Baxter, A. N. 1996. Portuguese and Creole Portuguese in the Pacific and Western Pacific Rim. In *Atlas of Languages of Intercultural Communication in the Pacific, Asia and the Americas*, Vol. II.1, eds. S. A. Wurm, P. Mühlhäusler and D. T. Tryon, 299–338. Berlin: Mouton de Gruyter.

Bernardes de Carvalho, R. 2012. A "snapshot" of a Portuguese community in Southeast Asia: The Bandel of Siam, 1684–86. In *Portuguese and Luso-Asian Legacies in Southeast Asia, 1511–2011*, Vol. 2: *Culture and Identity in the Luso-Asian World: Tenacities and Plasticities*, ed. L. Jarnagin, 44–66. Singapore: Institute of Southeast Asian Studies.

Cardoso, H. C. 2006. Challenges to Indo-Portuguese across India. In *Proceedings of the FEL X*, eds. R. Elangayan, R. McKenna Brown, N. Ostler and M. K. Verma, 23–30. Mysore: Central Institute of Indian Languages.

Cardoso, H. C. 2009. The Indo-Portuguese Language of Diu. PhD dissertation, University of Amsterdam.

Cardoso, H. C. 2010. African slave population of Portuguese India: Demographics and impact on Indo-Portuguese. *Journal of Pidgin and Creole Languages* 25 (1): 95–119.

Cardoso, H. C., and U. Ansaldo. eds. 2009. Accounting for commonalities among the Portuguese-lexified creoles of Asia. *Journal of Portuguese Linguistics* 8 (2) (Special issue).

Clements, J. C. 1996. *The Genesis of a Language. The Formation and Development of Korlai Portuguese* [Creole Language Library 16]. Amsterdam: John Benjamins.

Clements, J. C. 2000. Evidência para a existência de um pidgin português asiático. In *Crioulos de Base Portuguesa*, eds. E. d'Andrade, M. A. Mota and D. Pereira, 185–200. Braga: Associação Portuguesa de Linguística.

Clements, J. C. 2009. *The Linguistic Legacy of Spanish and Portuguese: Colonial Expansion and Language Change*. Cambridge: CUP.

Clements, J. C., and A. J. Koontz-Garboden. 2002. Two Indo-Portuguese creoles in contrast. *Journal of Pidgin and Creole Languages* 17 (2): 191–236.

Dalgado, S. R. 1913. *Influência do Vocabulário Português em Línguas Asiáticas*. Coimbra: Imprensa da Universidade.

Fernández, M. 2001. Por qué el chabacano? *Estudios de Sociolingüística* 2 (2): i–xii.

Fernández, M. 2006. Las lenguas de Zamboanga según los jesuitas y otros observadores occidentales. *Revista Internacional de Lingüística Iberoamericana* 7: 9–26.

Fernández, M. 2010. Leyenda e historia del chabacano de Ermita. Paper presented at the *10th ACBLPE conference*, CNRS, Paris, July 1–3.

Ferreira, J. S. 1978. *Papiá Cristám di Macau – Dialecto Macaense*. Macau: Tipografia da Missão do Padroado.

Forman, M. L. 1972. Zamboagueño Texts with Grammatical Analysis: A Study of Philippine Creole Spanish. PhD dissertation, Cornell University.

Frake, C. O. 1971. Lexical origins and semantic structure in Philippine Creole Spanish. In *Pidginization and Creolization of Languages; Proceedings of a Conference held at the University of the West Indies, Mona, Jamaica, April 1968*, ed. D. Hymes, 223–242. Cambridge: CUP.

Hancock, I. F. 1969. The Malacca Creoles and their language. *Afrasian* 3: 38–45.

Hancock, I. F. 1973. Malacca Creole Portuguese: A brief transformational account. *Te Reo* 16: 23–44.

Hancock, I. F. 1975. Malacca Creole Portuguese: Asian, African or European? *Anthropological Linguistics* 17 (5): 211–36.

Holm, J. 1989. *Pidgins and Creoles*, Vol. 2: *Reference Survey*. Cambridge: CUP.

Ing, R. 1968. A Phonological Analysis of Chabacano. PhD dissertation, University of London.

Ivens Ferraz, L. 1987. Portuguese creoles of West Africa and Asia. In *Pidgin and Creole Languages: Essay in Memory of John E. Reinecke*, ed. G. G. Gilbert, 337–360. Honolulu HI: University of Hawaii Press.

Jackson, K. D. 1990. *Sing Without Shame. Oral Traditions in Indo-Portuguese Creole Verse* [Creole Language Library 5]. Amsterdam: John Benjamins.

Keesing, R. 1988. *Melanesian Pidgin and the Oceanic substrate*. Stanford, CA: Stanford University Press.

Knowlton, E. J. Jr. 1964. Malaysian Portuguese. *The Linguist* 26 (211–213): 239–41.

Ladhams, J. 2009. The formation of the Portuguese-based Creoles: Gradual or abrupt? In *Gradual Creolization: Studies Celebrating Jacques Arends* [Creole Language Library 34], eds. R. Selbach, H. C. Cardoso and M. van den Berg, 279–303. Amsterdam: John Benjamins.

Lipski, J. 1987. Modern Spanish once-removed in Philippine Creole Spanish: The case of Zamboagueño. *Language in Society* 16: 91–108.

Lipski, J. 1988. Philippine Creole Spanish: Assessing the Portuguese element. *Zeitschrift für Romanische Philologie* 104: 25–45.

Lipski, J., P. Mühlhäusler, and F. Duthin. 1996. Spanish in the Pacific. In *Atlas of Languages of Intercultural Communication in the Pacific, Asia and the Americas*, Vol. II.1, eds. S. A. Wurm, P. Mühlhäusler and D. T. Tryon, 271–298. Berlin: Mouton de Gruyter.

Llamado, L. C. 1969. An Analysis of the Basic Structures of Cavite Chavacano. MA dissertation, Philippine Normal College.

Lopes, D. 1936. *A Expansão da Língua Portuguesa no Oriente nos Séculos XVI, XVII e XVIII*. Barcelos: Portucalense Editora.

Luís, A. R. 2008. Tense marking and inflectional morphology in Indo-Portuguese creoles. In *Roots of Creole Structures: Weighing the Contribution of Substrates and Superstrates* [Creole Language Library 33], ed. S. Michaelis, 83–121. Amsterdam: John Benjamins.

Maurer, P. 2012. *The Former Portuguese Creole of Batavia and Tugu (Indonesia)*. London: Battlebridge.

McKaughan, H. P. 1954. Notes on Chabacano grammar. *Journal of East Asiatic Studies* 3: 205–26.

Meyerhoff, M. 2008. Forging Pacific pidgin and creole syntax: Substrate, discourse and inherent variability. In *Handbook of Pidgin and Creole Studies*, eds. S. Kouwenberg and J. Singler, 48–72. Oxford: Wiley-Blackwell.

Michaelis, S., P. Maurer, M. Haspelmath, and M. Huber. eds. Forthcoming. *Atlas of Pidgin and Creole Structures*. Oxford: OUP.

Morais Barbosa, J. 1968. A língua portuguesa de Macau. *Colóquios Sobre as Províncias do Oriente* 2: 147–59.

Mühlhäusler, P. 1980. Structural expansion and the process of creolization. In *Theoretical Orientations in Creole Studies*, eds. A. Valdman and A. Highfields, 19–56. New York NY: Academic Press.
Parkvall, M. 2002. Cutting off the branch. In *Pidgin and Creole Linguistics in the Twenty-First Century*, ed. G. Gilbert, 355–368. Frankfurt: Peter Lang.
Pereira, D. 2006. *Crioulos de Base Portuguesa*. Lisbon: Caminho.
Pinharanda Nunes, M. 2011. Estudo da Expressão Morfo-Sintáctica das Categorias de Tempo, Modo e Aspecto em Maquista. PhD dissertation, Universidade de Macau.
Riego de Dios, M. I. 1976. The Cotabato Chabacano verb. *Philippine Journal of Linguistics* 7: 48–59.
Romanillos, E. L. A. 2006. *Chabacano Studies: Essays on Cavite's Chabacano Language and Literature*. Cavite: Cavite Historical Society.
Sankoff, G., and S. Laberge. 1973. On the acquisition of native speakers by a language. *Kivung* 6: 32–47.
Santos y Gómez, A. 1924. Caviteño dialect. MA thesis, University of the Philippines.
Siegel, J. 1987. *Language Contact in a Plantation Environment: A Sociolinguistic History of Fiji*. Cambridge: CUP.
Sippola, E. 2006. Hacia una descripción del Ternateño. *Revista Internacional de Lingüística Iberoamericana* 7: 41–54.
Sippola, E. 2011. Una Gramática Descriptiva del Chabacano de Ternate. PhD dissertation, University of Helsinki.
Smith, I. R. 1977. Sri Lanka Creole Portuguese Phonology. PhD dissertation, Cornell University.
Smith, I. R. 1979. Substrata vs. universals in the formation of Sri Lanka Portuguese. In *Papers in Pidgin and Creole Linguistics* 2, ed. P. Mühlhäusler, 183–200. Canberra: Pacific Linguistics.
Smith, I. R. 1984. The development of morphosyntax in Sri Lanka Portuguese. In *York Papers in Linguistics*, eds. M. Sebba and L. Todd. York: University of York.
Steinkrüger, P. O. 2008. The puzzling case of Chabacano: Creolization, substrate, mixing and secondary contact. *Studies in Philippine Languages and Cultures* 19: 142–57.
Taylor, D. R. 1957. Review of Whinnom (1956), *Spanish Contact Vernaculars in the Philippine Islands*. *Word* 13: 489–99.
Theban, L. 1977. Indo-Românica. Estruturas sintácticas em contacto. *Revue Roumaine de Linguistique* 22: 245–48.
Thompson, R. W. 1957. Review of Whinnom (1956), *Spanish Contact Vernaculars in the Philippine Islands*. *Revista Portuguesa de Filologia* 8: 369–71.
Thompson, R. W. 1960. O dialecto português de Hongkong. *Boletim de Filologia* 19: 289–93.
Thompson, R. W. 1961. A note on some possible affinities between the creole dialects of the old world and those of the New. *Creole Language Studies* 2: 107–13.
Tomás, M. I. 1992a. A presença africana nos crioulos portugueses do Oriente: O crioulo de Damão. In *Actas do Colóquio sobre Crioulos de Base Lexical Portuguesa*, eds. E. d'Andrade and A. Kihm, 97–108. Lisbon: Colibri.
Tomás, M. I. 1992b. *Os Crioulos Portugueses do Oriente; Uma Bibliografia*. Macau: Instituto Cultural de Macau.
Vázquez Veiga, N., and M. Fernández. 2006. Marcadores de énfasis: Gayod, gale y gane en el chabacano de Zamboanga. *Revista Internacional de Lingüística Iberoamericana* 7: 27–40.
Wallace, S. 1978. What is a creole? The example of the Portuguese language of Tugu, Jakarta, Indonesia. In *Contemporary Studies in Romance Linguistics*, ed. M. Suñer, 340–377. Washington DC: Georgetown University Press.

Whinnom, K. 1956. *Spanish Contact Vernaculars in the Philippine Islands*. Hong Kong: Hong Kong University Press & Oxford: OUP.

Whinnom, K. 1965. Contacts de langues et emprunts lexicaux: The origin of the European-based creoles and pidgins. *Orbis* 14: 509–27.

Wurm, S. A., and S. Hattori. eds. 1984. *Language Atlas of the Pacific Area*, Part II: *Japan Area, Philippines and Formosa, Mainland and Insular South East Asia*. Stuttgart: Geocenter.

Wurm, S. A., P. Mühlhäusler, and D. T. Tryon. eds. 1996. *Atlas of Languages of Intercultural Communication in the Pacific, Asia and the Americas*. 3 vols. Berlin: Mouton de Gruyter.

Notes on the phonology and lexicon of some Indo-Portuguese creoles

J. Clancy Clements

In this study, the focus is on three key differences in five Indo-Portuguese creoles: differences in phonological inventory, in the core lexicons, and in the syllable structure of the creoles. An account for these is based on two criteria and the distinction between borrowing and shift. The criterion used to account for the differences in the phonological inventories and the core lexicons is a dynamic of borrowing, shown to be sensitive to the chronology of the Portuguese presence in the different communities. The distinct treatment of the Portuguese post-tonic syllables, by contrast, is argued to be part of a shift dynamic.

1. Introduction

In classifying the Indo-Portuguese (IP) creoles[1], Ivens Ferraz (1987: 338) distinguishes between those creoles in northern India with an Indo-Aryan language substrate (those spoken in Diu, Daman, and Korlai today) and those creoles in southern India with a Dravidian substrate (those spoken just north of Kozhikode [also known as Calicut], in Kannur [also known as Cannanore] and Sri Lanka today).[2]

The purpose of this contribution is, first, to argue that these different substrates, along with the factor of typological distance, offer a reasonable account for the retention of post-tonic syllables in SLP and CANN and their respective loss in DAM, DIU, and KOR. Secondly, I will propose a simple account for the differential nature of the respective phonological inventories and core lexicons in the creoles, based on the argument that the length of the Portuguese presence in the respective settlements is consistent with the presence of key differences in the phonological inventories and the core lexicons of the creoles. I start with this second topic in Sections 3–5, and in Section 6 take up that of the post-tonic syllables in the IP creoles under discussion. Section 7 contains concluding remarks, including a rationale for why certain components of the grammar were affected as they were and not differently. Why, for example, were the core lexicons and

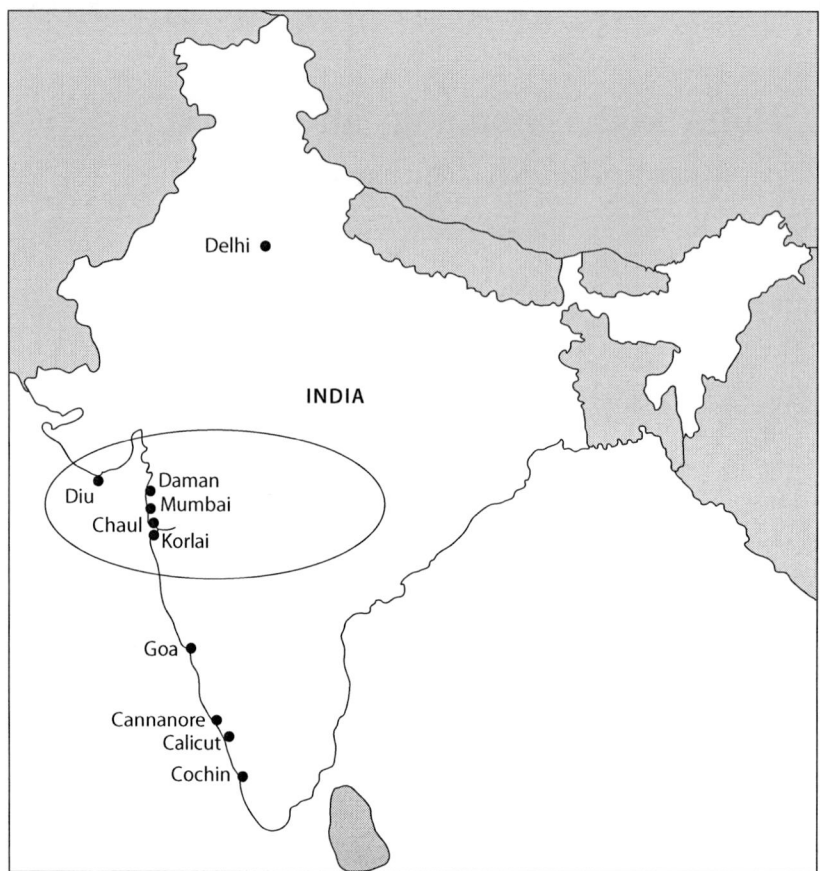

Figure 1. Map of important cities and locations where IP creoles are spoken. The encircled localities indicate where the northern IP creoles are still spoken, and their proximity to Mumbai, the major metropolitan area of the region.

the phoneme inventories affected by the presence of Portuguese, but the syllable structure in the respective creoles was not? I offer a response to this question by appealing to the distinction made by Thomason & Kaufman (1988) and Croft (2000) (among various others) between L2-acquistion/shift related phenomena vs. borrowing-related phenomena, which will be discussed in Section 2.

2. Some theoretical preliminaries

2.1 Languages and their speech communities

Typically, a language (or language variety) is spoken, at the very least, by one speech community. Here I adopt the definition of a speech community from sociolinguistics as a group of speakers who share what they perceive as a single linguistic code. This definition is based on the degree of social consciousness a given group has or has developed regarding a certain linguistic variety (their code) that they use among themselves for communication. Thus, as expressed by Croft, "conventional linguistic units such as words or constructions have not only a form (signifier) and meaning (signified) but a third dimension, the social domain/community in which they are used" (2000:91). In bi- or multi-lingual situations, there may be domains or communities according not only to languages spoken, but also to groups of speakers within the communities based on age, social class, gender, etc. In a given speech community, the language variety or varieties used contain lexical, structural and social features and these features constitute the linguistic feature pool of the speech community. In language contact situations, linguistic features, lexical, structural, as well as social, are present from different language varieties which can make the linguistic feature pool more diverse.

In the formation of pidgins and certain creole languages, the notion of speech community is fluid and undefined because a novel communication system in such cases is in the process of forming. At this incipient stage, it is difficult to talk of a group of speakers defined by communicative intercourse among themselves. Of course, pidgins and abrupt creoles initially start out as individual solutions to the problem of intercommunication, similar to immigrants' individual solutions to their problem of intercommunication with native speakers of the host country.[3] For example, in the latter part of the 15th and the first part of the 16th century, the African population in southern Portugal – making up 10–15% of the population there (Tinhorão 1997[1988]:92, 102–03) – arguably spoke immigrant Portuguese, portrayals of which found their way into popular plays of the era (cf. Lipski 2005:14–32, Clements 2009:42–48). Many of the features found in these portrayals are the same or very similar to those found in the Indo-Portuguese creoles, which are arguably abruptly formed creoles (see Clements 1996:11–12, 51–54). I assume that this is the case, not because there is a direct evolutionary link between the Africans speaking immigrant Portuguese in the 15th–16th century and the first speakers of the Indo-Portuguese creoles, but rather because the common features are a result of the untutored acquisition of the variety (or varieties) of Portuguese to which both sets of speakers had access in their communication with the Portuguese. Over time, many of these features conventionalized in the process of 'negotiated' solutions among the speakers. Revealingly, other immigrant language varieties, such as the ones involving Chinese and Spanish discussed in Clements (2003; 2009, Chapter 6) also exhibit features similar to those found in African L2 Portuguese and the IP creoles. This is not surprising given the finding by Klein & Perdue (1992) that many immigrant language varieties display similar characteristics, which taken together comprise what they have called the "basic variety".

For the discussion of the five IP creoles in question, it is important to take into account not only how they initially formed, but also the various influences on the communities of speakers over time. For the particular purposes of this article, the notions of language shift (which affects the initial stages of creole formation) and borrowing (which comes into play in the subsequent development of creoles) are important and will now be discussed.

2.2 Borrowing vs. shift situations and the feature pool

Thomason & Kaufman (1988) identify two general tendencies in contact-induced language phenomena: borrowing and shift. The extent of borrowing or shift depends on factors prevalent in the contact situation in question. For borrowing, Thomason & Kaufman (1988:73–75) propose a borrowing scale, whereby the more intense the contact situation, the more lexical and structural features tend to be borrowed. Briefly, the borrowing-community speakers initially borrow words from one or more of the source languages and, if the contact intensity is stronger, they begin to borrow linguistic structure as well.[4] In such a situation, bilingualism is a prerequisite for borrowing, at least at the moment an element is first borrowed.

In the case of shift, however, there need be no bilingualism involved prior to the shift, although a degree of bilingualism could develop in such a situation, as shifting speakers learn the target language vocabulary. As they learn the target language, they typically carry their native-language structures into the language to which they are shifting. Thus, Thomason & Kaufman (1988) note that in such situations one expects to find in their new variety structural features from the source languages but not necessarily core lexicon from the source languages, as the shifting speakers are targeting precisely this vocabulary.

The general developmental paths of borrowing and shift are given below (cf. Croft 2000:213–21).

(1) Borrowing → Extensive Borrowing → Death by Borrowing
(primary parent language is typically the language of the borrowing community)

(2) **Natural Second Language Acquisition** → **Semi-Shift** → **Total Shift**
(primary parent language is typically the language targeted by the new language learners)

In both borrowing and shift situations, key factors should be considered. These are contact intensity as just defined, markedness of a linguistic feature to be borrowed or to be learned in language shift, and the typological fit among the languages involved in the contact situation.

In such situations, Portuguese, as long as it was present in the communities, was considered to be the socially dominant language, although in terms of number of speakers it may not have been dominant. In the case of the IP creoles, the indigenous languages were: Marathi for Korlai, Gujarati for Daman and Diu, Malayalam for Kannur, and Tamil and Sinhala for Sri Lanka Creole Portuguese. So long as Portuguese was used in the church, education, and government, it was the dominant language, from a cultural and social perspective, although as mentioned this may have not been so numerically. Once Portuguese was replaced by one of the regional languages, or by another colonial language, the replacing language became the socially and culturally dominant language.

For Diu and Daman, the socially and culturally dominant language is assumed to be Portuguese up until the Indian government took over these areas in 1961. In the early part of the 20th century, English began to spread as an influential language of the Catholic church in urban areas. For its part, after partition in 1947, Hindi began to gain prestige, most particularly in northern India. Today, the Catholic communities in Diu and Daman have a polyglossic situation: IP creole speakers speak their respective creole with family and friends, and they speak Gujarati, Hindi and/or English at work when need be. Church services are in English and Portuguese in Diu and Daman. In both localities, all Catholic children go to English-medium Catholic schools. It is noteworthy, nevertheless, that Portuguese remains a somewhat prestigious variety in Daman and Diu, and that there is still some contact between Diu and Daman on the one hand, and Portuguese on the other through media (the Portuguese international television service is available) and emigration of Daman and Diu residents to Portugal and other countries, etc.

In Korlai, Kannur, and Sri Lanka, the respective situations are markedly different from those just described. In Korlai, Portuguese has had minimal to no presence since around 1740. Marathi, the adstrate language, is currently the most dominant language of the community, both socially and culturally, as well as in terms of overall number of speakers in the area. In Kannur and Sri Lanka, Portuguese ceased to be a major presence in the mid-17th century. Malayalam is the overall dominant language in Kannur, as are Tamil and Sinhala in Sri Lanka. Because of the social, cultural, and numeric dominance of these Indic languages in Korlai, Kannur, and Sri Lanka, Indic-language features such as aspirated stops, retroflex consonants, postpositions, OV order, etc. are well represented in terms of frequency of occurrence in the feature pool. In addition, English-language features are also well represented in all communities except Korlai, where English has a minimal presence.

Much or all of what has just been discussed involves either bilingualism (borrowing-type phenomena) or L2 acquisition (shift-type phenomena) and thus has significant ramifications for the structure of contact-induced language change, including pidgin/creole formation. In a given speech community in which there is substantial language contact, the feature pool contains a host of linguistic features – both lexical and structural – from the languages involved. To the extent that the languages in contact are typologically similar (for example, if they share the features of suffixal verb morphology), their respective features may reinforce each other in the feature pool of the speech community, as in the case of the preterit-imperfect distinction in Spanish and Italian. Lack of a clean typological fit among languages in a contact situation can lead to the reanalysis of certain particles. A well-known example involves the Korlai particle *su*, arguably from the Portuguese feminine possessive determiner *sua* 'his, her, their' (e.g. *sua(s) casa(s)* 'his, her, their house(s)'), which in Korlai became the genitive particle, as in *pay su kadz* [Lit. father GEN house] 'father's house(s)' (cf. Baxter, *this volume*). Arguably, *sua(s)* was targeted by the Marathi speakers creating Korlai IP. One reason for this may have been the functional and phonic similarity of *sua(s)* to the Marathi postpositional forms *tsa, tsə, tsi, tse* (e.g. *Teru tsə ghər* [Lit. Teru GEN-NT house.NT] 'Teru's house'). This Marathi structure could account for the shift from Portuguese *casa de Teru* (possessum + genitive + possessor) to Korlai *Teru su kadz* (possessor + genitive + possessum), which in turn would be accounted for by the dominance in the feature pool of the possessor + genitive + possessum structure in the area where predominantly Marathi speakers lived.[5]

Having briefly reviewed some of the theoretical preliminaries, we now discuss the influence of the Portuguese presence in the communities in question.

3. The presence of the Portuguese in the Indo-Portuguese communities

For the communities under consideration, the ecology of each situation is important to consider in order to understand the nature of the changes found in the phonological inventories and core lexicons, one focus of this study. In our particular case, the part of language ecology that seems most revealing is the chronology of the Portuguese presence in each community. As just noted, I argue that it is a significant predictor in the makeup of the phonological inventories and core lexicons of the creoles in question. Some simple and straightforward predictions can be advanced with regard to the Portuguese presence in the communities under discussion. Specifically, the more recent a substantial presence of the Portuguese is attested in an IP creole-speaking community, the less the phonological inventories and core lexicons will have been influenced by the adstrate language(s). Conversely, the more remote a substantial presence of the Portuguese is attested in an IP creole-speaking community, the more the phonological inventories and core lexicons will have been influenced by the adstrate or other superstrate language(s).

In each of the communities under discussion, the presence of the Portuguese has a different history. Before discussing the manner in which I distinguish the different groupings in light of the Portuguese presence, I need to 'unpack' the notion of 'Portuguese presence'.

When the Portuguese arrived on the Indian subcontinent, they encountered a society for the most part made up of Hindus, who maintained (and still maintain today to a large extent) a caste system, in which members of different castes did not intermarry for reasons of purity and pollution. That is, a given caste member married within the caste to retain purity and avoid pollution of another caste. Those Hindus who ultimately became slaves and/or concubines of the Portuguese, and later converted to Christianity, were lower caste Hindus seeking a better lot for themselves (Boxer 1963: 59–61). In each community, I assume that it was these Indians who were the co-creators of the IP creoles in question.[6] The important point in this is that all IP communities under discussion were isolated by their religion (Christianity), as well as their caste (low) in a society in which the caste system was ubiquitous, even in Christian communities (cf. Boxer 1963: 62–83). In each community, the presence of the Portuguese and Portuguese language provided a linguistic target. In those communities in which the Portuguese presence ended early on (mid-17th century in Korlai, mid-16th century in Kannur and Sri Lanka), the IP creole-speaking communities had no choice but to interact more with speakers of the regional languages in each contact situation. When I use the expression 'Portuguese presence' in this study, I'm referring to the working assumption that it was the socially and culturally dominant language in each of the IP creole-speaking communities.

With regard to the degree of Portuguese presence in the communities under discussion, three different groupings can be distinguished: (1) In Diu and Daman, the Portuguese presence lasted until very recently; (2) in Korlai the Portuguese left the area in 1740 as the result of a military confrontation; (3) in Kannur and Sri Lanka the Portuguese presence was ended by the Dutch takeover of these communities in 1663 and 1658, respectively. In the brief historical notes that follow, we will see more clearly the basis for distinguishing the groupings.

Daman and Diu: Although they arrived later in Diu, the Portuguese established a settlement there by 1535, whereas it took them until 1580 to accomplish the same task in Daman. During the 17th century, the Portuguese suffered the loss of many of their colonies in Asia, most notably to the Dutch. During this time, the kingdom of Portugal also became part of Spain from 1580 to 1640, which of course also had a detrimental effect on its hold on the colonies it had established throughout the 16th century in India, Malaysia, Indonesia, and China. With respect to its possessions in India, it lost many of them during the 17th and 18th centuries. Goa had already become the main seat of power in the late 16th century. When in 1740 the Marathas took the Portuguese Northern Provinces (save Diu), they allowed the Portuguese to retain Goa and Daman. While Goa remained the center of the 'Estado da Índia', both Diu and Daman were reduced to a relatively minor administrative presence. However, a Portuguese cultural and linguistic presence was maintained in both communities until their respective takeover by India in 1961. Today, however, few of the Diu and Daman Catholic inhabitants still speak European Portuguese, but many of them (around 250 in Diu, around 4000 in Daman) still speak their respective IP variety.

Korlai: In the area where Korlai IP is currently spoken, the most prominent city in the 15th century was Chaul, which had been a trading center for centuries before the Portuguese first arrived there in 1505. The major commercial influence from the Portuguese happened in Chaul in their first 100 years after settling in the area. By 1640, when Portugal regained its independence from Spain, Chaul was already in sharp decline, due in part to the political situation but also to the fact that the estuary where it was situated and which served as a harbor for trade became too shallow for ships due to the siltation of the river (Clements 1996).

With the takeover of the area by the Marathas in 1740, the governmental, social, and cultural presence of Portugal was replaced by Marathi. At that time, all the Portuguese lay people, along with the native Christians with the necessary means, abandoned the area for Goa, leaving behind the lower caste Indian Christians, and some clergy. From 1740 till 1963, there was one or more Portuguese-speaking parish priests taking care of the Christian community in Chaul as well as in Korlai, situated south of Chaul where a Catholic farming community had formed. Between around 1930 and 1963, only one Portuguese-speaking parish priest was assigned to the entire area, and from 1963 to the present, the priest assigned to Korlai has been Marathi-speaking. Thus, we can say that there has been no significant Portuguese presence in Korlai since 1740 and absolutely no Portuguese presence since around 1963 (Clements 1996).

Kannur and Sri Lanka: The Portuguese arrived to the Indian subcontinent, in Kozhikode in 1498 and by 1505 had established themselves as a presence in Kannur, which lie 300 kms to the north. By 1550, they had also established themselves in Sri Lanka. As with Korlai above, the Portuguese presence in these areas was reduced because of the incorporation of Portugal by Spain between 1580 and 1640. Moreover, the Dutch began to challenge the Portuguese in the beginning of the 17th century. Thus, by 1658, the Dutch had taken over the Portuguese possessions in Sri Lanka and they captured Kannur in 1663. In contrast to the Portuguese, who used one or more varieties of Portuguese to communicate with members of the IP community, the Dutch did not use Dutch as the language of communication but rather adopted Portuguese for this purpose. For their part, the English ended Dutch control in Sri Lanka in 1802 and in Kannur in 1792. In the case of Kannur and Sri Lanka, then, the strong governmental and cultural presence of the Portuguese already began to diminish at the beginning of the 17th century and ceased entirely by around 1663. Although there are no exact numbers regarding present-day speakers of SLP, we can assume that some speakers remain in Batticaloa and possibly elsewhere, given that these SLP speakers may have been displaced because of the civil war there. In Kannur proper, there are seven known speakers, three siblings, two older men who still understand the language, a female school teacher, and a woman who currently lives in Doha, Qatar. All are in the sixties or older.

Table 1 summarizes the length and degree of the Portuguese governmental and cultural presence in the communities in question.

Table 1. The length and degree of Portuguese presence in Diu, Daman, Korlai, Kannur, and Sri Lanka

	Strong Portuguese presence	Diminished Portuguese presence	Strongly reduced to absence of Portuguese presence
Diu and *Daman*	1540–1580 to around 1740	Around 1740 to 1961	1961 to present
Korlai	1520 to around 1640	1640 to 1740	1740 to present
Kannur and *Sri Lanka*	1505–1530 to the beginning of the 17th century	Beginning of the 17th century to 1658–1663	1658–1663 to present

Based on the foregoing, a series of concrete predictions can be advanced regarding the makeup of the phonological inventories and the core lexicons of the IP creoles under discussion. Specifically, the greater the length of the Portuguese presence, the less likely the phonological inventories and core lexicons will diverge from European Portuguese because the presence of the Portuguese would imply the presence of the Portuguese language and its presence would be expected to hinder the possibility of adstrate and/or superstrate language influence on the IP creoles.[7] For Diu and Daman, where the governmental presence ended only 50 years ago, we expect there to be little to no divergence in the respective phonological inventories and core lexicons of DIU and DAM. For CANN and SLP, where the Portuguese government ceased its presence in the mid-17th century, we expect to find considerable divergence given the presence of Dutch and, later, English and also that of the adstrate languages Malayalam for CANN and Tamil and Sinhala for SLP. For KOR, the situation is relatively less complex: after 1740 there was no Portuguese governmental presence and minimal to no Portuguese language presence. And since Marathi was the only adstrate language in the area for as long as the Portuguese were present in the Chaul-Korlai area, it has always been a two-language contact situation. Thus, we would expect substantial influence from Marathi on KOR.

With these predictions in mind, we now survey the phonological inventory in Section 4 and core lexicons of the IP creoles under study in Section 5.

4. Phonological inventories of DIU, DAM, KOR, CANN, and SLP

I discuss the vowel and consonant inventories separately. In Table 2, I include the vowel inventories of 15th/16th-century Portuguese, as well as of the IP creoles under study. A cursory examination of the information shown in Table 2 reveals, as predicted, that the inventories of the creoles which ceased to have a significant Portuguese presence the earliest have developed the most differences as compared to 15th/16th-century Portuguese. In the case of CANN, it has lost three nasal vowels and the nasal vowels it has retained have become mid-lax vowels, whereas in 15th/16th-century Portuguese they were mid-tense vowels. Moreover, CANN has developed the phoneme /æ/, which from the data available appears in stressed position (e.g. ['pæ li] 'skin, bark', [ma 'tæ] 'kill'. Since the data from CANN are recent and have not been exhaustively studied, it could be that [æ] and [ɛ] are allophones of either /æ/ or /ɛ/. Be that as it may, the presence of [æ], as a phoneme or an allophone, is an innovation and not found in any other creoles except SLP. A preliminary study of the CANN vowel system suggests that length is not phonemic, as it is in Malayalam, the adstrate language (Velayudhan & Howie 1974). Of all the creoles under discussion, SLP has undergone the most innovations: it has developed length as a phonemic distinction in its vowel inventory, it has lost all nasalized vocalic phonemes and, as just mentioned, it now has [æ] as a major realization of /a/. Moreover, it no longer has /ɛ/ and would probably be without /ɔ/ and /ɔ:/ as well, were it not for the lexical items incorporated from Dutch having a lax midback rounded vowel.

As for KOR, it has retained almost all phonemes of 15th/16th-century Portuguese. The only alteration found is in the mid nasal vowels, which have become lax but were tense in the Portuguese of the relevant period. The adstrate language, Marathi also has nasal vowel phonemes but is losing them, which seems to also be the case in KOR, where several frequently used words have also lost their nasal vowel, such as the present-tense copula *tɛ* (< 16th-c. Ptg. *tem* [tẽ] 'have-3SG', *têm* [tẽ:] 'have-3PL'; cf. Teyssier 1984:41). KOR's laxing of its mid nasal vowel phonemes cannot be due to direct Marathi influence given that, historically, Marathi does not have mid-lax vowel phonemes and it only has three nasal phonemes (Clements 1996:60). However, it may well be the case that one or more of the Southern Indian IP creoles may have had an influence in the creation of KOR and that KOR /ɛ̃/ and /ɔ̃/ may be due to influence from CANN or a close relative of it (such as Kochi Creole Portuguese), a possibility that will be explored in the discussion of the lexicons in Section 4. In the case of DAM, all vowel phonemes have remained the same, which is also the case for DIU with the exception of the mid nasal vowels, which display both a mid-high and mid-low realization, in free variation (Cardoso 2009:87).

So, it is arguably the case that mid-low nasal vowels are dominant in the IP creoles, suggesting a common origin. The fact that DIU and DAM have largely the same vowel inventory as Portuguese of the relevant period is not surprising given that the Portuguese presence for these varieties existed up until 1961 with a reduced presence up to the present, because of which the adstrate-language influence has been held in check with regard to these vowel inventories. So far, then, the factor of the length of a significant Portuguese presence in each of the communities can be appealed to for the degree of innovation found in each of the creoles.

In a slightly different format than in Table 2, I list in Table 3 the consonant inventory of 15th/16th-century Portuguese in the lefthand column and show which phonemes are present or absent in the IP creoles in question. All creoles here have retained 15 of the 26 phonemes from 15th/16th-century Portuguese: the stops /p, b, t, d, k, g, m, n/, the sibilants /f, s/, the liquids /ɾ, l/, the affricates /tʃ, dʒ/, and the glide /j/. All creoles except acrolectal DAM realize the 15th/16th-century Portuguese /v/ and /w/ as /ʋ/, an expected outcome given that the phoneme /ʋ/ is found in all Indo-Aryan and Dravidian languages in India.[8] And all the creoles have lost the apico-alveolar voiceless and voiced sibilants /ś/ and /ź/, as well as trilled photic /r/, although Diu and Daman retain it as an allophone of /ɾ/ in word-initial position.

Table 2. Vowel inventories of 15th/16th-century Portuguese, DIU, DAM, KOR, CANN, and SLP

Language	Vowel inventories
15th/16th-c. Portuguese	Oral: /i, e, ɛ, a, ɐ, ɔ, o, u/ (8)† Nasal: /ĩ, ẽ, ã, õ, ũ/ (5) (Clements 1996:60)
DIU	Oral: /i, e, ɛ, a, (ə), ɔ, o, u/ (8) Nasal: /ĩ, ẽ, ã, õ, ũ/ (5)
DAM	Oral: /i, e, ɛ, a, ə, ɔ, o, u/ (8) Nasal: /ĩ, ẽ, ã, õ, ũ/ (5)
KOR	Oral: /i, e, ɛ, a, ə, ɔ, o, u/ (8) Nasal: /ĩ, ɛ̃, ã, ɔ̃, ũ/ (5)
CANN	Oral: /i, e, ɛ, æ, a, ə, ɔ, o, u/ (9) Nasal: /ɛ̃, ɔ̃/ (2)
SLP	Oral: /iː, i, eː, e, æː, æ, aː, ə, (ɔː, ɔ), oː, o, uː, u/ (14) Nasal: -----

† With reference to the evolution of the Portuguese vowel system from the 14th century to the present, Teyssier (1984:42–43) posits the mid-central phoneme /ä/ both in stressed as well as in unstressed syllable. He situates this phoneme between the tense and lax mid vowels, the vowel space where we find /ə/ in IPA.

Table 3. Consonant inventories of 15th/16th-century Portuguese, DIU, DAM, KOR, CANN, and SLP

15th/16th-century Portuguese phoneme	DIU	DAM	KOR	CANN	SLP
p	+	+	+	+	+
b	+	+	+	+	+
t	+	+	+	+	+
d	+	+	+	+	+
k	+	+	+	+	+
g	+	+	+	+	+
m	+	+	+	+	+
n	+	+	+	+	+
ɲ	−	+	−	+	+
ɾ	+	+	+	+	+
r	− (present as allophone)	− (present as allophone)	−	−	−
f	+	+	+	+	+
v	−	+ (acrolectal)	−	−	−
s	+	+	+	+	+
z	+	+	−	+	+
š	−	−	−	−	−
ž	−	−	−	−	−

Table 3. (*continued*)

15th/16th-century Portuguese phoneme	DIU	DAM	KOR	CANN	SLP
ʃ	+	+	+	+	−
ts†	−	−	+	−	−
dz	−	−	+	−	−
tʃ	+	+	+	+	+
dʒ	+	+	+	+	+
j	+	+	+	+	+
w	−	−	−	−	−
l	+	+	+	+	+
ʎ	−	+	−	+	−
TOTALS:	17	20	18	19	17

† Both /ts/ and /dz/ are found only in KOR, very likely due to Marathi influence. For example, in Marathi /z/ or [z] is not found (Pandharipande 1997: 541). Thus, Portuguese *casa* [ˈka zɐ] is /kadz/ in KOR. /ts/ is found is various borrowed forms from Marathi, as in KOR /kats/ 'glass' and /potsu/ 'accompany (someone to a location)'.

Table 4 lists the consonantal phonemes that have been added to the inventories of the creoles in question.

Table 4. Consonants present in DIU, DAM, KOR, CANN, and SLP that are not from Portuguese

Language	New consonantal phonemes
DIU	/ʋ,(ŋ)/ (1 [or 2])†
DAM	/ʋ, (ŋ)/ (1 [or 2])
KOR	/bh, th, ʈ, ʈh, dh, ɖ, kh, gh, ʋ/ (9)
CANN	/ʋ/ (1)
SLP	/ʋ/ (1)

† Cardoso (2009: 92–93) argues for the phonemic status of [ŋ]. His main argument is that both [n] and [ŋ] can occur in coda position /fin/ 'small' vs /tiŋ/ 'had/there was'. This argument also applies to Daman, as well, in that [n] and [ŋ] are also found in coda position (cf. /pɛn/ and /tiŋ/).

Given the discussion in Sections 2 and 3 above, as well as the discussion of the vowel inventories just seen, we might expect that SLP would have diverged the most from Portuguese and DAM and DIU the least from Portuguese. The actual picture looks at first to be quite different. DIU has only 16 of the Portuguese phonemes, as does SLP. A closer look, however, reveals that SLP has lost /ʃ/, whereas DIU has not. SLP, then, seems to have diverged more than DIU. DAM has diverged the least, and even possesses sounds that developed later in Portuguese, such as [ʒ], and [ʟ], an allophone of /l/. Moreover, we would expect CANN and SLP to have similar or identical inventories, but CANN has retained the palatals /ʎ/ and /ʃ/ (e.g. /peʃi/ 'fish', /muʎɛr/ 'woman, wife') not present in SLP. KOR has by far the most affected consonantal inventory, having added nine new phonemes, retained the affricates /ts, dz/ (due arguably to Marathi influence, cf. Clements 1996: 67), and lost /ʎ/, which in KOR is realized as /l/, as in /mu-lɛr/ 'woman, wife', or reanalyzed as /ly/, as in /bal-'ya/ 'dance (v.)'.

To sum up this section, if we take into consideration both the vowel and consonant inventories of the IP creoles being analyzed, the predictions made in Sections 2 and 3 are overall borne out. Those creoles that have experienced the absence of a strong Portuguese presence the longest, i.e. CANN and SLP, have diverged the most from Portuguese in their phoneme inventories. The lack of newly adopted consonants could be the result of the influence of Dutch and English on the creoles in question, which kept at bay the influence of the regional indigenous languages Malayalam and Tamil/Sinhala, respectively. However, if this were the case, we would not necessarily expect the massive addition to the vowel system apparent in SLP. Thus, the predictions formulated in Sections 2 and 3, while pointing us in the right direction, cannot account for some of the sticky details. With respect to KOR, part of a two-language contact situation since its formation, the presence of nasal vowels and their recent decline, as well as the adoption of nine new consonants, is fairly clearly attributable to Marathi influence, apart from the lack of influence from other colonial languages, such as Dutch or English. Finally, DAM is the closest to Portuguese both in its vowel as well as consonant inventories. It not only has maintained all Portuguese vowels, as has DIU, but it still possesses all of the Portuguese consonants, including the more recently developed /ʒ/ and [ʟ] (not present in DIU), although these two are only found in acrolectal DAM. Essentially, then, the predictions are valid, but they do not account for the complexity of the sound inventories in the IP creoles under study. The phenomenon that underlies the changes is, of course, borrowing. In the absence of Portuguese in the communities under discussion, the creole-language speakers came to be more intensely in contact with the adstrate and/or other colonial languages. The consequence of this change was that it became more likely to borrow new sounds from these new languages. This also happened with lexical items, as we will now see in the discussion of the core lexicon in the next section.

5. The core lexicons of DIU, DAM, KOR, CANN, and SLP

The list of core lexical items for the five IP creoles is found below in the Appendix. It is difficult to compare the lists of the creoles because in SLP and DIU there are various missing items. To deal with this, I will assume that whatever the origin of a lexical item in DAM is, it will be the same in DIU.[9] This is based on the fact that 95% (197/208) of the Portuguese lexemes are the same in Daman and Diu. In the case of SLP, we can use our information about CANN and follow the same strategy in adjusting its lexical item inventory. In Table 5, I list the breakdown of the core lexicons of the five creoles in question, using the adjustments just described.

Table 5. Breakdown of the core lexicons (208 items) in DIU, DAM, KOR, CANN, and SLP

Language	From Portuguese	From adstrate/substrate	Unknown origin
DIU (adjusted)	206 (99.038%)	1	0
DAM	205 (98.557%)	2	1
KOR	188 (90.385%)	18	2
CANN	187 (89.903%)	20	1
SLP (adjusted)	194 (93.270%)	12	2

What is apparent is that there is a substantial difference in percentages of Portuguese core vocabulary retained between DAM and DIU on the one hand, and KOR, CANN, and SLP on the other. This division falls out directly from the criterion we have been using. Those communities where the Portuguese have been absent longer (from 1740 onward for Korlai, from the 1660s onward for Kannur and Sri Lanka) have incorporated more lexical items into their respective core vocabularies from the substrate or adstrate languages. In contrast, those communities in which the Portuguese presence lasted until recently (until 1961 for both Daman and Diu), there is substantially less impact on their respective core vocabularies.

Thus, for both the phonological inventories and the lexicons of these creoles, the length of the Portuguese presence coincides with more lexical borrowing and also a stronger tendency to borrow new segments. And these two phenomena are related in the sense that the more adstrate/substrate lexicon is borrowed, the greater the likelihood that new sounds will also be incorporated into the respective phonological systems.

Before discussing post-tonic syllables in the IP creoles, I offer an interesting fact about the connection between the south and the north. It is generally assumed that speakers of an Indo-Portuguese pidgin or newly developed creole in the south may have had an impact on the formation of northern creoles. Although it is sparse, the evidence is found in the form of two lexical items from

Malayalam. The Malayalam word *appam* 'unlevened rice flour handbread' is found in all northern IP creoles as *ap*. Malayalam *kaduva* 'tiger' is found in KOR as *khadya* 'tiger'. In a Diuese song, Cardoso (p.c. December 2011), found *patá*, which Dalgado (1919) argues is from Malayalam *patta* 'sash'. If these words traveled north, they were likely carried by speakers of a southern IP creole from Kochi, Kannur, and/or Kozhikode where Malayalam was and continues the regional language. If lexical items found their way into the northern IP creoles, I suggest that there was a numerically sizable number of speakers of a southern IP creole who had an impact on the northern IP varieties. We know that contact, both cultural and linguistic, did take place between one or more Portuguese colonial communities in the south and the northern communities where IP creoles were and/or are spoken today.

6. Portuguese post-tonic syllables in DIU, DAM, KOR, CANN, and SLP

In Sections 3–5, we have seen that the criterion of the length of the Portuguese presence in the communities where the creoles under discussion have been and are still spoken offers a reasonable account for the greater number of non-Portuguese lexical items in SLP, CANN, and KOR and relatively fewer of them in DAM and DIU. This same criterion also provides a sensible explanation for the general developmental trends in the phonological inventories of these creoles. The phenomenon underlying these changes is borrowing.[10] In the absence of the Portuguese and their language, the regional languages in the affected areas, and/or other colonial languages imposed, began to serve as sources for new lexical items and new sounds: CANN has borrowed from Malayalam and English, SLP from Tamil, Sinhala, and Dutch, KOR from Marathi, and DAM and DIU from Gujarati and English.

What we find in the creoles in question is a fundamentally different way of dealing with syllable structure in word-final position. Table 6 includes a comparison of key lexical items in the creoles that illustrate how the Portuguese post-tonic syllables are treated in each of the creoles. The systematic difference is striking: the creoles in the Indo-Ayran Sprachraum systematically drop the Portuguese post-tonic syllable, incorporating the onset consonant of the post-tonic syllable into the tonic syllable. In contrast, the creoles in the Dravidian Sprachraum retain the Portuguese post-tonic syllable.

Interestingly, with word-final coda in /ɾ/, CANN and SLP add a vowel to create a CVCV structure rather than maintaining a CV/ɾ/ structure. However, they permit CVC when /l/ (/saːl/, /sal/) is the coda. For SLP, /ʋ/ can also appear in coda, as in /raːʋ/ and /aːʋ/.

Table 6. Portuguese post-tonic syllables in KOR, DAM, DIU, SLP, and CANN

	PTG	Indo-Aryan creoles			Dravidian creoles	
		KOR	DAM	DIU	SLP	CANN
-p	tripa 'guts'	trip	trip	trip	triːpa	tripə
-b	rabo 'tail'	rhab	rrab	rab	raːv	rabə
-t	preto 'black, dark'	prɛt	prɛt	prɛt	prɛːtu	pretə
-d	pedra 'stone'	pɛd	pɛd	pɛd	pɛːdra	pædrə
-k	boca 'mouth'	bok	bok	bok	bɔːka	bɔkə
-g	água 'water'	ag	ag	ag	aːv	agə
-m	homem 'man'	ɔm	ɔm	ɔm	ɔːmi	ɔmi
-n	pena 'feather'	pɛn	pɛn	pɛn	pɛːna	pænə
-s	grosso 'thick'	gros	gros	gros	groːsu	grosə
-ʃ	peixe 'fish'	peʃ	peʃ	peʃ	peːsi	peʃi
-r	mar 'sea'	mar	mar	mar	maːra	marə
-l	sal 'salt'	sal	sal	sal	saːl	sal
	sol 'sun'	sɔl	sɔl	sɔl	sɔːl	sɔl

This notwithstanding, the pattern is clear. The question is why is this so? The answer can be found in the respective syllable structures of the Indo-Aryan languages on the one hand, and the Dravidian languages on the other. In her study of syllable structure in Malayalam, Mohanan (1989) compared syllable structures using Hindi- as well as Malayalam-speaking informants.[11] What she found was a systematic difference on how codas are treated, noting that, "[t]he distinction between speakers of Hindi and Malayalam could probably be generalized as a distinction between speakers of the Indo-Aryan and Dravidian languages in India" (1989:593). In general, Indo-Aryan languages allow virtually all consonants in coda position, as well as complex codas. Dravidian languages, by contrast, do not allow codas. Mohanan found the most dramatic evidence of this difference in the results of an experiment carried out on an individual speaker who spoke Kannada (a Dravidian language) and Konkani (an Indo-Aryan language) as native languages. This speaker was taught a word game that applies to syllables whereby the syllable *pa* is added to the beginning of each syllable of a word. For example, English *portal* would be *papor-patal* and *folder* would be *pafol-pader*. The informant, a child, was taught the *pa* language by her father, a linguist. She was then given a number of clearly Kannada words to elicit their respective versions in the '*pa* language'. Once the Kannada mode was set, the Kannada words were interspersed with the words (names) *naṇḍiṭa*, *uṭpala*, and *urmila*, that occur in all Indian languages. The informant's rendition of these words are in given in (3). The father then switched to Konkani, using clearly recognizable Konkani as input. When the same names were interspersed with these words, the informant rendered them as in (4).

(3) *Input in Kannada mode*   *Informant output in the 'pa language'*
    naṇḍita   pana-paṇḍi-paṭa
    uṭpala   pau-paṭpa-pala
    urmila   pau-parmi-pala

(4) *Input in Konkani mode*   *Informant output in the 'pa language'*
    naṇḍita   panaṇ-paḍi-paṭa
    uṭpala   pauṭ-papa-pala
    urmila   paur-pami-pala.

What is clear from these data is that the informant implemented different syllable structure rules in each language, which affected coda position of the word-initial syllable. For our purposes here, we assume that this difference in syllable structures in the Dravidian languages Malayalam and Tamil on the one hand, and in the Indo-Aryan languages Marathi and Gujarati on the other, affected the word-final syllables, as well, the great majority of which in Portuguese were post-tonic syllables. The result of this is visible in Table 6.

The next question is why these patterns found their way into the creoles. To answer this, we appeal to the notion of a shift dynamic that we assume was operative in the formation of these creoles. In the formation of these creoles, certain speakers of Tamil, Malayalam, Marathi, and Gujarati sought to acquire Portuguese. The speakers who first targeted one or more versions of Portuguese that led in each case to the formation of a creole language were speakers of Indic languages: of Dravidian languages in the south and of Indo-Aryan languages in the north. Consequently, when contributing to the formation of the respective creoles, these speakers would have been targeting Portuguese lexical items, but would have introduced structures from their respective native languages, among which they would have introduced some version of the syllable structure patterns found in their native languages. The preference of CV structure and non-tolerance for codas would have been introduced into CANN and SLP by speakers of Malayalam and Tamil (and possibly Sinhala), respectively. The speakers of Marathi and Gujarati, by contrast, would have introduced their strong tolerance for coda consonants into their variety of Portuguese. The overwhelming tendency in the northern IP creoles for word-final stress is not derivable from Marathi or Gujarati. Given that Portuguese post-tonic syllables disappeared in DIU, DAM, and KOR, and that the verbal systems in these languages took the Portuguese infinitival, 3SG preterit and past participle forms as the basis for verbal paradigm construction, there was a strong preponderance of forms with word-final stress in the newly forming creoles. Because of the sheer frequency of occurrence of this stress pattern, it may have been generalized in all three creoles, independently of one another. This matter still needs to be further studied.

7. Concluding remarks

In this study, I have focused on three key differences in the Indo-Portuguese creoles spoken in Diu, Daman, Korlai, Kannur, and Sri Lanka: differences in phonological inventory, in the core lexicons, and in the syllable structure of the creoles. We have suggested an account for these differences based on the chronology of the Portuguese presence and the distinction between borrowing and shift.

The criterion used to account for the differences in the phonological inventories and the core lexicons is the extent of Portuguese presence and borrowing in the communities. More specifically, the prediction is that the more recent the Portuguese presence, the less change one expects to find in the phonological inventories and core lexicons. This largely seems to be true. In Diu and Daman, where the Portuguese were present up to 1961, there is relatively less change in their respective phonological inventories and core lexicons. By contrast, in Korlai, Kannur, and Sri Lanka, the Portuguese presence ended well over 250 years ago and we find relatively more change in their respective phonological inventories and core lexicons. The underlying dynamic is, I argue, the borrowing dynamic. Once the Portuguese were absent in Korlai, Kannur, and Sri Lanka, the relevant indigenous languages and subsequent colonial languages took the place of Portuguese. The creole speakers then began to borrow from these languages over the last two and a half centuries.

The distinct treatment of the Portuguese post-tonic syllables, on the other hand, was not a borrowing phenomenon, but rather was part of a shift dynamic. As Thomason & Kaufman (1988) remind us, in a shift situation speakers target a language for acquisition. As a consequence, they seek to learn target-language vocabulary, but transfer their native-language structures into the language variety they are attempting to communicate in. In targeting Portuguese vocabulary, they learned this lexicon but at the same time carried their native-language structures into the variety of Portuguese they were helping to form. Concretely, the speakers of Gujarati, Marathi, Malayalam, Tamil, and Sinhala incorporated into the new variety of Portuguese they were forming the syllabic structure of their respective native languages. Based on this shift dynamic, the prediction regarding the syllabic structures to be found in the different Portuguese creole varieties is clear: to a greater or lesser extent, depending on the circumstances of each contact situation, the creoles will have the syllable structures of the native languages of the shifting speakers. The Dravidian no-coda constraint is found to obtain in word-final position in the Dravidian creoles, clearly apparent in how Portuguese post-tonic, final syllables are treated in CANN and SLP. By contrast, the Indo-Aryan creoles exhibit the constraints of Marathi and Gujarati in that they allow virtually all consonants in coda position and complex codas. As for the strong presence of word-final stress in the northern IP creoles, I have offered an account based on a frequency argument. With rare exceptions, all nouns underwent post-tonic syllable loss, which had as a consequence that they came to have word-final stress. Moreover, as stated above, the base forms for the verbal systems in these creoles had word-final stress, either directly from Portuguese, as with the infinitival and 3sg preterit forms, or indirectly through post-tonic syllable loss as in the case of the past participle. The result of these developments was the strong presence of word-final stressed forms, both in the nominal and verbal system. While I suggest that the strong presence of such forms may have led to a generalization of stress assignment in these creoles, it is also clear that the problem deserves more study.

Finally, there are some traits that are only traceable to those founding members in each settlement, evoking the Founder Principle, which is used to refer to speakers of the colonial languages who were instrumental in founding the settlements where creoles eventually formed (Mufwene 2001: 28–29). Two illustrative examples are the retention of the affricate /ʧ/ in words such as 'rain' (/ʧu/ in DAM and KOR, /ʧuʋ/ in DIU, /ʧuːʋa/ in SLP and /ʧuʋa/ in CANN), although one might expect the deaffricatization /ʧ/ → /ʃ/ that took place in the 17th century in Portuguese to have affected KOR, and especially DIU and DAM (Teyssier 1984: 53–54), and the form ɔs '2sg [familiar]' (< Ptg. *vos* '2pl, 2sg [formal]') in DAM, which ceased to be used from the 19th century onwards.

Notes

1. I consider the IP creoles a type of fort creole, that is, varieties that emerged and were nativized through the contact between colonials (the Portuguese in this case) and one or more groups of people in or around the fort, usually as slaves or workers of the colonizers. As such, the IP creoles are endogenous creole languages, that is, varieties that emerged in areas where the native languages of the creole-creating population were spoken. For Diu and Daman the creolizing population spoke Gujarati, for Korlai it was Marathi, for Kannur it was Malayalam, and for SLP they were Tamil, and possibly Sinhala, but to a lesser extent.

2. Unless otherwise indicated, the sources consulted for the different creoles are: Cardoso (2009) for Diu; Clements & Koontz-Garboden (2002) for Daman and Korlai, in addition to Clements (1996) for Korlai; Smith (1977) for Sri Lanka; and for Cannanore Edakkad (2010) and field notes taken by myself and Hugo Cardoso. I would like to thank Hugo Cardoso for facilitating my access to the speakers of Cannanore IP. The following abbreviations will be used: DIU = Diu IP, DAM = Daman IP, KOR = Korlai IP, CANN = Kannur IP, SLP = Sri Lanka IP.

3. Abruptly formed creoles are different from creoles that develop from stable pidgins, as for example, Tok Pisin. See Smith (2002) for a discussion of this.

4. For the IP creoles under discussion here, I understand contact intensity as the extent to which institutions such as the church, education, and government entities in the communities of IP creole speakers introduced languages other than Portuguese, and the extent to which these speakers were/are affected by such changes. More will be said about such changes below.

5. Alternatively, the possessor + genitive + possessum structure could have been brought from South India, where the Malayalam genitive marker *ude* appears in the same possessor + genitive + possessum structure and would have been mapped onto forms such as *sua* and *suas* (Essey et al. 2009; cf. also Krishnamurti 2003: 224, 233). However, the principle would be the same in that due to the dominance of the possessor + genitive + possessum structure in the Malayalam-speaking area in Kochi, Kozhikode, and Kannur.

6. We also know that there was input in the northern IP creoles (Korlai, Daman, and Diu) from speakers of southern IP creoles. For example, in Korlai, Diu, and Daman we find the Dravidian word *ap* 'handbread' (< Malm. *appam* 'handbread').

7. The presence of Portuguese and its function in the communities in question evoked for one reviewer the concept of the Founder Principle. Following Mufwene (2001: 28–29), the Founder Principle typically refers to speakers of the colonial languages who were instrumental in founding the settlements where creoles eventually formed. In the case of the IP creoles, there are some traits that are only traceable to those founding members in each settlement (such as /tʃ/ in words such as DIU, DAM, KOR /tʃega/ 'arrive' (today /ʃegar/ in modern Portuguese) or the form ɔs '2SG [familiar]' (< Ptg. *vos* '2PL, 2SG [formal]') in DAM, which is absent today in modern Portuguese. The Founder Principle can be evoked here and is compatible with the historical facts of the founding of these communities as I know them.

8. In word-final position, [w] is an allophone of /ʋ/, as in [paw] 'stick' in DIU, DAM, and KOR. To a far lesser extent, [w] is also found in CANN, as in [friw] 'cold'. Smith (1977: 182) states that [w] is also an allophone in SLP.

9. There are at least two ways to deal with the missing lexical items. Either we can make calculations based only on those items present in all five creoles or we can make certain assumptions about the nature of the missing items. Following the first option forces us to discard a significant number of items. The second forces us to make assumptions that might be erroneous, although they are probably true. I prefer the second option because it allows us to include more data.

10. It is entirely feasible that in shifting from an Indic language to some version of Portuguese, speakers in Diu, Daman, Korlai, Kannur, and Sri Lanka would also carry their native phonological inventories into the variety they ended up shifting to. This would account well for the presence of /ʋ/ in all creoles.

11. I use here the working assumption, based on the stability of the syllable structure in Marathi from the 16th century to the present, that the respective, current syllable structures of Gujarati, Hindi and Malayalam have been stable for the last four centuries.

References

Boxer, C. 1963. *Race Relations in the Portuguese Colonial Empire*. Oxford: Clarendon.
Cardoso, H. C. 2009. The Indo-Portuguese Language of Diu. PhD dissertation, University of Amsterdam.
Clements, J. C. 1996. *The Genesis of a Language: The Formation and Development of Korlai Portuguese* [Creole Language Library 16]. Amsterdam: John Benjamins.
Clements, J. C. 2003. The tense-aspect system in pidgins and naturalistically learned L2. *Studies in Second Language Acquisition* 25: 245–81.
Clements, J. C. 2009. *The Linguistic Legacy of Spanish and Portuguese: Colonial Expansion and Language Change*. Cambridge: CUP.
Clements, J. C., and A. J. Koontz-Garboden. 2002. Two Indo-Portuguese creoles in contrast. *Journal of Pidgin and Creole Languages* 17 (2): 191–236.
Croft, W. 2000. *Explaining Language Change. An Evolutionary Approach*. London: Longman.
Dalgado, S. R. 1919. *Glossário Luso-Asiático*. Coimbra: Imprensa da Universidade.
Edakkad, S. 2010. *Vasco da Gama and the Unknown Facts of History*. Kerala: Eye Books.
Essey, S., E. Silkensen, and L. Spangler. 2009. Malayalam. Ms.
Ivens Ferraz, L. 1987. Portuguese creoles of West Africa and Asia. In *Pidgin and Creole Languages: Essay in Memory of John E. Reinecke*, ed. G. G. Gilbert, 337–360. Honolulu HI: University of Hawaii Press.
Klein, W., and C. Perdue. 1992. *Utterance Structure: Developing Grammars Again* [Studies in Bilingualism 5]. Amsterdam: John Benjamins.
Krishnamurti, B. 2003. *The Dravidian Languages*. Cambridge: CUP.
Lispki, J. 2005. *A History of Afro-Hispanic Language: Five Centuries, Five Continents*. Cambridge: CUP.
Mohanan, T. 1989. Syllable structure in Malayalam. *Linguistic Inquiry* 20 (4): 589–625.
Mufwene, S. 2001. *The Ecology of Language Evolution*. Cambridge: CUP.
Pandharipande, R. V. 1997. *Marathi*. London: Routledge.
Smith, G. 2002. *Growing up with Tok Pisin*. London: Battlebridge.
Smith, I. R. 1977. Sri Lanka Creole Portuguese Phonology. PhD dissertation, Cornell University.
Teyssier, P. 1984. *História da Língua Portuguesa*. Lisbon: Sá da Costa.
Thomason, S. G., and T. Kaufman. 1988. *Language Contact, Creolization, and Genetic Linguistics*. Berkeley, CA: University of California Press.
Tinhorão, J. R. 1997 [1988]. *Os Negros em Portugal. Uma Presença Silenciosa*. Lisbon: Caminho.
Velayudhan, S., and J. M. Howie. 1974. Acoustical measurements of distinctive vowel quantity in Malayalam. *Language and Speech* 17: 95–102.

Appendix

No	English	Portuguese	Korlai IP	Daman IP	Diu IP	Sri Lanka IP	Kannur IP
1	all	todo/tudo	tud	tud	tud	tudu	tud(ə)
2	and	e	ani	i, ku	i, ku	kum	kum (with NPs; there is no conjunction for clauses)
3	animal	animal	animal	animal	animal	animal	animal
4	ashes	cinza	sints	sĩz	sĩz	siːnza	sinzə
5	at	em	su pert (< Ptg. *perto* 'near'), nə (< Ptg. *no* 'in the'), də (< Ptg. *de* 'of')	nə, də	pert də, jũt də (< Ptg. *no* 'in the')	-ntu (LOC)	∅
6	back (body)	costas	kɔs	kɔs, kwɔs	kɔs	kɔːsta	kɔstə
7	bad	mal(o)	maw	maw	mal	maːl	mizəral
8	bark (v.)	urrar, uivar, ladrar	hubya	ladra	ladra	bɔlfa	rónkə
9	bark (tree)	casca	alb su kas	kas	kask	paːʈa (< Tamil *paṭṭai*)	ælvəri sə pæli
10	because	porque	karən	purke	pɔrke, purke, kawz [də]	kiː-pa seː	swidə
11	belly	barriga	bharig	barig	barig	bariːya	barrigə
12	big	grande	gran	tɔmoyŋ, gran (acrolectal)	gran	graːndi	grandi
13	bird	pássaro	pas	pasariŋ	pasariŋ	paːstru	pastrə
14	bite	morder	murde	murde, da dentad	murde	murda	murdɛ
15	black	preto	pret	prêt	pret	preːtu	pretə
16	blood	sangue	sayŋ	sayŋ	saŋ	saːngi	sangi

No	English	Portuguese	Korlai IP	Daman IP	Diu IP	Sri Lanka IP	Kannur IP
17	blow	soprar, ventar	supra	supra	asupra	sufra:	supra
18	bone	osso	os	os	os	o:su	osə
19	breast	peito	peyt	pet	pet	pe:tu	petə
20	breathe	respirar, suspirar	suskar tuma	reʃpra	---	---	---
21	burn	queimar	kima	kima, pega fog	kima	kima:	kima
22	child	criança	kriyãs	kriyãs	kriãs	kriya:nsa	kriyansə
23	claw	garra	undʑ	uɲ	uɲ	---	uɲə
24	cloud	nuvem	ɖɦəg	nuʋ	nuʋ	mo:ʋis	cloud, mekham
25	cold	frio	friw	fri	fri	fri:yu	friw
26	come	vir	ʋi	ʋi	ʋi	ʋi:	ʋi
27	count	contar	kota	konta	kõta	konta:	konte, kontɛ
28	cut	cortar	korta	korta	korta	korta:	kɔrta
29	day	dia	di	di	di	di:ya	di(y)ə
30	die	morrer	mhure	mata	mure	mura	murre
31	dig	cavar	kava	kava	faze burak	---	gəʋatə
32	dirty	sujo	sudʑ	sudʑ	sudʑ	su:y	sudʑi
33	dog	cão, cachorro	kãw	kãw	kãw	kaʃo:ru	kaʃor
34	drink (v.)	beber	bebe	bebe	bebe	beʋa	bebe, bebɛ
35	dry	seco	sek	sek	sek	se:ku	sæke
36	dull	sem corte	bhoʈəl	buntu	---	brɔm	aguɖə nu tɛ̃ 'not sharp'
37	dust	pó	rhen	puyér	puer	suːy, pɔ	barə
38	ear	orelha, ouvido	oʋid	uʋid, oreʎ	uʋid	oreːya, oʋiːdu	uʋid
39	earth	terra	ter	ter	ter	teːra	barə
40	eat	comer	kume	kume	kume	kuma	kume
41	egg	ovo	ob	oʎ	oʋ	oːʋ	eʋə
42	eye	olho	ol	oʎ	oyl	oːy	oi

Notes on the phonology and lexicon of some Indo-Portuguese creoles 39

No	English	Portuguese	Korlai IP	Daman IP	Diu IP	Sri Lanka IP	Kannur IP
43	fall	cair	kaí	kai	kai	kaj	kaj
44	far	longe	lɔj	lɔj	lɔj	lɔːnɖi	lɔnɖi
45	fat/grease	manteiga, gordura, azeite 'oil'	manteg, adzejt	gordur, manteg, azejt	azet, mãteg	gurduːra, azeːti	azeti, mantegə 'ghee'
46	father	pai	paj	paj	paj	paːj	paj
47	fear	medo	med	med	med	meːdu	mɛdə
48	feather	pena, pluma	pɛn	pɛn	pɛn	pɛːna	pæːnə
49	few	poucos	pok	pok, tajn, pukin	pok, pokʃin	poːku, gɔːta (< Ptg. gota 'drop')	pok
50	fight (v.)	lutar	luta	luta, ʤuga	---	brija (< Ptg. brigar 'fight, quarrel')	pilʤe
51	fire	fogo	fog	fog	fog	foːʊ	fog(ə)
52	fish	peixe	peʃ	peʃ	peʃ	peːsi	peʃi
53	five	cinco	sink	sink	sĩk	siːnku	sinkə
54	float	boiar	tarta hika	nada	---	nadaː	---
55	flow	fluir	wahun anda	vaza	vaza	---	(ag su ribə tə vaj 'goes on top of the water')
56	flower	flor	ful	flor	flor	fuːla	fula
57	fly (v.)	voar	awga	agwa	uva	awgaː	agwa, agwɛ
58	fog	nevoeiro	fumas	orvaʎ	uva	uruvaːja 'dew, snow'	fog
59	foot	pé	pe	pe	pe	peː	pɛ
60	four	quarto	kwat	kɔt, kwɔt	kwɔt	kaːtru	katrə
61	freeze	gelar	bəraf hika	mara, fika ʤel	fika ʤel	---	freeze
62	fruit	fruta	frujt	frut	furt	froiːta	frute
63	full	cheio, enchido	iʧid	inʃid	chej	inʃiːdu	inʃid

No	English	Portuguese	Korlai IP	Daman IP	Diu IP	Sri Lanka IP	Kannur IP
64	give	dar	da	da	da	da:	da
65	good	bom	buni (< Ptg. bonito 'pretty')	bõ, lind, bunit	bõ, bunit	bo:m	bõ
66	grass	erva, grama	pal (< Ptg. palha 'straw')	paʎ	ɛrʊ	ɛ:rʊa	grasə (< Eng. grass)
67	green	verde	vɛrd	vɛrd	vɛrd	ve:rdi	vɛrdi
68	guts	tripa	trip	trip	trip	tri:pa	tripə
69	hair	cabelo	kabel	kabil	kabel	kabe:l	kabeli
70	hand	mão	mãw	mãw	mãw	ma:m	mɔ̃
71	he	ele	el 's/he'	il	el	eli	eli
72	head	cabeça	kabes	kabes	kabes	kabe:sa, kavasa	kabesə
73	hear	ouvir	ovi	uvi	uvi	ovi:	oí
74	heart	coração	korsãw	kursãw	kursãw	korsa:m	korso
75	heavy	pesado	peɖzad	pezad	pezad	peza:du	pezad
76	here	aqui	aki	aki, ka	aki	aki:	ɛki
77	hit	dar uma pancada, bater	dal (< Ptg. dá-lhe 'hit him/her')	bate	bate	--	dali
78	hold (take)	tomar	tuma	tuma	tuma, leva	toma:	tama, təma
79	horn	corno, chifre	ʃiŋ	dãnʃ	ʧif	ko:rnu	--
80	how	como	kilɛ (< Ptg. que laia 'what manner')	kilaj, kɔm	kɔm	kila:j	kelej
81	hunt	caçar	kasad birka	vay kasad	--	--	--
82	husband	marido	marid	marid	ɔm	mari:du	maridə
83	I	eu	yo	yo	yo	e:ʊ	yo
84	ice	gelo	bərəf	ʤel	ʤel	--	ajs (< Eng. ice)

Notes on the phonology and lexicon of some Indo-Portuguese creoles   41

No	English	Portuguese	Korlai IP	Daman IP	Diu IP	Sri Lanka IP	Kannur IP
85	if	se	ʃi	si	si	se;, kanda, kam- (< Ptg. quando 'when')	sə
86	in	em	nə, də, det	nə, dent, də	nə, dət [də]	-ntu 'LOC'	dentrə
87	kill	matar	mata	mata	mata	mata:	matæ
88	knee	joelho	dhopa	inveʎ, (indʒwel - acrolectal)	dʒwej	indʒuvej	---
89	know	conhecer, saber	kwise, sab(e)	kwise (kuɲse – acrolectal), sabe	kuɲse, sabe	kunsa, sava	kunse, sabɛ
90	lake	lago	tala	tænk	tãk	ta:nki	---
91	laugh	rir	rhi	ri	ri	ri:	rihe (also riɛ)
92	leaf	folha	fol	fol	foj	fɔʎa	fɔʎə
93	leftside	à esquerda	dawri (badzu)	iʃkerd	lad iskerd	mayskɑːrda (< Ptg. mão esquerda)	left,
94	leg	perna	pe (< Ptg. pé 'foot') 'leg and foot'	pe 'leg and foot'	pe 'leg and foot'	pe: 'leg and foot'	pɛ 'leg and foot'
95	lie	estar deitado	korp pichad	diskensa	diskənsa	deta:	detɛ
96	live	viver, morar (in a place)	vib hika, hika	vive, tɛ ku ʋid, fika	vive, fika	mora: (obs.) para: 'live, stay, stop, wait'	---
97	liver	fígado	fig	fig	fig	fiːdu	liver (< Eng. liver)
98	long	comprido	koprid	kumprid	kõprid	kumpri:du	kumpridə
99	louse	piolho	pijol	pjoʎ	piol	pijoːj	pioji
100	man	homem	ɔm	ɔm	ɔm	ɔːmi	ɔmi
101	many	muitos, -as	mɔt (< Ptg. monte 'mountain')	mwi(t)	muʲt, bastãt (< Ptg. bastante 'enough')	muʲtu, bastantə	bəstantə

No	English	Portuguese	Korlai IP	Daman IP	Diu IP	Sri Lanka IP	Kannur IP
102	meat	carne	kharm	karn	kar	ka:rni	karni
103	moon	lua	luvar	luvar, (lu – acrolectal)	lu	luma:ra	luvə, luvare
104	mother	mai	maj	maj	mãj	maj	maj
105	mountain	serra, outeiro, monte, montanha	sɛr	ojter (small), muntaŋ	ojter	monta:ɲa	montaɲə
106	mouth	boca	bok	bok	bok	bo:ka	bɔka
107	name	nome	nom	nom	nom	nɔ:mi	nɔmi
108	narrow	estreito	tʃũntʃ	estret	---	istre:tu	idungiya (Malayalam), narrow (English)
109	near	perto	pɛrt	pɛrt	pɛrt	pe:rtu	pɛrtə
110	neck	pescoço	biskos	piskos	gargát (< Ptg. garganta 'throat')	garga:ntu, gɔrgal	piskos, garganta, gargəntə
111	new	novo	nob	nov	nov	nov	ɛʋə
112	night	noite	anot	anot	nojt	ano:ti	nojti
113	nose	nariz	naris	naris	naris	na:ris	naris
114	not	não	nu, ni	nun, nin	nã, nãw	na:, nu(n/m)-	nu, na
115	old	velho	vɛʎ	vɛʎ	vɛj	vɛj	væli, veliz
116	one	um	ũ	ũ	ũ	uɲ(a)	uɲa
117	other	outro, mais um	maj(z)ũ	ot, majzũ	ot	o:tru	otrə, dusre (< Hindi dusra, dusri, dusre)
118	person	pessoa	piso	piso	piso, peso	pesa:m	peso
119	play	jogar, brincar	birka	dʑuga, brinka	dʑuga, brika	brinka:	brinke
120	pull	puxar, tirar	puʃa	puʃa, rranka	ráka, tira	pusa:	pwise, pwiʃe
121	push	empurrar	loʈu	empurra	atara	taʎi	puʃɛ
122	rain	chuva	tʃu	tʃu	tʃuʋ	tʃu:ʋa	tʃuʋə

Notes on the phonology and lexicon of some Indo-Portuguese creoles 43

No	English	Portuguese	Korlai IP	Daman IP	Diu IP	Sri Lanka IP	Kannur IP
123	red	vermelho, encarnado	birmel	enkarnad	vermej	bruma:j	brəmel
124	right/correct	direito, justo, correcto	dretur, ʤus	dret, sert, ʤus	dret, verdad	dre:tu, ʤu:stu	ʤusta
125	rightside	à direita	maw dret	lad dret	lad dret	mandre:tu, ma:m dre:tu	rightside
126	river	rio, ribeiro	rhiber	rri, rriber	riber, ri	ri:ɔ	river (English)
127	road	caminho	kami	kamiɲ, estrad	kamiɲ, istrad	kami:m	kamiɲə
128	root	raiz	rhajs	rrajz	raiz	rɛzə	root
129	rope	corda	kɔrd	kɔrd	kɔrd, liɲ	ko:rda	kɔrdə
130	rotten	podre	pod	pod	pod	po:dri, roti:du	a podrə, podrid
131	round	redondo	gol	redɔnd	redɔnd	rɔnt (< Dutch)	redondə
132	rub	esfregar	masa	iʃprega	---	rusa:	rub (English)
133	salt	sal	sal	sal	sal	sa:l	sal
134	sand	areia	reti	are	arej	ari:ja	barrə
135	say	dizer, falar	hala	fala	fala, dize	fala:	fala
136	scratch	arranhar	rhaɲa	rraɲa	raspa, raɲa	---	raɲɛ, raspɛ
137	sea	mar	mar	mar	mar	ma:ra	marə
138	see (perception)	ver	parse	parse	aparse	parsa	parsɛ
139	seed	semente	simet	siment	simẽt	---	frujtɛ
140	sew	coser, costurar	kudze	kuʃtra	kustara	kuza	kuze
141	sharp	agudo	agud	agud	agud	aʋdu	agud
142	short (object length)	curto	kurt	kurt, piken	kurt, piken	ku:rtu	kurtɛ
143	sing	cantar	kata	kanta	kanta	kanta:	kantɛ
144	sit	sentar	data	santa	sẽta	santa:	santɛ

No	English	Portuguese	Korlai IP	Daman IP	Diu IP	Sri Lanka IP	Kannur IP
145	skin	pele	pɛl	pɛl	pɛl	pɛːli	pæli
146	sky	céus	sews	sɛw	sɛw	sɛʋ	heaven (English)
147	sleep	dormer	durmi	durmi	durmi, drumi	drumiː	drumi
148	small	pequeno, fino	piken, fin	piken	piken, tʃɛr ʋi	pikiniːm	piken
149	smell	cheirar	tʃer ʋi	tʃera	tʃera, tʃer ʋi	tʃeraː	tʃerə
150	smoke (n.)	fumo, fumaça	fum	fum, fumas	fum	fuːmu	fumə
151	smooth	liso	lidʒ	liz	---	liʃiːn	---
152	snake	cobra	kɔb	kɔb	kɔb	---	kɔbrə
153	snow	neve	bərəf	dʒel (< Ptg. gelo 'ice')	---	---	ice (English)
154	some	algum	angu	algũ	ãgu	alũŋ, pisiɲə	---
155	spit	cuspir	kuspi	kuspi	kuspi	kuspiː	kuspi
156	split	partir	abri	abri	raʃa, kebra	fenda	abri
157	squeeze	apertar	dabu	tʃapa	apreta	masaː	piɲɛ, piɲə
158	stab/pierce	furar	fura, bəsku	fura	fura, firi	firiː	tʃutʃɛ 'poke'
159	stand	estar em pé	ipe tɛ/hika	fika impe	ẽpe, leũta	impɛ, irigiː 'be standing'	igri, impɛ
160	star	estrela	istrel	istrel, iʃtrel	istrel	istrɛːla	istrelə
161	stick	pau	paw	paw	paw	paːʋ	kanə
162	stone	pedra	ped	pɛd	pɛd	pɛːdra	pædrə
163	straight	direito, recto	dret	dret	dret	iirti (< Ptg. hirto 'stiff')	dretə
164	suck	mamar, sugar	mama, mama da	mama, tʃupa	---	tʃupaː	tʃupɛ
165	sun	sol	sol	sɔl	sɔl	sɔːl	sɔl
166	swell	inchar	itʃa	inʃa	itʃa	inʃaː	inʃə
167	swim	nadar	nada	nada	nada	---	---

No	English	Portuguese	Korlai IP	Daman IP	Diu IP	Sri Lanka IP	Kannur IP
168	tail	rabo	rhab	rrab	rab	ra:ʋ	rabə
169	that	isso, aquilo	ake	akel, əkel	ikəl	aka	akəl
170	there	aá, ali	ali, aklad, ake badzu	ali, əkelband, əkelad	ali, ikalad	ala:	ali
171	they	eles, elas	elo	ilot, elz	el, elz	etus	olot
172	thick	grosso	gros	gros	gros	gro:su	grosə
173	thin	ralo, fraco, magro, fino, delgado	rhal, frak, dalgad, fin	rral, agwadm mag	mag, fin	fi:nu, ma:gru	finə
174	think	pensar	viʃʃar hedze	pensa, bate kabes	pêsa	lembra:	lembra, lembre
175	this	este, esta, isto	ye	es	es	isti	isti
176	thou	tu	wɔ (< Ptg. vós 'you.pl')	sɔ	use (< Ptg. você 'you.formal')	bo:s, ʋo:s	bosə
177	three	três	trej	trej	trej	tre:s	tresə
178	throw	atirar	piʃʃa, atra	atra	atəra	pinʃə	pinʃə
179	tie	amarrar	mhara	marra	amərə	mara:	mare, marə
180	tongue	língua	liŋ	liŋ	liŋ	li:ŋgu	liŋə
181	tooth	dente	dɛt	dent	dɛt	de:nti	denti
182	tree	árvore	alb	arʋ	arʋ	a:lʋri	alʋri
183	turn	girar, virar	vira hedze	ʋira	ʋira	ʋira:	ʋirə
184	two	dois, duas	doj	doj	doj	do:s	dos
185	vomit	vomitar	gumita	lansa	---	gumita:	gumta, gumtɛ
186	walk	andar, marchar	marʃa	marʃa	ãda	maʃa:	marʃa
187	warm	quente	kɛt	kent	kɛt	ke:nti	kenti ('warm, hot')
188	wash	lavar	lava	lava	lava, lipa, faze lip	lava:	ænsəgə, lavə
189	water	água	ag	ag	ag	a:ʋ	age

No	English	Portuguese	Korlai IP	Daman IP	Diu IP	Sri Lanka IP	Kannur IP
190	we	nós	nɔ	nɔs	nɔs	noːs	nɔzə
191	wet	molhado	muljad	muljad	mujad	mujaːdu	muʌad
192	what	que	ki	ki	ki	kiː	ki
193	when	quando	kɔr (< Ptg. que hora 'what hour'), ki, kɔr ki	kwan, kɔm	kwɔn	kijɔːra	kiɔra, ɔrsə, əzə
194	where	onde	un	un, dun	ɔn	oːndi	ɔndi
195	white	branco	brak	brank	brãk	braːnku	brankə
196	who	quem	kẽ	kẽ	kẽ	keːm	kẽ
197	wide	largo, larga	larg	larg	larg	---	larg
198	wife	mulher, esposa	muler	muʌer	mujer	mujeːra, dʒifrau (< Dutch je vrouw 'your wife')	muʌerə
199	wind	vento	vẽt	vent, ventoz	vẽt	vɛːntu	væntə
200	wing	asa	adʒ, pənkhə	az	az	aːsa	azə
201	wipe	limpar	lipa ku pan	limpa ku trap	lipa, faze lip	limpaː	limpə
202	with	com	-kosid, ku	ku, dʒunt	ku, dʒũt də	juːntu	dʒunta, suntadə, dʒuntadə
203	woman	mulher	muler	muʌer	mujer	mujeːra	muʌer
204	woods	mato	mat	dʒəngəl	jungle	maːtu	matə
205	worm	bicho	biʃ	biʃ, lombrig	biʃ	biːʧi	lumbrigə
206	ye	você, vós	use	use	use	botus (< Ptg. vós outros)	bosə
207	year	ano	an	an	an	aːnu	anɛ, anə
208	yellow	amarelo	marel	marel, safrãw	amrel	safraːm	marɛl

A closer look at the post-nominal genitive in Asian Creole Portuguese

Alan N. Baxter and Augusta Bastos

The chapter discusses the post-nominal genitive present in many varieties of Asian Creole Portuguese and derived from a Portuguese prenominal possessive. The text builds on Clements' Malabar Pidgin Portuguese hypothesis, and Dalgado's vision of an easterly spread of Indo-Portuguese features. The role of Dravidian substrate in genitive restructuring is stressed. Possessives in 6 varieties of Asian Creole Portuguese are compared and a grammaticalization path for the post-nominal genitive is proposed. The extension of post-nominal genitives to further inter-NP functions is discussed, focusing on the creoles of Korlai and Malacca. Some extended post-nominal genitive functions may represent early Indo-Portuguese Pidgin/Creole use. Quantitative analysis of post-nominal genitive in Malacca Creole reveals a preference for + HUM possessors, and traits of a 3rd person prenominal possessive typical of 16th-century Portuguese. This suggests early consolidation of the structure.

1. Introduction

The post-nominal genitive (PNG), exemplified in (1), is a characteristic of Asian Creole Portuguese varieties extending from Korlai to Macau (Hancock 1975; Ferraz 1987; Holm 1989; Clements 1996).

(1) Malacca Creole (Baxter, fieldwork May 2011)
   aké   belu   sa   prau
   DEM   old   GEN   boat
   'The old man's boat'.

As such, it falls within a set of features shared by many varieties of Asian Creole Portuguese (ACP), including a future-irrealis marker *lo(gu)* <Ptg. *logo*, its negative equivalent *nad(i)* <Ptg. *não há de*, and the interrogative *k(il)ai* <Ptg. *que laia* (Ferraz 1987).

For the descriptive purposes of this chapter, it is assumed that the post-nominal genitive is an associative structure within a single DP_a which has the following format: $[DP_a[X [DP_b] + \text{GEN}] [NP]]$. Thus, within Example (1), the DP_b *aké belu*, and its post-position, genitive *sa*, function as a modifier (X) of the NP *prau*. The term genitive represents the fact that one of the salient semantic functions of this construction is the expression of possession. In this relationship, the owner entity is typically referred to as the POSSESSOR and the entity which is its property is referred to as the POSSESSEE (Croft 2003: 32; Heine 1997: 34). In Example (1), *aké belu + sa* functions as POSSESSOR, and the NP *prau* functions as the POSSESSEE.

The chapter considers aspects of the development and role of the post-nominal genitive in the possessive systems of a range of varieties of ACP. Following a discussion of the genesis and spread of PNG among these creoles, attention focuses on the comparative possessive systems of two sets of ACPs, one set being southern Indo-Portuguese and the other being Southeast/East Asian. Subsequently, discussion turns to the extension of the PNG to the representation of a wide range of semantic relationships including, among others, those of attribution, worth and composition. Korlai Creole and Malacca Creole data provide a focus for these considerations. Subsequently, quantitative data from Malacca Creole is analyzed in order to better assess the location and vitality of PNG in the grammar of this particular creole. It will be seen in both the comparative study and in the single quantified study that PNG retains certain core functions that appear to have crystallized early in the histories of the varieties of ACP considered here.

2. Background

Ferraz (1987: 349) considered the post-nominal genitive to be sufficiently pervasive in the varieties of ACP that it must have become established during the development phase of these creoles. Clements (2000) proposes a southern Indian origin for such items as *k(il)ai* and *lo(gu)*, through a pidgin centered on the first Portuguese trading posts, such as Cochin, where the Portuguese established a *feitoria* in 1502 and built a fortress in 1503 (Morais 1993: 27). In the 16th century, Cochin was the initial seat of government and administrative base for Portuguese activities in Asia. Along the Malabar (Kerala) coast *feitorias* were established in these early years at Cannanore, Calicut, Quilon, and Mangalore. Fortresses were built and garrisoned at many of these locations, such as at Cannanore in 1505 and Quilon in 1518 (Morais 1993: 28, 45).

Following Clements' proposal, a similar source is suggested for the origin of the post-nominal genitive. In this setting, in an early stage of contact, incipient pidginized Portuguese would have been influenced by areal features of the languages of South Asia. Subsequently, emergent varieties would have been propagated from the first southern Portuguese establishments to other locations as the Portuguese ventured further afield. These endeavors involved contingents of Portuguese and (often large numbers of) non-Portuguese military/maritime elements and sundry camp followers from India and further afield. The Portuguese chroniclers of the 16th century mention the heterogeneous compositions of the armadas (Cardoso 2009: 49–51). For example, it is reported that the conquest of Malacca, from Cochin, in 1511, involved some 800 Europeans and 600 Indian troops (Wilkinson 1912: 73). Such mixed groups would have been the initial purveyors of emergent pidgin to other locations. Subsequent population movements associated with colonial administration, missionary activities and principally maritime trade, would have spread creole elements.[1] This reality was first referred to by Dalgado (1917). The shared set of linguistic features documented from Korlai to Macau suggests an easterly process of linguistic spreading, whereby features crystallized in establishments founded earlier were spread to those locations established subsequently.

In the 16th century, varieties of pidgin Portuguese in the southern Indian *feitorias* formed in contact with local languages with strict post-positional configurations and with mutually similar genitive structures. It would appear that early stage acquisitional transfer from these languages guided the development of a post-nominal genitive tendency in the emergent Portuguese contact varieties. Thus, in Cochin, the local language is Malayalam, which indicates noun and pronoun possessors by a suffix *-uṭe* on nouns, as in (2a), and *-ṟe / -uṭe /* on singular and plural subject pronouns respectively, as in (2b):

(2) Malayalam (Asher & Kumari 1997: 173)
    a. *sittayuṭe viiṭə*
       Sita-GEN house
       'Sita's house'
    b. *enṟe tala*
       1SG-GEN head
       'My head'

From the perspective of a Malayalam speaker looking to identify genitive case in a Portuguese contact situation, it seems plausible that the ACP post-nominal possessive would have originated through a reanalysis of genitive structures wherein the marker of the genitive relation precedes the POSSESSEE. This is the case of the Portuguese possessive determiners in Table 1, all of which are assumed to have been present in the early 16th century.

Table 1. Possessive determiners in early 16th-century Portuguese†

Person ↓	Singular		Plural	
	Masculine	Feminine	Masculine	Feminine
1	meu	minha	nosso	nossa
2	teu	tua ~ ta		
	vosso	vossa	vosso	vossa
3	seu	sua‡	seu	sua

† All the forms in this table inflect for plural number by adding -s.

‡ The Medieval Portuguese unstressed possessive determiner *sa* is found occasionally in documents at the very beginning of the 16th century, such as the *Carta de Caminha* (written in 1500).

This was the pool of forms in which the L2 acquirer/observer of Portuguese would have detected a genitive function marker prior to a POSSESSEE NP. Later, in the 17th and 18th centuries, Portuguese incorporated *você* (<*vossa mercê* 'your grace') as a second person pronoun, accompanied by the use of *seu* (and variants) as its 2nd person possessive (Silva 1996: 169; Teyssier 1997: 89; Faraco 1996; Lopes & Duarte 2003; Menon 2006).[2]

In addition to evolving a genitive based on Portuguese 3SG/3PL possessive determiners, most of the ACPs have incorporated the possessive determiner *minha*. In these developments, the role of phonological salience and frequency of occurrence would have been significant. Indeed, a search on the possessive determiner paradigm in the diachronic corpus of Portuguese (Davies & Ferreira 2006) is instructive. Thus, in 16th-century documents of fiction, albeit only an indirect indicator of discourse, the following distribution is of possessives is found: 1SG *meu(s) / minha(s)* 16.65%; 2SG *teu(s) / tua(s)* 2.08%; 2SG/2PL *vossa(s) / vosso(s)* 2.6%; 3SG/3PL *seu(s) / sua(s) / su(s) / sa(s)* 68%; 1PL *nossa(s) / nosso(s)* 10.4%. The acquisition of forms based on the 1SG and 3SG/3PL series seems logical. At the same time, in some situations of language contact, the possibility of an acquirer/learner associating *seu(s) / sua(s) / su(s) / sa(s)* with the second syllable of the forms *nossa / nosso / vossa / vosso* might also be relevant. In contexts where the acquirer's L1 was Malayalam, the Portuguese subject pronouns *vós* 'you SG/PL' and *nós* 'we' could facilitate such an analysis, because Malayalam indicates pronominal possession by a *nominative pronoun + genitive suffix* structure. Overall, it does not seem logically difficult for a speaker of a language with a POSSESSOR-GEN + POSSESSEE structure to detect the Portuguese GEN + POSSESSEE pattern and thence assign a frequent Portuguese possessive determiner to an L1 structure. Portuguese pronominal *seu / sua* could thus be restructured as a post-nominal genitive following the (initially) Dravidian DP typology. However, while forms derived from Portuguese *minha* and *sua* are widespread, the latter principally as a post-nominal genitive, yet also partially as a possessive determiner, these are not the only possessive markers that entered the ACPs. Thus, a number of the latter creoles also display possessive determiners and pronominals based on Portuguese *nosso* and *vosso*, yet also based on Portuguese subject pronouns *nós* and *você* (see Tables 2a, 2b, 3a and 3b below).

2.1 Propagation further afield

Dalgado (1917:50) proposes that the post-nominal genitive would have been propagated on the basis of *sua* associated with the second person pronoun *você* and the possessive *vosso*; initial *sua* reducing to *su* or *sa*, and spreading to other pronouns. However, the history of Portuguese possessives and the pronoun *você*, plus the fact that 3rd person possessors would be the most represented in the input, and the consistent post-nominal genitive suffix in the southern Indian substrates, would seem to support an initial propagation by means of the 3rd person possessive determiners.

An early pidgin originating on the Malabar Coast, and spreading to other locations, in many cases would have come into contact with local languages sharing some features of the Dravidian language family. Thus, in the context of Chaul, speakers of contact Portuguese arriving from the southern region to establish a *feitoria* and later, in 1519, a fortress (Morais 1993:45), came into contact with Marathi, an Indo-Aryan language, which also has post-nominal possessives, as in (3). Clements (1996:139–140) has proposed the reanalysis of Portuguese *seu/sua* under the influence of the Marathi possessive suffixes *-tsa/-tsi/-tsə*, as in Example (3).

(3) Marathi (Clements 1996:140)
Kapil- tsa ghər
Kapil GEN house
'Kapil's house'

Marathi pronouns also receive a possessive suffix, *-dza* for the 1st and 2nd person, and *-tsa* with the 3rd person. The latter suffix, being present on nouns and pronouns, could have reinforced the reanalysis, yet possession with pronouns in Korlai Creole is indicated by possessive pronouns and not by the genitive marker (Clements 1996:103).

It seems reasonable to assume that any post-nominal genitive tendency already crystallized in the contact Portuguese of the Malabar Coast would have been readily assimilated during acquisition-development of the contact language by speakers of Marathi. In the south, initial contacts with Ceylon (Sri Lanka) in

1506 were also established from the Malabar Coast (Morais 1993:31). Later, in 1518, a fortress was built in Colombo (Morais 1993:45). In this southern setting, Malabar contact Portuguese met Sinhala, in which possessive DPs occur with a genitive morpheme that attaches to a personal pronoun or to a noun (Gutiérrez Morales 2006), and Tamil, wherein similar facts apply (Smith 1977; Krishnamurti 2003). The genitive structure in the contact precursor of Sri Lanka Creole Portuguese (SLP) would have been further guided by these two forces.

Much further afield, in Southeast and East Asia, this southern Indian areal feature would have met substrates with analytic genitives, in the same configuration: POSSESSOR + GEN + POSSESSEE. In Malacca Creole the post-nominal genitive is conditioned by such structures in Vehicular Malay and Baba Malay (4) and Hokkien (5), (Baxter 1988:92; Yap 2007), although it may also have had early reinforcement from the languages of the local Indian population.[3] In Bidau Creole, in East Timor, it coincides with an analytic structure in Tetum, in Example (6), and in the case of Macau Creole, a similar structure is also to be found in Cantonese, in Example (7) below.[4] In each of these local languages, the possessor may be either a noun or a nominative pronoun.

(4) Baba Malay (Baxter 1988:92)
 gua punya rumah
 1SG POSS house
 'my house'

(5) Hokkien (Baxter 1988:92)
 huà é cchŭ
 1SG GEN house
 'my house'

(6) Tetum (Baxter 1990:14)
 António nia carau
 António GEN buffalo
 'António's buffalo'

(7) Cantonese (Matthews & Yip 1994:108)
 léih ge pàhngyáuh
 2SG LP friend
 'your friend'

2.2 ACP post-nominal genitives compared

Research for the resent paper revealed that the post-nominal genitive occurs in the following 11 ACPs: Korlai, Mangalore, Mahé, Cannanore, Cochin, Nagapattinam, Sri Lanka, Malacca, Batavia/Tugu, Bidau (Timor) and Macau.[5] The retention of this feature in such a wide set of ACPs is likely to be owed to three factors: (1) its early crystallization in Indo-Portuguese Pidgin; (2) convergence with other languages that have a similar mechanism, in further geographic locations throughout the region; and, (3) ongoing reinforcement from Indo-Portuguese Creoles as connections between the diverse outposts developed and stabilized (Baxter 2010a).

Unfortunately, the data for many of these ACPs are scant, and allow little insight into their possessive systems. Nevertheless, there is a geographically well distributed subset of ACPs with a richer set of data, permitting an interesting comparison. The creoles in question are: Korlai, Mangalore, Sri Lanka, Malacca, Batavia and Macau. When information on the distribution of possessives within these ACPs is tabled, it is evident that the degree of grammaticalization of Ptg. *sua* varies considerably. In each of the ACPs compared, the post-nominal genitive shares space with other possessive markers, the extent of which varies from creole to creole. This may in part be due to differences in the extent of contact with Portuguese. Metropolitan Portuguese (and Asian derivatives thereof) had a prolonged presence in many of these locations, by way of missionaries and traders, and this could have helped retain certain forms closer to Portuguese. In the case of Macau, this contact was constant and led to decreolization over the past two centuries (Pinharanda Nunes 2011).

However, a degree of caution is warranted when interpreting the significance of variant forms in particular ACPs. The competing systems evident in the data on certain creoles may have several sources. The variants may represent elements of different registers: a colloquial register and a formal register (as, for example, in the case of Korlai Creole 2SG), more basilectal versus more acrolectal styles (for example, in Macau Creole), or a missionary register (for example in the Creole Portuguese of Sri Lanka). Missionary sources may impose novel interpretations on existing creole variants and also may introduce forms derived from Modern Portuguese (Smith 1998).

With the preceding observations in mind, Tables 2a and 2b (for the Southern Indo-Portuguese varieties) and 3a and 3b (for the Southeast and East Asian varieties) were prepared. Tables 2a and 3a compare the prenominal possessive determiners and their function as possessive pronouns. Tables 2b and 3b compare post-nominal genitives occurring with pronominal possessors and nominal possessors, and whether the pronominal possessor with this structure can function as a possessive pronoun.

Table 2a. Possessive determiners and possessive pronouns in Asian Creole Portuguese: three Southern Indo-Portuguese varieties[†]

	Possessive determiners [Poss.DET.] + NP				Possessive pronoun
	1SG <Ptg. *meu, minha*	2SG/2PL <Ptg. *vossa/o, vós, você*	3SG/3PL <Ptg. *seu, sua, sa*	1PL <Ptg. *nossa/o, nós*	= Possessive determiner
KORLAI	*mi* Cl:103.	*vosso* 2sGI, *usé* 2sGF[††], *udzo* 2PL Cl:103.	*su, sus* Cl:103.	*nɔ,* Cl:103.	All Poss.Dets.
MANGALORE	*minha, minh* S:885, 887.	*voss, bossa, vossa, vossu* S:887–890	*su* S:890, *sua*[‡] S:898	No data located.	2SG *vossu* S:891
SRI LANKA	*minha, minhe* C:21.	*vosso*[‡‡] C:21	*sua* D:148; *suve* C:21.[*]	*nosso* C:21.	All Poss.Dets. C:21.

[†] The abbreviated page number references in each row are: Korlai: Cl = Clements (1996; p.c. July 2011); Mangalore: S = Schuchardt (1883); Sri Lanka: C = Callaway (1820), D = Dalgado (1998[1900]).

[††] Clements registers a difference in formality in the second person singular: informal (2SGI) versus formal (2SGF).

[‡] The data item with *sua* has 2nd person reference.

[‡‡] In the singular, there seem to be two levels of formality, *vosso* or *vosse-su*, and the possessive determiner *tua*, however Callaway (1820) does not clarify this. Yet, he registers (p. 21) three levels of formality in the second person plural: *volotros-su* '2PL inferiors', *vosotros-su* '2PL equals', *vosse-ellotros-su* '2PL superiors'.

[*] Presumably *suve* is the same as *sua*, the letter 'v' representing a /w/ glide. This is the only instance of *suve* in the Callaway text, which otherwise is consistent in its use of genitive *su*. The use of *sua* in the texts in Dalgado (1998[1900]) possibly results from a convention of the 19th-century Protestant missionary register of SLP and, to judge from the presence of genitive *su* in modern SLP, was probably not representative of the 19th-century colloquial register (cf. discussion in Smith 1998).

Table 2b. Post-nominal genitives in Asian Creole Portuguese: Southern Indo-Portuguese varieties

	Pronominal possessor [[Pronoun]+GEN]+NP	Nominal possessor [[DP]+GEN]+NP	Possessive Pronoun =[[Pronoun]+GEN]
KORLAI	*x* Does not occur	*su* Cl:162–165.	*x* Does not occur
MANGALORE	2SG *boz's* S:892.	*'s* S:896.	No data located.
SRI LANKA	2SG *vosse-su*† C:21, *vosse* C:35, *vos-su* C:44. 3SG *elle-su, ella-su* C:21. 2PL *volotros-su, vosotros-su, vosse-ellotros-su* C:21. 3PL *elles-su, ellotros-su* C:21.	*sua* D:148; *su* C:13	2SG *vosse-su* C:21. 3SG *elle-su, ella-su* C:21. 1PL *nosse* C:41. 2PL *volotros-su, vosotros-su, vosse-ellotros-su* C:21. 3PL *elles-su, ellotros-su* C:21.

† Callaway (1820) does not list the form *vossa*. As he presents two orthographic forms for the 1SG possessive, *minha* and *minhe*, both presumably with a final /a/ vowel unstressed, it seems likely that *vosse* is derived from Ptg. *vossa* and not Ptg. *você*. The same comment applies to the 1PL possessive *nosse* (Callaway 1820:41).

Table 3a. Possessive determiners in Asian Creole Portuguese: three Southeast and East Asian varieties[†]

	Possessive determiner [Poss.DET.] + NP				Possessive pronoun
	1SG <Ptg. *Meu, minha*	2SG/PL <Ptg. *vossa/o, vós, você*	3SG/PL <Ptg. *seu, sua, sa*	1PL <Ptg. *nossa/o, nós*	= possessive determiner
MALACCA	*minha, mio* R:66.	x Does not occur.	*sa, sua* R:80–81.	x Does not occur.	*x mio, minha, sua* R.:66. Only *sa* has vitality currently.
BATAVIA	*mienja* S:100.[††]	*boos* S:95, *vossé*, S:100.	*soe* S:106; *soea* S:100.	No data located.[‡]	*soea* S:101.
MACAU	*minha* F:237.	*vosso* F:237.	*sua, sa* B:30, 348.	*nosso* F:237	*minha, bosso, nosso* F:237–238; *sua, sa* B:30, 348

[†] The abbreviated page number references in each row are – Malacca: R = Rêgo (1998[1942]), Batavia / Tugu: S = Schuchardt (1890); Macau: F = Ferreira (1996:237–238), B = Barreiros (1943–44).

[††] In the Tugu Creole data, the 1SG possessive is an adnominal genitive: *meessoewah* (Shuchardt 1882:69).

[‡] In the Batavia data, the only 1PL possessives take the postnominal genitive. The form *nos* is found in the Tugu Creole data: *nos paij* 'our father' (Schuchardt 1890:67).

Table 3b. Post-nominal genitive markers in Asian Creole Portuguese: Southeast and East Asian varieties

	Pronominal possessor [[Pronoun] + GEN] + NP	Nominal possessor [[DP] + GEN] + NP	Possessive Pronoun = [[Pronoun] + GEN]
MALACCA	*sa, sua* (arch.)† R:66: 1SG: *yo sa* 2SG: *bos sa* 3SG: *eli sa* 1PL: *nus sa* 2PL: *bolotu sa* 3PL: *olotu sa*	*sa, sua* R:66.	R:66: 1SG: *yo sa* 2SG: *bos sa* 3SG: *eli sa* 1PL: *nus sa* 2PL: *bolotu sa* 3PL: *olotu sa*
BATAVIA	S:100: 2SG *boos soea* 1PL *noos soea, noosoter soea* 2PL *vosoter soea* 3PL *iloter soea*	*soe, soea*, S:122.	S:100–101: 1SG *mienja soea* 2SG *bosée soea* 1PL *noosoter soea* 2PL *vosoter soea* 3PL *iloter soea*
MACAU	F:237–238: 1SG *iou-sua*†† 2SG *vosso-sua, vôs-sua* 3SG *êle-sua*‡ 1PL *nôs-sua* 2PL *vosôtro-sua* 3PL *ilôtro-sua*	*sa*, B:483, *sua*, B:30.	F:237–238: 1SG *iou-sua* 2SG *vosso-sua, vôs-sua* 3SG *êle-sua* 1PL *nôs-sua* 2PL *vosôtro-sua* 3PL *ilôtro-sua*

† Coelho (1886:722) reports both *sua* and *su* as occurring with pronominal possessors, with the same range of pronouns listed here for Malacca. Additionally, he lists *minha sua* or *minha su* as a 1SG pronominal possessor.

†† The form *sa* is common in recordings of Macanese speakers made by Charpentier (1992) and by Mário Pinharanda Nunes of the Department of Portuguese at the University of Macau.

‡ In the 3rd person, Barreiros (1943–44:483) also registers *sua-ça*: "*sua-ça mamã*" 'her mother'.

All of the varieties compared in the preceding tables display some use of prenominal possessive determiners based on Ptg. *minha* and Ptg. *sua*. In several cases they also display prenominal possessives based on Ptg. *vossa/o, vós, você* and Ptg. *nossa/o, nós*. However, the latter may result from the nature of the register reported or from the viewpoint of the persons who wrote these forms down. It is difficult to say whether the forms *nossa, vossa*, although written as units in the creole texts, in some creoles might have been analyzed by speakers as PRO + GEN. Hence, while all the ACPs considered here have a post-nominal genitive derived from Ptg. *sua*, the extent of its incorporation into the grammar in each case may vary.

The creoles of Korlai and Malacca represent two extremes. Korlai Creole relies on prenominal possessive determiners to represent pronominal possession and independent possessive pronouns (Table 2a), and only has the post-nominal genitive with nominal possessors (Table 2b). However, Malacca Creole has incorporated the post-nominal genitive (Table 3b) to such an extent that it expresses possession with both nominal and pronominal possessors and it constitutes the only means of representing independent possessive pronouns. Nevertheless, in Table 3a, Malacca Creole shows evidence of prenominal determiner functions of *sa/sua*, and vestigial *minya*.

On the other hand, Mangalore Creole, partially, and SLP more significantly, show evidence of pronominal possession represented both through prenominal possessive determiners (Table 2a) and through the post-nominal genitive (Table 2b). In SLP the post-nominal genitive has grammaticalized to represent most pronominal possessors and independent possessive pronouns. These structures show that the post-nominal genitive has lost the 3rd person semantics of its Portuguese etymon. Furthermore, from Callaway's (1820) consistent representation of the genitive as *su*, it appears that the phonological form of the genitive in modern SLP was present in the early 19th century. The form *sua*, reported by Dalgado (1998) may well be a fiction of the register popularized by the British protestant missionaries (Smith 1998). Although 19th-century SLP shows some evidence of a wide range of prenominal pronominal possessives functioning as independent possessive pronouns (Table 2a), caution is again warranted when considering the missionary sources. However, among the pronominal possesives in prenominal position, *minha* is the only means of representing the 1SG possessive, a detail that gains some support by comparison with the other varieties.

In Southeast Asia, 18th-century Batavia Creole suggests a similar distribution, with the role of the post-nominal possessive firmly extended to all functions (Table 3b): pronominal possessor, nominal possessor and independent possessive pronoun. However, the 1SG possessive, while expressed as a prenominal determiner, *mienja* (Table 3a), is also found with the post-nominal genitive (Table 3b), representing the 1SG possessive pronoun: *mienja soea* 'mine', which suggests that *mienja* was being used as a person-number marker, without its possessive feature.

Compared with 18th-century Batavia Creole, the distribution of possessive forms in 20th-century Malacca Creole seems to represent the next step in grammaticalization and spread of the post-nominal possessive. In Malacca Creole there is no sign of prenominal possession by 1PL <Ptg. *nosso/nossa, nós* and 2SG/2PL <Ptg. *vosso/vossa, vós, você*. These possessive functions are only represented by the post-nominal construction, and 1SG possession is also predominantly represented by the same means as *yo sa* 'mine, my', with the 1SG possessive determiner and possessive pronoun *minya* being obsolete. Malacca Creole now has a uniform genitive paradigm for all persons and numbers, consisting of pronoun + *sa*. Only a handful of elderly speakers maintain the 1PL possessive determiner *minya*, which today is mainly used with immediate kin terms. Thus a speaker who uses *minya* will also use the analytical structure *yo + sa* more generally. The presence of the form *minha sua* 'my' in the 19th-century Singapore offshoot of Malacca Creole (Coelho 1886:722) provides a parallel with the weakening of the possessive value of *mienja* evident in the presence of the pronominal possessive *mienja soea* 18th-century Batavia Creole data and in the presence of *messoewah* (Schuchardt 1890:73) in Tugu.⁶ To judge from the Malacca case, the extension of the post-nominal genitive to the 1SG pronoun is the final stage of this restructuring process. In this scenario, the Portuguese 3SG prenominal possessive determiner grammaticalizes first to function as an post-nominal genitive for the 3rd person, subsequently it spreads to the 1PL, 2SG and 2PL and, finally, it takes over the 1SG possessive functions. The development may be resumed as follows:

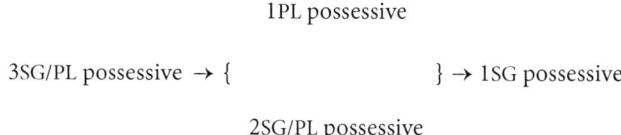

Figure 1. Spread of the post-nominal genitive <Ptg. *sua, seu* in personal possessives

Finally, the third extreme case is that of Macau Creole. On the one hand, it displays the full set of prenominal determiner uses (Table 3a), with the prenominal determiners also representing a pronominal function, as in Portuguese. The ongoing presence of Portuguese would have helped maintain this distribution. On the other hand, Macau Creole also displays strong post-nominal genitive use (Table 3b) in the representation of pronominal possessors and possessive pronouns, in addition to its representation of full DP possessors. The latter instance appears to be a minor function of this genitive marker.

However, the grammaticalization of Ptg. *sua, seu* as a post-nominal genitive does not end here. The following section considers the extension of the post-nominal genitive to functions beyond those of basic possession.

3. Extension of the functions of the genitive marker

Reanalysis and convergence of pre-POSSESSEE genitives of Portuguese and substrate origins may lead to the integration of additional functions associated with the substrate genitive. Thus, Clements (1996: 139–142) reports that the Korlai Creole genitive suffix, -*su* matches 10 functions of its Marathi post-nominal genitive -*sta* counterpart. The semantic functions of Kor. -*su* paralleled in Marathi, and the grammatical function of complementizer, are listed below:[7]

1. possession/origin (*x-su* = belongs to/is from *x*);
2. distributive (*x-su y* = a frequency of *y* relative to *x*);
3. purpose (*x-su* = for the purpose of *x*);
4. 'worth' (*x-su* = amount/worth of *x*);
5. 'composed of' (*x-su* = composed of *x*);
6. attributive (*x-su* = type of *x*);
7. complementizer 'for/to';
8. causal (*x-su* = because of *x*);
9. instrumental (*x-su* = with *x*);
10. immediate source (*x-su* = immediately from *x*).

Clements (1996: 142–143) also notes that Korlai Creole *su* has several functions that are not found in Marathi. These are the grammatical functions of adjective and adverb derivation, nominalization, marking of locative adverbials, and the semantic function of partitive (Clements 1996: 144).[8] In Malacca Creole, the *sa* genitive, in addition to expressing possession, as in Example (1) performs a number of the other functions found in Korlai Creole, including some of those not found in Marathi. Thus, for example, Malacca Creole *sa* can convey expression of "possession/source", as in (8a); "part of", as in (8b); expression of "worth", as in (8c); "material composition", as in (8d); marking of a locative adverbial, as in (8e); and an attributive function, as in (8f):

(8) Malacca Creole (Baxter, fieldwork May 2011)
    a. *Singapura sa jenti lo beng Malaka*
       Singapore GEN person FUT come Malacca
       'People from Singapore will come to Malacca'.

b. *prau sa tabu podri*
   boat GEN plank rotten
   'The boat's planks (= the planks of the boat) are rotten.'
c. *trinta sen sa sukri*
   thirty cent GEN sugar
   'Twenty cents worth of sugar'
d. *akeli prau madera sa*
   DEM boat wood GEN
   'That boat is made of wood.'
e. *naké casa sa dianti teng ngua albi koku*
   LOC+DEM house GEN front EXST 1 tree coconut
   'In front of that house there is a coconut palm.'
f. *quatu inch sa tabu podi sibrí*
   four inch GEN plank can use
   '4-inch planks can be used.'

Also, resembling the Korlai Creole genitive marker repertoire, in Malacca Creole the post-nominal genitive may enter into nominalization processes, as in (9):[9]

(9) Malacca Creole (Baxter 1988: 94)
eli sa kumí ńgka retu
3SG GEN eat NEG correct
'Her eating (i.e. diet) wasn't correct.'

In expanding into these functions, the *sa* construction competes with a Portuguese-based prepositional construction employing *di* 'of, from'. In Malacca Creole, with the exception of nominalization, the functions in (8) and (9) may be expressed by POSSESSEE + *di* + POSSESSOR structures (cf. Baxter 1988). In such cases, the use of Malacca Creole *di* reflects the functional range of its etymon in Portuguese. Thus, for example, the content of (8b) may be paraphrased as (10):

(10) Malacca Creole (Baxter, fieldwork May 2011)
tabu di prau podri
plank of boat rotten
'the planks of the boat (= the boat's planks) are rotten.'

The distribution of the Malacca Creole *sa* and *di* associative structures will be compared in Section 5, below.

In the different varieties of Asian Creole Portuguese that have the postpositional genitive, the extent to which this structure replaces the Portuguese-based prepositional variant in associative structures varies. Whereas Malacca Creole retains a certain presence of the prepositional structure, Korlai Creole, for example, privileges the postpositional structure and restricts the prepositional variant to one or two locative functions only, and even then, the postpositional structure is preferred:

(11) Korlai Creole (adapted from Clements 1996: 144)
mew   də   mar
middle of   sea
'in the middle of the sea'

Modern Sri Lanka Creole (Smith 1977) also displays a similar, essentially exclusive use of the postposition. The limited materials available for the other Indo-Portuguese varieties that have the postpositional structure suggest a similar tendency already in the 19th century.

The degree of retention of the prepositional structure in certain varieties may have several sources. In some substrate languages, certain functions cannot be represented by their postpositional genitive. Thus, for example, Malayalam uses a different postposition for locatives and Malacca Vehicular Malay employs prepositional representation of sources and spaces. Such 'exceptions' in the face of the extensive functions of a postpositional genitive in individual substrate languages, coupled with an ongoing presence of Portuguese, could have facilitated the presence of preposition *di*. Owing to limitations of space, this topic will not be explored further in the current chapter.

In addition to the functions mentioned above, the Malacca Creole genitive *sa* displays some divergent functions which appear to be peculiar to this variety. It occurs in complex modifiers resembling left branching relative clauses, as in (12), and it occurs in a very frequent structure, shown in (13), where it has an emphatic or stance function:

(12) Malacca Creole (Baxter 1988: 94)
eli   ngka   sistí   na   kaza   sa   jenti
3SG   NEG   stay   LOC house GEN person
'He isn't a person who likes to sit around at home (Lit. a stay-at-home person)'.

(13) Malacca Creole (Baxter, fieldwork 1980)
isi   cheru   bomong   forsa,   mizu   di   gadratu   sa
DEM   scent   very   strong   urine of crocodile GEN
'The scent/smell was very strong, (like) crocodile urine *truly*'.

Malacca Creole Examples (9), (12) and (13) point to the influence of Baba Malay and local Vehicular Malay. However, while these varieties of Malay constituted substrates in 16th-century Malacca, and the creoles are traditionally bilingual in colloquial Malay, it is not Malay itself that is the ultimate source here. Rather, it is

Hokkien and other Chinese languages, such as Hakka, Cantonese and Chaozhou (Yap 2007). Malacca Creole *sa* is similar to Baba Malay and Vehicular Malay post-nominal genitive *punya* (<Mal. lexical noun/verb *empunya* 'possess') which, Yap (2007, 2010) explains, has developed following a similar grammaticalization pattern in these Chinese languages. Vehicular and Baba Malay *punya* and Hokkien *e* (< Hok. noun classifier *e*) both have grammaticalized as genitive markers and, subsequently, as nominalizers, relative clause markers and markers of stance (Yap 2007; 2010).[10] Owing to limitations of space, the topics suggested by Examples (9), (12) and (13) will not be discussed further in the current paper.

In other varieties of ACP that have post-nominal genitives, it may be the case that functions beyond the basic possession role of the genitive are also present. Limitations of the data available for most of these varieties make it difficult to assess this issue. Nevertheless, some of the wider functions of the genitive observed in Korlai Creole and Malacca Creole are evident. These functions include, for example, the marking of a locative adverbial in Mangalore Creole in (14), worth (or, possibly, attribution) in Sri Lanka Creole (15), attribution in Tugu Creole, (16); and attribution again, in Cochin Creole, (17):

(14) Mangalore Creole (Schuchardt 1883: 896)
libro ki teng bureau sa riba
book REL EXST desk GEN top
'the book on top of the desk'

(15) Sri Lanka Creole (Dalgado 1998[1900]: 149)
33 cents sua vinho ellotros ja bebê
33 cents GEN wine 3PL PST[11] drink
'33 cents of wine (33 cent wine) they drank'

(16) Tugu Creole (Schuchardt 1890: 99)
trees peo so foendo
three foot GEN deep
'three feet deep (= a depth of three feet)'

(17) Cochin Creole (Schuchardt 1882: 6)
hojo su pescaria
today GEN fishing
'today's fishing (= fishing of today / these days)'

In view of these parallels, two questions arise. Firstly, to what extent do such properties reflect an earlier pidgin or earlier Asian creole(s) containing a common set of features in the period when regular maritime communication existed between the locations where different ACP communities developed? Secondly, to what extent do these properties represent individual, local developments attributable to indigenous areal effects? Table 4 lists the 14 Korlai Creole features expressed by the post-nominal genitive (Clements 1996: 141–144) and compares their representation in Marathi, Korlai Creole, Malacca Creole and Malacca vernacular Malay.

Table 4. Functions of post-nominal genitives in Marathi, Korlai Creole Portuguese, Malacca Creole Portuguese and Malacca Vehicular Malay

Functions	Marathi	Korlai Creole	Malacca Creole	Malacca Vehicular Malay†
1. Possession	✓	✓	✓	✓
2. Distribution	✓	✓	✗	✗
3. Purpose	✓	✓	?	✗
4. Worth	✓	✓	✓	✗
5. Composition	✓	✓	✓	✗
6. Attribution	✓	✓	✓	✓
7. Complementization	✓	✓	✗	✗
8. Causal	✓	✓	✗	✗
9. Instrumental	✓	✓	✗	✗
10. Immediate source	✓	✓	✗	✗
11. Derivation: adverb / adjective		✓	✗	✗
12. Partitive		✓	✗	✗
13. Nominalization		✓	✓	✓
14. Marking of locative		✓	✓	✗

† I thank Dr Yap Foong Ha (p.c. June 2011) for useful comments on this distribution. It must be stressed that Malacca Vehicular Malay, spoken in a multilingual setting, displays a great deal of variation, and it is possible that certain lects may represent more of these functions via the post-nominal genitive. Furthermore, a survey of the languages spoken by the Malacca Chinese community may reveal further parallels. These matters can only be addressed by further research.

Table 4 shows that post-nominal genitives in Korlai Creole and Malacca Creole have 7 functions in common. Five of these are also found in the substrate of Korlai Creole, Marathi. Of these five, three are also matched by the post-nominal genitive in the substrate of Malacca Creole, Vehicular Malay. A further feature, the marking of locatives, is found only in the two creoles. Among the functions beyond possession that were identified in certain other ACPs in the previous discussion, it is notable that these fall within the set shared by the Malacca and Korlai varieties. The tentative conclusion is that these 7 shared features could possibly constitute traces of early Indo-Portuguese Pidgin/Creole use, a by-product of regional substrates. A topic for future research would be to investigate how Malayalam handles these 14 functions.

In the discussion so far, a qualitative review shows that the *sa* genitive in Malacca Creole shares features with other ACPs that go beyond a basic possession relation, while displaying yet other functions that seem local. At the same time, it was noted that the *sa* genitive overlaps with the *di* prepositional construction. However, just because *sa* is possible in certain functions doesn't necessarily mean that it is specialized in those functions. For this reason, it was proposed to survey the distribution of the *sa* genitive quantitatively, in order to gain a clearer view of its locus in the system of Malacca Creole. The grammar of *sa*, and its interplay with the *di* associative structure might throw further light on the connection between Malacca Creole and other ACPs.

4. The place of *sa* genitive in Malacca Creole: data and method

A database was prepared from a 1980 corpus of 21 traditional Malacca Creole stories from five different story tellers in the same age-group (now 80–90 years). These stories all contain dialogues and narrative description. 903 instances of *sa* and 188 instances of prepositional *di* were identified in structures relating two denotations.[12] These data were codified for the semantics of the 'linking' relationship, the structure of the POSSESSEE and the POSSESSOR, and the separation of POSSESSEE and POSSESSOR. Subsequently, comparative tables were generated by the MAKECELL sub-program of the GOLDVARB-X statistical package (Sankoff, Tagliamone & Smith 2005).

In the following sections, four topics will be considered, presenting some key aspects of a larger quantitative analysis of Malacca Creole *sa* currently in progress:

1. the distribution of the *sa* and *di* constructions, according to the semantic functions of the genitive relationship;
2. the structure of possessor DPs in the *sa* and *di* constructions;
3. the degree of separability of possessor and possessee in *sa* constructions; and
4. the nature of distanced possessor DPs in *sa* constructions.

Unless otherwise indicated, language examples in the ensuing discussion are from the Malacca Creole traditional oral story corpus.

5. Semantic functions expressed by post-position *sa* and preposition *di*

The range of semantic functions represented by these two linking constructions covers, broadly, the areas of possession and post-nominal modification. It is relatively common cross-linguistically to find the same formal means representing these relations (Heine 1997; Nikolaeva & Spencer, *forthc.*). Where possession is concerned, in the literature, the prime distinctions of inalienable/alienable, or that of intrinsic/extrinsic possession, constitute a basic descriptive matrix (Nikolaeva & Spencer, *forthc.*: 4–7). Nevertheless, languages vary greatly as to whether this distinction is represented formally (Heine 1997), and while the notion of inalienable possession is clear enough, alienable possession may express a broad range of semantic values more akin to post-nominal modification, often quite removed from the notion of possession.

Bearing in mind the evident absence of a cross-linguistic commonality defining alienable and inalienable possession, (Heine 1997; Nikolaeva & Spencer, *forthc.*: 5) and aware that the *sa* and *di* constructions express meanings beyond the basic possession functions, in the current paper it was decided to classify these constructions in terms of a broad set of 9 semantic classes based partly on Baxter (1988).[13] The aim was to capture any finer tendencies in the distribution. Table 5 shows the overall distribution of the 903 *sa* genitives in terms of these semantic classes.

Table 5. Distribution of *sa* and *di* constructions by semantic function

Function ↓		*sa*			*di*		
		Nº	% of total *sa*	% per function	Nº	% of total *di*	% per function
a.	Kinship	500	55.4	100%	0	0	0
b.	Body part	80	8.9	96%	3	1.6	4%
c.	Ownership	250	27.7	94%	16	8.5	6%
d.	Other interpersonal relationship	40	4.4	89%	5	2.6	11%
e.	Classificatory	6	0.7	50%	6	3.2	50%
f.	Part-whole	8	0.9	42%	11	5.9	58%
g.	Spatial/locative	10	1.1	16%	51	27.1	84%
h.	Origin/source	5	0.6	13%	34	18.1	87%
i.	Material composition	4	0.4	6%	62	33	94%
	TOTAL	903	100%		188		

The above nine factors are exemplified respectively for the *sa* and *di* constructions in (18a–i), for the *sa* construction, and (19a–i), for the *di* construction, below.

(18) Malacca Creole (Baxter, fieldwork 1980)
    a. bos sa fila
       2SG GEN daughter
       'your daughter'

b. *e(li) sa garganta*
   3SG GEN throat
   'his throat'
c. *eli sa prau*
   3SG GEN boat
   'his boat'
d. *el sa dama*
   3SG GEN mistress
   'his mistress'
e. *isi nasang sa pastu*
   this type GEN bird
   'this type of bird'
f. *ngua barku sa kodra*
   one boat GEN line
   'a boat's mooring line'
g. *yo sa kaza sa dianti*
   1SG GEN house GEN front
   'the front of my house'
h. *aké mpoku Rome sa jenti*
   that few Rome GEN people
   'those few people from Rome'
i. *papel sa pastu*
   paper GEN bird
   'a bird (made) of paper'

(19) Malacca Creole (Baxter, fieldwork 1980)
   a. [no examples in corpus]
   b. *rosto di sa inyu*
      face of GEN godfather
      'the face of his godfather'
   c. *palasu di re*
      palace of king
      'the palace of the king'
   d. *akeli re di demoni*
      that king of demon
      'the king of the demons'
   e. *isti prispi di buntal*
      this prince of puffer-fish
      'the puffer-fish king (= prince turned into a puffer-fish)'
   f. *isi matera di trigi*
      this pus of tiger
      'the pus of the tiger'

(19) g. *dianti di kaza*
       front of house
       'the front of the house'
   h. *kletura di mundu*
       creature of world
       'earthly creature'
   i. *albi di oru*
       tree of gold
       'golden tree'

In Table 5, *sa* occurs in 9 functions, and *di* in 8. The strong presence of *sa* in the functions of kinship, body-part, ownership and other interpersonal relationships shows that it is preferred by exclusively human possessors. These also happen to be the functions in which, the bulk of the *sa* data occur in the corpus, when considered independently from *di*. The exclusive use of *sa* with kin term POSSESSORs points to a specialization of *sa* for this function. Nevertheless, the fact that ownership, with human POSSESSOR, is strongly represented by the *sa* construction shows that the inalienable/alienable distinction is not differentially represented.

However, *sa* is weakly represented in the remaining functions, and in two functions, part-whole and classificatory, *sa* shows a degree of competition with *di*. This corresponds to some extent with the observation in Baxter (1988) that part/whole, and origin/source are areas where *sa* overlapped with *di*.

Where the *di* construction is concerned, although it is an alternative for all functions except the kin relationship, it shows a strong presence in functions (f), (g), (h) and (i), functions with a preponderance of [-human] POSSESSORs, and functions in which the *di* data, counted independently from *sa*, register the greatest numbers. The results for functions (e) and (f), especially the former, should be treated with caution, as the data numbers are rather small.

Generalizing, from this distribution one can say that the *sa* and *di* constructions show evidence of a complementary variable distribution: in numeric terms, although they do overlap, where one tends to get *sa* one will tend not to get *di*. The next section considers briefly the structure of the possessor DP.

5.1   The structure of the POSSESSOR DP

For the analysis of the structure of the possessor DP, five categories were established according to whether the DP was represented by (a) a deleted head: [Ø]; (b) a pronoun: [PRO]; (c) a NP with a pre-nominal modifier (that does not itself contain a *sa* or *di* structure), and that is accompanied or not by post-nominal modifiers: [XNX]; (d) an DP itself determined by a post-nominal genitive: [(X) + sa + SN]; or, (e) a bare noun: [N]. The resulting comparative distribution of *sa* and *di* structures by POSSESSOR structure is shown in Table 6:

Table 6. Structure of the POSSESSOR

POSSESSOR DP ↓		sa			di		
		N°	% of total sa	% per function	N°	% of total di	% per function
a.	Deleted [[Ø] + sa]	291	32.2	100%	0	0	0
b.	Pronoun [PRO] + sa	474	52.5	99.60	2	1.10	0.40
c.	[XNX] + sa	42	4.5	68	20	10.60	32
d.	[(X) + sa + DP] + sa	20	2.20	66.66	10	5.30	33.33
e.	Noun only [N] + sa	76	8.4	32.70	156	83	67.30
	TOTAL	903	100%		188	100%	

The above factors are exemplified for these two genitive constructions respectively in (20a–e), for *sa*, and in (21a–e), for *di*:

(20) Malacca Creole (Baxter, fieldwork 1980)
  a. Ja lá   chomá ku   [Ø] sa fila
     PRF EMPH call ACC   GEN daughter
     'So he called his daughter'.
  b. Bo mpodi   drumí ku   yo sa familia
     2SG NEG-can sleep   with 1SG GEN offspring
     'You can't sleep with my daughter'.
  c. Eli panyá aké tigri sa matera
     3SG take that tiger GEN pus
     'He took the (dead) tiger's pus'.
  d. Ja kabá   bendé bai e(li) sa dama   sa kaza
     PRF finish sell go 3SG   GEN mistress GEN house
     'After selling (it) he went to his mistress' house'.
  e. Ago Luzia sa pai   ta   ubí
     now Luzia GEN father PROG hear
     'Now Luzia's father was listening'.

(21) Malacca Creole (Baxter, fieldwork 1980)
  a. [no examples in corpus]
  b. Yo misti kai yo sa korsang riba di eli
     1SG must fall 1SG GEN heart   top of 3SG
     'I must fall for him (Lit. my heart must fall on top of him)'.

(21) c. *Nang   ubí   palabra di yo   sa   pai*
       NEG-IMP hear   word   of 1SG GEN father
       'Don't listen to the words of my father'.
    d. *Abu Nawas pasá   **dianti di   re   sa   rua***
       Abu Nawas pass front   of   king GEN   street
       'Abu Nawas passed in front of the King's street'.
    e. *Eli   ja   bai tomá   ngua,   basu   di   ngua albi*
       3SG PRF go   take   one   beneath of one   tree
       'She went and took a, shelter under a tree (lit. underneath of a tree)'.

Table 6 shows that only 4 categories of possessor DPs are represented by both the *sa* and *di* structures, and in three thereof the *sa* genitive is predominant. With category (b), pronominal possessor heads, the *sa* construction predominates, accounting for 99.6% of cases. Indeed, the pronoun is the most frequent head in *sa* post-nominal genitives, accounting for 52.5% of *sa* structures in the corpus. This seems a perfectly natural finding given the high frequency of human participants in these traditional stories, and in discourse normally.

The *sa* construction also predominates (68%) with category (c) DP possessor heads that have pre-nominal modifiers not containing *sa* genitives, and that are optionally accompanied by post-nominal modifiers. Finally, in the remaining categories permitting both structures, the *sa* genitive also predominates in category (d) when the possessor DP itself is determined by a *sa* genitive. On the other hand, when the possessor is a bare noun, category (e), the *di* structure is doubly predominant (67.3% with *di*, versus 32.7% for the *sa* structure). In fact, 83% of the items of the *di* corpus alone are bare [+count, ±human, ±animate] nouns. Evidently the *sa* structure, with the possessor in initial position of the DP, offers both the advantage of informational prominence, and the convenience of conveying more information within the possessor NP.

The fifth category of possessor DPs, category (a), deleted possessors, is only found with the *sa* construction. It accounts for 32.2% of the *sa* constructions in the corpus. Although mentioned in Rêgo (1998 [1942]), the Malacca Creole *sa* structure with a deleted possessor head has until now gone relatively unnoticed in studies of the language. Its salience in the corpus considered here was a surprise. The next section examines it more closely.

5.2 Headless Possessor DPs in the *sa* construction

This structure raises interesting questions about the extent of structural dependency between the items linked by *sa*. An immediate question concerns what type of head can be omitted. Examining the antecedents of headless *sa*, the distribution in Table 7 was obtained:

Table 7. The antecedents of headless POSSESSOR DPs

DP antecedent		Nº	%
a.	Pronoun	200	68.7
b.	Name	52	17.9
c.	(X)+N+(X)	39	13.4
	TOTAL	291	

Most (68.7%) of the antecedents of headless possessor DPs are pronouns. The remainder are mainly proper nouns, followed by a smaller number of DPs with common noun heads, with either pre-head and/or post-head modifiers. Closer inspection reveals that of the 91 non-pronominal DP possessors, 81 are [+human], 5 are [−human, +animate] and another 5 are [−animate]. Clearly, an animate, preferably human antecedent exerts strong licensing of the deletion of the DP head of the possessor structure, in the same way that anaphoric reference is licensed between possessor antecedents and possessive determiners in other languages. The three factors of Table 7 are exemplified as follows:

(22) Malacca Creole (Baxter, fieldwork 1980)
  a. <u>Eli</u> ja   beng   ta   buská,   Ø   sa   kaska   nté
     3SG PRF   come   PROG   search   GEN skin   NEG-EXST
     'He came and was searching (...) **his skin wasn't there**'.
  b. Sior re   ja   gitá   ku   Ø   sa   familia
     Mr. king   PRF   call   ACC   GEN offspring
     'His Majesty called <u>his child</u>'.
  c. Isi fila   ta   santá lá   churá ku   Ø   sa   mai
     this girl   PROG   sit   EMPH cry   with   GEN mother
     'The girl was sitting and crying about her mother'.

However, a further surprise here is that the pronominal antecedents are restricted to one form: all 200 pronouns in Table 6 are 3SG. Evaluation of the headless possessor structure with informants in Malacca reveals that the finding holds for both 3SG and 3PL. 1st and 2nd person, singular and plural, antecedents cannot support the headless SA construction, and their possessive structures must be stated in full, as PRO + SA + POSSESSEE:

(23) Malacca Creole (Baxter, fieldwork 2010)
     yo   ja   gitá   ku   yo   sa   mai
     1SG   PRF   call   ACC   1SG   GEN   mother
     'I called my mother'.

The headless structure, however, must be interpreted as having a third person antecedent:

(24) Malacca Creole (Baxter, fieldwork 2010)
<u>Bos</u> ta santá lá churá ku Ø sa mai
2SG PROG sit EMPH cry ACC (3SG) GEN mother
'You are/were sitting there crying about his/her mother.'

This suggests that *sa* carries not only a genitive function derived from its Portuguese etyma but also retains some of their additional information regarding person. Moreover, the latter information is intrinsic to deletion of the possessor head under identity with a 3SG or 3PL pronoun or a non-pronominal DP. These points show that the Malacca Creole system retains some strong features of the 16th-century Portuguese possessive determiner system, wherein the *sa* etyma are associated with 3rd person possessors but not yet with 2nd person possessors.[14] Local influence from Vehicular Malay genitive *punya* with strong third person reference would have provided reinforcement for any pre-existing tendency arriving from the Southern India regions. However, Vehicular Malay *punya* does not occur in a pre-nominal construction without the preceding possessor.

A further fact lending support to the possessive determiner characteristic of *sa*, is the considerable degree of separability permitted between the antecedent possessor and the headless possessor structure. Table 8 shows two degrees of distance: from 1 to 9 words, and 10 or more words:

Table 8. Distance between antecedent DP and headless possessor structure

Distance between antecedent DP and headless possessor structure	Nº	%
From 1 to 9 words	175	60.1
10 or more words	116	39.9
TOTAL	291	

While the majority of headless possessor structures in the corpus considered here have their antecedents within the same clause, it is also the case that a considerable degree of distance is permissible. In the following examples, (25a) shows the antecedent and its co-referent headless possessor within the same clause, while Example (25b) shows both items in different clauses:

(25) Malacca Creole (Baxter, fieldwork 1980)
a. *Maria bai kaza falá ku Ø sa pai tudu* (…).
Maria go house speak DAT GEN father all
'Maria went home and told her father all (…)'.

b. *Aké fila ja subí brabu, sé? Ja subí*
   that girl PRF rise annoy know? PRF rise
   brabu ku Ø sa pai
   annoy with GEN father
   'The girl got annoyed, you know? (She) got annoyed with her father'.

As the other ACPs considered here show some evidence of a similar behavior, this 3rd person quality of *sa* may constitute a further typological dimension of these languages. In part, this would derive from the function of the 16th-century Portuguese possessive determiner *seu/sua*, which was 3rd person, and not yet 2nd person. Yet, it may also be related to those southern Indian substrates wherein the possessive suffix on nominals shows overlapping with those of pronominals.

The strong 3rd person quality of *sa* is also partly evident in the other Indo-Portuguese Creoles that have the post-nominal genitive. The limited data show headless possessor structures only with 3SG nominal or pronominal antecedents. The Examples (26) through (30) represent headless 3rd person possessor structures in the creoles of Cochin, Mangalore, Batavia, Tugu and Macau, respectively:

(26) Cochin Creole   (Schuchardt 1882:804)
     governo com outro su jenti ja parti por Trivandrum
     governor with other GEN person PST leave for Trivandrum
     'The governor and his entourage left for Trivandrum'.

(27) Mangalore Creole   (Schuchardt 1883:890)
     elle ja manda por elle un su varj par cria porc
     3SG PST send ACC 3SG where GEN land to raise pig
     'He$_i$ sent him to his$_i$ field to raise pigs'.

(28) Batavia Creole   (Schuchardt 1890:94)
     Anda olla kantoe <u>akel sienjoe</u> teeng cajoe. Vala
     go see if that gentleman EXST house say
     eo manda mienja reccadoe. E manda pergoenta
     1SG send my regard and send ask
     klaay teeng koen <u>soea saodie</u>
     how EXST with GEN health
     'Go and see if that/the gentleman is at home. Tell him I send my regards and inquire as to his health'.

(29) Tugu Creole   (Schuchardt 1890:43)
     Djenti kampong Toegoe** papija **soeä linggoe Portegies
     person village Tugu speak GEN language Portuguese
     'People in Tugu village speak their Portuguese language'.

(30) Macau Creole   (Barreiros 1943–4: 30; text 1865)
tudu poço agora tem sua cobertor bem feto
all   well now   have GEN cover   well made
'All wells now have a decent cover'.

Where an ACP has had closer contact with Portuguese, or where a text has been transcribed by someone with a knowledge of Portuguese, or with pre-conceived notions of the creole (perhaps a missionary), the 3SG possessive determiner quality of the genitive marker may be influenced by Portuguese or even English. In these respects, the early texts of Macau Creole data need to be treated with caution, just as do Indo-Portuguese texts supplied to Schuchardt and, notably, texts compiled by British missionaries in former Ceylon. Furthermore, the ongoing presence of Portuguese in some contexts may have influenced the feature in question: the extent to which possessor and possessee may be separated.

In this respect, a significant problem arises in relation to the strong 3rd person characteristic of the headless possessor (i.e. pre-possessee determiner-like) instances of the post-nominal genitive. Namely: how can one know if one is dealing with an early stage effect in the development of the creole, or a more recent development caused by ongoing contact with Portuguese? The answer may lie in the Batavia/Tugu data, and possibly in early SLP data. The history of the Batavia/Tugu variety (Schuchardt 1890; Holm 1989), in particular, suggests that it had less ongoing and probably little latter day contact with Portuguese, yet in the texts in Schuchardt (1890) the headless genitive is frequent and only occurs with 3SG antecedent possessors, and permits distant separation of antecedent and possessee. So the characteristic in question could be old in this variety. Certain 19th-century Sri Lanka Creole texts might support a similar argument if the influence of missionary Portuguese or missionary creole can be discounted. However, in Tugu Creole the feature in question could have been reinforced in the late 16th century and in the 17th century by the influx to Batavia of speakers of Indo-Portuguese Creoles from ports formerly under Portuguese control (Lopes 1969).

On the other hand, when contemplating the data on Macau Creole, the effect of ongoing and recent contact with Portuguese must be taken into account. It might be said that, in a situation of decreolization, the point of reintroduction of the Portuguese pre-nominal possessive determiner in ACP is similar to the original departure point for the creole reanalysis that yielded the post-nominal genitive.

6. Conclusion

This has been an initial exploratory study which, building on Clements' (2000) Malabar Coast Pidgin hypothesis and Dalgado's (1917) idea of easterly and reciprocal transmission, sketches the development of PNG across a subset of ACPs. The structure from the Malabar region was assimilated to similar post-nominal possessives in different substrate typologies in different geographical settings. In the southern Indian region, the Portuguese pre-nominal possessive grammaticalized with suffixal qualities, whereas when transplanted to Southeast and East Asia, the already crystallized post-nominal suffix arriving from India, and the Portuguese pre-nominal determiner, developed an analytic post-nominal structure.

In the different settings post-nominal GEN acquired wider functions. The limited data show some evidence of shared features, such as in the case of the locative, attributive and worth. In the case of Korlai Creole and Malacca Creole, there are 7 functions in parallel, of which 5 match the Marathi substrate in Korlai, 3 match Malay substrate in Malacca, and 1 feature (location) is not matched in either substrate. These 7 features may represent vestiges of early southern Indo-Portuguese Pidgin/Creole use.

It is proposed that the starting point for the reanalysis of 16th-century Portuguese 3rd person *sua / seu* would have been the third person possessive and association with the genitive suffixes in the substrate languages in Southern India, and not the 17th- and 18th-century Portuguese 2nd person *sua / seu*. The latter form would have been relevant in later periods. The spread of the genitive to the pronouns *nós* and *vós*, found, for example, in the ACPs of Mangalore, Nagapattinam and Sri Lanka, as well as in all the varieties east of India, could have been facilitated by reanalysis of their respective possessives, *nosso/nossa* and *vosso/vossa*, thanks to an analogy between the nascent 3rd person genitive and the second, unstressed syllables of these possessive forms and, again, the genitive suffixes in the substrate. In some of the ACPs the earlier grammaticalization from the 3SG may be reflected in the ability of the post-nominal possessive marker to represent headless possessor phrases.

The cases of Malacca Creole and Korlai Creole exemplify how different ACPs grammaticalized the original Portuguese possessive determiner to different degrees. Whereas Korlai Creole retains prenominal possessive determiners and restricts the post-nominal genitive to full DP possessors, Malacca Creole generalizes the post-nominal genitive to all possessive structures. Furthermore, where full DP possessors are concerned, Korlai Creole displays a greater spread of the post-nominal genitive to functions beyond basic possession. The range of such functions in Malacca Creole falls within the set found in the Korlai variety. Yet

Malacca Creole *sa* shows specialization for basic possession relations (ownership, kinship, other interpersonal relations, body part), and plays only a minor role in non-possessive associative relations (origin, space, composition, attribution (classification). Malacca Creole *sa* also displays some entirely local characteristics matching Vehicular Malay: functioning as a stance marker and as relativizer.

However, unlike Korlai Creole, in Malacca Creole, the range of semantic functions of the post-nominal possessive marker is also represented by the prepositional associative structure with *di* 'of'. The prepositional structure specializes for those functions which *sa* expresses marginally: non-possessive associative relations. This is very different from the situation in the ACPs of Korlai and Sri Lanka, where the post-nominal genitive predominates and the linking item derived from Portuguese *de* 'of' is very marginal. In Malacca Creole, *di* still retains some vitality. This is possibly related to the longstanding presence of Portuguese missionaries, from the early 18th century until the 1990s, and the persistence of a degree of diglossia into the first half of the 19th century (Baxter 2010b). On the other hand, the strong 3SG quality of Malacca Creole *sa* seems more likely to be the product of early-stage development, in the 16th and early 17th centuries.

Notes

1. An easterly extension of cultural influences is supported by the chronology of Portuguese expansion in South, Southeast and East Asia and the firm retention of an administrative base in India, initially at Cochin and subsequently at Goa. On the other hand, the notion of a network of port communities exerting mutual influences is supported by shared creole folklore traditions (Jackson 1990) and by evidence of continued trade among ports with Creole Portuguese communities during the Dutch period (Baxter 2010a, 2010b).

2. Faraco (1996) asserts that different forms of *vossa mercê* were in variation in the 16th century, and places the consolidation of *você* as a 2nd person pronoun in the 17th century. Menon (2006) also places the introduction of *você* in the 17th century. However, Lopes & Duarte (2003), on the basis of theatre texts, place it in the 18th century.

3. Thomaz (1985) observes that, at the beginning of the 17th century, most of the local Christian converts in Malacca were of Indian origin.

4. Matthews & Yip (1994) note that the use of *ge* is somewhat formal with a pronominal POSSESSOR. However, it does occur fairly freely with nominal DPs.

5. Dalgado (1917) notes that it is also found in Norteiro in a song. This appears to be a marginal phenomenon, not representative of the grammar of that variety.

6. Another interesting aspect of the Malacca system is that its 2SG pronoun is only derived from Ptg. *vós*, and there is no evidence of Ptg. *você*. This may be taken as evidence that the forms derived from *você* in the other ACPs postdate the presence of forms derived from Ptg.

vós. Where Batavia Creole is concerned, the presence of possessives derived from *você* could have two sources. On the one hand, it could be related to the introduction into Batavia of Creole Portuguese speakers originating from Indo-Portuguese ports taken over by the Dutch long after the siege of Malacca in 1642 (Lopes 1969[1936]) and who had acquired some sensitivity to the new generalized 2SG use of *você*. On the other hand, it seems more plausible that it reflects documentation of the creole by individuals who were influenced by Modern (i.e. post-18th century) Portuguese. In this sense it is instructive that Hugo Cardoso (p.c. December 2011) in fieldwork in Cochin and Cannanore (in the Dutch sphere of influence) only found the form 2SG *bos*.

7. The labels are adapted from Clements (1996), with the addition of a bracketed gloss.

8. Asher & Kumari (1997: 226–238) demonstrate that in Malayalam, while some locatives are marked by the dative, others are marked by PNG. This would appear to lend support to the idea of a Malabar coast origin for the creole PNG structure, since Marathi does not use such a mechanism with locatives. Further support for this view comes from Sri Lanka Portuguese. Ian Smith (p.c. March 2012) points out that Sinhala would not have provided a model for PNG marking of the locative function. While he suggests that Indo-Aryan influence may have provided input to the structure, via inter-colony contacts, the idea of a southern Indian origin seems reasonable, especially in view of the early 16th-century history of Portuguese presence in the region.

9. In Malacca Creole nominalization of both verbs and adjectives is possible (Baxter 1988: 99). While not mentioned in Clements (1996), Korlai Creole also admits de-verbal nominalization:

    (i) Korlai Creole   (Clements, p.c. June 2011)
        uskre   su:
        write   GEN
        'stuff having to do with writing'

10. Direct sources of Hokkien influence are also relevant. Traditionally, the Malacca creoles and Hokkien Chinese lived in contact in the Trankerah and Banda Hilir areas of Malacca. This led to a degree of fluency in Malacca Creole on the part of Hokkien Chinese, some marrying into the Malacca Creole speaking community, and a degree of fluency in Hokkien on the part of certain Malacca creoles. It is still possible to find Hokkien Chinese speakers of Malacca Creole, and Malacca creoles speakers of Hokkien in the Banda Hilir and Ujong Pasir areas of Malacca.

11. While it is unclear whether this item represents tense or aspect, for current purposes it has been glossed as a tense particle.

12. In addition to these 903 genitive *sa* data there were other instances of *sa* in the texts, corresponding principally to the function of stance marker, mentioned above.

13. This classification, being entirely semantic, subsumes and details the semantic functions reported by Clements (1996) for Korlai Creole *su*.

14. It was noted in Section 2 that, in the Portuguese of the late 17th century and in the 18th century, the 3rd person possessive *seu* (and variants) was introduced as the possessive associated with the newly introduced 2nd person pronoun *você*. The facts considered here show that this subsequent development did not affect the Malacca Creole possessive system.

References

Asher, R. E., and T. C. Kumari. 1997. *Malayalam* [Descriptive Grammars Series]. London: Routledge.
Barreiros, D. L. 1943-44. *O Dialecto Português de Macau: Antologia*. Macau: Renascimento.
Baxter, A. N. 1988. *A Grammar of Kristang (Malacca Creole Portuguese)* [Pacific Linguistics. Series B; no. 95]. Canberra: Pacific Linguistics.
Baxter, A. N. 1990. Notes on the Creole Portuguese of Bidau, East Timor. *Journal of Pidgin and Creole Languages* 5 (1): 1-38.
Baxter, A. N. 2010a. Vestiges of etymological gender in Malacca Creole Portuguese. *Journal of Pidgin and Creole Languages* 25 (1): 120-54.
Baxter, A. N. 2010b. Malacca Portuguese in the 19th century – evidence of a wider lectal range? Paper presented at the *10th ACBLPE conference*. CNRS, Paris, July 1-3.
Callaway, J. 1820. *A Vocabulary in the Ceylon Portuguese and English Languages, with a Series of Familiar Phrases*. Colombo: Wesleyan Mission Press.
Cardoso, H. C. 2009. The Indo-Portuguese Language of Diu. PhD dissertation, University of Amsterdam.
Charpentier, J.-M. 1992. A survivance du créole portuguais "makaísta" en Extrême-Orient. In *Actas do Colóquio sobre "Crioulos de Base Lexical Portuguesa"*, eds. E. d'Andrade and A. Kihm, 81-95. Lisboa: Colobri.
Clements, J. C. 1996. *The Genesis of a Language: The Formation and Development of Korlai Portuguese* [Creole Language Library 16]. Amsterdam: John Benjamins.
Clements, J. C. 2000. Evidência para a existência de um pidgin português asiático. In *Crioulos de Base Portuguesa*, eds. E. d'Andrade, M. A. Mota and D. Pereira, 185-200. Braga: Associação Portuguesa de Linguística.
Coelho, F. A. 1886. Os dialectos românicos ou neo-latinos na África, Ásia e América. Novas notas complementares. *Boletim da Sociedade de Geographia de Lisboa* 6 (12): 705-55.
Croft, W. 2003. *Typology and Universals*. Cambridge: CUP.
Dalgado, S. R. 1917. Dialecto Indo-Português de Negapatão. *Revista Lusitana* 20: 40-53.
Dalgado, S. R. 1998 [1900]. *Dialecto Indo-Português de Ceilão*. Lisboa: Comissão Nacional para as Comemorações dos Descobrimentos Portugueses.
Davies, M., and M. Ferreira. 2006. *Corpus do Português: 45 Million Words, 1300s-1900s*. http://www.corpusdoportugues.org (accessed May 19, 2011).
Faraco, C. A. 1996. O tratamento *você* em português: Uma abordagem histórica. *Fragmenta* 13: 51-82.
Ferraz, L. I. 1987. Portuguese creoles of West Africa and Asia. In *Pidgin and Creole Languages; Essays in Memory of John E. Reinecke*, ed. G. G. Gilbert, 337-360. Honolulu HI: University of Hawaii Press.
Ferreira, J. S. 1996. *Papiaçám di Macau*. Macau: Fundação Macau.
Gutiérrez Morales, S. 2006. Morphosyntactic expressions of possession and existence in Sinhala. *Santa Barbara Papers in Linguistics* 17: 20-28.
Jackson, K. D. 1990. *Sing Without Shame; Oral Traditions in Indo-Portuguese Creole Verse* [Creole Language Library 5]. Amsterdam: John Benjamins.
Hancock, I. F. 1975. Malacca Creole Portuguese: Asian, African or European? *Anthropological Linguistics* 17: 211-36.
Heine, B. 1997. *Possession; Cognitive Sources, Forces and Grammaticalization*. Cambridge: CUP.
Holm, J. 1989. *Pidgins and Creoles*, 2 Vol. Cambridge: CUP.

Krishnamurti, B. 2003. *The Dravidian Languages*. Cambridge: CUP.
Lopes, C. R. S., and M. E. L. Duarte. 2003. De *vossa mercê* a *você*: Análise da pronominalização denominais em peças brasileiras e portuguesas setecentistas e oitocentistas. In *Análise Contrastiva de Variedades do Português: Primeiros Estudos*, eds. S. F. Brandão and M. A. Mota, 61–76. Rio de Janeiro: In-Fólio.
Lopes, D. 1969 [1936]. *A Expansão da Língua Portuguesa no Oriente Durante os Séculos XVI, XVII e XVIII*, 2nd ed, revised and commented by Luís de Matos. Porto: Portucalense Editora.
Matthews, S., and V. Yip. 1994. *Cantonese: A Comprehensive Grammar*. London: Routledge.
Menon, O. P. S. 2006. A história de *você*. In *Teoria e Análise Linguísticas: Novas Trilhas*, eds. M. Guedes, R. A. Berlinck and C. Murakawa, 99–160. Araraquara: UNESP.
Morais, C. A. de. 1993. *Cronologia Geral da Índia Portuguesa*. Macau: Instituto Cultural de Macau.
Nikolaeva, I., and A. Spencer. Forthcoming. Possession and modification – a perspective from canonical typology. In *Canonical Typology*, eds. D. Brown and G. Corbett, 1–47. New York: OUP.
Pinharanda Nunes, M. 2011. Estudo da Expressão Morfo-sintáctica das Categorias de Tempo, Modo e Aspecto em maquista. PhD dissertation, Universidade de Macau.
Rêgo, A. S. 1998 [1942]. *Dialecto Português de Malaca – e Outros Escritos*. Lisboa: Comissão Nacional para as Comemorações dos Descobrimentos Portugueses.
Sankoff, D., S. Tagliamonte, and E. Smith. 2005. *GOLDVARB-X – A Multivariate Analysis Application*. Toronto: Department of Linguistics, University of Toronto & Department of Mathematics, University of Ottawa.
Schuchardt, H. 1882. Kreolische Studien II. Über das Indoportugiesische von Cochim. *Sitzungsberichte der Kaiserlichen Akademie der Wissenschaften zu Wien (Philosophisch-historische Klasse)* 102: 799–16.
Schuchardt, H. 1883. Kreolische Studien VI. Über das Indoportugiesische von Mangalore. *Sitzungsberichte der Kaiserlichen Akademie der Wissenschaften zu Wien (Philosophisch-historische Klasse)* 105 (III): 882–904.
Schuchardt, H. 1890. Kreolische Studien IX. Über das Malaioportugiesische von Batavia und Tugu. *Sitzungsberichte der Kaiserlichen Akademie der Wissenschaften zu Wien (philosophisch-historische Klasse)* 122 (9): 1–256.
Silva, G. M. O. 1996. Estertores da forma seu na língua oral. In *Padrões Sociolingüísticos: Análise de Fenômenos Variáves do Português Falado na Cidade do Rio de Janeiro*, eds. G. M. O. Silva and M. M. P. Scherre, 168–181. Rio de Janeiro: Tempo Brasileiro.
Smith, I. R. 1977. Sri Lanka Creole Portuguese Phonology. PhD dissertation, Cornell University.
Smith, I. R. 1998. Introdução. In *Dialecto Indo-Português de Ceylão*, ed. S. R. Dalgado [1900]. Lisboa: Comissão Nacional para as Comemorações dos Descobrimentos Portugueses.
Teyssier, P. 1997. *História da Língua Portuguesa*. São Paulo: Martins Fontes.
Thomaz, L. F. 1985. The Indian merchant communities in Malacca under Portuguese rule. In *Indo-Portuguese History; Old Issues, New Questions*, ed. T. R. de Souza, 56–72. New Delhi: Concept.
Wilkinson, R. J. 1912. The capture of Malacca, AD 1511. *Journal of the Straits Branch of the Royal Asiatic Society* 61: 71–76.
Yap, F. H. 2007. On native and contact-induced grammaticalization: The case of Malay *empunya*. Ms, Department of Linguistics and Modern Languages, Chinese University of Hong Kong.
Yap, F. H. 2010. Referential and non-referential uses of nominalization constructions in Malay. In *Nominalization in Asian Languages: Diachronic and Typological Perspectives* [Typological Studies in Language 96], eds. F. H. Yap, K. Grunow-Hårsta and J. Wrona, 627–658. Amsterdam: John Benjamins.

Luso-Asian comparatives in comparison*

Hugo C. Cardoso

In this article I compare and contrast the comparative constructions in the Luso-Asian Creoles, establishing their similarities and dissimilarities with Portuguese as well as with all the most relevant adstrate languages. Through a detailed look at a particular construction, this study aims to uncover the various creoles' degree of reliance on either lexifier or adstrate models and unearth potential links between them. The results of this study are then articulated with a number of comments previously made about the Luso-Asian creoles in particular (such as their interrelatedness, and the perceived impact of socio-historical differences on linguistic structure) and language contact in general (such as the role of congruence in the selection of linguistic features).

1. Introduction

The Luso-Asian Creoles, or the Portuguese-lexified creoles of Asia, were earlier scattered throughout a vast portion of coastal Asia (v. Teza 1872; Coelho 1880; Schuchardt 1889a; Vasconcellos 1901; Lopes 1936). Although few of the previous varieties subsist, several of them have been recorded in one way or another. Drawing on these corpora, I will analyse prototypical comparative constructions in as many Luso-Asian Creoles as possible and contrast them both with their main lexifier, Portuguese, and the adstrate languages which were relevant in their specific settings. My definition of 'adstrate' is encompassing, including those languages which were involved in the very formative stages of the creoles and which would traditionally be classified as 'substrata'. In the case of the Luso-Asian Creoles, the substrate/adstrate opposition is cancelled, first and foremost, by the fact that most – though possibly not all – are endogenous creoles in the sense of Chaudenson (1974), having remained in contact with languages which were part of their formative ecology. One complicating factor in this respect is the possibility that the various Luso-Asian Creoles establish relationships of progeny and/or diffusion (cf. Ansaldo & Cardoso 2009); this will be taken into account in the discussions below, where the results will be interpreted in light of this hypothesis.

The remainder of the article is divided into 3 distinct parts. Section 2 introduces a typology of comparative constructions and defines key terms which recur in the following descriptive sections. Given that the available sources of data differ in nature and detail, not all of the Luso-Asian Creoles may be included in this study;[1] a discussion of the reliability of primary data therefore introduces each of the descriptive subsections in 3. After describing the comparative constructions in all the relevant languages, I will collate the data for 8 creoles, as well as for their lexifier and adstrate(s), in Section 4, and abstract some generalisations and conclusions from their comparison.

2. Comparative constructions

For the purposes of this study, and in the interests of cross-linguistic validity, comparatives are defined as the strategies a language uses to express the "mental act by which two objects are assigned a position on a predicative scale" (Stassen 2008). I will also impose the following conditions:

a. the position of the two elements on the scale must be different; this excludes *similatives* (e.g. *Tokyo is as expensive as Hong Kong*), which, although logically related to comparative constructions, do not always employ the same formal means;
b. the comparison must be based on a single property applicable to both parts: this simultaneously excludes cases in which two properties of the same participant are compared (e.g. *Macau is more compact than it is large*) and the comparison of the degree of different properties for each of the two participants (e.g. *Bangkok is more humid than Delhi is ancient*);
c. the elements being compared must not be co-referential: this excludes logically odd but grammatical instances such as e.g. *Singapore is more forward-thinking than itself*.

What we are left with is what Dixon (2008) considers "prototypical comparatives", in which two participants are compared in terms of a single property. From the point of view of their formal expression, the components that I will term *essential constituents* are:

A. Comparee (NP)
B. Parameter (often a predicative adjective, in some languages involving a copular frame)
C. Standard (NP)

In addition, certain constructions also include:

D. Index
E. Comparative marker (which marks one of the participants as the standard)

(1) English
<u>Daman</u> is <u>more</u> <u>hectic</u> <u>than</u> <u>Diu</u>.
A   D   B   E   C

The discussion will concentrate mostly on the comparison of superiority, as in (1), rather than the comparison of inferiority (e.g. *Diu is less hectic than Daman*), because the former is the one typically reported in descriptive grammars, and not all languages actually have the means to express the comparison of inferiority. Nonetheless, I will include examples of comparatives of inferiority, where available, to clarify the formal links they establish with comparatives of superiority.

2.1 A typology of comparative constructions

Comparative constructions have been the object of cross-linguistic comparative studies in the past (Andersen 1983; Stassen 1984, 1985, 2008; Dixon 2008), resulting in some relevant generalisations. Stassen's (see e.g. 1984, 2008) typology of comparatives is essentially based on the encoding of the standard NP and identifies the categories represented in Figure 1:

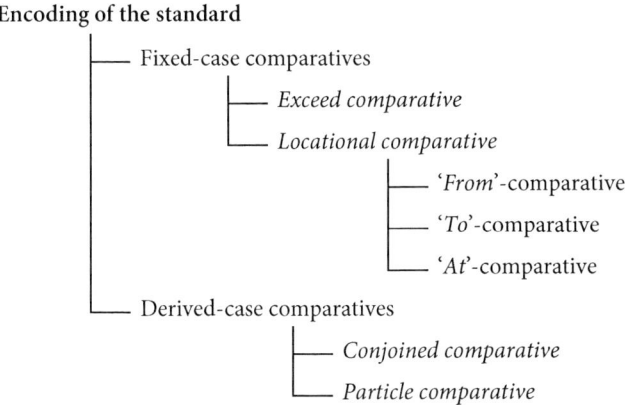

Figure 1. A representation of Stassen's typology of comparative constructions

Fixed-case comparatives are those in which the standard is always assigned the same case, irrespective of the function and case of the comparee.[2] These can be further subdivided into two large groups: (a) *Exceed comparatives*, in which the standard NP is treated as the object of a verb meaning 'to exceed, to surpass';[3] and (b) *Locational comparatives*, in which the standard NP receives a case used elsewhere typically for spatial reference, whether denoting source[4] (*'from'*-comparatives or, in Stassen's terminology, *separative comparatives*), goal or benefactive (*'to'*-comparatives) or location (*'at'*-comparatives).[5]

In *derived-case comparatives*, the case of the standard is the same as that of the comparee. These can be subdivided into: (a) *Conjoined comparatives*, involving the expression of two predicates or a repetition of the same with different polarity values, in separate clauses usually in juxtaposed or in disjunctive coordination (e.g. *X is a, (but) Y is not a*; *X is a, (but) Y is b*); and (b) *Particle comparatives*, in which, by contrast, the comparee and the standard are not constituents of separate clauses and the predicate need not be repeated, instead using a comparative particle (which can double as something else in the language's syntax, e.g. relativiser, temporal adverb, subordinating conjunction, etc.) to flag the clause as comparative. As an example, it may be useful to note that the comparative construction in English, as in many of the major languages of Europe (see Stassen 2008), is a particle comparative using the particle *than* – see Example (1).

These types are meant to classify particular constructions rather than a language as a whole, as some languages admit competing constructions of different types. But it is sometimes also difficult to fit individual constructions into these categories because certain constructions combine characteristics of more than one type, producing what Stassen (1984: 147) calls "mixed comparatives". A recurrent mixed type in the languages under study here is one in which a comparative marker establishes no synchronically identifiable links to any other case-assigning element in the language (thereby functioning as a comparative particle) and yet imposes a specific case on the standard nominal regardless of that of the comparee (thereby constituting a fixed-case comparative). For the purposes of this study, I will term these *mixed fixed-case comparatives*.

Finally, it is often difficult to ascertain whether a construction is of the fixed-case or derived-case type, for whereas in some languages nominals show morphological case in general, in others it is only so for certain subsets of nominals (as in English or Portuguese, in which morphological case distinctions occur in the personal pronoun paradigm) or not at all. Nonetheless, the general categories identified will be useful to grasp the extent to which the comparative constructions of particular creoles coincide with either the lexifier or other languages in the ecology, particularly when they provide significantly different models.

2.2 Comparative constructions in Portuguese

In order to understand the development of comparatives in the Luso-Asian creoles, one must be aware of the models contributed by both their adstrate languages and their main lexifier. The description of these constructions in the relevant Asian languages can be found in Section 3. The present section deals with comparatives in Portuguese. I will focus on what can be gathered from Portuguese texts and grammars of the Classical period (mid-16th to 18th century; see Cuesta & Luz 1980; Castro 1991). One must of course admit that the 'Portuguese' input to the formation of the Luso-Asian Creoles may have included restructured or L2 varieties (see e.g. Clements 2000; Holm 2009; Cardoso 2010), but also bear in mind that Standard Portuguese remained influential in several of their locations for a long time after initial contact.

In terms of the typology introduced in 2.1, Portuguese can be said to adhere to the *particle comparative* type. Typically, the case of the standard is derived from that of the comparee; consider the following examples:

(2) European Portuguese
*Tu   és   mais alto   que   eu   / *mim.*
2SG.SBJ   COP.PRS.2SG   more tall   CMPR   1SG.SBJ   1SG.OBJ
'You are taller than me.'

The Portuguese personal pronoun paradigm codes a distinction between subject and object forms. In (2), where the comparee is the subject of a copular construction, the only form of the pronoun admitted as the standard is the subject form, not its object variant. Conversely, in the Portuguese Example (3), the comparee is an indirect object; therefore, the standard of comparison must also be treated as an indirect object, in this case taking the oblique form of the pronoun preceded by the dative preposition *a* 'to':

(3) European Portuguese
*Dei-lhe   melhor   nota   que   a ti   / * tu.*
give.PRF.1SG=3SG.IOBJ   better   grade   CMPR   to 2SG.OBJ 2SG.SBJ
'[I] gave a better grade to him than to you.'

In terms of the order of the essential constituents, the basic configuration is Comparee > Parameter > Standard. In Modern Portuguese, the comparative particle may either be *que* or the complex *do que*. In prototypical comparatives of the kind that form the basis of this analysis, they occur in free distribution:

(4) European Portuguese
Tóquio é   mais   cara | que   Hong Kong.
                                   | do que
Tokyo COP.PRS.3SG more expensive.F CMPR Hong Kong
'Tokyo is more expensive than Hong Kong.'

At the time of the first contacts between Portuguese and Asian languages, in the late 15th century, the situation was only slightly different. In a study of 14th-century Portuguese texts, Mattos e Silva concludes:

> A comparação entre qualidades é expressa pelo Qt *mais/mēos* que precede o Ql e ao qual sucede o subordinante *que* ou *ca*, só mais tardiamente *do que*. [...]:
> – ... *mais* poderosos *ca* nossos enmiigos
> – Verdade firme e *mais* clara *que* a luz   (Mattos e Silva 1993: 35)[6]

In grammars of Portuguese up to the 18th century, the only particle reported is *que*. Example (5) is taken from the 16th-century grammar of João de Barros', the one in (6) is given in Contador de Argote's 18th-century description:

(5) Classical Portuguese   (Barros 1540)
    Eitor   foy   milhór   caualeiro   que   Achiles.
    Hector be.PST.3SG better   knight   CMPR   Achilles
    'Hector was a better knight than Achilles.'

(6) Classical Portuguese   (Contador de Argote 1725)
    A   Cidade   de Lisboa   he   mayor que   a
    ART.F   city   of Lisbon   be.PRS.3SG bigger CMPR   ART.F
    do   Porto.
    of.ART.M Porto
    'The city of Lisbon is bigger than Porto.'

The prevalence of the particle *que* in prototypical comparatives over *do que* at this time is supported by a study of written sources from the 14th century onwards. The figures in Table 1 refer to the occurrence of *que*[7] and *do que*[8] in comparative constructions in the 45 million word-strong *Corpus do Português* (Davies & Ferreira 2006). The figures are plotted on a chart in Figure 2, showing the diachronic progression of the relative contribution of the competing forms to the total number of tokens per century.

Table 1. Portuguese *que* / *do que* comparative particles in the Davies-Ferreira corpus

	14th c.	15th c.	16th c.	17th c.	18th c.	19th c.	20th c.
que	94	290	468	356	232	1325	1776
do que	7	37	71	36	70	915	1647

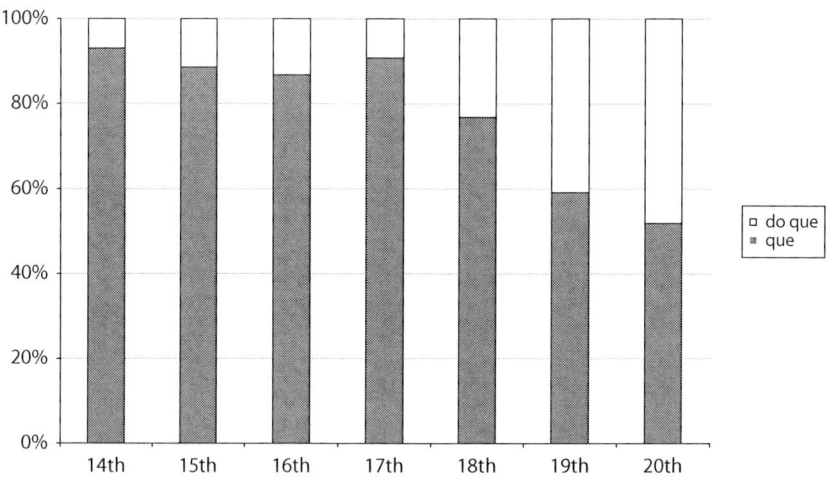

Figure 2. Portuguese *que* / *do que* comparative particles: percentages per century

These data reveal that, although the *do que* comparative particle was already used in the 14th century, it remained marginal in the written production at least until the 18th century. Even discounting the well-known time-lapse between an innovation in oral language and its reflection in the written medium, one would expect the particle *que* to have been the dominant variant during the formation of the Luso-Asian creoles and throughout a good deal of their history. It is therefore surprising that some of the creoles which lost significant contact with Portuguese earlier nonetheless retain forms of the particle derived from *do que* – see Sections 3.2.2, 3.3.3 and 3.4.3.

3. Luso-Asian comparatives

In this section, I will describe the comparative constructions of the various Luso-Asian Creoles for which there is sufficient information. The discussion will be divided into subsections according to their major adstrates, whose comparative constructions will be described first so as to set the stage for understanding the sources and development of creole constructions. The subsections are geographically organised in a roughly west-to-east direction.

3.1 Gujarati adstrate

In the Gujarati-speaking region around the Gulf of Cambay (modern Khambhat), in north-western India, Portuguese-lexified creoles are still vital in Diu and in Daman. As a result of geographical proximity, a history of administrative unity (both territories were Portuguese colonies until 1961, and now constitute a single Union Territory of the Republic of India) and population exchange, the two creoles are similar in many respects. This does not, however, preclude some important differences. One important feature of modern-day Daman Creole is the coexistence of two rather different varieties associated with two different neighbourhoods: Small Daman, and Badrapur-Big Daman; a socio-historical interpretation of the differences is given in Clements (2009), and summarised in Section 4 below.

Both the creole of Diu and that of Daman have received scholarly attention recently and, as such, a significant body of oral data, both narrative and elicited, is available, providing a rich source of information. To understand the development of comparative constructions in both these languages, however, I will first describe the model provided by Gujarati, the dominant language in the region and their primary adstrate.

3.1.1 Gujarati

Locational comparatives are an areal feature of South Asia, but they are not the only ones in the languages of the Indian subcontinent. Gujarati, an Indo-Aryan language, has two different constructions. The first of these is a clear example of a locational *'from'*-comparative, with the standard receiving the ablative/instrumental case marker *-thi*, which Cardona (1965: 90) describes as "a clitic [...] meaning 'from, by'". Standard NPs, including personal pronouns, must occur in the dependent (oblique) form so as to accommodate the ablative/instrumental suffix:

(7) Gujarati (Cardona 1965: 90)
 a. *a chokr-o pel-a chokr-a-thi moṭ-o che.*
  PROX boy-M DEM-OBL boy-M.OBL-from big-M COP.PRS
  'This boy is bigger than that boy.'
 b. *pel-uN a-thi sɔst-uN che.*
  DEM-NT PROX-from cheap-NT COP.PRS
  'That one is cheaper than this one.'

The second comparative is similar, but instead of the ablative/instrumental marker it employs *kərtaN*, "an enclitic adverbial [...] used only in comparison" (Cardona 1965: 90, 91). Again, the standard nominal takes on its oblique form, regardless of the case of the comparee; this construction is therefore a fixed-case construction and, given that *kərtaN* appears not to establish any (synchronic) links with other operators in the language, the construction will be classified as a mixed fixed-case comparative (see 2.1):

(8) Gujarati (Cardona 1965: 90)
a. e   mahra   kərtaN   moṭ-o   che.
   DIST   1SG.OBL   CMPR   big-M   COP.PRS
   'He is bigger than me.'
b. pel-a   ghər   kərtaN   a   ghər   sundər   che.
   DEM-OBL house   CMPR   PROX house   beautiful COP.PRS
   'This house is more beautiful than that one.'

As can be seen from the previous examples, the order of comparee and standard is interchangeable, but the parameter of comparison is consistently placed after both. The order of essential constituents will therefore be represented as Comparee <> Standard > Parameter. In both constructions, an index *vadhu/vadhaare* 'more' may be inserted optionally just before the parameter. Comparison of inferiority is possible, but its markedness can be gauged from the fact that, while an index is optional in the comparison of superiority, the inferiority index is obligatory.

3.1.2 Diu Creole

Schuchardt's (1883b) 19th-century corpus of Diu Creole does not contain any instance of a comparative construction, but we may refer to a recent description of the language by Cardoso (2009). In modern Diu Creole, comparatives defy classification into any of Stassen's cardinal types. While normally making use of a comparative particle, the standard typically receives a different case from the comparee, being introduced by the ablative/possessive preposition *də*.[9] The prototypical construction is of the following type:

(9) Diu Creole (Cardoso 2009: 183)
galiŋ   ε   mays   barat   ki   də   karner.
chicken COP.NPST more   cheap CMPR from mutton
'Chicken is cheaper than mutton.'

In this configuration, the construction can only be classified as a mixed fixed-case comparative, for whereas the comparative marker *ki* is elsewhere a non-case-assigning element (as a complementiser, a relativiser, etc.), standards of comparison are always preceded by the ablative preposition *də*. In free-flowing speech, not only the index but also the comparative particle may be omitted, resulting in an entirely typical locational *'from'*-comparative much like the Gujarati model:

(10) Diu Creole (Cardoso, constructed from field notes)
use ɛ (may) gran (ki) də mĩ.
2SG COP.NPST more big CMPR from 1SG.OBL
'You are bigger than me.'

Portuguese still plays a considerable normative role in Diu (Cardoso 2007), as a result of which elicited material tends to be highly variable. In response to the same prompt [viz. *Aline is taller than us*], different informants produced the following translations:

(11) Diu Creole (Cardoso, field notes)
Aline ɛ may alt | də kə nɔs.
| u kə
| u kə də
| ki də
Aline COP more tall CMPR 1PL
'Aline is taller than us.'

As shown in Figure 3, however, only the *ki də* and *də* types occur in free-flowing speech, which supports the observation that they constitute the basic comparative markers in present-day Diu Creole.

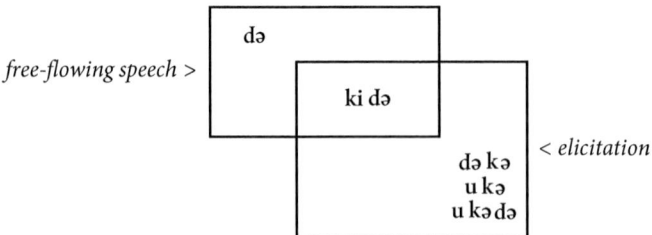

Figure 3. Contextual distribution of comparative markers recorded in Diu Creole

The typical order of essential constituents in comparative constructions is Comparee > Parameter > Standard.

It is also worth pointing out that, when the standard NP happens to be introduced by possessive *də*, speakers have the option of whether or not to respect the juxtaposition of *də + də*. In Example (12), one *də* has been suppressed:

(12) Diu Creole (Cardoso, field notes)
yo ɛ may gran ki d-use irmãw.
1SG COP.NPST more big CMPR of-2SG brother
'I am bigger than your brother.'

The index *may* 'more' is used in the overwhelming majority of comparatives in the corpus, but in some instances (particularly in the speech of children and young speakers) it is left out. Conversely, the only speakers to produce a comparative of inferiority through the replacement of *may* 'more' with *men* 'less' are older speakers who had particularly high exposure to Portuguese.

3.1.3 Daman Creole

Although the creole of Daman is, in many respects, very similar to that of Diu, the evidence from recently published descriptive work nonetheless suggests a slightly different comparative construction. This is exemplified in (13):

(13) Daman Creole (Clements & Koontz-Garboden 2002: 225)
 Pedru tɛ may fin də ki Mario.
 Pedro COP.PRS more small CMPR Mario
 'Pedro is smaller than Mário.'

Damanese informants consulted in Macau in June 2011 confirm this construction, and add that the comparative particle may either be *də ki* or simply *ki*.[10]

The Damanese comparative appears to side with Portuguese in virtually all parameters, from the Comparee > Parameter > Standard order of essential constituents down to the form of the complex comparative marker *də ki* and the fact that the case of the standard appears to match the comparee.

3.2 Marathi adstrate

The Marathi-speaking region of western India saw the development of various Portuguese settlements, from which the Portuguese retreated before the end of the 18th century. Portuguese-lexified creoles are likely to have sprung up in several locations, including Bassein (modern Vasai), but we only have access to linguistic data from two of these: the creole(s) of the Bombay (modern Mumbai) region, now extinct, and the creole of Korlai, still vital and accurately documented. Since constant contact with Marathi typifies both of them, it is essential to first acknowledge how this language may have influenced their comparative constructions.

3.2.1 Marathi

Just like neighbouring Gujarati, Marathi is an Indo-Aryan language, and comparatives in the two languages are somewhat similar. The standard of comparison may be marked by either a postposition *pekṣā* reserved for comparative constructions, or by the ablative postposition *hūn*. In both cases, the standard nominal can receive the possessive/genitive postposition *tSyā* (which functions as a generic linker to construct complex adpositions); this is obligatory for pronominal standards and optional for any others:

(14) Marathi   (Pandharipande 1997: 222–223)
   a. *anū   madhū(-tSyā)   pekṣā/hūn   ūtsa   āhe.*
      Anu   Madhu-POSS   CMPR/ABL   tall   COP
      'Anu is taller than Madhu.'
   b. *ti-tSyā   pekṣā/hūn   to   huśār   āhe.*
      3SG.F-POSS   CMPR/ABL   3SG.M   intelligent   COP
      'He is more intelligent than her.'

Both constructions are, therefore, of the fixed-case type. While the *hūn* comparative is a clear instance of a locational '*from*'-comparative, the fact that *pekṣā* is exclusive to comparatives does not permit a semantic classification of that kind; this construction will therefore be treated as a mixed fixed-case comparative.

Optionally, an index *ədhik* or *jastə* 'more' (alternatively *kəmi* 'less' for comparisons of inferiority) may be used immediately preceding the parameter of comparison (Dhongde & Wali 2009: 57). The comparee and the standard are interchangeable in order, although the initial position of the standard normally means it is emphasised. The parameter is placed after them towards the end of the clause. The order of essential constituents in this construction is therefore Comparee <> Standard > Parameter.

3.2.2 Bombay Creole

According to all sources, the creole of the Bombay region is now extinct. All the data available is that collected for Sebastião Rodolfo Dalgado and published by him in the early 20th century (Dalgado 1906), a small corpus consisting of a parable, some short stories and dialogues, poems and riddles. Since we lack information about the informants, the collectors and their methods, there is reason to question the accuracy and reliability of the data, especially when Dalgado himself reports that, among the creolophone community in the Bombay region:

> As classes ilustradas manifestam desamor à sua língua maternal, pela consciência e pejo que têm da sua corrupção, e procuram descartar-se dela, servindo-se ou do português legítimo ou do inglês, língua oficial, principalmente em Bombaim e nos subúrbios   (Dalgado 1906)[11]

It therefore comes as no surprise that, despite the intention of the transcribers to represent the phonological and lexical specificities of the language, all instances of comparative constructions in the corpus adhere closely to the Portuguese model in most respects, including the variation between particles *que* and *do que*:

(15) Bombay Creole (Dalgado 1998[1906]: 126; 133)
   a. *Amigo fals é   mais mau do que inimig.*
      friend false COP.PRS more bad CMPR enemy
      'A false friend is worse than an enemy.'
   b. *Est   noss ala-palá,   est   noss gauntí é*
      PROX our herbal.remedy PROX our local COP.PRS
      mais melhor que mezinh do Europ.
      more better CMPR remedy of Europe
      'This local herbal remedy of ours is better than the remedies of Europe.'

While it is relevant to report on it here, I do not consider the corpus available for Bombay Creole to be sufficiently large or necessarily representative of unconstrained speech. For that reason, this creole is excluded from the comparative study in Section 4.

3.2.3 *Korlai Creole*
In contrast to the creole of the Bombay region, Korlai Creole has been extensively documented in recent times by J. Clancy Clements, which gives us access to much more complete and reliable data. In the literature, the comparative construction reported has the following configuration:

(16) Korlai Creole (Clements & Koontz-Garboden 2002: 225)
   Luiz mayz ki Pedru piken tɛ.
   Luís more CMPR Pedro small COP.PRS
   'Luís is smaller than Pedro'

According to Clements (p.c. June 2011), the Comparee and Standard are interchangeable, and therefore the order of essential constituents is represented as Comparee <> Standard > Parameter. In addition, a surprising characteristic is that the index *mayz* is not adjacent to the parameter, instead preceding the standard and comparative marker. As Clements (1996: 169) points out, this is a peculiarity of Korlai Creole which is not shared with either Portuguese or Marathi.

In a set of recordings made in Korlai by the author of this article, in 2006, an alternative comparative construction occurred in the speech of a teenage boy. This is transcribed below:

(17) Korlai Creole (Cardoso, field notes)
   gran tə mi   pekṣā.[12]
   big COP 1SG.POSS CMPR
   '[He] is bigger [older] than me.'

It is clear that this construction derives from the application of the Marathi comparative particle *pekṣā* and that, as in Marathi, it attributes a specific case to the standard. The pronoun appears in its possessive form, which may explain the omission of the multifunctional (genitive, possessive, attributive, etc.) postposition *su*, normally selected to link with a postposed element to form complex postpositions such as e.g. *X su mew* 'in the middle of X' (Clements 1996: 144).

Since we do not have many recorded occurrences of this construction, it is impossible to assess its current distribution, and the effect of ellipsis on examples such as (17) makes it difficult to provide a complete description. The fact that this construction has been recorded at all is, however, highly relevant to our discussion of the creoles' reliance on lexifier or adstrate models. Therefore, it will be considered in Section 4 as a secondary construction of Korlai Creole of the mixed fixed-case type, with a P > S partial order of essential constituents, a postposed comparative marker and a copular element (the obligatoriness of which cannot be ascertained). However, as there is no evidence that both constructions described are equally established in the language (unlike in Diu Creole), only the particle construction – the only one recorded in published descriptions – will be admitted in the initial quantitative analysis.

3.3 Malayalam adstrate

Along the coast of what is now the south-western Indian state of Kerala, the Malayalam heartland, Indo-Portuguese communities flourished in many towns and villages from the 16th century onwards. Over time, their Portuguese-lexified creoles have dwindled and, according to the latest accounts, only that of Cannanore (modern Kannur) remains. Late 19th-century data is available for the creoles of Cannanore/Mahé and Cochin (modern Kochi), and fieldwork with some of the last creole speakers was carried out recently, in both Cannanore and Cochin, by the author of this article. I will begin by describing the structure of comparative constructions in Malayalam, before concentrating on the region's Portuguese-lexified creoles.

3.3.1 *Malayalam*

In Malayalam, a language of the Dravidian family, there are two basic comparative constructions. One of these is a clear case of a locational '*at*'-comparative: the standard is in the locative case (identified by the suffix *-il*) and hosts the clitic *-um*, a multifunctional element whose prototypical function is that of a coordinator:

(18) Malayalam (Asher & Kumari 1997: 170)
    atə   it-il-um   nallatə aaɳə.
    DIST   PROX-LOC-and   good   COP.PRS
    'That is better than this.'

The other construction is also a fixed-case comparative, but the standard receives accusative case and is followed by a comparative postposition *kaaḷ(um)* or *kaaṭilum*:

(19) Malayalam (Asher & Kumari 1997: 169)
raaman kṛṣṇan-e   kaaḷum miṭukkan aaṇə.
Raman Krishnan-ACC CMPR   clever   COP.PRS
'Raman is cleverer than Krishnan.'

Since the literature does not establish any synchronic link between *kaaḷum* and any case-assigning element in the language, the construction will be classified as a mixed fixed-case comparative.

Although the parameter may be preceded by an index, which takes the form of intensifiers *kuuṭutal* or *adhikam* expressing 'respectively notions of excess and superiority' (Asher & Kumari 1997: 169), it is most often not used and only becomes compulsory if the standard is elided.

According to my informants, the copula may easily be left out in the first construction but not so in the second. The comparee and the standard are interchangeable in order. Although the comparee may be placed after the parameter when it consists of a clause rather than a simple nominal, I have not found any such examples for the type of prototypical comparatives which form the basis of this study. Therefore, the order of essential constituents will be represented as Comparee <> Standard > Parameter.

3.3.2 *Cannanore Creole*

The data available for Cannanore and nearby Mahé is a good example of how careful one must be when interpreting material collected at the turn of the 19th century, in the early days of academic interest in creole languages. In this particular case, I refer to a short corpus collected for Hugo Schuchardt and published in 1889. The corpus consists of a few isolated sentences, a short story and five songs. In it, we do not find examples of prototypical comparatives according to my strict definition, but other comparatives appear to suggest the constructions did not differ significantly from the Portuguese model, using a comparative particle *que* and an index *mais* 'more'. Notice the following example:

(20) Cannanore/Mahé Creole (Schuchardt 1889b: 521)
Eu   amey   avos,   Maquita / Mais que minha vida.
1SG love.PST ACC.2   Maquita   more CMPR my   life
'I loved you, Maquita, more than my life.'

Linguists familiar with the modern Indo-Portuguese creoles will recognise some creole traits in (20), such as the use of the dative/accusative preposition *a*, and other traits which appear highly acrolectal, including the Portuguese-style declension of the verb (*amey*, from Ptg. *amei* 'love.PST.2SG'). The comparative of inferiority recorded in the corpus, with the Portuguese index *menos* 'less', is also uncommon in the modern Indo-Portuguese creoles:

(21) Cannanore/Mahé Creole (Schuchardt 1889b: 517)
Vos te durmi menos que nos.
2 IPFV sleep less CMPR 1PL
'You (are) sleep(ing) less than us.'

What is striking, in this respect, is that recent fieldwork with the last creole speakers in Cannanore yielded entirely different constructions:[13]

(22) Cannanore Creole (Cardoso, field notes)
a. Ana nɔs-sə mas fɔrti.
 elephant 1PL-from more strong
 'Elephants are stronger than us.'
b. bɔz ku yo Olivia-sə mas kūprid tẽ.
 2 CNJ 1SG Olivia-from more tall COP
 'You and I are taller than Olivia.'

Here, comparatives involve an index *mas* 'more' and a structure of essential constituents with the configuration Comparee > Standard > Parameter, after which a copula may or may not be expressed. The standard is flagged by postposed *-sə*, a highly multifunctional grammatical element in Cannanore creole. One of its functions, that of ablative marker, is shown in (23):

(23) Cannanore Creole (Cardoso, field notes)
bɔz ɔndi-sə jə vi?
2 where-from PST come
'Where did you come from?'

Therefore, the Cannanore construction can be safely said to constitute a locational '*from*'-comparative. There appears to be no comparison of inferiority, since the elicitation of 'less X than' meets with the structure 'more ~X than'.[14]

Regarding the discrepancy between the 19th-century data and that recorded in the 21st century, one could certainly posit that the creole underwent significant change since the collection of the earlier corpus; yet, the problems with the ethnography of the period are well-known (see Cardoso 2012), and therefore it is the modern data that will be contemplated in the comparative study in Section 4.

3.3.3 Cochin Creole

Unfortunately, the data available for the Creole of Cochin is less extensive than that of Cannanore. The short collection of texts published by Schuchardt in 1882 contains a few instances of comparative constructions, yet they appear mostly in ecclesiastical texts showing significant influence from Portuguese, including person-number inflection in verbs (*sou*) and number inflection within NPs (*outros*). Below are two examples:

(24) Cochin Creole (Schuchardt 1882: 806; 809)
    a. *não por causa que sou pela natureza*
        NEG for cause that be.PRS.1SG by.ART nature
        melhor do que outros
        better CMPR other.PL
        'not because I am by nature better than others'
    b. *Melhor palha do que nada.*
        better straw CMPR nothing
        'Straw is better than nothing.'

I was able to conduct fieldwork in Vypeen, near Cochin, between 2007 and 2010 with the person who appeared to be the last fluent speaker in the region. Unfortunately, instances of comparison are rare in the recorded speech; in all such cases, the speaker, an elderly gentleman who had not spoken the language for a few years, produced sentences of the following type:

(25) Cochin Creole (Cardoso, field notes)
    ĩdu tẽ, moyrmorə mas tẽ.
    hindu be muslim~muslim more be
    'There are more muslims than hindus (there).' [Lit. 'There are hindus, there are more muslims.']

Fieldwork in Cochin and Cannanore reveals that the two variants are to a very large extent equivalent, and therefore one might expect a locational '*from*'-comparative from the speaker in Cochin. The construction in (25), however, falls into the *conjoined comparative* type in Stassen's typology, as the comparee and the standard are embedded into separate clauses. Given the circumstances in which the Cochin data were collected (from only one informant who showed signs of language obsolescence), it is unclear whether this is to be taken as representative of the Creole of Cochin in its vital days. I must therefore exclude this creole from the comparative study in Section 4.

3.4 Tamil adstrate

For the purposes of our study, it is important to point out that Tamil is the dominant language not only of Southeastern India (the modern-day state of Tamil Nadu) but also of Northeastern Sri Lanka. In this wide region, Luso-Asian communities sprung up in many coastal locations, and their creoles were once widespread (see Schuchardt 1889a). According to recent fieldwork visits to the region, the creoles of the Indian Tamil-speaking region are now extinct. However, we do have a very short corpus of linguistic data collected in Nagapattinam and published by Dalgado in 1917. Unfortunately, this corpus contains no data relevant for a study of comparatives, and therefore the Creole of Nagapattinam will not be treated here.

The Creole of Sri Lanka, on the other hand, appears to have been spoken in many towns across the island, not only in Tamil-majority regions but also in Sinhala-speaking areas. This creole is discussed here under the Tamil heading because the most recent and extensive linguistic data available, gathered from the work of Ian Smith, was collected in the Tamil-majority city of Batticaloa. However, for historical reasons, Sinhala needs to be considered as an additional relevant adstrate, not only because it has in recent times come to be dominant in the country, but also because we do not yet know whether Sri Lanka Creole was ever fragmented into highly divergent varieties – which raises the additional question of the extent to which the various Lankan varieties arose independently or spread from an initial location. Therefore, I also include a description of Sinhala comparatives in 3.4.2 (see also the discussion in Section 4).

3.4.1 *Tamil*
Tamil, a language of the Dravidian family, has a large number of competing comparative constructions. One of the most common involves the use of a marker *viḍa*, which is etymologically related to the verb 'to leave', placed after an accusative-marked standard. Despite its diachronic roots in the expression of movement from a source, the modern construction does not fit any of the types in Stassen's typology entirely, and it will therefore be classified as a mixed fixed-case comparative:

(26) Tamil (Schiffman 1999: 127)
Anda viiṭṭe viḍa inda viiḍu perusaa irukku.
DIST house.ACC CMPR PROX house big.ADV COP
'This house is bigger than that house.'

Admittedly, whereas the most accessible descriptions of Tamil are based on the Indian variety, the language spoken in Sri Lanka may present some differences. However, the comparative construction reported by Smith (1979: 207) for the variety of Tamil spoken in the Batticaloa region is equivalent to the one in Example (26).

Another common construction in Tamil is a locational '*at*'-comparative very similar to the one described for Malayalam in (18) above:

(27) Tamil (Stassen 1985: 151)
At-il-um   ittu   cinnatu.
DIST-LOC-and PROX big
'This is bigger than that.'

Alternative constructions for Tamil include a different locational '*from*'-comparative (28a) and a locational '*to*'-comparative (28b):

(28) Tamil (Stassen 1985: 244)
a. *Ten-in-um   initu   enna?*
honey-ABL-and what sweet
'What is sweeter than honey?'
b. *Ittu-ku   atu   nallatu.*
this-DAT that good
'That is better than this.'

As can be seen from the previous examples, Tamil comparatives do not include an index, and a copular verb may or may not be expressed. The order of essential constituents is Standard > Comparee > Parameter.

3.4.2 Sinhala

In Sinhala, the Indo-Aryan language which is numerically and politically dominant in modern Sri Lanka, comparative constructions have the following configuration:

(29) Sinhala (Chandralal 2010: 9)
kaḍuwə-ṭə   waḍaa   pæænə   baləwat.
sword-DAT more pen powerful
'The pen is mightier than the sword.'

The Sinhala comparative makes use of an index, the adverb *waḍaa* 'much, more', immediately after a standard flagged by the dative suffix *-ṭə*. In addition to marking indirect objects and the subjects of particular verbs, among several other functions, *-ṭə* also marks physical goals, as in the following sentence

(30) Sinhala (Chandralal 2010: 11)
kaḍee-ṭə ya-nn-e Ranjit.
shop-to go-NPST-FOC Ranjit
'It is Ranjit who is going to the shop.'

Therefore, the Sinhala comparative may be said to fall into the locational 'to'-type category. Notice that no copula is expressed in Sinhala comparatives. As for the order of essential constituents, it will be represented as Comparee <> Standard > Parameter, given that the standard and the comparee are interchangeable.

3.4.3 Batticaloa Creole

In Batticaloa Creole, comparative constructions involve the operation of a comparative particle *dikə*, which occurs after the standard:

(31) Batticaloa Creole (Smith 1979: 207)
eli dikə go:rdu
he CMPR fat
'fatter than him'

Smith (1979: 207) clarifies that the standard is typically in nominative case, although accusative is also an option. Smith (p.c. May 2011) sees the use of the accusative in this function as a clear instance of Tamil influence (cf. Example (26)), and provides the following example:

(32) Batticaloa Creole (Smith, field notes)
noos-pə dikə graandi jeentis fɔɔra naandə say
1PL-ACC CMPR big people outside NEG.POT go.out
'People older than us won't get out.'

In both variants, according to Smith (p.c. May 2011), the case of the standard is not derived from the case of the comparee, which is not what would be expected of a prototypical particle-type comparative. The construction will therefore be classified as a mixed fixed-case comparative.

The Batticaloa Creole comparative construction makes no use of an index or a copula, and the order of essential constituents is Standard > Parameter > Comparee.

3.5 Malay adstrate

Portuguese-lexified Creoles have been documented both in the Malay Peninsula, viz. Malacca, and the Indonesian island of Java, viz. the region of Batavia [presently Jakarta] and nearby Tugu. Malacca Creole, also known as Papia Kristang, is still vital and conveniently documented, whereas for the extinct creole of Batavia and Tugu one must rely on a substantial collection of texts published by Hugo Schuchardt in 1890.

Previous historiographical studies clarify that the creole recorded in Batavia and Tugu developed essentially from an offshoot of that spoken in Malacca, from 1641 onwards (see e.g. Tomás 2009: 59–60), with additional input from South Asia (see Lopes 1936). Malay would remain a fundamental adstrate in its new Javanese setting. Although one must admit the influence of other languages of the island, it seems clear that Malay was particularly current among the creolophone community. Not only is the speech recorded in Schuchardt (1890) laced with Malay loans (content as well as function words), the informants themselves reflect on the issue thus:

(33) Tugu Creole (Schuchardt 1890: 43)
Djenti kampong Toegoe papija soeä linggoe Portegies
people village Tugu speak POSS language Portuguese
ki dja tjempra koe linggoe Malay.
REL PST mingle with language malay
'The villagers of Tugu speak their Portuguese language which has intermingled with the Malay language.'

An additional source of initial input may have been Bazaar Malay, a restructured form of Malay prevalent in 16th-century commercial hubs of the region. Modern descriptions of Bazaar Malay report a comparative construction which is entirely similar to that of standard Malay, alongside an alternative which, however, does not reflect on any of the Malayo-Portuguese creoles. As for standard Malay, presently there are differences between *Bahasa Malaysia*, the variety of Malaysia, and *Bahasa Indonesia*, its Indonesian counterpart. However, with respect to comparative constructions, these are not significant. Therefore, their description is unified under the generic appellation 'Malay' in Section 3.5.1, which is followed by a study of the two creoles of the region.

3.5.1 *Malay*

The standard comparative construction in Malay is exemplified in (34):[15]

(34) Bahasa Indonesia (Sneddon 1996: 179, quoted in Dixon 2008: 798)
Dia lebih tinggi dari saya.
3SG more tall CMPR 1SG
'He is taller than me'

Although Example (34) is taken from a description of Bahasa Indonesia, it is also applicable to Bahasa Malaysia. In spoken Malay, the index particle *lebih* may be replaced with *lagi*, with equivalent semantics. No copula is employed in prototypical comparatives, and the order of essential elements is Comparee > Parameter > Standard. In formal and written Malay, the form of the comparative particle is *daripada* rather than *dari*. Given that *daripada* is an ablative marker in Malay, the construction is of the locational '*from*'-type.

According to a description of modern-day Singaporean Bazaar Malay, comparative constructions are perfectly equivalent to those in Standard Malay (Aye 2005: 122, 123; but see note 16), with the exception that the comparative particle *dari* may be replaced with *sama*, a multifunctional preposition which expresses comitative, instrumental or locative (*at*) case, marks objects/agents, and also effects NP conjunction (Aye 2005: 84, 85). As we shall see below, these alternative readings provided by Bazaar Malay are not reflected in any of the Malayo-Portuguese creoles. The significance of Bazaar Malay as opposed to Standard Malay for the development of Malayo-Portuguese comparatives is therefore disproved; as a result, it will not be considered as a separate adstrate in the discussion in Section 4.

3.5.2   Malacca Creole

The creole of Malacca, or Papia Kristang, has been extensively described in recent times. The comparative constructions reported are of the following type:

(35)   Malacca Creole   (Baxter 1988: 184)
   a.   eli   más   altu   di   Pio
        3SG   more   tall   CMPR   Pio
        'She is taller than Pio.'
   b.   John   más   kaninu / menus   altu   di   Peter
        John   more   small   less   tall   CMPR   Peter
        'John is smaller/less tall than Peter.'

This is a locational '*from*'-comparative, given that the particle *di* which precedes the standard NP is, among other things, the ablative preposition meaning 'from' (Baxter 1988: 65). The order of essential constituents is Comparee > Parameter > Standard, and no copular element is used. The obligatory index *más* 'more', as exemplified in (35b), construes the comparison of superiority in opposition to the index of inferiority *menus* 'less'.

An earlier grammatical sketch of the language, published in 1941–1942 by Rêgo, attests the same construction but adds yet another, a particle construction using the Portuguese-like particle *qui* exemplified in (36):

(36)   Malacca Creole   (Rêgo 1998[1941–42]: 65)
       êste   binho   más   miór   qui   aquel'outro.
       PROX   wine   more   better   CMPR   DIST.other
       'This wine is better than that one.'

This reference raises a number of questions, in particular because, while (36) is given as an example of a typical comparative of superiority, the example provided of a comparative of inferiority marks the standard with the preposition *di* (Rêgo 1998[1941–42]: 66). In addition, the comparative particle seems not to be the only approximation to Portuguese in this sentence: *miór*, derived from the synthetic comparative/superlative Portuguese form *melhor* 'better' – see also (15) and (24) above – has no currency in modern Malacca Creole; Rêgo (1998[1941–42]: 65) himself, in the same description, provides the analytical counterpart *más bom* 'more good'. One may therefore expect this construction to have been produced by a speaker with some contact with standard Portuguese. A look at the distribution of the two constructions in Rêgo's corpus also reveals an interesting fact. The particle construction almost only occurs in ecclesiastical written texts, highly acrolectal if not entirely Portuguese at times:

(37) Malacca Creole (Rêgo 1998[1941–42]: 217)
Muito mais pena me daes / Do que
much more suffering 1SG.OBL give.2PL CMPR
me da minha morte.
1SG.OBL give.3SG my death
'[You] give me much more suffering / Than my death does.'

The religious context was at the time dominated by Portuguese-speaking priests, a good source of lexifier input. In more popular texts, however, the only construction recorded by Rêgo is the locational '*from*'-comparative described above. (38a) is taken from a song (which is likely to preserve older constructions and forms), while (38b) is one of several isolated sentences recorded in Malacca:

(38) Malacca Creole (Rêgo 1998[1941–42]: 89; 148)
a *Pastorinho berde, / Más bêrde di rico flôr.*
bird.DIM green more green CMPR rich flower
'Little green bird, / Greener than the richest flower.'
b *Eu más idade di êle. Ele más crença*
1SG more old CMPR 3SG 3SG more child
di eu.
CMPR 1SG
'I am older than him. He is younger than me.'

It is therefore safe to assume that the particle construction was the prerogative of an acrolectal register, while the locational '*from*'-comparative appears to have been dominant throughout the history of the language. For this reason, and because it is the only construction reported in more scientific descriptions, only the latter construction will be considered for the comparative study in Section 4.

3.5.3 Batavia/Tugu Creole

All the data available for the creole of Batavia and Tugu comes from a corpus published by Hugo Schuchardt in 1890. Nevertheless, the collection, comprising songs and speech of various kinds, is long enough to contain various occurrences of comparatives, two of which are transcribed below:

(39) Batavia/Tugu Creole (Schuchardt 1890: 70; 61)
  a. *Noszotter kompra na Mester kanie baka; aka mas*
     1PL buy LOC Mester meat cow DEM more
     sabrodjoe darie karnie boefra.
     tasty CMPR meat buffalo
     'We buy beef from Mester [master?]; it is tastier than buffalo meat.'
  b. *soewah predjoe mas dari otter soeker, sebab ellie*
     POSS price more CMPR other sugar reason 3
     soewah dosie finjoe.
     POSS sweet fine
     'its price is higher [lit. 'more'] than other sugars, because of its fine sweetness.'

(39a) is the clearest example of a prototypical comparative. As can be seen, comparatives in the Batavia/Tugu corpus employ the Malay ablative/comparative *dari/darie*, and their syntax is also quite similar to that of Malay: it makes use of an index *mas* 'more', there is no intervening copular element, and the order of essential constituents is Comparee > Parameter > Standard.

A look at the corpus reveals that the typical ablative preposition in Batavia/Tugu Creole is the Portuguese-derived *die* 'from', as shown in (40):

(40) Batavia/Tugu Creole (Schuchardt 1890: 99)
  say die akel loegaar.
  leave ABL DEM place
  'leave from that place.'

The question therefore arises whether *dari/darie* also has ablative semantics in the creole corpus, in which case this construction could be classified as a locational '*from*'-comparative. If it does not, then – unlike the Malay or Malacca Creole constructions – the Batavia/Tugu comparative would be more accurately treated as a particle construction. As it turns out, the corpus does contain a few instances of ablative *dari/darie* indicating source:

(41) Batavia/Tugu Creole (Schuchardt 1890: 66)
  Sijoew dari ondie? – Ijoh darie ciedadie.
  sir ABL where 1SG ABL city
  'Where is sir from? – I am from the city.'

While it is impossible to ascertain whether the speakers who produced such sentences as (39a, b) were the same for whom *dari/darie* marked the standard of comparison, it appears that comparatives in Batavia/Tugu Creole were also of the locational *'from'*-type.

3.6 Cantonese adstrate

The Cantonese-speaking region of southern China witnessed the development of a Portuguese-lexified creole in the city of Macau, which then travelled with the Macanese diaspora to several locations around the world. Significant linguistic similarities with Malacca Creole and other Asian creoles suggests the development of Macau Creole, also known as Maquista or Patuá locally, to have owed a great deal to previously creolised varieties further to the west (see the discussion in Section 4). In Macau, however, contact with Cantonese, which was particularly intense after the 18th-century (see Baxter 2009: 278; Pinharanda Nunes, *this volume*), made this language the major adstrate in the development of Macau Creole. Therefore, I will begin by describing Cantonese comparative constructions, in 3.6.1, before turning to Macau Creole.

3.6.1 *Cantonese*
In modern Cantonese, prototypical comparatives (i.e., with the overt expression of all essential constituents) rely on two major constructions. The first of these, the most common in colloquial speech and the one Ansaldo (2010: 926) considers unmarked in the language, marks the standard with a preceding element *gwo*; this is, in fact, a verbal element meaning 'cross' or 'pass' (Matthews & Yip 1994: 167), making this a good example of an *'exceed'*-type comparative:

(42) Cantonese (Matthews & Yip 1994: 166)
Gāmyaht yiht gwo kàhmyaht.
today hot CMPR yesterday
'Today is hotter than yesterday.'

Certain degree adverbials – such as *hóu dō* 'very much', *síu~síu* 'little~little' and *dī~dī* 'some~some' – may optionally be added after the standard to indicate the degree of comparison. As shown in (42), this construction requires no copular element or an index, and the order of essential constituents is Comparee > Parameter > Standard.

Another comparative construction, used in formal speech, involves a different order of essential constituents, with the configuration Comparee > Standard > Parameter:

(43) Cantonese (Matthews & Yip 1994: 167)
A-Wàhn béi kéuih mùihmúi leng.
A-Wan CMPR 3 younger.sister pretty
'Wan is prettier than her (younger) sister.'

The marker of the standard, in this case, is *béi*, also used predicatively with the meaning 'to give', and as a marker of indirect objects; although the morphological simplicity of Cantonese makes it difficult to impose the fixed-case vs. derived-case distinction, this construction nonetheless appears akin to the locational '*to*'-type (the definition of which, as seen in 2.1, involved not only cases associated with goals but also benefactives). A variation of this second construction involves the comparative marker *béihéi*:

(44) Cantonese (Matthews & Yip 1994: 167)
Nī gāan gūngsī béihéi kèihtā gūngsī gōukāp dī.
PROX CLF store CMPR other store high-class a.bit
'This department store is more high-class than the others.'

Both constructions admit the addition of a degree adverbial or aspectual markers; but only in the locational '*to*'-type constructions may the parameter be optionally followed by *dī* 'a bit', which essentially functions as an index of comparison and occurs only in what Ansaldo (2010: 925) calls '"short" comparatives", i.e. those in which the standard is not expressed.

The fact that the *béi/béihéi* construction is said to have been modeled on Mandarin (Matthews & Yip 1994: 167; Ansaldo 2010: 925)[16] presumably indicates it is a more recent comparative in Cantonese than the *gwo* construction. Therefore, there is reason to suspect the '*exceed*'-type comparative would have had a greater chance to influence Macau Creole.

3.6.2 Macau Creole

Various sources may be used to research the highly endangered creole language of Macau, from 19th-century collections of texts through 20th century grammatical sketches and fieldwork data recently collected by Mário Pinharanda Nunes. These sources record more than one type of construction to express comparison, differing not so much in syntactic terms as with respect to the comparative marker selected. With a long history of contact with Portuguese and a history of formal education in this language, it is hardly surprising that the most common construction in printed materials is relatively close to the Portuguese model, as exemplified in (52) with a sentence from a 19th-century feuilleton:

(45) Macau Creole (Barreiros 1943–44: 352)
ôtro vez falá que nôs tudo [...] sã más émada
other time say that 1PL all COP more glutton
que cusinheiro
CMPR cook
'some other times [he] will say that we [i.e., women] are all more gluttonous than a cook'

In addition to the Portuguese-derived *que* particle, the same source also records *de que*. In a short grammatical sketch published in 1978, only the first variant is recorded:

(46) Macau Creole (Ferreira 1990[1978]: 234)
Toneca sã menos/ más arviro qui su máno.
Toneca COP less more naughty CMPR POSS brother
'Toneca is less naughty/naughtier than his older brother.'

Interestingly, the set of interviews recently recorded among older-generation Macanese residing in Macau and abroad, more reliable as a representation of unconstrained oral language production, presents a more complex picture. Contrast the following sentences:[17]

(47) Macau Creole (Pinharanda Nunes, field notes)
a. *Eles mais pior que japonês.*
   3PL more bad CMPR Japanese
   'They [were] worse than the Japanese.'
b. *E ela mais velha de que eu.*
   and 3SG.F more old CMPR 1SG
   'And she [was] older than me.'
c. *Iloutro ung pouco mais alto grau de nós.*
   3PL one little more high grade CMPR 1PL
   'They [were] a little higher-class than us.'

In all three cases, the order of essential constituents is Comparee > Parameter > Standard, an index is used but no copular element. However, while (47a) and (47b) use the comparative particles *que* and *de que* previously identified, (47c) uses the preposition *de* 'from' we may recognize from other Asian creoles, and which is also the standard ablative preposition in Macau Creole. In the oral corpus, both *que* and *de* are well represented in this function, with *de que* occurring less frequently.

4. Discussion

In this section, I will begin by collating the linguistic data presented in the previous sections for the 8 creoles for which a reliable description of comparatives is possible (Diu, Daman, Korlai, Cannanore, Batticaloa, Malacca, Batavia/Tugu and Macau), alongside their lexifier (Portuguese) and adstrates (Gujarati, Marathi, Malayalam, Tamil, Sinhala, Malay and Cantonese). I will then draw some generalisations and make some observations from a comparative analysis of the data.

4.1 Data

Figures 4a–e show the patterns of coincidence between the various creoles and their respective lexifier and/or adstrate, with respect to five typological parameters involved in the expression of prototypical comparatives:

a. the type of comparative construction according to the general typology presented in 2.2 (Figure 4a);
b. the order of essential constituents (Figure 4b);
c. the position of the comparative marker in relation to the standard (Figure 4c);
d. the presence, absence or optionality of an index (Figure 4d);
e. and the presence, absence or optionality of a copular element (Figure 4e).

In these figures, solid boxes encircle the type(s) of the creoles – in the middle column – and extend to include the cells of the lexifier and/or adstrate if at least one of their values matches those of the creole. Parenthesised values refer to constructions considered secondary in their respective languages, and dotted lines (in the case of Korlai Creole) indicate the typological links established by a secondary construction. In the case of Batticaloa Creole, as explained earlier, I will consider both Tamil and Sinhala as potentially relevant adstrates; the 'Adstrate(s)' cell adjacent to this creole therefore contains two sets of values separated by </>, the first of which refers to Tamil, and the second one to Sinhala.

Even a cursory look at these figures reveals that both lexifier and adstrate input are necessary to explain the characteristics of the creoles' comparative constructions. There are also some instances in which creole constructions do not side with either the lexifier or the adstrate (see e.g. Cannanore Creole and the second value for Macau Creole in Figure 4a). In other cases, the creoles match the values of both the lexifier and the adstrate, whether because the two are typologically equivalent (see e.g. Malacca, Batavia/Tugu and Macau values in 4b) or because the creole admits two different constructions siding with either one (see e.g. the case of Korlai Creole in Figure 4c). In Table 2, which quantifies the typological links established by each creole with regard to the five parameters, I have

	LEXIFIER	CREOLE	ADSTRATE(S)
Diu	Particle	Loc. *from*; Mix. fixed	Loc. *from*; Mix. Fixed
Daman	Particle	Particle	Loc. *from*; Mix. Fixed
Korlai	Particle	Particle; (Mix. fixed)	Loc. *from*; Mix. fixed
Cannanore	Particle	Loc. *from*	Loc. *at*; Mix. fixed
Batticaloa	Particle	Mix. fixed	Loc. *at, to, from*; Mix. fixed/Loc. *to*
Malacca	Particle	Loc. *from*	Loc. *From*
Batavia/Tugu	Particle	Loc. *from*	Loc. *From*
Macau	Particle	Particle; Loc. *from*	Exceed; (Loc. *to*)

Figure 4a. Type(s) of comparatives

	LEXIFIER	CREOLE	ADSTRATE(S)
Diu	C > P > S	C > P > S	C <> S > P
Daman	C > P > S	C > P > S	C <> S > P
Korlai	C > P > S	C <> S > P; (P > S ?)	C <> S > P
Cannanore	C > P > S	C > S > P	C <> S > P
Batticaloa	C > P > S	S > P > C	S > C > P/C<>S >P
Malacca	C > P > S	C > P > S	C >P >S
Batavia/Tugu	C > P > S	C > P > S	C > P > S
Macau	C > P > S	C > P > S	C > P > S; (C > S > P)

Figure 4b. Order of essential constituents

	LEXIFIER	CREOLE	ADSTRATE(S)
Diu	Preposed	Preposed	Postposed
Daman	Preposed	Preposed	Postposed
Korlai	Preposed	Preposed; (Postposed)	Postposed
Cannanore	Preposed	Postposed	Postposed
Batticaloa	Preposed	Postposed	Postposed
Malacca	Preposed	Preposed	Preposed
Batavia/Tugu	Preposed	Preposed	Preposed
Macau	Preposed	Preposed	Preposed

Figure 4c. Position of case/comparative marker in relation to Standard

therefore opted for considering four different categories: *L* (for 'lexifier') refers to the number of instances in which the creole reflects the model provided by the lexifier only; *A* (for 'adstrate') counts the number of instances in which the creole sides only with the adstrate; *L/A* (for 'lexifier and adstrate') refers to instances in which the creole matches the values of both the lexifier and the adstrate because they coincide;[18] and *O* (for 'others') represents those instances in which a creole

	LEXIFIER	CREOLE	ADSTRATE(S)
Diu	Present	Optional	Optional
Daman	Present	Present	Optional
Korlai	Present	Present; (?)	Optional
Cannanore	Present	Present	Optional
Batticaloa	Present	Absent	Absent/Present
Malacca	Present	Present	Present
Batavia/Tugu	Present	Present	Present
Macau	Present	Present	Absent; (Optional)

Figure 4d. Index in comparatives of superiority

	LEXIFIER	CREOLE	ADSTRATE(S)
Diu	Present	Present	Present
Daman	Present	Present	Present
Korlai	Present	Present; (Present ?)	Present
Cannanore	Present	Optional	Optional; Present
Batticaloa	Present	Absent	Optional/Absent
Malacca	Present	Absent	Absent
Batavia/Tugu	Present	Absent	Absent
Macau	Present	Absent	Absent

Figure 4e. Copular element in comparisons of superiority

type does not reflect either the lexifier or its immediate adstrate. The sum of the figures for each creole is 5: if a creole has a single value for a given parameter, this is counted as 1; if a creole has two values (e.g. Macau Creole in 4a), each one accounts for 0.5.

Based on the figures in Table 2, we may now calculate for each creole a measure of its reliance on the typological model provided by the lexifier in detriment of the adstrate. The *Index of Reliance on Lexifier* (IRL), given in Table 3, is calculated according to the following formula:

$$IRL = \frac{L}{L + A}$$

This procedure at once discounts the instances of divergence (O) and those for which the lexifier and the adstrate provide comparable input (L/A). Reliance on the lexifier has been selected as an arbitrary parameter, but the IRL also provides an inverse indication of reliance on the adstrate: an IRL closer to 1 represents a

Table 2. Distribution of typological links

	L	L/A	A	O
Diu	2	1	2	0
Daman	4	1	0	0
Korlai†	3	1	1	0
Cannanore	1	0	3	1
Batticaloa	0	0	4	1
Malacca	0	3	2	0
Batavia/Tugu	0	3	2	0
Macau	1.5	2	1	0.5

† It must be repeated that the types associated with Korlai Creole's mixed fixed-case construction are not taken into consideration in this table, given my doubts regarding the currency of the construction.

Table 3. *Index of Reliance on Lexifier*

	IRL
Diu	.5
Daman	1
Korlai	.75
Cannanore	.25
Batticaloa	0
Malacca	0
Batavia/Tugu	0
Macau	.6

greater degree of reliance on the lexifier in the typological tug-of-war between lexifier and adstrate (see Section 4.4.; cf. Smith, *this volume*), an IRL closer to 0 shows the adstrate take the upper hand.

For the correct interpretation of the IRL, it is important to remember that it measures the significance of the lexifier input only with relation to the features in which it diverges from the adstrate, and not overall similarity with the lexifier; this explains why, for instance, Malacca Creole receives an IRL = 0 even though it does share a considerable number of traits with Portuguese (see column L/A in Table 2). The figures in Table 2 are plotted on a chart in Figure 5, with the creoles presented in decreasing order of IRL; notice that the IRL is the same for Malacca, Batavia/Tugu (given according to the order in which they were treated in Section 3) and Batticaloa (shown last because it has a lower value of overall similarity with the lexifier, i.e., L + L/A).

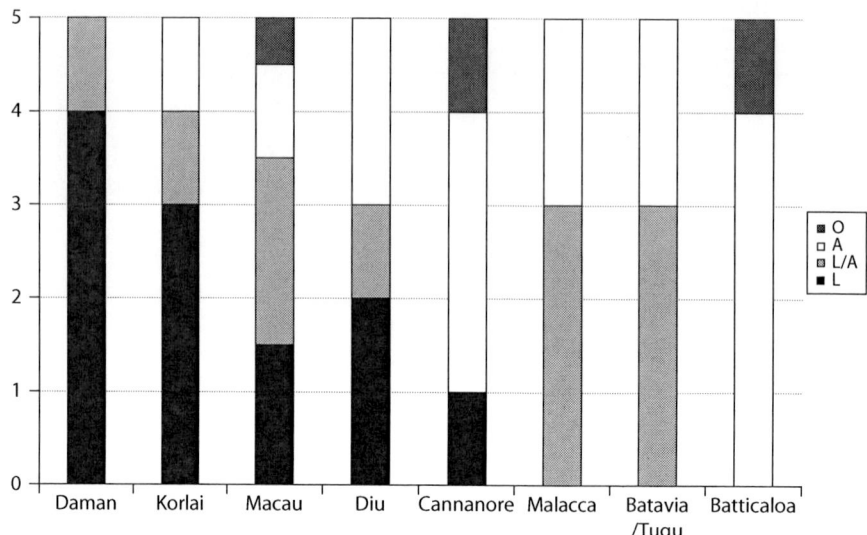

Figure 5. Relative distribution of typological links (in decreasing order of IRL)

4.2 Typological alignment

Let us start by observing the patterns of typological alignment represented in Figures 4a–e. We have already noticed that the creoles may align with one of their ancestor languages, with both, or with none. The only solid generalisation is that instances of innovation only occur when the input of the adstrate and the lexifier are incompatible. That is to say that whenever the adstrate and lexifier coincide, the creole selects their common feature, thereby lending support to the notion that *congruence* is an essential factor in the selection of features for a contact variety (see e.g. Siegel 1999, 2008; Mufwene 2001; Aboh & Ansaldo 2007).

A variation on the interpretation of congruence posits that, if a contact language received input from more than two languages (including the lexifier and two or more relevant sub-/adstrates), matching types would be particularly likely to be selected. In this discussion, I have considered both Tamil and Sinhala as relevant adstrates for Batticaloa Creole, so I may now discuss the significance of the results from this perspective. As it turns out, this type of congruence does not appear to be particularly significant as an explanation for the structure of Batticaloa Creole comparatives. The two adstrates share three values (locational 'to' type of comparatives, S > C > P order of essential constituents, postposed comparative marker in relation to Standard), yet only one of these is reflected in the creole (postposed comparative marker). In addition, Portuguese and Sinhala coincide with respect to the obligatory presence of an index, yet it is absent from the creole, which in this case sides with Tamil. This raises the point of whether we should downgrade the relevance of one of the adstrates, presumably to the benefit of Tamil on account of its overall dominance in the Batticaloa region. There appears to be some validity to this proposal. An observation of Figures 4a–e reveals that Batticaloa Creole shares 2 values with Tamil only, 1 with Sinhala only, and 1 with both. Therefore, while it is justifiable to accept Tamil as the strongest adstrate model for Batticaloa Creole, removing Sinhala from the picture would cancel the closest model for the strict absence of the copular element in the creole (see Figure 4e). The question of the role of Sinhala can only be resolved with further comparative work and a clearer understanding of the socio-historical conditions of the creation and development of Batticaloa Creole.

A different question concerns the exact relationship between the *Norteiro* 'northern' Indo-Portuguese creoles (i.e., those of Diu, Daman, Bombay and Korlai) and those of the South (Southern India and Sri Lanka). Whereas the northern and the southern groups differ with respect to their history and the taxonomy of their adstrates, their development is expected to be connected to some extent. On the one hand, the fact that the first Portuguese settlements in South Asia were located in the south could suggest some form of unilateral continuity between these creoles and the northern group; on the other hand, historical evidence increasingly suggests that the various Portuguese settlements in the region formed a network through which populations and culture flowed in multiple directions (see e.g. Dalgado 1917; Thomaz 1994; Ansaldo & Cardoso 2009; Tomás 2009; Pinharanda Nunes, *this volume*). This study of comparative constructions provides little evidence of one or the other processes, especially because the local adstrates for each of the various Indo-Portuguese creoles are to a large extent typologically equivalent. For most of the features analysed, the values of individual creoles can be found in their immediate ecology (including the lexifier). The only exceptions are:

a. Batticaloa Creole's peculiar word order;
b. Cannanore Creole's locational '*from*'-type of comparative.

With respect to (a), we should note that none of the languages involved in this study provide a suitable model, and therefore we cannot read a diffusion scenario in it. However, in the case of (b), similar types can be identified in languages further north (Gujarati, Marathi, also modern Diu Creole) and further east (Tamil, also Malay and the Malayo-Portuguese Creoles).[19] This raises a number of interesting possibilities, which this particular study is insufficient to settle: (1) Cannanore Creole's locational '*from*'-comparative could reflect a previously widespread Asian form of restructured Portuguese – Clements' (2000) *pidgin asiático* 'Asian pidgin' –, of which the pioneering contact between Portuguese and Malayalam was not the (sole) relevant source; (2) the locational *'from'*-comparative could have been diffused to Cannanore Creole from elsewhere (including other Luso-Asian varieties); (3) languages spoken in Cannanore (including Malayalam) may have in the past accommodated a similar comparative construction; (4) Cannanore Creole may have developed a locational *'from'*-type of comparative *ab ovo* (in which case one should recall the dominance of this particular type in the languages of the world).

Elsewhere, the analysis does lend support to the better-understood linguistic and historical links between Macau Creole and Malacca Creole (see e.g. Batalha 1965–66; Baxter 2009). One will notice that, except for the addition of a Portuguese-style particle construction in Macau Creole, its values are perfectly equivalent to those of Malacca Creole and Batavia/Tugu Creole. Crucially, that happens to the detriment of the input provided by Cantonese, revealing that Malacca Creole and Malay are the significant sources of Macau Creole comparatives. With regard to comparative constructions, the Cantonese adstrate could even be entirely disregarded, for whenever it is at odds with Malay/Malacca Creole, it is the input of the latter that prevails.

4.3 Interpreting the *Index of Reliance on Lexifier*

To proceed with the discussion which closed the previous subsection, if Malay and/or Malacca Creole were to be counted as adstrates instead of Cantonese, the distribution of Macau Creole's typological links in Table 2 would be: $L = 0.5$; $L/A = 3$; $A = 1.5$; $O = 0$, producing a significantly lower IRL = .33. This would place it lower than Diu Creole in the IRL scale, leaving the *Norteiro* Creoles (Daman, Diu, Korlai) to occupy the top three spots.[20] This part of the distribution is not surprising. It has been noticed before that the modern *Norteiro* Creoles, alongside Macau Creole, are relatively close to the lexifier within the context of the Luso-Asian Creoles. This fact would, with the possible exception of Korlai Creole, reflect a long period of colonial domination and a recent decolonisation: in 1999 for Macau, in 1961 for Diu and Daman, but as early as the 1740s for the Korlai region.

What may be surprising here is that the relative position of Daman Creole, Korlai Creole and Diu Creole in the IRL scale contradict Clements' (2009) observation that, in many respects, Diu Creole and the Small Daman variety of Daman Creole have a preference for acrolectal (i.e. lexifier-influenced) features where Korlai Creole and the Badrapur-Big Daman variety of Daman Creole opt for basilectal features. I do not think my analysis of comparative constructions – a single construction among many – undermines the overall validity of this generalisation. However, it does hint at the fact that Diu Creole need not be strictly acrolectal in all respects, and it introduces the possibility that certain changes in the creoles may have been triggered and/or generalised after the (relative) demotion of the Portuguese language, upon decolonisation, in ways that are not entirely predictable.

Inversely to what has just been pointed out in relation to the *Norteiro* and Macau varieties, the creoles occupying the lower half of the IRL scale (IRL < .5) are those whose territories had a shorter period of colonial domination by Portugal. Cannanore (as well as Cochin), Malacca and Sri Lanka were taken by the Dutch in the mid-17th century, and Batavia and Tugu were never administered by Portugal. This fact lends support to the notion that, in the typological tug-of-war between lexifier and adstrate(s) in which the creoles develop, colonial domination favoured the lexifier, and that this was generally neutralised with decolonisation. The only exception in this study, one could say, is the relatively high IRL of Korlai Creole. But notice that I have chosen to ignore a secondary mixed fixed-case construction, as it has not been established whether it is a regular and productive construction in the language. If it turned out to be (or became) used on a par with the particle construction, the figures for Korlai Creole in Table 2 would be: $L = 2.5$; $L/A = 1$; $A = 1.5$; $O = 0$. This would produce an $IRL = .63$, resulting in an approximation to the adstrate, yet not enough to alter the creole's position in the IRL scale relative to the other creoles under consideration.

4.4 Contact and change

The situation that was earlier described as a 'typological tug-of-war' refers to the fact that, as long as both lexifier and adstrate(s) remain active in the ecology, they may both exert some degree of metatypic pull onto the creole, thereby influencing its development. Naturally, the effects of this tug-of-war will be particularly visible among endogenous creoles with a protracted history of contact with their lexifier (as in the case of Diu or Macau).

This is a dynamic process sensitive to changes in the sociolinguistic context. Under the influence of both lexifier and adstrate(s), a certain equilibrium may be produced in which the creoles are pressured into reflecting the input of both. What this comparative study reveals is that they may do so in two different ways: (1) by licensing two competing constructions, as appears to be the case in Macau Creole; (2) by conflating the input of both ancestors into a novel construction, as appears to be the case of the Diu Creole mixed fixed-case comparative, which essentially consists of appending to its Gujarati-influenced locational *from*-comparative a redundant particle *ki* from Portuguese. In the case of Korlai Creole, the diverging source of the competing constructions is clear, although in this case it would be difficult to defend a contemporary role for Portuguese at all. What this suggests is that, if one of the actors in the typological tug-of-war is removed, there may still be a conflict between, on the one hand, the pressure to converge towards an adstrate and, on the other hand, community-internal resistance to change.

It remains to be seen whether or not conflated constructions like the mixed fixed-case comparative of Diu Creole are simply transitional products of a significant change in the relative social weight of the ancestor languages. After all, language contact has often been invoked as the source of typological rarities (e.g. Tosco 2000; Bisang 2006), leaving open the possibility that such constructions could indeed crystallise.

The results also clarify the need to enforce a distinction between what Matras (2009) calls "matter replication" (roughly, the borrowing of lexical and grammatical forms) and "pattern replication" (roughly, the borrowing of syntactic, morphological, semantic combinatory principles). Let us look at Malacca Creole and Batavia/Tugu Creole as an example. Because the etymological source of comparative markers was not admitted as a parameter for the present comparative study, the typological configuration of these two creoles emerges as precisely the same, reflecting their shared history and similarities in their ecology. However, as described earlier, they differ in formal terms in that Malacca Creole uses a Portuguese-derived comparative marker, whereas Batavia/Tugu uses a Malay form. Arguably, since the communities of Batavia and Tugu received a considerable influx of Malaccan population, this change would have occurred in the new setting. However, if the comparative construction in Malacca Creole was then similar to what it is now, it was already entirely Malay in terms of its structure. It is, therefore, clear that matter and pattern need not be transferred at the same time, although they may be – as in the rise of Korlai Creole's secondary mixed fixed-case comparative construction.

5. Conclusions

In this article, I have collated data on the expression of prototypical comparatives from all Luso-Asian Creoles for which sufficient and reliable data is available, as well as from their lexifier (Portuguese) and principal adstrates. I then performed a comparative study based on five typological parameters involved in such constructions, which revealed complex patterns of typological alignment with their source languages.

This study has shown that, whereas congruence between lexifier and adstrate is a powerful factor in blocking the typological divergence of the creole, it was not as univocal in explaining the options of the creole for which two relevant adstrates were posited (Batticaloa Creole). This raises the possibility that Tamil provided a more influential input for Batticaloa Creole than Sinhala did, although the latter may not easily be removed from the equation. Similarly, it was shown that Macau Creole comparatives produce a closer typological match with both Malay and Malacca Creole than with Cantonese, reinforcing the historical evidence which points towards a strong ancestral influence from Malacca on the traditional Macau Creole-speaking community. With respect to the Indo-Portuguese creoles, the presence in Cannanore Creole of a comparative type which is absent from its immediate ecology opened the door to the possibility of either diffusion or language-internal change.

In terms of the relative reliance on the lexifier model in detriment of the adstrate model, a certain inverse correlation emerged with time elapsed since break of significant contact with Portuguese. Therefore, unsurprisingly, the *Norteiro* Creoles and Macau Creole reveal the most exclusive links with the lexifier, even if Korlai Creole appears an outlier – in its case, however, there is evidence of what could be or could become a competing construction modelled on the local adstrate.

I have argued that, while addressing the diachrony of these creoles, it is important to posit a dynamic competition between the input of the lexifier and that of the adstrate(s). This assists in accounting for instances of variation, change and innovation. Finally, it was shown that actual forms and combinatory principles are transferred into a contact language independently from each other, and that this should be recognised in order not to obscure relevant similarities and differences.

Given that this study is based on a comparative analysis of a single construction – even if some of the parameters are expected to interact with wider features of the languages (e.g., 'Order of essential constituents'/'Position of case/comparative marker in relation to Standard' and headedness) –, my generalisations must be taken as hints rather than as holistic, established facts. Nevertheless, to a certain extent, this comparative exercise allowed us to raise questions and test previous proposals. Hopefully it can provide a framework for future comparative studies and add to their results in order to produce a more solid picture of the Luso-Asian Creoles, their sources and their inter-relationships.

Notes

* Given the cross-linguistic nature of this article, I have had to rely not only on published sources but also the generous consultancy of many colleagues and informants (on various issues). Special thanks go to Umberto Ansaldo, Sónia Ao Sio Heng, Alan Baxter, Gonçalo Cardoso, Clancy Clements, Renjith Leen, Mário Pinharanda, Ian Smith and Himanshu Upadhyaya. Any possible shortcomings are my own responsibility.

1. The Creole of Mangalore could not be included because the only source of data available (Schuchardt 1883a) contains only one example of a comparative construction, in a seemingly acrolectal context. As for the Creole of Nagappatinam, as explained in 3.4, the short corpus published by Dalgado (1917) contains no comparatives. The corpus of the Creole of Bidau (Timor) studied in Baxter (1990) contains only one comparative, which, though insufficient to justify the inclusion of this creole in the study, is of a unique type among the Luso-Asian Creoles – see note 4.

2. I assume here a broad, semantic definition of case, in that case may be expressed not only through morphology but also by other means (including adpositions).

3. Among the Luso-Asian Creoles, that of Bidau (East Timor) does display an '*exceed*'-type comparative, in harmony with the corresponding construction in Tetum (Baxter, p.c. September 2011):

    (i) Bidau Creole   (Baxter 1990:25)
        eu ˈaltu ˈpasa ˈdʒuli.
        1SG tall pass Julio
        'I am taller than Julio.'

4. This type of standard marking is highly common in the languages of the world: comparative-ablative marker syncretism was observed in 30% of the languages in Stassen's (1984) sample, and Dixon (2008:795) also notes its predominance.

5. Grammaticalization processes by which spatial markers come to mark standards in comparative constructions are well-documented around the world, in languages which could not have developed in synch either on account of genetic inheritance or contact. For an overview of the ABLATIVE > COMPARATIVE, LOCATIVE > COMPARATIVE, UP > COMPARATIVE grammaticalization paths, see Heine & Kuteva (2002).

6. 'The comparison of qualities is expressed by the Qt [quantifier; H. C.] *mais/mẽos* which precedes the Ql [qualifier; H. C.], after which comes the subordinator *que* or *ca*, only later *do que* [...]

    – ... *more* powerful *than* our enemies
    – Truth firm and *more* clear *than* light'

7. Figures for *que*: (a) search command <ma?s [j] qu?> (where ? stands for a variable segment and [j] elicits an adjective), which yielded sequences of the type *mais venturosas que*, *mays ventoso que*, *mais nobre qui*; (b) deduct results of search command <[at] ma?s [j] qu?> (where [at] stands for an article), which produced instances of superlatives of the type *a mays honrrada que, os mais acertados que*.

8. Figures for *do que*: (a) search command <ma?s [j] d? qu?>, which yielded sequences of the type *mais velha do que, mays enteyras do que*; (b) deduct results of search command <[at] ma?s [j] d? qu?>, which produced instances of superlatives of the type *ha mays natural que, o mays brauo de que*.

9. Ablative-Possessive syncretism is common among the Luso-Asian creoles, reflecting a similar syncretism in Portuguese: Ptg. *de* 'from, of'. The reason why, in such cases, the ablative function of syncretic markers is stressed in this article derives from the fact that, as described in Section 2.1, the use of ablative markers in comparatives is especially common in the languages of the world.

10. This form occurs also in a text collected in Small Daman and transcribed in Clements (2001), which, however, shows some acrolectal features:

(ii) Daman Creole (Clements 2001: 12)
kriad   ki   fik   nə   kaz   də   mew   pay   te   miλor
servant REL   stay   LOC house of   my   father have better
kumid   ki   yo   apá~yə~ aki.
food   CMPR 1SG   get   here
'The servants who live in my father's house have better food than what I get here.'

11. 'The educated classes reveal lack of love for their mother tongue, because of their conscience of its corruption and their disdain for it, and they attempt to distance themselves from it, using instead either legitimate Portuguese or English, the official language, particularly in Bombay and its suburbs'.

12. The actual pronunciation of this instance was *gran də mi pekṣā*, with what seemed like a preposition *də*. However, a native-speaker informant identified it in this context with a copular element which underwent initial voicing, a phenomenon which, according to Clements (p.c. June 2011), is not uncommon in Korlai Creole.

13. All Cannanore data other than that credited to Schuchardt (1889b) was collected by the author of this article from 2006 onwards. The orthography used here is not to be taken as final, since a complete phonological study of the creole of Cannanore is yet to be carried out.

14. Example (iii) was the elicited response to the prompt 'Olivia is less tall than us':

(iii) Cannanore Creole (Cardoso, field notes)
Olivia nɔs-sə   mas   kurtə tē.
Olivia 1PL-LOC   more   short COP
'Olivia is shorter than us.'

15. Stassen also reports for Malay an entirely different construction of the conjoined type:

(iv) Malay (Stassen 2008)
kayu   batu   bĕrat batu
wood   stone heavy stone
'Stone is heavier than wood.'

This construction met with considerable unrecognition on the part of all my informants (including a native speaker of the Malaysian variety), therefore raising questions as to its actual extent and context of use. A similar – though not identical – comparative construction is however reported for modern-day Bazaar Malay as spoken by elderly Singaporeans:

(v) Bazaar Malay (Aye 2005: 123)
John tinggi. Jimmy pendek.
John tall   Jimmy short
'John is taller than Jimmy.'

16. In the cognate construction in Mandarin, the order of essential constituents is also Comparee > Standard > Parameter, and the marker of the standard is *bǐ*, which doubles as a verb meaning 'to compare, to match' (see Sun 2006: 210).

17. All three examples were collected by Mário Pinharanda Nunes in San Francisco, United States of America: (47a) was produced by a Macau-born 82-year-old woman; (47b) was produced by a Hong Kong-born 78-year-old woman; (47c) was produced by a Hong Kong-born 81-year-old man.

18. This category reveals that the level of typological correspondence is not the same for every lexifier-adstrate pair: for instance, Portuguese and Malay coincide in 3 out of 5 parameters, whereas Portuguese and Tamil never coincide.

19. The languages of Cannanore's colonial occupiers after the Portuguese (Dutch and English) could not have been the source of this type of comparative, as in both of them comparative constructions are of the particle type.

20. The number of variables involved in the calculation of the IRL is relatively small, and as a result the statistical significance of any change is too large. A higher number of parameters would result in more solid IRL values.

References

Aboh, E. O., and U. Ansaldo. 2007. The role of typology in language creation: A descriptive take. In *Deconstructing Creole* [Typological Studies in Language 73], eds. U. Ansaldo, S. Matthews and L. Lim, 39–66. Amsterdam: John Benjamins.
Andersen, P. K. 1983. *Word Order Typology and Comparative Constructions* [Current Issues in Linguistic Theory 25]. Amsterdam: John Benjamins.
Ansaldo, U. 2010. Surpass comparatives in Sinitic and beyond: Typology and grammaticalization. *Linguistics* 48 (4): 919–50.
Ansaldo, U., and H. Cardoso. 2009. Introduction. In *Accounting for Commonalities Among the Portuguese-Lexified Creoles of Asia* [Special issue of *Journal of Pidgin and Creole Languages* 8(2)], eds. H. C. Cardoso and U. Ansaldo, 3–10.
Asher, R. E., and T. C. Kumari. 1997. *Malayalam* [Descriptive Grammars Series]. London: Routledge.
Aye, D. K. K. 2005. Bazaar Malay: History, Grammar and Contact. PhD dissertation, National University of Singapore.
Barreiros, D. L. 1943–44. *O Dialecto Português de Macau: Antologia*. Macau: Renascimento.
Barros, J. de. 1540. *Grammatica da Lingua Portuguesa*. Lisbon: Lodouicum Rotorigiũ Typographum.

Batalha, G. 1965–66. A contribuição malaia para o dialecto macaense. *Boletim do Instituto Luís de Camões* 1 (1): 7–19; 1 (2): 99–108.
Baxter, A. N. 1988. *A Grammar of Kristang (Malacca Creole Portuguese)* [Pacific Linguistics. Series B; no. 95]. Canberra: Pacific Linguistics.
Baxter, A. N. 1990. Notes on the Creole Portuguese of Bidau, East Timor. *Journal of Pidgin and Creole Languages* 5 (1): 1–38.
Baxter, A. N. 2009. O português em Macau: Contacto e assimilação. In *Português em Contato*, ed. A. M. Carvalho, 277–312. Madrid-Frankfurt: Vervuert-Iberoamericana.
Bisang, W. 2006. Linguistic areas, language contact and typology: Some implications from the case of Ethiopia as a linguistic area. In *Linguistic Areas. Convergence in Historical and Typological Perspective*, eds. Y. Matras, A. McMahon and N. Vincent, 75–98. Hampshire: Palgrave MacMillan.
Cardona, G. 1965. *A Gujarati Reference Grammar*. Philadelphia, PA: University of Pennsylvania Press.
Cardoso, H. C. 2007. Linguistic traces of colonial structure. In *Linguistic Identity in Postcolonial Multilingual Spaces*, ed. E. Anchimbe, 164–181. Newcastle upon Tyne: Cambridge Scholars.
Cardoso, H. C. 2009. The Indo-Portuguese Language of Diu. PhD dissertation, University of Amsterdam.
Cardoso, H. C. 2010. African slave population of Portuguese India: demographics and impact on Indo-Portuguese. *Journal of Pidgin and Creole Languages* 25 (1): 95–119.
Cardoso, H. C. 2012. Oral traditions of the Luso-Asian communities: local, regional and continental. In *Portuguese and Luso-Asian Legacies in Southeast Asia, 1511–2011, Vol. 2: Culture and Identity in the Luso-Asian World: Tenacities and Plasticities*, ed. L. Jarnagin, 143–166. Singapore: Institute of Southeast Asian Studies.
Castro, I. 1991. *Curso de História da Língua Portuguesa*. Lisbon: Universidade Aberta.
Chandralal, S. 2010. *Sinhala* [London Oriental and African Language Library 15]. Amsterdam: John Benjamins.
Chaudenson, R. 1974. *Le Lexique du Parler Créole de la Réunion*. Paris: Honoré Champion.
Clements, J. C. 1996. *The Genesis of a Language: The Formation and Development of Korlai Portuguese* [Creole Language Library 16]. Amsterdam: John Benjamins.
Clements, J. C. 2000. Evidência para a existência de um pidgin português asiático. In *Crioulos de Base Portuguesa*, eds. E. d'Andrade, M. A. Mota and D. Pereira, 185–200. Braga: Associação Portuguesa de Linguística.
Clements, J. C. 2001. Acrolect evolution and stigmatized speech in Daman Creole Portuguese. Paper presented at the *Annual Meeting of the ACBLPE*, Coimbra, Portugal, June 29–30.
Clements, J. C. 2009. Accounting for some similarities and differences among the Indo-Portuguese creoles. *Journal of Portuguese Linguistics* 8 (2): 23–47.
Clements, J. C., and A. J. Koontz-Garboden. 2002. Two Indo-Portuguese creoles in contrast. *Journal of Pidgin and Creole Languages* 17 (2): 191–236.
Coelho, F. A. 1880. *Os Dialectos Românicos ou Neo-Latinos na África, Ásia e América*. Lisbon: Sociedade de Geographia de Lisboa.
Contador de Argote, J. 1725. *Regras da Lingua Portugueza, Espelho da Lingua Latina, ou Disposiçaõ para Facilitar o Ensino da Lingua Latina pelas Regras da Portugueza*. Lisbon: Officina da Musica.
Cuesta, P. V., and M. A. M. Luz. 1980. *Gramática da Língua Portuguesa*. Lisbon: Edições 70.
Dalgado, S. R. 1917. Dialecto Indo-Português de Negapatão. *Revista Lusitana* 20: 40–53.

Dalgado, S. R. 1998. *Estudos sobre os Crioulos Indo-Portugueses*. Lisbon: Comissão Nacional para as Comemorações dos Descobrimentos Portugueses (Includes 1906. Dialecto Indo-Português do Norte. *Revista Lusitana* 9: 142–166; 193–228).

Davies, M., and M. Ferreira. 2006. *Corpus do Português: 45 Million Words, 1300s-1900s*. http://www.corpusdoportugues.org

Dhongde, R. V., and K. Wali. 2009. *Marathi* [London Oriental and African Language Library 13]. Amsterdam: John Benjamins.

Dixon, R. M. W. 2008. Comparative constructions; A cross-linguistic typology. *Studies in Language* 32 (4): 787–817.

Ferreira, J. S. 1990. *Doci Papiaçám di Macau*. Macau: Instituto Cultural [Includes 1978. *Papiá Cristâm di Macau: Epitome de Gramática Comparada e Vocabulário – Dialecto Macaense*. Macau: Tipografia da Missão].

Heine, B., and T. Kuteva. 2002. *World Lexicon of Grammaticalization*. Cambridge: CUP.

Holm, J. 2009. Atlantic features in Asian varieties of Creole Portuguese. *Journal of Portuguese Linguistics* 8 (2): 11–22.

Lopes, D. 1936. *A Expansão da Língua Portuguesa no Oriente nos Séculos XVI, XVII e XVIII*. Barcelos: Portucalense Editora.

Matras, Y. 2009. *Language Contact*. Cambridge: CUP.

Matthews, S., and V. Yip. 1994. *Cantonese: A Comprehensive Grammar*. London: Routledge.

Mattos e Silva, R. V. 1993. *O Português Arcaico. Morfologia e Sintaxe*. São Paulo: Contexto.

Mufwene, S. S. 2001. *The Ecology of Language Evolution*. Cambridge: CUP.

Pandharipande, R. V. 1997. *Marathi*. London: Routledge.

Rêgo, A. S. 1998. *Dialecto Português de Malaca e Outros Escritos*. Lisbon: Comissão Nacional para as Comemorações dos Descobrimentos Portugueses (Includes 1941–1942. Apontamento para o estudo do dialecto português de Malaca. *Boletim Geral das Colónias* 17 (198): 3–78; 18 (203): 9–71; 18 (208): 3–88).

Schiffman, H. F. 1999. *A Reference Grammar of Spoken Tamil*. Cambridge: CUP.

Schuchardt, H. 1882. Kreolische Studien II. Über das Indoportugiesische von Cochim. *Sitzungsberichte der Kaiserlichen Akademie der Wissenschaften zu Wien (Philosophisch-historische Klasse)* 102: 799–816.

Schuchardt, H. 1883a. Kreolische Studien VI. Über das Indoportugiesische von Mangalore. *Sitzungsberichte der Kaiserlichen Akademie der Wissenschaften zu Wien (Philosophisch-historische Klasse)* 105 (III): 882–904.

Schuchardt, H. 1883b. Kreolische Studien III. Über das Indoportugiesische von Diu. *Sitzungsberichte der Kaiserlichen Akademie der Wissenschaften zu Wien (Philosophisch-historische Klasse)* 103: 3–18.

Schuchardt, H. 1889a. Beiträge zur Kenntnis des creolischen Romanisich. V. Allgemeineres über das Indoportugiesische (Asioportugiesische). *Zeitschrift für Romanische Philologie* 13: 476–516.

Schuchardt, H. 1889b. Beiträge zur Kenntnis des kreolischen Romanisch: VI. Zum Indoportugiesischen von Mahé und Cannanore. *Zeitschrift für Romanische Philologie* 13: 516–524.

Schuchardt, H. 1890. Kreolische Studien IX. Über das Malaioportugiesische von Batavia und Tugu. *Sitzungsberichte der Kaiserlichen Akademie der Wissenschaften zu Wien (philosophisch-historische Klasse)* 122 (9): 1–256.

Siegel, J. 1999. Transfer constraints and substrate influence in Melanesian Pidgin. *Journal of Pidgin and Creole Languages* 14 (1): 1–44.

Siegel, J. 2008. In praise of the Cafeteria principle: Language mixing in Hawai'i Creole. In *Roots of Creole Structures: Weighing the Contributions of Substrates and Superstrates* [Creole Language Library 33], ed. S. Michaelis, 59–82. Amsterdam: John Benjamins.
Smith, I. R. 1979. Convergence in South Asia: A creole example. *Lingua* 48: 193–222.
Sneddon, J. N. 1996. *Indonesian: A Comprehensive Grammar*. London: Routledge.
Stassen, L. 1984. The comparative compared. *Journal of Semantics* 3: 143–82.
Stassen, L. 1985. *Comparison and Universal Grammar*. Oxford: Basil Blackwell.
Stassen, L. 2008. Comparative constructions. In *The World Atlas of Language Structures Online*, eds. M. Haspelmath, M. S. Dryer, D. Gil and B. Comrie. Munich: Max Planck Digital Library. http://wals.info/chapter/121 (accessed May 10, 2011).
Sun, C. 2006. *Chinese: A Linguistic Introduction*. Cambridge: CUP.
Teza, E. 1872. Indoportoghese. *Studi Filologici* 5.
Thomaz, L. F. 1994. *De Ceuta a Timor*. Lisbon: Difel.
Tomás, M. I. 2009. The role of women in the cross-pollination process in the Asian-Portuguese varieties. *Journal of Portuguese Linguistics* 8 (2): 49–64.
Tosco, M. 2000. Is there an "Ethyopian Language Area"? *Anthropological Linguistics* 42 (3): 329–65.
Vasconcellos, J. L. 1901. Esquisse d'une Dialectologie Portugaise. PhD dissertation, Université de Paris.

Measuring substrate influence
Word order features in Ibero-Asian Creoles*

Ian Smith

Word order characteristics of the Ibero-Asian creoles are examined in order to determine the extent of influence of the lexifier and substrate(s) and to correlate this with the strength and extent of lexifier presence in the history of each creole. The design and application of a numerical metric is discussed. The creole most influenced by its substrate is Sri Lanka Portuguese and the least influenced is the creole of Macau. Overall, the degree of substrate influence displays strong negative correlation with the strength of the lexifier presence. Each creole has thus been subject to a "tug-of-war" between lexifier and substrate. Arguably, early Ibero-Asian creoles adopted word order similar to their lexifier, and weakened lexifier presence allowed former substrates to exert adstrate influence on them.

1. Introduction

One of the characteristics that makes the Ibero-Asian creoles interesting in comparison with the better-known creoles of the Caribbean is that, as "settler" creoles (Reinecke 1937, cited in Holm 2000: 40), they have remained in contact with their substrates (which, post-creolization, become adstrates and, after decolonization, may develop socio-politically into superstrates).[1] Creoles that are in contact with their lexifiers are known to adopt features from them, at least in their upper registers. For example, the WH-relative pronouns in Diu (though English likely plays a role here too – Hugo Cardoso, p.c. May 2011), occasional SVO word order in Ternateño (Eeva Sippola, p.c. August 2010). Similarly, creoles that remain in contact with their substrates continue to be influenced by them. For example, the ongoing word order shift in Korlai from SVO to SOV (Clements 1991). Where lexifier and substrate are typologically different, they pull the creoles in different directions. Although all the Ibero-Asian creoles have maintained contact with their substrates, they have not all maintained the same contact with their lexifier. Thus when the Dutch put an end to approximately 140 years of Portuguese presence in Sri Lanka, the island's Portuguese-based creole developed for the following three and a half centuries in the near total absence of lexifier influence. At the other end of the spectrum, the creole Portuguese of Macau remained in contact with its lexifier for its entire existence. The longer the presence of contact with the lexifier, the greater opportunities for its post-creolization influence on the creole and the stronger the brake on substrate influence. Therefore, the following hypothesis suggests itself:

Ibero-Asian creoles that have longer and more intense contact with their lexifiers will show more influence from their lexifiers and correspondingly less substrate influence.

The 'tug-of-war' scenario embodied in this hypothesis is consonant with research findings such as Clements (2009a), who finds that the difference between the degree of Portuguese presence in Daman and Diu, on the one hand, and Korlai, on the other, accounts for the greater substrate influence in the latter on lexicon, consonant inventory and SOV and NP – ADP word-order relationships and stronger lexifier influence in the former on question words and pronoun forms. The hypothesis is worth testing on a broader selection of creoles for the light that it may throw on the evolution of creole languages after they have formed when no direct evidence is available.

The fact is sometimes ignored that creoles evolve like other languages; so the current structure of a long-standing creole can be quite different from its early structure (cf. Cardoso 2009a: 17 citing Arends 1989: 89). The effect of the lexifier on creoles with which it remains in contact is well known from the Caribbean creoles. The substrates, however, have disappeared from the Caribbean, and only their early influence can be gauged. The Ibero-Asian creoles, on the other hand, remain in contact with their substrates, whose continuing influence in their role as adstrates must be considered. As a case in point, the head-final word order in modern Sri Lanka Portuguese (SOV, NP – ADP, etc.) matches that of the substrates in nearly every detail (with the exception of TAM markers). But was this a feature of the early creole, or is it a subsequent development? Texts from the 19th century have a more lexifier-like word order, but Smith (2011) argues that they are composed in a missionary-inspired literary 'high' variety, which masked a low already in conformity with the substrates (*pace* Bakker 2000a, 200b). If substrate features characterized the spoken language of the 19th century, were they present at an even earlier date? In the absence of direct records we can only answer this question through inferences such as that embodied in the above hypothesis.

This paper attempts to test the validity of the hypothesis numerically. The Ibero-Asian Creoles constitute an interesting field for such a test because the synchronic similarity of their lexifiers (as a consequence of their close diachronic relationship) establishes a common starting point and their continued contact with their substrates a common social context. The following section discusses the difficulties in establishing a metric for quantifying substrate influence in different creoles. Taking these difficulties into account as much as possible, Section 3 develops a metric for comparing substrate influence on word order relationships. The application of this metric to the Ibero-Asian creoles is discussed in Section 4. Finally, the results of this exercise are correlated with the differing socio-historical relationships of these creoles with their lexifiers.

2. Issues in comparing substrate influence

To establish a fair measure of the influence of one language on another is not a straightforward exercise, particularly given the diverse possible combinations of typologically similar and dissimilar languages. Before designing a metric to measure substrate influence, some issues must be clarified. Under what conditions is such a measure possible? What features should be measured and what encoding considerations arise?

We begin with the issue of pre- and post-creolization influences. Accommodation toward the lexifier and/or substrate(s) obscures the extent of the initial impact these languages had at the time of creolization. Teasing apart such differently timed influences requires the type of detailed historical or apparent-time sociolinguistic analysis that is beyond the scope of this study. Hence no attempt is made here to differentiate between substrate effects and adstrate effects and my use of the term *substrate* should be read to imply the more cumbersome *substrate/adstrate*.

A second consideration is the number of substrates. Much of creole typology has focussed on 'plantation' creoles, such as those in the Caribbean, where substrates are typically numerous and diverse. It has thus been assumed that these reflect the prototypical social context of creolization – cf. Thomason's stipulation that "prototypical creoles develop in a contact situation involving *more than two* groups of speakers" (1997:78, emphasis mine). Most of the Ibero-Asian creoles, however, result from contact between two languages, and when multilingual substrates exists (as, e.g., in Sri Lanka and the Philippines), they consist of typologically similar languages.[2] This focuses and strengthens the pressure of the substrate on these creoles. Fortunately for this exercise, it also simplifies the task of trying to quantify substrate influence.

A third consideration is the initial typological distance between lexifier and substrate. The greater the number of differences, the greater the number of opportunities for the influence of the substrate or superstrate to be felt on the resulting creole.[3] Thus, in order to compare substrate influence in two creoles where the distance between lexifier and substrate is different, a simple count of the influenced features is likely to favour the pair with the greater difference. For example, if the substrate and lexifier of creole A differed in 3 features, and the creole followed the substrate in all of these, then creole A should rank high for substrate influence. If substrate and lexifier of creole B differed in 8 features and the creole followed the substrate in only 4 of these then by a simple feature count, creole B would outrank creole A for substrate influence, even though it follows the substrate only 50% of the time. Therefore, an objective metric must somehow take account of these differences in starting points.

Fourth, we must consider what features to survey in the comparisons. Obviously the focus should be on structural, not lexical influence. The lexifier is aptly named as the source of nearly all of a creole's vocabulary. While the influence of a substrate on a creole's structure may be during or subsequent to creolization, any significant substrate (/adstrate) impact on its lexicon is likely to be post-creolization.

What features are to be selected in gauging the influence of one language on another? Even confining ourselves to structure still leaves a very large number of features. Moreover, it is an open set of features, since linguistic research is constantly revealing new ways in which structures may be classified. Thus the selection of a reduced set is necessary. Since it is possible to skew the results by carefully selecting the basis of comparison, some objective means of establishing features for comparison must be determined. One possibility would be to select the features of a given subsystem and to survey those features exhaustively. This would avoid the possibility of cherry-picked features, but one might be accused of cherry-picking a subsystem. Certainly the subsystem chosen would have to be a universal among the languages being compared. We must also be concerned with the possibility of interrelationship among the selected features, such as the well known correlation between OV word order and postpositions. Indeed, the use of a single subsystem of features in order to avoid a possible bias in the selection of features from different subsystems will likely have the unfortunate side-effect of producing more linked features. In compiling a metric that counts features, how much weight should be assigned to a group of related features?

A fifth concern is the availability of data. Some languages are well described, others less well so. So, even if it were possible to arrive at a set of unbiased features, there is no guarantee that data on these features would be available for all the languages under consideration.

Finally, we must be concerned with the quantification and interpretation of the data. The scoring system chosen needs to have as few biases as possible and to take into account differences in starting points and interrelationships among the features studied. Once a metric is constructed, how large a difference in score counts as significant? This partly depends on the number of features investigated, as differences based on only a few features could be subject to chance variation.

3. Methodology

3.1 Selection of features

The present study chooses to focus on word order relationships, partly because they constitute a universal structural subsystem on which data is usually available. Since a grammatical category may be encoded by an affix rather than an independent word, for the present study 'word order' will be interpreted liberally to include morpheme order. Word-order relationships can be subdivided ad libitum – for example, the Latin preposition *cum* 'with' encliticizes to pronouns (*mecum* 'with 1SG', *tecum* 'with 2SG' etc.) and it might therefore be useful to distinguish between Adposition – Noun and Adposition – Pronoun relationships. Consequently, a selection of word order relationships must be made. For convenience, I have taken as a starting point the word-order relationships listed in the online version of the questionnaire for the forthcoming *Atlas of Pidgin and Creole Structures* (APiCS) – see Table 1. This list was adapted from that of the *World Atlas of Language Structures* (henceforth WALS) (Haspelmath et al. 2005) for the purposes of a survey of creoles, and can thus be seen as unbiased for the present study. In the present study, the following features will be omitted:

1. the order of Definite Article – Noun and the order of Indefinite Article – Noun, since in many of the substrates definite and indefinite articles were not distinct from demonstratives and the numeral 'one', respectively;
2. the orders Demonstrative – Noun and Numeral – Noun, because, by and large in both lexifiers and all substrates the demonstrative and numeral precede the noun. With respect to the demonstrative, it should be noted that while in standard Malay demonstratives follow the noun they specify, in Bazaar Malay they precede it. In Ternateño (and presumably Zamboangueño) the demonstrative may also occur postnominally as a topic marker (Steinkrüger 2006: 374). With respect to the numeral, the sole exception is Sinhala where the order Noun – Numeral is found;
3. the placement of the Adverb "often" with respect to the Verb and Object, as data for several of the languages under study were not available;
4. the placement of Tense, Mood & Aspect Markers with respect to the Verb and the internal order of Tense, Mood and Aspect Markers, because of the sheer complexity and number of possibilities. A future study might attempt to subdivide these categories by focusing on specific markers.

Table 1. Word order features of the APiCS Questionnaire

Feature	APiCS feature nr.	WALS feature nr.
Subject, Verb, Object	1	81A
Possessor, Possessum	2	86A
Adjective, Noun	3	87A
Adposition, Noun Phrase	4	85A
Demonstrative, Noun	5	88A
Cardinal Numeral, Noun	6	89A
Relative Clause, Noun	7	90A
Degree Word, Adjective	8	91A
Definite Article, Noun	9	–
Indefinite Article, Noun	10	–
Adverb "often", Verb, Object	11	–
Position of Interrogative Phrase in Content Questions	12	93A
Tense Mood & Aspect Markers, Verb	43	69A (Tense and Aspect only)
Internal Order of Tense, Mood & Aspect Markers	44	–

Table 2 gives the features used in this study.

Table 2. Word order features in the present study

Subject, Verb, Object
Possessor, Possessum
Adjective, Noun
Adposition, Noun
Demonstrative, Noun
Cardinal Numeral, Noun
Relative Clause, Noun
Degree Word, Adjective
Position of Interrogative Phrase in Content Questions

3.2 Constructing a metric: Substrate influence score

Nine Ibero-Asian creoles (see Section 4) are surveyed here along with their lexifier and substrate(s). For each creole in the study, the features where substrate and lexifier have the same order are eliminated. For each feature where substrate and lexifier have a different order, points are assigned as follows:

a. −1 if the creole and lexifier are identical;
b. +1 if the creole and substrate are identical;
c. a value between −1 and +1 if the creole is partially like the lexifier and partially like the substrate.

For some features it is found that the lexifier and substrate are only partially different. These are assigned values in the range −0.5 to +0.5. (See 5.3 for discussion of an example.)

The substrate influence score (SIS) for the creole is the total number of points assigned, divided by the sum of the number of features for which values are assigned in the range −1 to +1 and half the number of features for which values are assigned in the range −0.5 to +0.5. The SIS, therefore, lies between −1 and +1; the closer it is to −1, the stronger the lexifier influence; the closer to +1, the stronger the substrate influence. Where there are multiple substrates that differed in their similarity to the lexifier, separate scores are calculated.

There are admittedly some defects to this metric. First, it does not address interrelationships among the features. Second, there is room for arbitrariness in assigning intermediate values when the creole does not agree fully with either substrate or superstrate. Despite these problems the SIS as formulated yields some striking results.

4. The languages

The nine Ibero-Asian creoles surveyed, together with their lexifiers and major substrates, are listed in Table 3. For Sri Lanka, both Sinhala and Tamil are listed as substrates even though the Portuguese contacts were first with the Sinhala-speaking area in the southwest. It is not clear whether the language was recreolized when the Portuguese expanded their control to Tamil-speaking areas. The remaining pockets of speakers are located in Batticaloa and Trincomalee, on the east coast where Tamil is the sole adstrate. Although the Dutch Burgher community, which developed after the Dutch took the island from the Portuguese, adopted creole as their home language, the possible influence of Dutch is ignored for the purposes of this exercise.[4] For the Malacca Creole (a.k.a. Kristang), I list Bazaar Malay (the interethnic restructured Malay of Malaysia) as one substrate, it being the likely lingua franca of Malacca at the time of Portuguese accession (Lach 1965:515, 518–19, cited by Baxter 1988:3); Tamil is listed because of the substantial Tamil-speaking merchant community that was resident in Malacca prior to the arrival of the Portuguese and of whom "a considerable part became Christian" (Thomaz 1985:64).[5] The Batavia community originated with a group from Malacca, who were reinforced by people from other former Portuguese colonies conquered by the Dutch, chiefly in Southern India and Ceylon (Daus 1989:30, who claims simplified Portuguese was already in use in the area for interethnic communication; Suratminto 2011:6). Bazaar Malay and Tamil are listed as substrates, the former also standing in for Betawi, the low Malay of Batavia (or probably more accurately Betawi-influenced Vehicular Malay) and the latter for Malayalam and Sinhala.[6] For Zamboangueño, Malayic & Hokkien are also listed by Steinkrüger (2006:9), but their influence seems to be minor. I also ignore the possible role of Portuguese as a co-lexifier for the Philippine creoles (Whinnom 1956; Lipski 1988; Steinkrüger 2006; Veiga & Fernández Rodriguez, *this volume*), the structure of the two lexifiers being identical in the traits surveyed here. Since the two Philippine creoles are also identical in the traits surveyed, and since the substrates are also identical, I will group the two Philippine creoles together as Chabacano. For Makista (Macau), Baxter (p.c. February 2012) argues that [Bazaar/Vehicular] Malay was the chief substrate in early Macau (mid-16th to mid-17th centuries), although other Southeast Asian, South Asian and East Asian ethnicities were also represented. Cantonese (and Hokkien) only became important (as adstrates) in the 17th century. This perspective is supported by Pinharanda Nunes (*this volume*), who provides a discussion of some of the key aspects of the sociolinguistics of early Macau.

Table 3. Ibero-Asian creoles, their lexifiers and chief substrates

Creoles	Lexifiers	Substrates
Daman	Portuguese	Gujarati
Diu	Portuguese	Gujarati
Korlai	Portuguese	Marathi
Sri Lanka	Portuguese	Sinhala/Tamil
Malacca	Portuguese	Bazaar Malay/Tamil
Batavia	Portuguese	Bazaar Malay/Tamil
Zamboangueño Chabacano	Spanish	Bisayan (esp. Cebuano/Hiligaynon)
Ternateño Chabacano	Spanish	Tagalog
Makista	Portuguese	Vehicular Malay/Cantonese

5. **The survey**

In this section, the word-order features listed in Table 2 are surveyed for the languages in Table 3.[7] For each feature a score is assigned to each creole in accordance with the rule set out in 3.2.

5.1 Subject, Verb, Object

The unmarked order of Subject, Verb, and Object in Portuguese and Spanish is SVO. The unmarked order of these elements in the creoles and their substrates is shown in Table 4. Minor word orders are shown in single parentheses, marginal orders in double parentheses. The Indo-Portuguese creoles have substrates with SOV order. Sri Lanka, exemplified in (1) has assimilated completely to the substrate order and therefore receives a score of 1.[8]

(1) Sri Lanka Portuguese (Smith, field notes #5115 [conversational])
avara nosa   mahan-aar-untu um pesaam alaa
now   1PL.GEN son-HON-LOC   one person there
ɔɔrta jaa-tomaa.
land   PST-buy
'Now one of our sons has bought land there.'

For Diu, on the other hand, O may precede V only as a marked order, when the O is focused (Hugo Cardoso, p.c. May 2011); thus Diu scores −1. Daman has predominantly SVO with occasional SOV, but it is not clear whether this alternative is also unmarked. I will assume that it partially resembles both lexifier and substrate, so must be assigned an intermediate score; −.9 reflects the fact that it "is decidedly a VO and prepositional language, displaying only the initial signs of becoming a head-final language" (Clements & Koontz-Garboden 2002: 223). In Korlai there is evidence of ongoing shift from earlier SVO to SOV, which now predominates (Clements 1991). As noted above, historical implications cannot be drawn for all creoles, and in order to maintain a level playing field for all languages and all features, I base the score on the present state of affairs and have assigned +.5 to reflect the dominance of SOV. For Malacca and Batavia, the substrates are different and therefore scored separately. Bazaar Malay has the same order as the

Table 4. Order of Subject (S), Verb (V) and Object (O)

	Creoles	Substrates	Score
Daman	SVO, ((SOV))	SOV	−.9
Diu	SVO	SOV	−1
Korlai	SOV, (SVO)	SOV	.5
Sri Lanka	SOV	SOV	1
Malacca	SVO	BM: SVO / T: SOV	n.a. / −1
Batavia	SVO	BM: SVO / T: SOV	n.a. / −1
Chabacano	VSO	VSO	1
Makista	SVO	SVO	n.a.

lexifier; consequently, this item is ignored in calculating the SIS; Tamil has SOV; so a score of −1 is awarded. For Macau, this item is ignored as the substrates have the same order as the lexifier. Chabacano has VSO unmarked word-order, like the substrates, and thus a score of +1 is assigned.

5.2 Possessor, Possessum

Both lexifiers have the possessive construction Possessum *de* Possessor, where the Possessor is non-pronominal.[9] The possessive structures in the Ibero-Asian creoles and their lexifiers are shown in Table 5. It is apparent that many of the Portuguese-based creoles have a structure modelled on Possessor-*sua* Possessum (where *sua* is the Portuguese 3rd person possessive pronoun showing feminine agreement). This structure, illustrated for Malacca in (2) is not present in the Afro-Portuguese creoles.

(2) Malacca (Baxter 1988: 94)
nus ja bai Johor ku Albert sa kareta
1PL PFV go Johor INS Albert GEN car
'We went to Johor in Albert's car.'

It is thus almost certainly a South-Asian development that found its way into the simplified Portuguese that lexified subsequent creoles, such as Malacca and Makista (Clements 2000; Baxter & Bastos, *this volume*). I will not try to associate this development with any specific creolization locus in South Asia – there was in any case considerable traffic among the various settlements. Consequently, I will assume that the simplified Portuguese – likely with some African-inspired structures – which functioned as the lexifier for all varieties of Indo-Portuguese (including Sri Lanka) had the Standard Portuguese construction with *de*. It is reasonable to assume that the simplified Portuguese that functioned as the lexifier for subsequent creoles also included some South-Asian-inspired structures and thus exhibited both the standard formation with *de* and the South Asian innovation with *sua*. In Sri Lanka the Portuguese-inspired construction is found only in frozen constructions such as *bɔvardaav* 'watermelon' < Ptg. *abóbora-d'agua* (id., lit. 'pumpkin of water'), folksongs, and the missionary-inspired 19th-century literature. Thus the only productive construction is identical with that of the substrate. In Diu the predominant order is Possessum *dǝ* Possessor, but a marginal pattern of *dǝ* Possessor Possessum is occasionally found, as illustrated in (3):

(3) Diu Indo-Portuguese (Cardoso 2009b: 169fn)
dǝ Tɛtɛ kaz jɔ bēze-w?
GEN Tɛtɛ house already bless-PST
'Has [he] already blessed Tɛtɛ's house?'

For Malacca and Batavia, I take the Bazaar/Vehicular Malay substrate expression to be Possessor-*punya* Possessum, rather than Standard Malay Possessum Possessor; Tamil has the same configuration, so no separate scoring is necessary here. In Malacca the *-sa/sua* expression is widespread, but the *de* expression survives productively in some contexts (Baxter 1988: 91–99). Since, as mentioned above, the South-Asian-inspired *-sa/sua* construction is assumed to have been available (alongside the Standard *de* construction) into the simplified/restructured Portuguese that lexified Malacca, a score of +.5 reflects the influence of the substrates in favouring the first variant. This item is ignored for the Philippine creoles since their substrates have the same order as Spanish. It is interesting nevertheless that Zamboangueño has a possible order that is found in neither lexifier nor substrates. Makista shows both orders that were present in the simplified/restructured Portuguese lexifier, for the Malay substrate I take the expression to be Possessor-*punya* Possessum, as for Malacca. Cantonese also has Possessor Possessum. Assigning a score is problematical because the creole is identical with its lexifier (which indicates −1) and partially identical with the substrates (which indicates an intermediate score). The score of −.75 reflects a somewhat subjective resolution of this conflict.

Table 5. Order of Possessor (Pr) and Possessum (Pm)

	Creoles	Substrates	Score
Daman	Pm də Pr	Pr-GEN Pm	−1
Diu	Pm də Pr, (də Pr Pm)	Pr-GEN Pm	−.5
Korlai	Pr-su Pm, (Pm Pr-su)	Pr-GEN Pm	.5
Sri Lanka	Pr-su Pm, ((Pm da Pr))	Pr-GEN Pm	1
Malacca	Pr-sa Pm, (Pm di Pr)	Pr-GEN Pm	.5
Batavia	Pr-su Pm	Pr-GEN Pm	1
Chabacano	Pm del Pr, (del Pr Pm)	Pm Pr	n.a.
Makista	Pm di Pr; Pr sua Pm	BM: Pr-GEN Pm / C: Pr Pm	−.75?

5.3 Adjective, Noun

The order of Adjective and Noun in the Ibero-Asian creoles and their substrates is shown in Table 6. Portuguese and Spanish have dominant Noun – Adjective word order with Adjective – Noun as a minor pattern. This fact immediately entails scoring difficulties for this feature: whatever the substrate order, it will be partially similar to the lexifier order. Because full identity of substrate and lexifier patterns would disqualify the feature from consideration, I discount this feature by awarding a score within the range of .−5 to +.5 and counting it as half the value of other features (see 3.2).[10] Daman, Diu and Sri Lanka, for example,

Table 6. Order of Adjective (ADJ) and Noun (N)

	Creoles	Substrates	Score
Daman	ADJ N	ADJ N	.5
Diu	ADJ N	ADJ N	.5
Korlai	ADJ N, N ADJ	ADJ N	0
Sri Lanka	ADJ N	ADJ N	.5
Malacca	N ADJ	BM: N ADJ / T: ADJ N	.25? / –.5
Batavia	N ADJ, (ADJ N)	BM: N ADJ / T: ADJ N	0 / –.25
Chabacano	ADJ N, (N ADJ)	ADJ N, N ADJ	0
Makista	N ADJ, (ADJ N)	BM: N ADJ / C: ADJ N	–.25? / –.5

are identical with their substrates with respect to this feature; therefore I award them +.5. Malacca, similarly, has only the Bazaar Malay pattern, but since this matches the dominant pattern of the lexifier, rather than the minor one, the value of choosing it seems less, perhaps +.25 rather than +.5. Since Malacca has eliminated the order found in Tamil, a score of –.5 is given for this substrate language.[11] Korlai has the same two options as the lexifier, but with a more balanced distribution; since this seems to reflect a partial movement toward the substrate, which has Adjective – Noun exclusively, I awarded a score of zero. Batavia has more or less the same options as the lexifier, but since adjectives which normally precede the noun in the lexifier may also follow it in the creole (e.g. *piklinu* 'small' and *bong* 'good'), again partial movement toward the substrate Bazaar Malay should be recognized; this movement is away from the second substrate, Tamil, as reflected in the score of –.25. There is disagreement in the literature over the order of Adjective and Noun in the Philippine creoles. Grant (2002: 22–23) notes that in Zamboangueño the order is as in Spanish, with the same adjectives in both languages being lexically specified as preceding the noun. Lipski & Santoro (2007: 390) give Noun – Adjective as the default order, noting that Adjective – Noun is "not lacking". Both their examples of the latter order conform to Spanish usage, however. Steinkrüger (p.c. October 2010), on the other hand, finds Adjective – Noun to be the most common order. Both orders are found in Forman's data, e.g. for the adjective *maduro* 'ripe' which follows the noun in Spanish, his texts have both *prúto madúro* 'ripe fruit' and *el madúro ságiŋ* 'the ripe banana(s)' (1972: 30). This would seem to indicate that there has been at least some movement toward the substrates, which allow both Adjective – Noun and Noun – Adjective. As with Korlai, therefore, I award a score of 0. Makista has the same distribution as the lexifier. Unlike Malacca, there has been no loss of the minor pattern, thus no movement towards Malay. But since

Malay has the lexifier's dominant pattern, Noun – Adjective, the lack of movement in the minor pattern is worth perhaps –.25 rather than –.5. Cantonese, on the other hand, has Adjective – Noun, the reverse of the dominant lexifier pattern; therefore it gets a score of –.5, the lowest available for this feature.

5.4 Adposition, Noun Phrase

While the lexifiers have prepositions, the substrates in South Asia have postpositions. Of the South Asian creoles, only Sri Lanka Portuguese exhibits postpositions exclusively, as in *kaaza pɛɛrtu* (house near) 'near the house'. Outside South Asia, the substrates have prepositions, like the lexifier, and therefore this feature is not counted. In the Indo-Aryan languages (except Sinhala) postpositions often require a genitive complement, and this requirement appears optionally in the Indian creoles. For pronominal complements (not shown in the chart) genitive is more common and even found in Sri Lanka, Batavia, and Makista, where no substrate counterpart is found. This indicates that the feature found its way into the simplified Portuguese contact language. From this chart on, I will discontinue justification of each score, since the general lines of reasoning should by now be clear.

Table 7. Order of Adposition (ADP) and Noun Phrase (NP)

	Creoles	Substrates	Score
Daman	ADP (de) NP	NP(Gen) ADP†	–.75
Diu	ADP (de) NP	NP(Gen) ADP	–.75
Korlai	NP su ADP, (ADP NP)	NP(Gen) ADP	.75
Sri Lanka	NP ADP	NP ADP	1
Malacca	ADP NP	BM: ADP NP / T: NP ADP	n.a. / –1
Batavia	ADP NP	BM: ADP NP / T: NP ADP	n.a. / –1
Chabacano	ADP NP	ADP NP	n.a.
Makista	ADP NP	ADP NP	n.a.

† *Gen* abbreviates Genitive.

5.5 Relative clause, Noun Phrase

The Indo-Aryan languages (Sinhala excepted) have a biclausal structure consisting of the relative clause and a 'correlative' (main) clause, as seen for Marathi in (4). They also have a Dravidian-style pre-nominal participial relative which, in most Indo-Aryan languages (but not Marathi), is of much more restricted use.

Korlai, alone among the Indian creoles has mimicked the correlative structure, as seen in (5). Sri Lanka has the typical Dravidian prenominal participial relative found in both of its substrates, as seen in (6). Beyond South Asia, the creoles exhibit the lexifier order of Noun followed by Relative clause:

(4) Marathi (Jyunghare 2002:163)
[jo mānus titha ubhā   āhe] [to mājhā bhāu   āhe.]
REL man   there standing is   he my   brother is
'The man who is standing there is my brother.'

(5) Korlai Portuguese (based on Clements 1996:185)
[akə ɔm   Mari ɔ̃t   ki   ulyo] [el tɛ aki oj.]
that man Mari yesterday REL see.PST 3SG is here today
'The man Mari saw yesterday is here today.'

(6) Sri Lanka Portuguese (Smith, field notes #5291 [conversational])
avara [nosa   soviŋ   sɛntar-untu tiña] meshiin
now   1PL.GEN sewing centre-LOC   be.PST machine
boom meshiin teem.
good machine be.PRS
'Now the machine that was in our sewing centre is a good machine.'

Table 8. Order of Relative Clause (REL) and Noun (N)

	Creoles	Substrates	Score
Daman	N REL	REL CORREL, ((REL N))	−1
Diu	N REL	REL CORREL, ((REL N))	−1
Korlai	REL CORREL, (CORREL REL)	REL CORREL, ((REL N))	1
Sri Lanka	REL N	REL N	1
Malacca	N REL	BM: N REL / T: REL N	n.a. / −1
Batavia	N REL	BM: N REL / T: REL N	n.a. / −1
Chabacano	N REL	N REL	n.a.
Makista	N REL	BM: N REL / C: REL N	n.a. / −1

5.6 Degree word, Adjective

The Degree word precedes the adjective in both lexifiers and all the creoles. The substrates have the same order except in the Philippines, where no order dominates. Since the Philippine substrates partially resemble the lexifiers, I will assign values between −.5 and +.5 and count the value of this feature as 0.5, as with Noun – Adjective order.

Table 9. Order of Degree word (Deg) and Adjective (ADJ)

	Creoles	Substrates	Score
Daman	Deg ADJ	Deg ADJ	n.a.
Diu	Deg ADJ	Deg ADJ	n.a.
Korlai	Deg ADJ, (ADJ Deg)	Deg ADJ	n.a.
Sri Lanka	Deg ADJ	Deg ADJ	n.a.
Malacca	Deg ADJ, (ADJ Deg)	Deg ADJ	n.a.
Batavia	Deg ADJ	Deg ADJ	n.a.
Chabacano	Deg ADJ	Deg ADJ, ADJ Deg	−.25?
Makista	Deg ADJ	Deg ADJ	n.a. / −1

5.7 Position of Interrogative phrase

In the absence of stylistic markedness, the lexifiers have interrogative phrases in initial position. The Indian creoles appear to have adopted the pre-verbal position of their substrates, as exemplified for Korlai in (7). Sri Lanka has adopted the variable position of Tamil, as seen in (8a,b). Interrogatives in Sinhala are generally non-initial, but generally follow a relevant constituent (such as the verb):

(7) Korlai Portuguese (Clements 1996: 179)
 yo ki lə hedze?
 1SG what FUT do
 'What will I do?'

(8) Sri Lanka Portuguese (Smith, field notes #5070, #2365 [conversational])
 a. *noos-pa kii ta-faya? etus-su poḍiyaas-pa kii ta-faya?*
  1PL-DAT what PRS-do 3PL-GEN child-DAT what PRS-do
  'What can they do for us? What can they do for their children?'
 b. *aka kii siñoor jaa-botaa inda ɔɔra?*
  that what gentleman PST-put this time
  'So, what did the gentleman put [into the machine] just now?'

Table 10. Position of interrogative phrase

	Creoles	Substrates	Score
Daman	pre-verbal	pre-verbal	1
Diu	pre-verbal	pre-verbal	1
Korlai	pre-verbal	pre-verbal	1
Sri Lanka	variable	S: post-X / T: variable	.5?/1
Malacca	initial, (non-initial)	BM: initial / T: variable	n.a. / −.5
Batavia	initial, non-initial	BM: initial / T: variable	n.a. / −.5
Chabacano	initial	initial	n.a.
Makista	initial	BM: initial / C: non-initial	n.a.

5.8 Substrate Influence Score

The calculation of the Substrate Influence Score (SIS) is outlined in Section 3.2. For example, adding up all the points awarded to Daman gives a total raw score of −2.15. The number of features for which Daman was scored (i.e. where lexifier and substrate differ) is 5.5 (Adjective–Noun order counts as 0.5 because lexifier and substrates are only partially different). The SIS for Daman is therefore −2.15/5.5 = −.39. The calculation for each of the creoles is shown in Table 13; in this table the creoles are listed in order from highest SIS to lowest. The final column lists the rank order of the creoles according to their SIS, which will be used in the statistical analysis below. For creoles with more than one substrate, the ranking is based on the greatest substrate influence detected (i.e. Bazaar Malay for Malacca and Batavia, Tamil for Sri Lanka). According to this metric, then, Makista is the least influenced by its substrate, while Sri Lanka is most influenced. Among the Indian creoles, Korlai is more substrate-influenced than Daman and Diu.

Table 11. Calculation of the Substrate Influence Score (SIS)

	Raw total	No. of features	SIS	SIS rank
Sri Lanka	S: 5 / T: 5.5	S: 6.5 / T: 5.5	S: .77 / T: 1.0	1
Korlai	3.75	5.5	.68	2
Batavia	BM: 1 / T: −2.75	BM 1.5 / T: 5.5	BM: .67 / T: −.5	3
Malacca	BM: .75 / T: −3.5	BM: 1.5 / T: 5.5	BM .50 / T −.64	4
Chabacano	.75	2.5	.30	5
Diu	−1.75	5.5	−.32	6
Daman	−2.15	5.5	−.39	7
Makista	BM: 1 / C: −3.25	BM: 1.5 / C: 3.5	BM: −.67 / C: −.93	8

6. SIS and Socio-historical context of the contact situation

In order to test the hypothesis that substrate influence is weaker as the lexifier presence is stronger, it is necessary to rate the length and intensity of contact between the creoles and Spanish or Portuguese. In order to avoid the possibility of bias in the selection and weighting of factors that contribute to such influence, I will adopt, with a few additions (viz. Batavia and Macau) and adaptations, the assessment provided by Clements (2009b: 53), itself based on information in Clements & Mahboob (2000). This appears in Table 14. I have ordered the creoles showing stronger lexifier presence higher in the table and provided a column with the rank order of each creole.

Table 12. Degree of lexifier influence in Ibero-Asian creoles (after Clements 2009b: 53)

Creole	Presence of Portuguese/Spanish	Rank
Makista	Relatively strong throughout.	1
Daman	Relatively strong up to the 19th century; less so but constant up to 1961; some presence has remained until the present.	2
Diu	Relatively strong up to the 18th century; less so but constant up to 1961; some presence has remained until the present.	3
Chabacano	Constant up to around 1580, relatively constant Spanish presence, starting in 1665.	4
Korlai	Relatively strong up to 1650 and constant up to 1740; very weak (parish priest) up to 1960s; no presence since the 1960s.	5
Malacca	Relatively constant up to 1640; weak to non-existent to the 17th century; weak to early 20th century.	6
Batavia	Relatively constant up to 1640 (in Malacca); weak to nonexistent thereafter (established pidgin/creole brought from Malacca).	7
Sri Lanka	Relatively constant up to 1658; occasional missionaries/priests to at least 1886.	8

Table 13 shows the correlation between lexifier-influence rank and SIS. By and large, the less the influence of the lexifier, the higher the substrate influence score, indeed this (inverse) correlation is highly significant statistically (Spearman Rank Correlation Coefficient (rho) = 0.93; critical value = 0.91, N = 8, 2-tailed test, .005 confidence level).[12] This result confirms our initial hypothesis and lends credence to the "tug-of-war" scenario between lexifier and substrate.

Table 13. Lexifier influence rank vs. SIS

Creole	Lexifier influence Rank	SIS	SIS rank
Makista	1	−.93	8
Daman	2	−.39	7
Diu	3	−.32	6
Chabacano	4.5	.3	5
Korlai	6	.68	2
Malacca	7	.5	4
Batavia	8	.67	3
Sri Lanka	9	1	1

7. Discussion

Three types of development may take place in a creole after its formation:

1. developments influenced by the lexifier;
2. developments influenced by the substrate(s)/adstrate(s);
3. developments influenced by neither lexifier nor substrate(s).

While the hypothesis suggesting a "tug-of-war" between lexifier and substrates has been validated, it addresses only (1) and (2); it does not preclude (3) but says nothing about such developments. Nor does the hypothesis address the early state of the creole. For example, in the case of Sri Lanka Portuguese, the hypothesis correctly predicts that the absence of Portuguese for the past 350+ years has allowed the sub/adstrate(s) to exert considerable influence on the language; it also predicts that prior to that time, the presence of Portuguese would have provided a counterbalance to such influence. These predictions allow for a range of possible early scenarios, however: the creole could have started out looking more like Portuguese and remained that way, or changed very slowly until the end of the Portuguese period, after which sub/adstrate influence would have been felt more strongly; or the creole could have started out with substrate characteristics already in place, some of which could have been replaced by lexifier characteristics during the Portuguese period; or the creole could have begun with a mix of lexifier and substrate characteristics, which remained more or less stable or developed in the direction of the lexifier during the Portuguese period. Lefebvre (1998: 38–40), following Lefebvre & Lumsden (1992), argues that in creole genesis the order of major category items follows that found in the lexifier, while substrate order prevails for functional category lexical items. To the extent that creolization embodies second language acquisition (particularly with respect to the lexifier as target), Lefebvre's position on the dominance of lexifier order is reinforced by Hickey's finding that Irish word order did not transfer to Irish English as Irish speakers shifted to English after the mid-17th century (2010: 161). Consequently, substrate influence on word order in creoles is essentially *adstrate* influence that takes place after creolization.

Thus, restricting ourselves to the major category orders examined here, Sri Lanka Portuguese and the other Ibero-Asian creoles were likely in their initial stages to have exhibited the following word order patterns: Subject – Verb – Object, Noun – Adjective (predominantly), Preposition – Noun Phrase, Cardinal Numeral – Noun, Noun – Relative Clause, Interrogative Phrase in sentence-initial position. Possibly both Possessor -*su(a)* Possessum and Possessum *de* Possessor were both present in the Portuguese-based creoles; while the Spanish-based creoles would have exhibited Possessum – Possessor, in agreement with both lexifier and substrates. In Sri Lanka Portuguese, the orders Subject – Object – Verb, Adjective – Noun, Noun Phrase – Postposition, Relative Clause – Noun, and Interrogative Phrase in non-initial position would have developed subsequently under sub/adstratum influence. Smith (2011) argues that these orders were already in place by the early 19th century; if the presence of Portuguese until the mid-17th century acted as a brake on the development of substrate features, then these orders would have developed during the period of Dutch rule, from the mid 17th to the late 18th century.

The conclusion that early creoles followed lexifier word order (for major categories) is also in line with the greater Substrate Influence Score for Bazaar Malay than for Tamil for Malacca and Batavia. The relatively higher score for Bazaar Malay reflects the fact that it (or Betawi-influenced Vehicular Malay, in the case of Batavia) was the chief adstrate after creolization. The low score for Tamil indicates that Tamil was no longer a significant adstrate. This is likely because the lingua franca of the larger communities in which Creole speakers were embedded was Bazaar Malay(/Betawi-influenced Vehicular Malay). One might expect a similar scenario for Makista, with Cantonese adstrate influence outweighing that of Malay; such is not the case because the continuing presence of the lexifier trumps all adstrate influence.

A background theme of this study has been the difficulty of constructing a measure of substrate influence on word order. Certain design problems, such as accounting for the different degrees of initial resemblance between lexifier and substrate can be overcome, but others, such as the interrelationships between word-order features, remain. Difficulties in scoring emerged when a creole partly resembled its lexifier and partly its substrate(s), or when lexifier and substrates were only partially different; in such cases a solution was found, but a certain level of subjectivity in assigning scores cannot be avoided. For the time being, then, the SIS is an unsophisticated overall measure of the penetration of substrate or superstrate word order patterns in the creole. While these problems are diminished by the robustness of the results, i.e. their high level of statistical significance, they should not be ignored. A further problem derives from the fact that some of the substrates are very similar to the lexifiers in their word-order typology, giving rise to an SIS calculated on the basis of very few features. This is particularly an issue for the creoles with Bazaar Malay(/Betawi-influenced Vehicular Malay) as adstrate: the SIS for Malacca and Batavia was based on only 1.5 features (i.e. two features, of which one – Adjective and Noun order – was discounted because of partial similarity between lexifier and substrate. Malacca and Batavia are the only creoles having an SIS Rank that does not reflect their Lexifier Influence Rank; we can speculate that this anomaly would be mitigated if more features were available on which to calculate the SIS. For the future, the development of a more broadly-based metric that takes into account morphosyntactic features beyond word-order would provide a fuller picture of lexifier and substrate influence. It would also provide a greater number of possible features on which to calculate the SIS, overcoming the reliability issue just raised. The *Atlas of Pidgin and Creole Structures* will be a useful source of such features, when it becomes available. A complementary approach would be to adopt the framework of computational phylogenetics, which Bakker et al. (2011) have demonstrated can be fruitfully exploited in creole studies.

Notes

* I am grateful to Alan Baxter, Hugo Cardoso and three anonymous reviewers for comments on earlier drafts. Remaining errors are mine.

1. For the purposes of this paper, 'creolization' may be taken to include both expansion and nativization.

2. An anonymous review points out that African substrates for some of the Caribbean creoles can also be argued to be typologically similar.

3. An anonymous reviewer suggests that frequency should also be taken into account, in that a feature that occurs more frequently would have greater impact. This point is perhaps debatable, but in any case, the substantial corpora needed to assess the frequency of morphosyntactic features are not available at present.

4. This is not to suggest that Dutch had no influence on Sri Lanka Portuguese; indeed, the passive structure in Sri Lanka Portuguese may be calqued from Dutch (Smith 2010), but for the features surveyed here, its influence is negligible. The Sri Lanka substrates differ from the lexifier, Portuguese, in most of the features surveyed, while Dutch agrees with the lexifier in most cases; in all cases Sri Lanka Portuguese follows one of the substrates.

5. Thomaz (1985:57) puts their number at over one thousand.

6. Paauw (2003), following Abdullah (1969), Lim (1988) and Adelaar (1991) restricts the term 'Bazaar Malay' to refer to "the contact language which has arisen in the multi-ethnic setting of West Malaysia". Following Smith and Paauw (2006), I use "Vehicular Malay" to denote the variety of Malay that for centuries served as a lingua franca throughout the Indonesian archipelago, Malaysia and Brunei.

7. Creole data are taken (or extracted) from the following sources: for Daman, Clements & Koontz-Garboden (2002), Clements (2009a) and Clements (n.d.); for Diu, Cardoso (2009b); for Korlai, Clements (1996), Clements & Koontz-Garboden (2002) and Clements (2007); for Sri Lanka, my own field notes; for Malacca, Baxter (1988); for Batavia, Maurer (2011), for Zamboangueño, Forman (1972), Steinkrüger (2006); for Ternateño, Sippola (2006), Steinkrüger (2007); for Makista, Fernandes & Baxter (2004). Substrate data are taken/extracted from WALS, Masica (1991) and, for Gujarati, Cardona (1965); for Sinhala, Fairbanks et al. (1968), Gair &

Paolillo (1997); for Tamil, my own knowledge; for Bazaar Malay, Bao & Aye (2010), Alan Baxter (p.c. October 2010 – February 2012)); for Javanese, Samarmurti (2008); for Cebuano, Bunye & Yap (1971), Wolff (1966); for Hiligaynon, Wolfenden (1971), Wolfenden (1975); for Tagalog, Ramos (1971). I would like to thank Philippe Maurer for providing me with pre-publication drafts of relevant parts of Maurer (2011).

8. For examples taken from other sources, morpheme divisions have silently been added where discernable and glosses have been made to conform to the Leipzig glossing rules to the extent possible.

9. Pronouns, which have genitive forms that precede the Possessum, will be excluded from this discussion.

10. Since the lexifier order is partly specified lexically and partly semantically conditioned, a more nuanced approach would look at individual adjectives and semantic specificities. I do not have the data at hand to pursue this option, however.

11. Alan Baxter (p.c. February 2012) points out that in emphatic usage, the Tamil-inspired order ADJ + DET + N is used, as in *grandi ungua omi* 'a BIG man'.

12. The SIS and Spearman rho were calculated using an Excel spreadsheet. Critical values for rho were obtained from Zar (1972).

References

Abdullah, H. 1969. Bahasa Melayu pasar di Malaysia barat. *Dewan Bahasa* 13: 207–18.
Adelaar, K. A. 1991. Some notes on the origin of Sri Lanka Malay. In *Papers in Austronesian Linguistics no. 1* [Pacific Linguistics Series A-81], ed. H. Steinhauer, 23–37. Canberra: Australian National University.
Arends, J. 1989. Syntactic Developments in Sranan: Creolization as a Gradual Process. PhD dissertation, University of Nijmegen.
Atlas of Pidgin and Creole Structures (APiCS), Questionnaire. 2010. http://lingweb.eva.mpg.de/apics/index.php/APiCS_Questionnaire (accessed April 20, 2011).
Bakker, P. 2000a. Convergence intertwining: An alternative way towards the genesis of mixed languages. In *Languages in Contact*, eds. D. Gilbers, J. Nerbonne and J. Schaeken, 29–35. Amsterdam: Rodopi.
Bakker, P. 2000b. Rapid language change: Creolization, intertwining, convergence. In *Time Depth in Historical Linguistics*, 2 vol., eds. C. Renfrew, A. McMahon and L. Trask, 585–619. Cambridge: The McDonald Institute for Archaeological Research.
Bakker, P., A. Daval-Markussen, M. Parkvall, and I. Plag. 2011. Creoles are typologically distinct from non-creoles. *Journal of Pidgin and Creole Languages* 26: 5–42.
Bao, Z., and K. K. Aye. 2010. Bazaar Malay topics. *Journal of Pidgin and Creole Languages* 25: 155–71.
Baxter, A. N. 1988. *A Grammar of Kristang (Malacca Creole Portuguese)* [Pacific Linguistics. Series B; no. 95]. Canberra: Pacific Linguistics.

Bunye, M. V. R., and E. P. Yap. 1971. *Cebuano for Beginners*. Honolulu HI: University of Hawaii Press.

Cardona, G. 1965. *A Gujarati Reference Grammar*. Philadelphia, PA: University of Pennsylvania Press.

Cardoso, H. C. 2009a. Jacques Arends' model of gradual creolization. In *Gradual Creolization; Studies Celebrating Jacques Arends* [Creole Language Library 34], eds. R. Selbach, H. C. Cardoso and M. van den Berg, 13–23. Amsterdam: John Benjamins.

Cardoso, H. C. 2009b. The Indo-Portuguese Language of Diu. PhD dissertation, University of Amsterdam.

Clements, J. C. nd. Four texts in Daman creole Portuguese. Ms.

Clements, J. C. 1991. Two Indo-Portuguese creoles: Languages in transition. *Hispania* 74: 637–46.

Clements, J. C. 1996. *The Genesis of a Language: The Formation and Development of Korlai Portuguese* [Creole Language Library 16]. Amsterdam: John Benjamins.

Clements, J. C. 2000. Evidência para a existência de um pidgin português asiático. In *Crioulos de Base Portuguesa*, eds. E. d'Andrade, M. A. Mota and D. Pereira, 185–200. Braga: Associação Portuguesa de Linguística.

Clements, J. C. 2007. Korlai (Creole Portuguese) *or Nɔ Liŋ*. In *Comparative Creole Syntax* [Westminster Creolistics Series 7], eds. J. Holm and P. Patrick, 153–173. London: Battlebridge.

Clements, J. C. 2009a. Accounting for some similarities and differences among the Indo-Portuguese creoles. *Journal of Portuguese Linguistics* 8: 23–47.

Clements, J. C. 2009b. *The Linguistic Legacy of Spanish and Portuguese: Colonial Expansion and Language Change*. Cambridge: CUP.

Clements, J. C., and A. J. Koontz-Garboden. 2002. Two Indo-Portuguese creoles in contrast. *Journal of Pidgin and Creole Languages* 17: 191–236.

Clements, J. C., and A. Mahboob. 2000. Wh-words and question formation in pidgin/creole languages. In *Language Change and Language Contact in Pidgins and Creoles* [Creole Language Library 21], ed. J. McWhorter, 459–497. Amsterdam: John Benjamins.

Daus, R. 1989. *Portuguese Eurasian Communities in Southeast Asia*. Singapore: Institute of Southeast Asian Studies.

Fairbanks, G. H., J. W. Gair, and M. W. S. De Silva. 1968. *Colloquial Sinhalese*, parts I & II. Ithaca NY: Cornell University South Asia Program.

Fernandes, M. S., and A. N. Baxter. 2004. *Maquista Chapado: Vocabulary and Expressions in Macao's Portuguese Creole*, translated by M. I. Macleod. Macau: Instituto Cultural de Macau.

Forman, M. L. 1972. Zamboangueño Texts with Grammatical Analysis: A Study of Philippine Creole Spanish. PhD dissertation, Cornell University.

Gair, J. W., and J. C. Paolillo. 1997. *Sinhala* [Languages of the World: Materials 34]. Munich: Lincom Europa.

Grant, A. P. 2002. El Chabacano Zamboangueño: Una lengua mezclada. *Papia* 12: 7–40.

Haspelmath, M., M. Dryer, D. Gil, and B. Comrie. 2005. *World Atlas of Language Structures (WALS)*. Oxford: OUP; Munich: Max Planck Digital Library. http://wals.info/

Hickey, R. 2010. Contact and language shift. In *The Handbook of Language Contact*, ed. R. Hickey, 151–169. Chichester: Wiley-Blackwell.

Holm, J. 2000. *An Introduction to Pidgins and Creoles*. Cambridge: CUP.

Lach, D. C. 1965. *Asia in the Making of Europe*, Vol. 1: *The Century of Discovery*, Book 2. Chicago IL: University of Chicago Press.
Lefebvre, C. 1998. *Creole Genesis and the Acquisition of Grammar: The Case of Haitian Creole* [Cambridge Studies in Linguistics]. Cambridge: CUP.
Lefebvre, C., and J. S. Lumsden. 1992. On word order in relexification. *Travaux de Recherche sur le Créole Haïtien* 10: 1–22 (Université du Québec à Montréal).
Lipski, J. 1988. Philippine creole Spanish: Reassessing the Portuguese element. *Zeitschrift für Romanishce Philologie* 104: 25–45.
Lipski, J., and M. Santoro. 2007. Zamboangueño creole Spanish. In *Comparative Creole Syntax*, eds. J. Holm and P. Patrick, 373–398. London: Battlebridge.
Lim, S. 1988. Baba Malay: The language of the 'Straits-born' Chinese. In *Papers in Western Austronesian Linguistics* no. 3 [Pacific Linguistics Series A No. 78.], ed. H. Steinhauer, 1–61. Canberra: Australian National University.
Masica, C. P. 1991. *The Indo-Aryan Languages*. Cambridge: CUP.
Maurer, P. 2011. *The Former Portuguese Creole of Batavia and Tugu (Indonesia)*. London: Battlebridge.
Paauw, S. 2003. What is Bazaar Malay? Paper presented at the Seventh International Symposium on Malay/Indonesian Linguistics (ISMIL 7), Nijmegen.
Ramos, T. V. 1971. *Tagalog Structures*. Honolulu HI: University of Hawaii Press.
Reinecke, J. E. 1937. Marginal Languages: A Sociological Survey of the Creole Languages and Trade Jargons. PhD dissertation, Yale University.
Samaramurti, W. 2008. Tak and Kok in Javanese Language. MA dissertation, Utrecht University.
Sippola, E. 2006. Hacia una descripción del ternateño. *Revista Internacional de Lingüística Iberoamericana* 4: 41–53.
Smith, I. R. 2010. Grammaticalization in Creoles: The Sri Lanka Portuguese Passive. Paper presented at the *10th International Conference of the ACBLPE*, CNRS, Paris, July 1–3.
Smith, I. R. 2011. Diglossia in Sri Lanka Portuguese: The role of Anglophone missionaries. Ms.
Smith, I. R., and S. Paauw. 2006. Sri Lanka Malay: Creole or convert? In *Structure and Variation in Language Contact* [Creole Language Library 29], eds. A. Deumert and S. Durlemann, 159–181. Amsterdam: John Benjamins.
Steinkrüger, P. O. 2006. The Puzzling Case of Chabacano: Creolization, Substrate, Mixing and Secondary Contact. Paper presented at *Tenth International Conference on Austronesian Linguistics*. Puerto Princesa, Palawan, Philippines, January. http://www.sil.org/asia/philippines/ical/papers /Steinkrueger_The_Puzzling_Case_of_Chabacano.pdf (accessed April 24, 2011).
Steinkrüger, P. O. 2007. Notes on Ternateño (a Philippine Spanish creole). *Journal of Pidgin and Creole Languages* 22: 37–77.
Suratminto, L. 2011. Creol Potuguese [sic] of the Tugu village: Colonial heritage in Jakarta based on the historical and linguistic review. *Tawarikh: International Journal for Historical Studies* 3: 1–30.
Thomason, S. G. 1997. A typology of contact languages. In *The Structure and Status of Pidgins and Creoles*, eds. A. K. Spears and D. Winford, 71–88. Amsterdam: John Benjamins.
Thomaz, L. F. F. R. 1985. The Indian merchant communities in Malacca under the Portuguese rule. In *Indo-Portuguese History: Old Issues, New Questions*, ed. T. R. de Souza, 56–72. New Delhi: Concept.

Whinnom, K. 1956. *Spanish Contact Vernaculars in the Philippine Islands.* Hong Kong, Hong Kong University Press/Oxford: OUP.

Wolfenden, E. P. 1971. *Hiligaynon Reference Grammar.* Honolulu HI: University of Hawaii Press.

Wolfenden, E. P. 1975. *A Description of Hiligaynon Syntax.* Norman OK: Summer Institute of Linguistics of the University of Oklahoma.

Wolff, J. U. 1966. *Beginning Cebuano.* New Haven CT: Yale University Press.

Zar, J. H. 1972. Significance testing of the Spearman Rank Correlation Coefficient. *Journal of the American Statistical Association* 67: 578–80.

Indefinite terms in Ibero-Asian Creoles

Eeva Sippola

This paper compares the indefinite terms in the Indian Creole Portuguese varieties of Diu and Korlai, Sri Lanka Creole Portuguese, Malacca Creole, Macau Creole and the Spanish-lexified creole languages in the Philippines, referred to as Chabacano of Cavite, Ternate and Zamboanga. The study uses functional criteria for the definition of indefinite terms that include not only pronouns, but also analytic constructions. The comparison builds on three functional categories: realis indefinites, free-choice indefinites and negative indefinites, and the main formal categories of special indefinites, generic-noun-based and interrogative-based indefinites. The comparison shows that both adstrate and superstrate structures have influenced the indefinite terms in these languages. It also reveals parallels between them, especially in areal subgroups, and shows a clear connection with wider cross-linguistic patterns.

1. Introduction

This paper presents, analyses and compares the indefinite terms in the Spanish and Portuguese creoles in Asia. Indefinite terms are pronouns and related constructions that express indefinite reference, and denote something unknown to the hearer. These include indefinites that express 'somebody' and 'something', terms that express free choice such as 'anybody' and 'anything', and their negative counterparts, such as 'nobody' and 'nothing', that express non-existence. As mentioned in Haspelmath (1997: 10), in many cases the indefinite terms are somewhere halfway on the grammaticalisation path from the lexicon to the grammar. For this reason, the present comparison includes not only pronouns, but also different types of formal categories under the common denomination 'term'.

The study of indefinite terms can provide insights into the processes of language change and language contact, as closely related languages often show very different indefinite pronouns and indefinite systems due to a relatively short lifespan and the diachronically unstable nature of the indefinite pronouns

(Haspelmath 1997: 235). Therefore, the present study can shed light on the current situation of the languages in the sample, reflected in the presence of the Portuguese, Spanish or adstrate uses of the indefinite terms.[1] The principal aim of the comparison across the creoles under study is to reveal parallels or differences between them and to identify possible areal subgroups within this group of creoles.

The initial idea for this study arose from the striking similarity of indefinite expressions in Malacca Creole and Chabacano. As in (1) and (2), both languages can make use of a generic noun as an indefinite, as in their adstrate languages, even though in the existing studies the formal typological classification of these constructions differs, as will be shown in this paper.

(1) Malacca Creole (Baxter 1988: 55, ex. 17)
    teng   jenti   na   fora
    be   person   LOC   outside
    'There is somebody outside.'

(2) Ternate Chabacano (Sippola, field notes 1 (2008))[2]
    Tyéni   hénti   ayá   na   pwéra.
    EXST   person   there   LOC   outside
    'There is someone outside.'

The comparison includes Manila Bay Chabacano and Zamboanga Chabacano,[3] Macau Creole and Malacca Creole in South East Asia, the Indian Creole Portuguese varieties of Diu and Korlai, and Sri Lanka Creole Portuguese. The data and examples were collected from published sources and from personal communication with the authors of unpublished works.[4] The examples, glosses and translations follow those of the above sources.

Our aim is not to offer a comprehensive description of the functions of indefinite terms for all languages under study, but to give an overview of the general patterns and their organization. The formal classification of the sample is rather straightforward, but the recognition and classification of the diverse functions is not complete by any means. Despite these shortcomings, many interesting general developments can be observed even on the basis of this limited sample of data.

The limitations of this study stem from the scarcity of the data and the generalizing bias of typological studies. Although there are a growing number of detailed descriptive grammars of the Ibero-Asian creoles, these seldom pay much attention, if any, to the range of functional properties of indefinites. Additionally, from a methodological point of view, using a typological categorization as a tool of analysis can imply some loss of depth in the description of individual languages, as it is challenging to include variation between different constructions or different lects within the pre-established typological categories. Therefore, we will try to proceed inductively while also discussing some questions related to the methodological framework of comparative creole studies.

The paper is organised as follows: Section 2 briefly presents the theoretical background of the study. This is followed, in Section 3, by a presentation of the languages considered. Section 4 constitutes the core of the paper, presenting the indefinite terms in Ibero-Asian creoles and discussing the different formal categories present in these languages. In the analysis, indefinite terms are classified according to their form and main semantic groups, and compared across the languages in question in order to uncover similarities, differences and possible common paths of development. The results of the comparison are discussed in the light of general typological work. The conclusion summarizes the findings and discusses their implications for our current understanding of the Spanish and Portuguese-lexified creoles of Asia.

2. Typological framework

The comparison of the indefinite terms in Ibero-Asian creoles builds on prior typological work on indefinite pronouns by Bhat (2004) and Haspelmath (1997, 2008).

Haspelmath (1997: 11) offers a rather simple functional definition of indefinite pronouns: "Indefinite pronouns express indefinite reference and denote something not known to the hearer." The definition includes a number of meanings associated with indefinites, ranging from unknown reference and indication of free choice to non-existence:

a. *someone, something, somewhere, somehow*; used in affirmative declarative sentences with realis modality.
b. *anyone, anything, anywhere, anyhow*; expressing free choice rather than indefiniteness, used in questions and conditional clauses.
c. *no one, nothing, nowhere, never*; expressing non-existence rather than indefiniteness, used in negative sentences.

In several languages, these diverse meanings are expressed by different formal series (Haspelmath 2008).

In his study, Haspelmath uses a formal definition of a pronoun in its broad sense, comprising not only pronouns that are grammatical items which may replace nouns or noun phrases, but also pro-adverbs, pro-adjectives, pro-verbs. This classification also includes indefinite determiners that clearly belong to a series of indefinite pronouns (Haspelmath 1997: 10). In the present study, we focus on terms that correspond to pro-nouns, but in some cases, terms corresponding to pro-adverbs are also discussed in order to offer a wider picture of the matter in specific languages. In addition, indefinite pronouns tend to indicate the epistemic domain of the replaced elements in much the same way as interrogative pronouns (Bhat 2004:182, Dixon 2009:118).

In our study, the vagueness of the word 'term' might create methodological problems. However, our aim is to follow functional criteria in order to include the different ways of expressing indefinite terms, and to obtain a realistic picture of the expression of indefinite terms in these languages.

In traditional grammars, the category of indefinite pronouns seems to function as a sort of wastebasket, including such elements as mid-scalar quantifiers (*few, many, several*), generic pronouns, identity pronouns/determiners (*other, same*) and universal quantifiers (*all, every*). It is true that there are close connections between distributive universal quantifiers (*every*) and indefinite pronouns which express irrelevance of choice (*any*), even though universally quantified noun phrases are semantically definite (Haspelmath 1997:11–12). This is reflected, for example, in the Spanish tradition whereby indefinite terms (*nada* 'nothing', *ninguno* 'no one', *nadie* 'nobody', *uno* 'one', *algo* 'something', *alguno* 'someone', *alguien* 'somebody') are generally classified as existential quantifiers (especially *alguno, ninguno*) or as indefinite quantifiers (together with *varios* 'several', *cualquiera* 'whichever') (Rigau 1999:336). In addition, indefinite pronouns share the same basic meaning of indefiniteness as, for example, the Spanish form *un* (Leonetti 1999:838). As in the lexifiers, all the languages studied here have an indefinite article that is identical to the numeral 'one', even though, from a typological point of view, there is no correlation of indefinite terms with the presence or absence of articles (Haspelmath 1997:238).

The shapes of the indefinite pronouns are fairly uniform across languages (Haspelmath 1997:235). They can either be closely related to interrogative pronouns (often with an indefiniteness marker, usually an uninflected particle), or be based on generic nouns like 'person' and 'thing'. Indefinite pronouns not related to anything else synchronically receive the label of special indefinites (Haspelmath 2008). Often, indefinite pronouns are formed by reduplication or the use of a scalar focus particle; moreover, bare interrogatives may also be used as indefinites. Yet other types with a clearly phrasal origin are indefinites derived from constructions such as 'don't know', 'want/please', 'it may be' ('whoever it may be') and 'no matter who' (Haspelmath 1997:237).

Looking closer at the formal types of indefinite markers, Haspelmath (1997:31) finds that indefinite pronouns normally occur in series which have one member for each of the major ontological categories such as person, thing, property, place, time, manner, amount… etc. We have chosen Portuguese to exemplify the types and ontological categories (from Haspelmath 1997:256).[5]

Table 1. Types of indefinites and interrogatives in Portuguese (Haspelmath 1997)

	Interrogative	*alg*-series	*qualquer*-series	*n*-series
person	quem	alguém	qualquer pessoa	ninguém
thing	que	alguma coisa, algo	qualquer coisa	nada
place	onde	algures, em algum lugar	em qualquer lugar	nenhures
time	quando	alguma vez	em qualquer altura	nunca, jamais
manner	como	de algum modo	de qualquer modo	
determiner	que, qual	algum	qualquer	nenhum

Categorizing the series according to the formal categories established, we find both special indefinites, such as *alguém, algo, nada, nunca*, and generic-noun-based indefinites, such as *alguma coisa, alguma vez*. Haspelmath mentions that the origin of the marker is generally still transparent, as in *alguém* compared with the interrogative *quem*, although the meaning can never be determined on a compositional basis alone due to the item's recent grammaticalisation. In the Portuguese series, the origins of the *alg*-series go back to the Latin *ali*-series, and *qualquer* is from *qual* 'which' plus *quer* 'wants'. We will return to the issue of transparency later on, when we discuss the analytic constructions used for indefinite reference in the languages under study.

In the geographic area where the Ibero-Asian creole languages are located, all of the three main formal typological categories are present. Special indefinites are scattered around Eurasia, represented especially by Indic languages. Interrogative-based indefinite pronouns are found in Eurasia as well, while the generic-noun-based indefinites are found in the Pacific Islands and on the African continent (Haspelmath 1997: 241, Haspelmath et al. 2008). As a result, the area where the Ibero-Asian creoles are located is clearly a meeting point for several areal clusters.

Haspelmath (1997: 236) forms the implicational map in Figure 1 on the basis of the functional distinctions of indefinite pronouns. The distribution of the Portuguese series exemplifies the implicational relations in the same figure. This map should be read such that if an indefinite term expresses two non-adjacent functions, it very probably also expresses all the other functions located in between (Haspelmath 1997: 236). In Portuguese, the *alg*-series is used in all non-emphatic functions from (1) to (5). In the specific-known function (1), only the *alg*-series is possible, while in the other functions (2)–(5) the *qualquer*-series is a possible alternative. The *qualquer*-series is used in (2)–(9), and the negative *n*-series in (6) and (7).

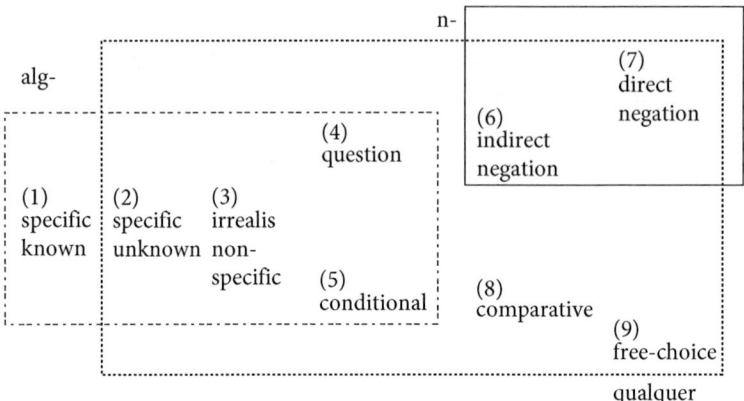

Figure 1. The implicational map of (Brazilian) Portuguese indefinite pronouns (after Haspelmath 1997:256)

3. Presentation of the sample

The current sample contains seven languages. Table 2 sets out the classification according to five categories: the geographic area, the Ibero-Romance lexifier language concerned, the main adstrate language, and the sources that were consulted to gather the information.

Table 2. Ibero-Asian creoles in the sample

Area		Lexifier	Adstrate	Language	Main sources
South Asia	Western India	Portuguese	Gujarati	Diu Creole	Cardoso 2009
			Marathi	Korlai Creole	Clements 1996
	Sri Lanka		Tamil, Sinhala	Batticaloa Creole	Smith, p.c. August 2010
SE Asia	Malay Peninsula		(Bazaar) Malay, (Hokkien)	Malacca Creole	Baxter 1988
	China Coast		Cantonese (Malay, Hokkien)†	Macau Creole	Ferreira 1967, 1978
	Philippines	Spanish	Tagalog	Manila Bay Chabacano	Riego de Dios 1989, Sippola 2011
			Cebuano, Hiligaynon, Tagalog	Zamboanga Chabacano	Forman 1972, Riego de Dios 1989, Miravite et al. 2009

† Substrate languages for Macau Creole (Batalha 1965–66, Tomás 2009).

The sample can be evaluated according to the following criteria: representativeness based on different lexifier and adstrate languages and the geographical distribution in the sample.

Based on a compilation of sources (Holm 1988, Bartens 1995, Cardoso 2006: 23, Cardoso 2009: 7), at least 12 Ibero-Romance lexifier languages are recognized and currently spoken in the area studied, although a greater number of varieties can be differentiated depending on the subdivisions within the twelve. Of those twelve, we have included seven (two Spanish- and five Portuguese-based) in our comparison. At present, Portuguese-lexified creoles survive in Diu, Daman, Korlai and Kannur (India);[6] and in Sri Lanka (Cardoso 2009: 7); in Malacca (Malaysia), with an offshoot in Singapore; and in the Macau/Hong Kong region. In the Philippines, Chabacano is still spoken in Zamboanga on Mindanao, and in Cavite and Ternate on the shores of Manila Bay. The Manila Bay varieties are treated here as a cluster, because of the shared main adstrate language Tagalog, even though there are some lexical and grammatical differences. Zamboanga Chabacano is differentiated from them, because of the different adstrate.

Portuguese is the lexifier of five languages in question, while Spanish is the main lexifier only for the Chabacano varieties. This however reflects the reality of the area, where there are more Portuguese-based creoles in general. It is also important to bear in mind that the typological distance between Spanish and Portuguese is minimal, and even less so regarding our topic. Due to the lack of documentation of the surviving languages in the sample, it is often difficult to know what kind of early Ibero-Romance varieties were spoken in the contact situations from which these creoles emerged.[7] In modern European Spanish and Portuguese, the differences concerning the indefinite pronouns are related to a few specific forms and registers, and probably existed at the time of the formation of these contact varieties. Examples are Portuguese *alguma coisa* vs. Spanish *algo* 'something' or the Portuguese pro-adverb *algures* vs. Spanish *algún lugar*. Despite these examples, when discussing indefinite terms, we should keep in mind that constructions such as *alguna cosa* 'some thing' in colloquial Spanish or *algo* and *algum lugar* in Portuguese are also possible alternatives to the forms presented above.[8]

The adstrate languages are typologically more divergent than the lexifier languages. The Indo-Portuguese varieties can be subdivided into clusters according to the endemic language of their environment: Diu and Korlai have Gujarati and Marathi as their adstrate, while Sri Lanka Creole Portuguese has both Sinhala and Tamil adstrate. Gujarati, Marathi and Sinhala are Indic languages from the Indo-European family, and Tamil is a Southern Dravidian language from the Dravidian family. Malay varieties form the Sundic adstrate of Malacca Creole, which was complemented by Hokkien. The Malay varieties were also present as a substrate for Macau creole, which has Cantonese, Malay and Hokkien as adstrate languages. Lastly, the adstrate of Chabacano varieties is formed by Tagalog in the Manila Bay and Cebuano, Hiligaynon and, more recently, Tagalog in Zamboanga.⁹ Of the languages mentioned, Malay and Philippine languages belong to the Western Malayo-Polynesian subfamily of the Austronesian family and the Chinese varieties belong to the Sino-Tibetan language family.¹⁰

Generally speaking, the sample is rather heterogeneous. The languages are quite discrete geographically and scattered in an area representing a variety of different adstrates. The sample is also biased towards the Portuguese lexifier creoles, which clearly outnumber the Spanish-based languages among creoles in general.

4. Analysis of the data

4.1 Presentation of the data by language

In the following, the different indefinite terms are presented for each creole in a geographical order, from West to East.

4.1.1 Diu Creole

According to Cardoso (2009: 132), Diu Creole uses two general formal series and a few other means of forming indefinite terms. One of the formal series is called the *aŋ-* series and it expresses both free choice and lack of knowledge; the other is termed the negative *n-* series by Cardoso. Other indefinite terms are formed with *kwɔlki* or *sɛrt* 'some, any'.

The only real pro-form in the *aŋ-* series is *aŋe* 'somebody', as it is not related to anything else synchronically. It expresses specific animate referents that are usually human, as in (3).

(3) Diu Creole (Cardoso 2009: 132, ex. 61a)
 aŋe fez fon
 somebody make.PST phone
 'Somebody called.'

For the expression of any other type of indefinite reference analytical constructions are used. These are formed with the existential quantifier *aŋũ* 'some, any' and a generic nominal reference to the corresponding epistemic domain. The resulting terms in analytic constructions are *aŋũ jẽt* 'some people', with the alternatives *kwɔlki jẽt* and *sɛrt jẽt* in (4), *aŋũ koys* 'something' in (5) and *kwɔlki di* 'someday' in (6).

(4) Diu Creole (Cardoso 2009: 132, ex. 61b)
aŋũ/kwɔlki/sɛrt jẽt pəd abr-i kok
some people can.NPST open-INF coconut
sẽ fak.
without knife
'Some people can open coconuts without a knife.'

(5) Diu Creole (Cardoso, p.c. September 2010)
Dig aŋũ koys a mī.
tell.NPST some thing DAT 1SG.OBL
'Tell me something.'

(6) Diu Creole (Cardoso 2009: 132, ex. 61c)
kurəsãw də makak kwɔlki di ad sa-i fɔr?
heart of monkey some day IRR.NPST leave-INF out
'Would a monkey's heart ever come out?'

In addition, interrogatives are used in non-specific complement clauses, expressing free choice indefinites as in (7).[11]

(7) Diu Creole (Cardoso 2009: 244–245, ex. 314)
 a. kẽ chig-a pimer a gaŋ-a prɛzẽt.
  who arrive-INF first IRR.NPST win-INF present
  'Whoever arrives first will receive a present.'
 b. yo uki fal-a use ti ki faz-e.
  1SG what say-INF 2SG AUX.NPST COMP do-INF
  'You must do whatever I say.'

The *n*-series of the negative indefinites in Diu contains suppletive simple forms not related to anything else synchronically. These are *nĩge* 'nobody', which replaces animate and usually human referents, as in (8a), and *nad* 'nothing', used for non-human referents as in (8b). There is also a form for the epistemic domain of time, *nuk* 'never', as in (8c). As can be observed from these examples, the use of these forms triggers negative concord on a syntactic level (Cardoso 2009: 115). It should also be noted that these forms are very similar to the Portuguese negative indefinites, presented earlier in Table 1.

(8) Diu Creole (Cardoso 2009: 211, ex. 236)
 a. nĩge nã apĩŋ-o pex.
  nobody NEG catch-PST fish
  'Nobody caught fish.'
 b. Tɛ agɔr nã vey nad.
  until now NEG come.PST nothing
  'Up until now, nothing has come.'

(8) c. el   nuk   nə   foy   sinem.
       3SG never NEG go.PST cinema
       'He never went to the movies.'

For all other domains, Diu Creole makes use of analytical constructions with the NP negator *niŋũ* 'no [X]', as in (9).

(9) Diu Creole   (Cardoso 2009: 172, ex. 146a)
    Tɛ   agɔr   niŋũ   rɛpos   nã   dew.
    until   now   none   answer NEG give-PST
    'So far, [they] have not given any answer.'

From a formal point of view, Diu Creole has special indefinites with suppletive forms, generic-noun-based and interrogative based indefinite terms. The generic-noun-based terms are formed by analytic constructions and used for the positive *aŋ-* series expressing realis and free-choice indefinite terms as well as the *n-* series for the negative terms (Cardoso 2009: 133). Constructions with interrogatives express free-choice indefinite terms.

4.1.2   *Korlai Creole*

For Korlai Creole, Clements (1996: 88) documents the positive forms *angé* 'someone' for animate humans, as in (10a), and *ankodz* 'something' for non-human referents, as in (10b). The origins of these forms are the Portuguese *alguém* 'someone' and *alguma coisa* 'something'. However, in contrast to the Portuguese indefinites, neither one of the Korlai Creole forms is an analytic construction. The Korlai forms are not synchronically related to any other items, such as generic nouns or interrogatives.

(10) Korlai Creole   (Clements, p.c. September 2010)
     a. *Angé   yawe?*
        someone   came
        'Did someone come?'
     b. *Jhiko   ankodz?*
        PST-be/become-PST something
        'Did something happen?'

Another means of expressing indefinites in Korlai Creole is to use the interrogative pronouns *kẽ* 'who' and *ki* 'what' with the meanings 'whoever' and 'whatever'. An analytic construction *ki təri* 'whatever' is also found (Clements, p.c. September 2010). Also Marathi, the main adstrate language of Korlai Creole, has interrogative-based indefinites (Haspelmath 2008).

Negative indefinites are special indefinites, such as *ningẽ* 'no one' for human referents, as in (11).

(11) Korlai Creole   (Clements, p.c. September 2010)
   a. *ningɛ̃   nu   yawe.*
      nobody NEG came
      'Nobody came.'
   b. *yo   nu   tɛ   ulyad   ku   ningɛ̃.*
      1SG NEG PRS see-PFV OBJ nobody
      'I didn't see anyone.'

Negative indefinites in Korlai Creole occur with predicate negation in preverbal and postverbal positions, as can be seen from the previous examples. The negative indefinite for inanimates is *nad* 'nothing', as in (12).

(12) Korlai Creole   (Clements, p.c. September 2010)
   nad   nu   tɛ   hedzid   el.
   nothing NEG PRS do-PTCP 3SG
   'S/he didn't do anything.'

In formal terms, Korlai Creole indefinite terms present largely suppletive special forms, with a few exceptions especially in the forms that express free choice. There are special indefinites in the positive realis and the negative categories. Bare interrogatives and analytic constructions based on interrogatives are used with free-choice meanings.

4.1.3 Sri Lanka Creole Portuguese

Sri Lanka Creole Portuguese presents somewhat different indefinite terms in comparison to the northern Indo-Portuguese varieties. In Sri Lanka Creole Portuguese, there are three similar indefinite constructions, all of which use interrogative words as their basis (Smith, p.c. August 2010).

The structure 'interrogative + conditional marker *see*' expresses indefinites as an equivalent to the English expression 'some X / any X', as in the following example:

(13) Sri Lanka Creole Portuguese   (Smith, field notes (1974–5: 1653))
   asii mee kii   see   pooy teem
   so   FOC what COND HBL   be
   'It may be something like that.'

Indefinite terms can be expressed in another way with the addition of the concessive marker *taam*, in which case *see* is sometimes omitted. The meaning of this construction is 'X-ever' expressing free choice in the categorisation within the theoretical framework employed here. If a dependent verb is involved in this construction, (e.g. 'whatever he touches'), the conditional and concessive markers usually follow the verb, as in (14) (Smith, p.c. August 2010).

(14) Sri Lanka Creole Portuguese (Smith, field notes (1974–5: 1087))
eli kii tokaa see taan[12] tafikaa ooru
3SG.M what touch COND CONC PRS.become gold
'Whatever he touches becomes gold.'

Yet another form of expressing indefinites is to use the indefinite marker *voo* after the interrogative word, as in (15). This construction gives an indefinite reading 'some X / some X or other'. *Voo* is used also to soften yes/no questions (Smith, p.c. August 2010).

(15) Sri Lanka Creole Portuguese (Smith, field notes (1974–5: 1378))
etuspa un diiyapa kii voo tadaa vesli
3PL.HON.DAT one day.DAT what INDF PRS.give Wesley
'Wesley is giving them something or other per day.'

In addition to these three interrogative-based constructions, there exist a few indefinite terms that have *aluŋ(-) as* the common element, forming both analytic constructions and independent forms. However, it is important to note that these forms are quite rare in actual discourse. The form *aluŋ* 'some' occurs only in some specific terms, such as the indefinite pronoun *aluŋas* 'some people' that has no singular form, as well as the constructions *aluŋ ooras* 'sometimes'[13] and *aluŋ jeentis* 'some people' that make use of generic nouns (Smith, p.c. August 2010).[14]

Negative indefinites in Sri Lanka Creole Portuguese are special indefinites, such as *naada* 'nothing' in (16a) and *niinga* 'nobody' in (16b), and they co-occur with predicate negation (Smith, p.c. August 2010).

(16) Sri Lanka Creole Portuguese (Smith, field notes (1974–5))
a. avara prendatu naada naa poy faya
now study.PFV.PST-PTCP nothing NEG.FUT HBL do
'Now, having studied, [he] won't be able to do anything [i.e. find work].'
b. niinga nukunistaa falaa daa
nobody NEG.need say give
'Nobody needs to teach [them].'

In sum, Sri Lanka Creole Portuguese indefinite terms are mainly based on interrogatives that are used with conditional, concessive and indefinite markers. Generic-noun-based constructions occur marginally in certain expressions. There is one positive special indefinite, while the negative indefinite terms for 'nobody' and 'nothing' have special forms that occur with a negator and are similar to the lexifier entries.

4.1.4 Malacca Creole

Moving on to the Malay Peninsula and Indonesian archipelago area, Malacca Creole too has several formal ways of expressing indefinite terms.

Baxter (1988: 55) identifies two subclasses of indefinite pronouns for Malacca Creole, based on the human / non-human distinction. The common noun *angkoza* 'something' is used for expressing non-human reference, as in (17) and, in the same way, the common noun *jenti* 'person' expresses human referents, as in (1) given in the introduction. As a proof of their classification as common nouns, both of these can also be preceded by *ńgua* 'one' (Baxter, p.c. October 2010).[15] These common nouns occur in existential constructions in the examples provided.

(17) Malacca Creole (Baxter 1988: 55, ex. 16)
   teng angkoza na   rentu
   be   thing   LOC inside
   'There is something inside.'

In this type of examples we might ask if the options with a generic noun *there is a thing* and with a pronoun *there is something*, as well as *there is a person* and *there is somebody* respectively, have the same meaning and if the constructions including generic nouns should be included in the comparison. Semantically, the two different options are nearly the same, and it can be difficult to decide if we are talking about just general lexical or syntactic ways of expressing indefiniteness. In this study, our functionalist explanations concentrate on the semantic motivation of a concept, while the form is language-dependant. First, our definition of indefinite term includes analytic constructions and second, in the case of Malacca Creole, the described expressions constitute the principal means of expressing indefinite terms, as there are no alternative, more grammaticalized forms for the indefinite expression with the same realis indefinite meaning.

Also in Malacca Creole, bare interrogatives express free choice as 'whoever' in (18a) and 'whatever' in (18b).

(18) Malacca Creole (Baxter 1988: 55, ex. 15)
   a. keng ganyá lo   ri   la
      who   win   FUT.IRR laugh EMPH
      'Whoever won would laugh.'
   b. ki   teng eli keré da   ku bos
      what have 3SG want give to 2SG
      'Whatever he has he wants to give you.'

In addition to the bare interrogatives as indefinites, there are also reduplicated forms of the interrogatives *ki* 'what' and *keng* 'who' conveying indefinite reference: *keng keng* 'anybody' and *ki ki* 'anything, whatever' (Baxter 1988:54).[16] The reduplicated forms are often followed by the adverb *pun* 'also', as in (19a). This seems more often to express the meaning 'anyone at all'. Occasionally, the bare interrogative followed by the adverb *keng pun* is observed in the function of 'anyone'. (Baxter, p.c. October 2010).

(19) Malacca Creole   (Baxter 1988:54, exs. 13, 14)
  a. keng   keng   pun podi balá
     anyone anyone also can   dance
     'Anyone can dance.'
  b. keng   pun podi bai nalá
     anyone also can go   there
     'Anyone can go there.'

Reduplicated interrogatives can also occur in the scope of negation with the same adverb. Its presence is required in the focused subject position (Baxter 1988:55).

(20) Malacca Creole   (Baxter 1988:55, exs. 19, 20)
  a. eli ngka olá   ki   ki   (pun)
     3SG NEG see   what what (also)
     'He didn't see anything (at all).'
  b. keng keng pun nté   na   kaza
     who who also NEG.be LOC   house
     'Nobody at all is in the house.'

The indefinite pronouns *keng keng* and *ki ki* have parallels in Malay: *siapa siapa* and *apa apa* respectively, which may occur in the scope of negation (Baxter 1988:56).

In addition to these forms, Baxter (1988:54) reports *kalkizera*, which has a free-choice meaning 'whichever (one)', probably from *qual quiser* (Fernández, p.c. August 2011). The form is interesting because the final -*a* is more typical of the modern Spanish than the Portuguese forms in similar *want*-constructions (see Table 1).[17]

The negative indefinites documented in Baxter (1988:55) are Portuguese-based *nada* 'nothing' and *nggéng* 'nobody' and they are always used with predicate negation, as in (21), *ngka* being the most frequent type of negator. Also reduplicated interrogatives can be used in negated clauses, with predicate negation or existential negation (Baxter, p.c. October 2010).

(21) Malacca Creole (Baxter 1988: 55)
    a. *nté   nada   na riba di meza*
       NEG.be nothing LOC top of table
       'There is nothing on the table.'
    b. *nggéng ńgka olá nada*
       nobody NEG see nothing
       'Nobody saw anything.'

In sum, Malacca Creole has both generic-noun-based indefinites for realis meanings and interrogative-based indefinites for free-choice meanings. The interrogatives can occur bare or in the reduplicated form and complemented with an empathic particle. Special indefinites are also found in Malacca Creole for the negative series, as well as a positive entry with a free-choice meaning 'whichever'. The negative indefinites occur in negative sentences with predicate negation.

4.1.5 Macau Creole

The Macau creole data provides the following indefinite pronouns: *alguim* 'somebody', as in (22a), and *ancuza* 'something', as in (22b), which also has the meaning 'thing' as a generic noun (Ferreira 1978: 256).[18]

(22) Macau Creole (Ferreira 1978: 241, 249)
    a. *alguim ta bate porta*
       somebody IPFV knock door
       'Somebody is knocking at the door.'
    b. *tudo dia istudá, assi tamêm non sabe ancuza bêm-fêto*
       all day study so also NEG know thing well-done
       'Study all day, even so does not know anything well.'

The negative indefinites are special indefinites not synchronically related to other items, such as generic nouns or interrogatives. *Ninguim* 'nobody' expresses the inexistence of human referents, as in (23a), and *nada* 'nothing' the inexistence of non-human referents, as in (23b). The negative indefinites can occur in negative sentences with predicate negation.

(23) Macau Creole (Ferreira 1978: 241)
    a. *ninguim já uví*
       nobody PST hear
       'Nobody heard.'
    b. *non-sabe fazê nada*
       NEG-know make nothing
       'Does not know to do anything.'

In addition, Ferreira (1978: 240) mentions that *qualquer* (sg.) and *quaisquer* (pl.) from Portuguese do not have corresponding terms in Macau creole, and that *quánto* is used as the non universal quantifier.[19]

Macau creole presents a mixed system with special indefinites and generic-noun-based indefinites in the positive series. In the negative series only special forms are found. No specific forms expressing only free choice have been found in the sources.

It does not seem very probable that free-choice indefinites would be completely absent from Macau creole. Unfortunately, we can only make assumptions of a possible influence of the Chinese or other substrate language indefinite structures. Chinese varieties have both generic-noun indefinites and existential constructions, and the first could have contributed to the generic-noun use of *ancuza* in Macau creole. Other creole varieties in the Malacca-Macau region might give insights to the possible indefinite constructions in Macau creole. For example, the Batavia and Tugu varieties once spoken in Indonesia have generic-noun-based indefinite expressions, such as *alung kudja* 'something' in (24a), and *alung pesua* [some person] 'somebody', as well as the use of reduplicated interrogative pronouns in free-choice indefinites, as in (24b) (Maurer 2011).[20] We thus obtain a very similar picture to the indefinite terms in Malacca Creole.

(24) Batavia/Tugu Creole (Maurer 2011: 34)
 a. Eo lo   konta alung kudja.
    1SG FUT tell   some   thing
    'I'll tell [you] something.'
 b. Yo   nunte   doy,   nunte   ki   ki.
    1SG   NEG.have   money NEG.have   what what
    'I don't have any money, I don't have anything.'

In addition, it is possible that Macau creole might use reduplicated interrogative pronouns in free-choice indefinites, just as do Malacca and Batavia/Tugu Creoles. However, in their study of Macanese reduplication constructions, Ansaldo & Matthews (2004) do not mention reduplication involving indefinite meanings.

4.1.6 *Chabacano*

In the Spanish lexified creoles of the Philippine archipelago there are various ways of expressing indefinite terms. A collection of dictionaries and wordlists of Manila Bay Chabacano (Riego de Dios 1989, Escalante 2005, Diccionario Chabacano 2008) presents mainly forms that correspond quite closely to the Spanish indefinite pronouns *algo* and *alguno*, but these same sources also mention analytic constructions.

Of the special indefinites, *algo* 'something' is used for expressing non-human reference, as in (25), and *alguno(s)* 'somebody' / 'someone' for human referents, as in (26). These forms are not in use in Ternate. They are more characteristic of the higher written variety used in Cavite, although there too they are rather rare.

(25) Cavite Chabacano (Escalante 2005: 6)
Mas   bueno que tiene tu   algo   que no
more good that have 2SG something than NEG
hay   nada.
EXST nothing
'It is better that you have something than nothing.'

(26) Cavite Chabacano (Sippola, field notes 1 (2007))
Ya   lliga alguno.
PFV   come   someone
'Someone came.'

Another way of expressing indefinite terms is by the use of the construction '*maski* 'even' + interrogative word', such as *maski kosa* 'anything'/'whatever', *maski kwal* 'anyone'/'whichever' and *maski kyen* 'anybody' / 'whoever' (Ocampo 1943, Riego de Dios 1989: 111, Diccionario Chabacano 2008, Escalante 2010: 28, Sippola 2011: 135).[21] These constructions express free choice and they can also be used in negative sentences, as in (27). The use of the concessive *masqui* 'even' reflects the Tagalog structures for concessive clauses with *maski*, *kahit* and *man*, and indefinite expressions with *kahit* and *man* (Schachter & Otanes 1972: 480–481, 531).[22]

(27) Ternate Chabacano (Nigoza 2007: 20)
Y   no   esti ta   platica masque cosa.
and NEG this IPFV say   even   thing
'And this [man] did not say anything.'

In addition to the earlier examples, the most common way of expressing indefinite functions in spoken language is through the use of existential constructions. These constructions often include interrogative or generic words, as was the case with the generic nouns in Malacca Creole Examples (17) and (1) above. Of the generic nouns in Manila Bay Chabacano, *hénti* 'someone' / 'somebody' is used in an existential construction, as in (2) presented in the introduction, but it is also found separately in a wordlist as *ung jenti* (Nigoza 2007: 86). However, as other elements can occur in these contexts, the occurrences of Chabacano generic nouns are generally classified as existential constructions, unlike the similar constructions in Malacca Creole. For example, interrogative words occur occasionally in the same existential structures, as in the following example:

(28) Ternate Chabacano (Sippola, field notes 1 (2008))
 Tyéni kyén tayá na pwéra.
 EXST who there LOC outside
 'There is someone outside.'

Furthermore, the bare existential plus free relative clause can be used with an indefinite meaning, as in (29). In this example, the relativizer is omitted. This typologically rare circumlocution is well known in the Philippine languages in general and in Tagalog in particular (Schachter & Otanes 1972: 276, Haspelmath 2008).

(29) Ternate Chabacano (Sippola, field notes 2 (2008))
 tyéni ta-kohré na estéyt
 EXST IPFV-run LOC state
 'Somebody goes to the States.'

Another instance of interrogatives expressing indefinite meaning is their reduplication in order to express free-choice indefinite meanings. These forms often have an additional universal meaning 'every X'.

(30) Ternate Chabacano (Nigoza 2007: 20)
 A habla eli cung quieng-quieng...
 PFV say 3SG OBJ whoever
 'He said to whoever/everyone...'

Interrogatives can also appear in another construction with the particle *si*: '*si* + interrogative' as in (31). This particle has the meaning 'if', but it could also reflect the Tagalog grammatical marker *kung*, which has the same meaning and has a variety of corresponding uses (Whinnom 1956: 63, Fernández 2008: 154).

(31) Cavite Chabacano (Escalante 2010: 96)
 si cosa tu ta sentí.
 if thing 2SG IPFV feel
 'Whatever you feel.'

The negative series of Manila Bay Chabacano includes both special negative indefinites and negative existential constructions.

The negative existential construction with *nuwáy* is the most common way of expressing indefinite terms that correspond to 'nobody' and 'nothing'.[23] The negation can be emphasized by means of preposed *ni*, as in *ni nuwáy*.[24] The construction can include interrogatives, as in (32a), or generic nouns, as in (33). In addition to the general problem of classifying these constructions as existential, generic-noun or interrogative-based, another classification problem emerges regarding the indefinite with non-human reference in (32b), in which *kósa* means both 'what' and 'thing'. The same example also presents the use of the concessive *máski*.

(32) Ternate Chabacano (Sippola, field notes 2 (2006))
 a. *Nuwáy   kyén   asé   suport.*
    NEG.EXST who   make support
    'Nobody supports [us].'
 b. *Nuwáy   yo   ya-mirá   máski   kósa.*
    NEG.EXST 1SG PFV-see   even   thing
    'I did not see anything.'

(33) Cavite Chabacano (Escalante 2005: 119)
 No hay   gente   na   casa   ahora.
 NEG EXST   people LOC home   now
 'There is no one at home now.'

The only special negative indefinite forms currently used in the spoken language in both Cavite and Ternate are *nada* 'nothing', as in (34), and *núnka* 'never', as in (35).[25]

(34) Ternate Chabacano (Sippola, field notes 2 (2006))
 No   sábi   yo   náda!
 NEG   know   1SG nothing
 'I don't/didn't know anything!'

(35) Cavite Chabacano (Escalante 2005: 121)
 Nunca eli   ya   tiene miedo na   mga   multo.
 never   3SG   PFV have   fear   of   PL   ghost
 'He has never been afraid of ghosts.'

Ninguno 'nobody' / 'no one' for human referents occurs only in Cavite Chabacano, as in (36). There is additionally an emphatic form *ni uno* 'no one' / 'not even one' very closely related to *ninguno* in Cavite and Ternate. Also, *nadye* 'nobody' is mentioned as a rare form in Cavite Chabacano (Riego de Dios 1989: 124). All the negative indefinites generally occur with predicate negation.

(36) Cavite Chabacano (Escalante 2005: 119)
 No   ya   parece   ninguno   de   ilos.
 NEG   PFV   appear   no-one   of   them
 'None of them appeared.'

The southern Chabacano of Zamboanga has largely the same indefinite terms as the Manila Bay varieties, with a few additions in the special category, such as *alguien* or *alkyen* 'somebody' and *algunos* or *algunus* 'someone' (Riego de Dios 1989, Quilis & Casado-Fresnillo 2008: 455, Miravite et al. 2009: 294).

(37) Zamboanga Chabacano   (Quilis & Casado-Fresnillo 2008: 455)
   Algunus   ya   saca el   mana pru
   someone   PFV   take DEF   PL   fruit
   'Someone took the fruit.'

Bare interrogatives with indefinite meanings *kosa* 'something'/'what' and *kyen* 'someone'/'who' are also listed (Forman 1972: 109, Riego de Dios 1989: 45), but with indefinite meanings they used in analytic constructions, with *algo* > *algo kosa* 'something' (Miravite et al. 2009: 107), with *si*, as in (38), or in existential constructions.

(38) Zamboanga Chabacano   (Fernández 2008: 150, ex. 10, Matthew 10: 42)
   Y   si   quien   dale   toma   maskin   un   vaso
   and if   who   give   take   even   a   glass
   lang   de   agua...
   only   of   water
   'And whoever gives [one of these little ones] even a cup of cold water...'

In the negative series of Zamboanga Chabacano, *nadye* 'nobody' is used for human referents, as well as *ninguno/ninggunos* and (*ni*) *nuway kyen,* while *nada* 'nothing', (*ni*) *nuway kosa* express non-animate referents. *Nungka* 'never' corresponds to the epistemic domain of time (Riego de Dios 1989: 124, Camins 1999: 11, Miravite et al. 2009: xxii). As in the Manila Bay varieties, there are also bare existentials with relative clauses.[26]

The Spanish fossilized expression *kwalkyera* 'whoever'/'whatever' is found in Riego de Dios (1989: 111), but the form seems to be rarely used currently, as it does not appear in other sources. Even though this form can be regarded as a pronoun with a clausal origin in Spanish, it can be considered partly transparent at least in Zamboanga and Cavite Chabacano, if not in Ternate Chabacano. However, it seems probable that it has been derived directly from Spanish, as only *kwal* occurs as such in Chabacano varieties, while the subjunctive *quiera* has not survived.

As in the Manila Bay varieties, *maskin* has an indefinite meaning when used preceding the interrogative pronouns, e.g., *maskin kyen* 'whoever', *maskin kosa* 'whatever' = 'anything' etc. (Miravite et al. 2009: 346).[27]

Indefinite terms among the different Chabacano varieties follow very similar patterns despite the wide range of possibilities for forming them. The most common type of indefinite terms in all the varieties of Chabacano is probably the use of the existential construction. Existentials are used both for the positive series 'something', 'somebody' and the negative series 'nothing', 'nobody'. Even though the existential construction seems to predominate, the indefinite constructions often include items that can be classified as generic nouns or interrogatives, or they may constitute proper existentials with a relative clause. However, the existence of such alternative, more grammaticalized forms of these indefinite terms is restricted to certain functions and registers. It is also worth noting that the negative indefinite term *nada* with non-animate reference has a special indefinite form in all the varieties, and the positive indefinite *algo* 'something' is also more widely found than the term *algyen* with human reference. For some reason, inanimate reference has favoured the retention (or modern introduction) of the Spanish form. Free choice is indicated with a construction that has the concessive *maskin* together with an interrogative. In conclusion, Manila Bay and Zamboanga Chabacano present basically a mixed type of indefinite terms, in which the use of the existential construction prevails.

The variation observed can be attributed to both geographical and sociolinguistic motivations. Ternate Chabacano data are largely from the spoken language, and even the written samples of this variety reproduce the spoken variety quite closely. Ternate Chabacano is the variety with the smallest number of Spanish indefinite terms in use. On the other hand, Zamboanga Chabacano has been considered the one with the most influence from modern Spanish, so it should not be surprising that it presents more Spanish terms.

4.2 The forms of the indefinites compared

As we have seen in the previous sections, the three basic formal categories (special indefinites, generic-noun-based indefinites and interrogative-based indefinites) are all reflected in the Ibero-Asian creoles. This section presents an overview of the indefinite forms based on the division between negative and positive items. A more detailed functional classification will follow in the next section.

Table 3 shows that the negative indefinites of the categories for 'thing' and 'human' have strikingly similar forms in all the languages under study. The vast majority closely resemble the forms of their Iberian lexifiers and they are generally used in negated clauses, which is a universal tendency also present in the superstrates.[28] The Iberian *ninguem/nadie* is the only form that seems not to be used in some registers of the modern varieties of Chabacano. In addition, Diu Creole, the Chabacano varieties and Malacca Creole show mixed systems in which some or all of the negative indefinite terms may be expressed by alternative forms. This is partly due to lectal variation, at least in the case of Chabacano.

Table 3. Formal classification of negative indefinite terms in Ibero-Asian creoles

	Special	Generic-noun-based	Interrogative-based
DIU	nĭge 'nobody' nad 'nothing' nuk 'never'	niŋũ 'no [X]'	
KOR	ningẽ 'no one' nad 'nothing'		
SLP	niinga 'nobody' naada 'nothing'		
MALC	nggéng 'nobody' nada 'nothing'		'NEG + Q.RD (EMPH)' 'nobody/thing'
MAC	ninguim 'nobody' nada 'nothing'		
Manila Bay CHA	ninguno 'nobody' nadye 'nobody' náda 'nothing' núnka 'never'	'(EMPH) NEG.EXST + X' nwáy X 'no X' ni úno 'no(t even) one'	'(EMPH) NEG.EXST + Q' 'nobody/thing'
Zamboanga CHA	nadye 'nobody' ninguno/ninggunos 'nobody' nada 'nothing' nungka 'never'	'(EMPH) NEG.EXST + X' (ni) nuway X 'no X' ni uno 'nothing', 'no(t even) one'	'(EMPH) NEG.EXST + Q' 'nobody/thing'

The positive indefinite terms across the languages under consideration reveal a somewhat more complex situation, which is presented in Table 4. Special indefinites are found in all the languages studied except in Malacca Creole, but the occurrence of these forms is limited to the high varieties in Manila Bay and Zamboanga Chabacano as well as Sri Lanka Creole Portuguese, in which other constructions are the most common way of expressing the respective indefinite terms. From a synchronic perspective, special indefinites are not clearly derived from other pronouns or nouns. Rather, they have been taken directly from the lexifier.

As for the second type of indefinite terms, generic-noun-based indefinites are documented for all the languages under consideration, except for Korlai Creole. However, it is important to note that, generic-noun expressions are marginal in Sri Lanka Creole Portuguese and, in the Chabacano varieties, generic nouns generally occur in existential constructions even though some sources mention them also separately as independent forms.

All the languages contemplated here have interrogative-based indefinites, which occur in diverse constructions. The Portuguese-based creoles share many question words, which are directly derived from the lexifier. Bare

Table 4. Formal classification of indefinite terms in Ibero-Asian creoles†

	Special	Generic-noun-based	Interrogative-based
DIU	aɲe 'someone'	aɲũ/kwɔlki/sɛrt koys 'something' aɲũ/kwɔlki/sɛrt jẽt 'some people'	kẽ 'whoever' uki 'whatever'
KOR	angé 'someone' ankodz 'some thing'		kẽ 'whoever' ki 'whatever' ki təri 'whatever'
SLP	aluŋas 'some people'	aluŋ òòras 'sometimes' aluŋ jeentis 'some people'	kii see 'something'/'anything' kii see taam 'whatever' kii voo 'something (or other)'
MALC		angkoza 'something' jenti 'somebody'	keng 'whoever' keng keng 'anybody' ki 'whatever' ki ki 'anything', 'whatever' kalkizera 'whichever (one)'
MAC	alguim 'somebody'	ancuza 'something'	quánto 'some'
Manila Bay CHA	algo 'something' alguno(s) 'somebody'/'someone'	'EXST + X' 'someone/thing' ung jenti 'someone'	si + Q 'X-ever' masqui + Q 'any-X'/'Xever'
Zamboanga CHA	algo 'something' algunus 'someone' algyen 'somebody' kwalkyera 'whoever'/'whatever'	algo kosa 'something' 'EXST + X' 'someone/thing'	'EXST + Q' 'someone' maski + Q 'X-ever'/'any-X' si + Q 'X-ever' Q.RD 'X-ever' kwalkyera 'whichever'/'whoever'

† The classification is synchronic. When possible, we have relied on the original classification given in the source.

interrogatives with an indefinite meaning are found in Diu, Korlai, Malacca and Macau. Furthermore, although the synchronic transparency is no longer evident, Portuguese indefinites, on which the Indo-Portuguese special indefinites are based, are themselves largely derived from interrogatives.

Reduplicated interrogatives occur in Malacca Creole and Chabacano varieties and reflect Austronesian adstrate structures. In many languages world-wide, indefinite pronouns have a reduplicated form and, as in the case of the languages studied, the most common cases are indefinites consisting of two full instances of the corresponding interrogative pronoun (Haspelmath 1997: 179).

4.3 Realis and free-choice indefinite terms compared

In this section we include observations on the meanings and similarities between the forms in the basic categories of realis indefinite terms and free-choice indefinite terms. Comparing Table 5 and Table 6, it becomes clear that the formal means for expressing free choice, 'any-X', and 'X-ever' present a wider scope of alternatives than the formal categories of realis indefinite terms expressing 'some-X'.[29]

Table 5. Forms of realis indefinite terms in Ibero-Asian creoles

Realis indefinite term	DIU	KOR	SLP	MALC	MAC	Manila Bay CHA	Zamboanga CHA
pronoun	x	x			x	x	x
analytic construction	x		x	x		x	x
generic	x		x	x	x	x	x
interrogative		x	x		x	x	x
conditional			x				
indefinite			x				
existential				[x]		x	x

For the realis meanings, both pronouns and analytic constructions are present across the languages contemplated. Here, interrogative words that occur alone or which are reduplicated are classified as pronouns, while analytic constructions include multiword-constructions, such as existential constructions and concessive or conditional markers occurring together with interrogative words. Korlai Creole and Macau Creole have pronominal forms, and Sri Lanka Creole Portuguese and Malacca Creole only present constructions classified as analytic. Diu Creole and the Chabacano varieties show a mixed system in which various alternatives coexist.

In the case of free-choice indefinite terms, as in the case of the realis meanings, both pronouns and analytic constructions are used across the languages studied. Interrogatives expressing free choice are found in all the languages in the study. The use of interrogatives expressing free-choice meaning reflects a similar typological tendency. Many languages can use bare interrogatives as indefinites, giving the same set of pronouns two different uses (Haspelmath 1997: 241; 2008). Bhat (2004: 227–228) points out that the same set of pronouns is used not

Table 6. Forms of free-choice indefinite terms in Ibero-Asian creoles

Free-choice indefinite term	DIU	KOR	SLP	MALC	Manila bay CHA	Zamboanga CHA
pronoun				x	x	x
analytic construction	x	x	x		x	x
generic	x					
interrogative	x	x	x	x	x	x
conditional			x		x	x
indefinite						
existential					x	x
concessive			x		x	x
reduplicated interrogative				x	x	x
emphatic marker				x	[x]	[x]

only as indefinite and interrogative pronouns, but also as the pronouns of relative clauses and exclamatory sentences in several languages. All these usages have the common characteristic of indicating an information gap. On the other hand, languages that use the same pronominal element in the formation of interrogative and indefinite pronouns generally use additional devices for differentiating between the two (Bhat 2004:183). For example, the languages of Oceania and Africa differentiate interrogatives and indefinite pronouns, but even among these, they may use the interrogative pronouns for denoting some of the indefinite meanings (especially the non-specific ones) as well (Bhat 2004:182). A glance at the Ibero-Asian creoles confirms this tendency, as the forms of interrogatives and indefinites are partly overlapping.

The creoles of the Malacca-Philippines axis employ reduplication of the interrogative pronouns for free-choice indefinite and negative indefinite meanings, something which is not documented for the Indo-Portuguese varieties. This reflects the typological tendency according to which reduplicated indefinites often express a free-choice or at least negative-polarity meaning, rather than a specific realis meaning. There is also a similarity between the free-choice function and the distributive universal function, which is widely used to express the meaning 'every', e.g. Tagalog *taon-taon* 'every year', as in the Chabacano Example (30) presented earlier (Haspelmath 1997: 180–181).

Conditionals and concessive markers are also found in some languages in the sample, such as Chabacano and Sri Lanka Creole Portuguese, the latter language also having an indefinite marker for a specific indefinite meaning. Adverbs and particles with emphasizing meanings are also found, at least in Malacca Creole and Chabacano.

To sum up, we find several areal differences, especially when looking at larger geographical areas, such as India / Sri Lanka compared with the Malacca-Philippines axis. Also, many of the similarities in these subgroups can be traced back to the adstrate languages. However, many of the shared features can be explained by superstrate influence, or by universal typological paths of development as well.

On the other hand, the great diversity of indefinite constructions reveals interesting questions concerning the methodology of comparative studies in relation to the linguistic distance between the languages and their superstrates. Distance from the superstrate indefinite pronouns seems to be one of the factors that can be used to explain the degree of separation between these languages. In the Philippines, for example, Cavite and Zamboanga were in closer contact with modern Spanish than Ternate, which is reflected in the developments of the indefinite pronouns, as it is for many other features as well. Following this concept, we could say that the northern varieties of Indo-Portuguese are closer to Standard Portuguese than Sri Lanka Creole Portuguese is, just as Macau Creole is closer to Standard Portuguese in comparison with Malacca Creole. At the same time, however, the limitations of the available data very probably influence the profile that we have sketched of the indefinite terms in these languages. It is probable that other terms not so closely related to the superstrate could be found by looking deeper into the data. Every case of an indefinite construction needs to be studied individually, taking context into account. First, we should establish the existence of alternative, more grammaticalized forms of indefinite terms and the functions or registers that are specific to them. Later, it is essential to consider whether these forms coexist functionally and sociolinguistically with the more general lexical and syntactic forms.

Further studies should investigate the adstrate influence more deeply and add a diachronic perspective to these issues. Unfortunately, we have no direct access to the varieties spoken in the settings where these languages emerged, even though the linguistic data explaining historical developments should ideally reflect the original contact situation. On the other hand, even if the synchronic nature of the typological studies may partly obscure language specific variation or historical developments, it is useful for general presentations and classifications of the structures.

5. Conclusions

Our study shows that the Ibero-Asian creoles studied display a wide variety of indefinite terms. This variation largely reflects the structures in their respective adstrate languages, which often have contributed significantly to the forms and uses of indefinite terms. This can be seen not only in cases of rather straightforward calques, as for Chabacano and Malacca Creole, but also in several instances where the constructions could also result from language-internal change or from convergence between the adstrate and superstrate structures. There are also clear traces of the influence of the superstrate languages, Portuguese and Spanish, especially in relation to the negative indefinites and the realis indefinite terms that correspond to *alguém/alguien* 'somebody' and *algo* 'something'. Nearly all the languages considered show very similar indefinite pronouns directly derived from the Iberian ancestors, especially if written and high varieties of the languages in the sample are to be included in the comparison. The occurrence of these special indefinites is often favoured by convergence of the superstrate and adstrate structures.

This study has raised important questions concerning the use of a typological model in comparative linguistic classification. The availability of the data and the nature of the data are of great significance. When comparing less studied languages, it is important to compare similar registers. In this study, for example, grammatical features of spoken language often present indefinite terms that are closer to adstrate structures, while dictionaries and high variety data have indefinites that resemble the superstrate indefinite pronouns. In addition, even very similar structures occurring in different creoles can be labelled differently because the criteria for the final classification have to be language internal. These similarities should be pointed out in order to evaluate possible connections between the varieties.

A comparison of the languages under study reveals parallels among them and it also shows a clear connection with a wider cross-linguistic pattern. Areal subgroups are based on the use of reduplication, generic nouns and interrogatives. However, areal groups cannot be merely attributed to the creoles' common history, because their adstrates belong to the same genetic groups. We can classify the majority of the indefinite terms in Ibero-Asian creoles either together with the indefinite terms in their superstrate languages or with their adstrate languages. This study therefore lends support to the traditional areal classification and the cross-linguistic groupings of these languages.

Notes

1. In this paper the term adstrate is used with a meaning that in certain cases includes substrate languages, as the majority of substrate languages of the Ibero-Asian creoles continue to be spoken as adstrates of these languages.

2. "Field notes 1" refers to elicitations carried out in Cavite or Ternate with native speakers of Chabacano. "Field notes 2" refers to narratives recorded in the context of an informal thematic interview in the same locations.

3. Manila Bay Chabacano represents the Northern Chabacano (varieties spoken in Cavite City and Ternate) and Zamboanga Chabcano the Southern Chabacano spoken in Mindanao.

4. I would especially like to thank the editors and reviewers Alan Baxter, Hugo Cardoso, Mauro Fernández and an anonymous reviewer for their comments and corrections, as well as Clancy Clements, Philippe Maurer and Ian Smith for their help with the data.

5. Haspelmath (1997) uses Brazilian Portuguese, but there is essentially no difference in our theme between Brazilian and European Portuguese.

6. In a 2010 interview, Cardoso reported the death of who may well have been the last speaker in Cochin (see Pradeep 2010).

7. Baxter (p.c. April 2011) points out that the Europeans who were present early on were probably of very diverse origins. Most of them would have been iliterate, and many of the average troops and sailors could have been of provincial origins. The varieties they spoke were very likely somewhat removed from what we know of early Portuguese or Spanish in writing.

8. In Portuguese, *algo* is very current in formal speech, as pointed out by Cardoso and Fernández (p.c. August 2011).

9. See Fernández (*this volume*) for a possible Kinaray-a substrate instead of Cebuano and Hiligaynon.

10. Information on the genetic classification of the languages is from Haspelmath et al. (2008).

11. In the main adstrate language Gujarati, reduplicated interrogative or relative pronouns express free choice indefinite terms (Fernández, p.c. August 2011).

12. From *taam*, I am following the original transcription.

13. Also 'perhaps' (Smith, p.c. August 2010).

14. In early documentation of Sri Lanka Portuguese (as noted in Dalgado 1900: 38) *alhuma* was used for Standard *alguém* and *algum*. Also other indefinites like *alhumas, alguems, quemseja, queseja, ninguem* and *nenhum* can be found in early works that represent formal style, such as *O Novo Testamento de Nossa Senhor* and *O Bruffador* (Dalgado 1900: 38, 65).

15. The form *ungua* exists as a phonological variant of *ñgua*, but there is no difference in meaning or function.

16. Here we assume that reduplication forms phonological words, even though in many sources the status of the reduplicated items as phonological words is not clear from the transcriptions.

17. Portuguese has the pluperfect form *quisera* but it is not used currently in similar expressions. In addition, it is also possible that, older (regional) varieties of Portuguese, and especially more proximate to Spanish-speaking areas, may have had the form *calquera*. Also, analogy might cause the appearance of the final -a. (Baxter, p.c. April 2011).

18. The Macau creole data should be treated with some caution, because the author was not a trained linguist (Baxter, p.c. April 2011).

19. An example of the use as a non universal quantifier is: *ele rispondê qui têm quánto* (Ferreira 1978: 240), [3SG respond that be some] 'He responded that there are some'.

20. The examples are presented according to the ortography in Maurer (2011), even though they are originally from Schuchardt (1890).

21. *Mas que* in Escalante's spelling.

22. *Masqui* is a Spanish loan in Tagalog, with the synonym *kahit na* (English 1986: 901). See also Vázquez Veiga & Fernández (*this volume*).

23. *No hay / nuay* in Cavite spelling.

24. See also Fernández (*this volume*).

25. Generally written *nunca* in the Cavite sources.

26. In lexicalized expressions even with a relativizer, as in *nuway ke ase* [NEG.EXST REL do] 'Free time [lit. There is nothing to do]' (Miravite et al. 2009: 89).

27. In the Manila Bay varieties *maskikwal* is used, but in Zamboanga *kwal* occurs only in the distributive *kaday kwal* 'each and every one' (Fernández, p.c. August 2011, see for example Miravite et al. 2009: 326).

28. Even though in the superstrate the negative concord only occurs when the negative pro-form precedes the VP.

29. Macau has been excluded from Table 6, as there was no data available to represent free-choice indefinites.

References

Ansaldo, U., and S. Matthews. 2004. The origins of Macanese reduplication. In *Creoles, Contact and Language Change. Linguistic and Social Implications* [Creole Language Library 27], eds. G. Escure and A. Schwegler, 1–19. Amsterdam: John Benjamins.

Baxter, A. N. 1988. *A Grammar of Kristang (Malacca Creole Portuguese)* [Pacific Linguistics. Series B; no. 95]. Canberra: Pacific Linguistics.

Bartens, A. 1995. *Die Iberoromanisch-Basierten Kreolsprachen: Ansätze der linguistischen Beschreibung*. Frankfurt: Peter Lang.
Batalha, G. 1965–66. A contribuição malaia para o dialecto macaense. *Boletim do Instituto Luís de Camões* I (1–2): 7–19: 99–108.
Bhat, D. N. S. 2004. *Pronouns*. Oxford: OUP.
Camins, B. S. 1999. *Chabacano de Zamboanga Handbook*. Zamboanga: Office of the City Mayor.
Cardoso, H. 2006. Challenges to Indo-Portuguese across India. In *Proceedings of the FEL X*, eds. R. Elangayan, R. McKenna Brown, N. Ostler and M. K. Verma, 23–30. Mysore: Central Institute of Indian Languages.
Cardoso, H. C. 2009. The Indo-Portuguese Language of Diu. PhD dissertation, University of Amsterdam.
Clements, J. C. 1996. *The Genesis of a Language: The Formation and Development of Korlai Portuguese* [Creole Language Library 16]. Amsterdam: John Benjamins.
Dalgado, S. R. 1900. *Dialecto Indo-Português de Ceylão*. Lisboa: Imprensa Nacional.
Dalgado, S. R. 1906. Dialecto Indo-português do Norte. *Revista Lusitana* 9: 142–166; 193–228.
Diccionario Chabacano del Ciudad de Cavite. 2008. Cavite City: Asociacion Chabacano del Ciudad de Cavite/Office of the City Mayor.
Dixon, R. M. W. 2009. *Basic Linguistic Theory*, Vol. I: *Methodology*. Oxford: OUP.
Escalante, E. 2005. *Chabacano… for Everyone. A Guide to the Chabacano Language*. Manila: Escalante/Baby Dragon Printing Press.
Escalante, E. 2010. *Learning Chabacano. A handbook*. Manila: Escalante/Baby Dragon Printing Press.
Fernández, M. 2008. Las interrogativas indirectas en el chabacano – un caso de acción del sustrato. In *Lenguas en Diálogo. El Iberorromance y su Diversidad Lingüística y Literaria. Ensayos en Homenaje a Georg Bossong*, eds. H. J. Döhla, R. Montero Muñoz and F. Báez de Aguilar González, 143–160. Madrid-Frankfurt: Iberoamericana-Vervuert.
Ferreira, J. S. 1967. *Macau sã Assi*. Macau: Tipografia da Missão do Padroado.
Ferreira, J. S. 1978. Dialecto Macaense; Gramática e Vocabulário. In *Papia Cristám di Macau*, 224–327. Macau: Tipografia da Missão do Padroado (Reprinted 1996. *Papiaçám di Macau*. Macau: Fundação Macau).
Forman, M. 1972. Zamboangueño Texts with Grammatical Analysis. A Study of Philippine Creole Spanish. PhD dissertation, Cornell University.
Haspelmath, M. 1997. *Indefinite Pronouns*. Oxford: OUP.
Haspelmath, M. 2008. Indefinite pronouns. In *The World Atlas of Language Structures Online*, eds. M. Haspelmath, M. S. Dryer, D. Gil and B. Comrie, Ch. 46. Munich: Max Planck Digital Library. http://wals.info/feature/46 (accessed September 10, 2010).
Haspelmath, M., M. S. Dryer, D. Gil, and B. Comrie, eds. 2008. *The World Atlas of Language Structures Online*. Munich: Max Planck Digital Library. http://wals.info (accessed August 15, 2010).
Holm, J. 1989. *Pidgins and Creoles*. Vol. 2. Cambridge: CUP.
Leonetti, M. 1999. El artículo. In *Gramática Descriptiva de la Lengua Española 1. Sintaxis Básica de las Clases de Palabras*, eds. I. Bosque and V. Demonte, 786–890. Madrid: Espasa.
Maurer, P. 2011. *The Former Portuguese Creole of Batavia and Tugu (Indonesia)*. London: Battlebridge.

Miravite, R. M., U. C. N. Sanchez, D. S. Tardo, S. J. B. Viloria, and Fr. D. J. M. De Los Reyes. 2009. *Chavacano Reader*. ed. by R. David Zorc. Hyattsville MD: Dunwoody Press.
Nigoza, E. 2007. *Bahra. Manga Historia, Alamat, Custumbre y Tradiciong di Bahra*. Cavite: Cavite Historical Society.
Ocampo, E. A. de. 1943. *The Ternateños. Their History, Languages, Customs and Traditions* (Reprinted 2007. Manila: National Historical Institute).
Pradeep, K. 2010. Tribute to Cochin Creole Portuguese. *The Hindu*, September 26. http://www.thehindu.com/news/cities/Kochi/article795353.ece?homepage=true (accessed September 17, 2011).
Quilis, A., and C. Casado-Fresnillo. 2008. *La Lengua Española en Filipinas. Historia. Situación actual. El Chabacano. Antología de Textos* [Anejos de la Revista de Filología Española, 101]. Madrid: CSIC.
Riego de Dios, M. I. O. 1989. *A Composite Dictionary of Philippine Creole Spanish (PCS)*. Manila: Linguistic Society of the Philippines and Summer Institute of Linguistics.
Rigau, G. 1999. La estructura del sintagma nominal: Los modificadores del nombre. In *Gramática Descriptiva de la Lengua Española 1. Sintaxis Básica de las Clases de Palabras*, eds. I. Bosque and V. Demonte, 311–362. Madrid: Espasa.
Schachter, P., and F. Otanes. 1972. *Tagalog Reference Grammar*. Berkeley CA: University of California.
Schuchardt, H. 1890. Kreolische Studien IX. Über das Malaioportugiesische von Batavia und Tugu. *Sitzungsberichte der Kaiserlichen Akademie der Wissenschaften zu Wien (philosophisch-historische Klasse)* 122 (9): 1–256.
Sippola, E. 2011. *Una Gramática Descriptiva del Chabacano de Ternate*. Helsinki: Unigrafia.
Tomás, M. I. 2009. The role of women in the cross-pollination process in the Asian-Portuguese varieties. *Journal of Portuguese Linguistics* 8 (2): 49–64.
Whinnom, K. 1956. *Spanish Contact Vernaculars in the Philippine Islands*. Hong Kong: Hong Kong University Press.

Maskin, maski, masque... in the Spanish and Portuguese creoles of Asia
Same particle, same provenance?

Nancy Vázquez Veiga and Mauro A. Fernández

While much of the scholarship on the subject of Ibero-Asian pidgins and creoles does contain some mention of the *maski/maskin/masque* particle, so far no detailed study has been made of the contrasting uses of the form in the different varieties. The prevailing wisdom holds that the particle originated solely from Portuguese *mas que*, based on the mistaken belief that the same construction in Spanish had no concessive value. In this paper, we will examine the significant variations in the meaning of this particle in the different Portuguese and Spanish creole languages of Asia. Building on that analysis, we will challenge the notion of a common Portuguese origin and show instead how the differences in meaning between Spanish-Philippine creoles and the other varieties in the region came about as a result of the contact that took place between Spanish and the indigenous languages of the Philippines.

1. Introduction

As every creolist knows, it was Whinnom (1956) who first suggested that the Spanish creoles of the Philippines came about as a result of the contact between Spanish and a Portuguese Malay pidgin believed to have been spoken in the Moluccan Islands. Over time, Whinnom grew more and more convinced of his theory, to the point of believing that he had in fact 'proved' it to be so. That is what is so strange about Whinnom's (1956) explanation of the origin of *masque* [máske], which he introduces in connection with this sentence from a story by Jesús Balmori entitled 'Na maldito arena', an example of what he called the 'Ermitaño' dialect: *y el viejo ta pensá na su vida, peliz agora, masque el madre de Pelisa ya morí de viejo*. Whinnom's gloss reads as follows:

masque. On the face of it, the translation of this phrase would seem to be a rather cynical, 'More so now, since Pelisa's mother died', taking *más* to be the Spanish *más*, 'more'. However it is more probable that *mas* is Spanish – and Portuguese – *mas*, 'but', so that the phrase might be literally rendered into English 'but that'. The sense of *masque* would then cover 'although', 'in spite of the fact that', and any concessive notion. *Masque* as a concessive does not exist in Spanish; but it might very easily have been formed under the influence of Tagalog *maskí* 'even if', if, indeed, *masque* is not a Hispanicized *maskí*. (Whinnom 1956: 38)

The surprising thing about Whinnom's explanation regarding the presence of a sub-stratum of Portuguese Malay pidgin in the history of Chabacano, is that he fails to make the further connection between this *masque* in the Spanish creoles of the Philippines and similar versions of the form occurring in other creole languages, some of them unmistakably Portuguese in origin. He might, for example, have noted the presence of concessive *masque* in Sri Lanka Creole Portuguese, or observed the relationship between it and the *maski* particles found in Malacca Creole Portuguese (or Papia Kristang) and Tugu Creole Portuguese, which also have a concessive meaning. At the very least, he might have remarked upon the similarities between it and the *masquí* item present in the creole of Macau, a variety still spoken at that time and substantially so among Macanese immigrants in Hong Kong, where Whinnom had been working as a university lecturer in Romance languages until the year before his study was published. There was, furthermore, the concessive *mas que* locution found in Papiamentu to consider, which Schuchardt (1883: 144) associated with the *ainda que* 'even though' meaning of the same phrase in Portuguese, as defined by Silva (1789: see entry for *mas*).

Apart from Portuguese creoles, Whinnom also failed to examine the connection that Schuchardt (1883: 144) had made earlier between *mas que* and the *maskee* [maskí] form heard on a daily basis on the streets of Hong Kong, where speakers of Chinese Pidgin English were still to be found. Documented as early as 1769, according to Baker & Mülhausler (1990: 100), this *maskee* item was very popular among Europeans in the region, and one of its uses was with the concessive meaning 'although, even, in spite of'.[1]

Various different theories have been proposed to explain the etymology of this emblematic lexical item in Chinese Pidgin English, and likewise for Papua New Guinea's Tok Pisin *maskí* and the *maskie* particle found in Cape Dutch Pidgin; majority opinion, though, not surprisingly, supports an origin in Portuguese *mas que*.[2] *Maski* and its different variants in other creole and non-creole languages have featured in many studies down through the years, before Whinnom's time and after him, although in general the commentary has been superficial or confined to a passing mention.[3]

Overlooking this tradition, Whinnom picks out Spanish *mas* in its adversative sense of 'but' as the primary origin of *masque*, while admitting that *mas* is also present in Portuguese. Neither does he look to Portuguese to account for the particle's concessive value but to the contact between Spanish *mas* and Tagalog *maskí*, which he treats as indigenous to the latter; in fact, he goes so far as to suggest that *masque* might not even be of Spanish origin after all, but an example of hispanicised Tagalog.

Whinnom was aware of the concessive value of *mas que* in Portuguese but not that the same was true of the phrase in Spanish. This is why, when confronted with the occurrence of the Zamboangueño form *maskin* in a purely concessive sense, he does not even consider the possibility of a Spanish or Portuguese origin but looks instead to Cebuano *maskin*, which he also seems to regard as a native item:

> **maskin.** Cebuano *maskin* 'even'. The word occurs in McKaughan texts where it is translated 'just'. Tagalog has *maskí*, 'even if'. (Whinnom 1956: 75)[4]

The critics, not surprisingly, were quick to react. Just a few months after the book appeared, Thompson (1957), who was also working at the University of Hong Kong, reproached Whinnom's failure to consider all the other *maski* forms, in particular the Hong Kong variant. He still hoped, nevertheless, that his colleague would rectify the oversight in a new work on the subject of Pidgin English which the latter had announced in the 'Preface' to *Spanish Contact Vernaculars in the Philippines* (Whinnom 1956: viii). Not long afterwards, from Macau, Batalha (1960) expressed a similar criticism in relation to the *masqui* form in Macanese and other languages.

We will begin this study by demonstrating the concessive value of the *masque/maski* particle adopted from Portuguese by the creole languages of Sri Lanka, Malacca, Macau and Tugu. Moving on from that, we will examine the presence of the form in the Spanish creole varieties of the Philippines. We will demonstrate the concessive use of *mas que* in Spanish at the time the languages came into contact and show that the same value was present among the varieties of Spanish spoken in the Philippines, thereby removing any doubt there may remain in this regard. We will analyse the different uses of *maskin* in Chabacano and observe how contact with the indigenous languages of the Philippines brought about various changes in the meaning of the form, though always in keeping with values already accounted for in the original Spanish. The particle has been adopted across all the creole languages of the Philippines, appearing as *masque*, for example, in the dialects spoken in Luzon (in areas such as Manila, Cavite, Ternate, Tayabas and possibly others; see Fernández 2011); or as *maskin* in Mindanao (in Zamboanga,

Basilan, Cotabato, Pollok and Davao). While the meanings we propose to study are common to all of these varieties, our analysis will focus on examples of the *maskin* form used in Mindanao.

2. *Masque/maski*: from Portuguese to the Portuguese creoles of Asia

Although the phrase *mas que* with concessive value has disappeared from modern Portuguese, its use in the past is well documented. Dalgado was aware of this and, in his account of the origins of concessive *masqui* and *masque* in the Portuguese creoles of Macau and Ceylon, he observes: "neste sentido aparece em clássicos portugueses" ['it appears in this sense in the classics of Portuguese literature'] (Dalgado 1913: 106), illustrating this point with two examples from the 17th century.[5] Batalha (1977: 217) makes the same reflection, using an example from the 18th century.[6] To this already sufficient collection of examples, we wish to add one further illustration, this time from the 16th century, from a letter sent by the Jesuit priest Luís Fernandes from Ambón on 9 May 1599, to Father General Claudio Acquaviva:

> Porque eu nunca serei de parecer que esteja Padre algum em cristandade soo sem companheiro, mas que tenha muito pouco que fazer nella, pelos muitos perigos e males que daqui se podem seguir e se experimentão.
> (Fr. Acquaviva; reproduced in Jacobs 1980: 458–462)[7]

The existence of concessive *mas que* is also recorded in early works of Portuguese lexicography, featuring in the dictionaries of both Bluteau (1712–1728) and Silva (1789). It makes perfect sense, therefore, that the form should have entered the language of all the Portuguese-based dialects of Eastern Asia, as noted by Thompson (1957). What follows is a brief survey of the way the phrase was assimilated into those creole varieties.

For Sri Lankan Creole Portuguese, Callaway (1820: 19) presents *masque* as an adverb with a meaning analogous to 'though' in English. Similarly, in the 19th-century edition of the New Testament (NT 1852, a corrected version of the translation prepared in 1826 by the Wesleyan missionary, Robert Newstead), there are a number of instances in which *masque* (or *mas que*) is used as a concessive particle – English translations of (1)–(5) consist of the corresponding verses in the *New King James Version* (1982):

(1) Sri Lanka Creole Portuguese   (NT 1852: Matthew XXVI: 35)
*Petros ja falla, **masque** eu lo deve per morre com ti, eu nada nega per ti.*
'Peter said to Him, "Even if I have to die with You, I will not deny You!"'

(2) Sri Lanka Creole Portuguese   (NT 1852: 2 Corinthians XIII: 4)
Parque, **masque** *per fraqueza elle tinha crucificado, com todo elle te vive de o poder de Deos.*
'For though He was crucified in weakness, yet He lives by the power of God.'

(3) Sri Lanka Creole Portuguese   (NT 1852: Philemon 8)
Poristo, **masque** *per mi tem liberdade per ordena per ti tua obrigação […].*
'Therefore, though I might be very bold in Christ to command you what is fitting […].'

(4) Sri Lanka Creole Portuguese   (NT 1852: Mark XIV: 29)
E Petros ja falla per elle: **Masque** *todos lo tropeça eu não tropeça.*
'Peter said to Him, "Even if all are made to stumble, yet I *will* not *be*".'

(5) Sri Lanka Creole Portuguese   (NT 1852: Colossians 2: 5)
Parque **mas que** *eu tem ausente ne o carne, ainda eu tem com vossotros ne espirito.*
'For though I am absent in the flesh, yet I am with you in spirit.'

The concessive use of the form is also collected in Dalgado's monograph study on the Indo-Portuguese dialect of Sri Lanka, in the section of the work that deals with vocabulary:

> **Maisque, masque** (mais us.), por mais que, ainda que, mas se. Dial. mac. *masqui,* que, segundo o sr. Marques Pereira, vem do malaio. Mas David Haex (*Dictionarium Malaico-Latinum et Latino-Malaicum*) diz o contrário: "*Quanvis ita sit*: mas que. *Quanto magis*: quanto mas". (Dalgado 1900)[8]

The form is also documented extensively in the creole language of Macau. Dalgado's allusion to the Macanese form in the previous illustration and the mention of it by Marques Pereira, which Dalgado references, are just two examples among many. In her *Glossário do dialecto macaense*, Batalha (1977: 217) adverts to the high frequency in Macau creole of *masquí* (*mas qui*) used in a concessive sense (*masqui seza preto* 'though it be black'). She also mentions a second meaning, which we have been unable to identify in any of the other Asian Portuguese creoles: the use of *masquí* to express agreement or acceptance. Batalha records that one of her informants recalled how, when she was a child, her father would reply *masquí* when he agreed to let her go out or do something. A further example of concessive *masquí* from the same work occurs in the following fragment, taken from a letter (*Carta de Maria Varê-Rua*) to the magazine *Ta-ssi-yang-kuo* (1888) and used by Batalha to illustrate the word *ampaz*:

> Certo que sã que tem bastante de triguera que sã bem chistosa, tanto que (…) dá capŏte pra quanto branco-branco, que masquí tem feção [a pesar de ter boas feições] sã ampaz sem sumo.   (quoted in Batalha 1977: 161, with a few corrections according to the original text)[9]

Batalha also looks at the occurrence of *masquí* in Macau creole in an earlier article on the similarities between Macanese and the Spanish creoles of the Philippines:

> *Masquí* é palavra que aparece com grande frequência nos textos em crioulo macaense. Tem um sentido concessivo de 'ainda que, a pesar de que, mesmo', que indubitàvelmente é o mesmo nos textos filipinos. (Batalha 1960: 301)[10]

Ferreira (1996) makes three references to Macau *masquí*: in his treatments of prepositive locutions and concessive conjunctions, and again in the section on vocabulary. In the first two cases, he suggests the equivalent meanings in Portuguese of 'apesar de' (*masquí grándi* 'apesar de grande') and 'embora', 'ainda que' (*masquí triste, tamêm sabe ri*) (Ferreira 1996: 244, 250). In the vocabulary section, he states: "[e]ste termo vem do malaio, significando: a pesar de; embora. *Masquí seza: embora seja* [...]" ['the term comes from Malay, meaning: in spite of; even though. *Masquí seza: although he may be* [...]'] (Ferreira 1996: 294).

The *maski* form in Papia Kristang, the creole spoken in Malacca, appears in work by Rêgo (1998[1941–42]) and Baxter (1988, 1996). Baxter (1996: 305), who also looks at the presence of the form in the Portuguese dialect of Tugu, proposes a Portuguese origin: "*maski* (<P. *Mais que* "more than"/ < P. *Mas que* "but that")". In his notes on the grammar of the Malaccan variety, Rêgo (1998[1941–42]: 69) lists *másqui* (*mais que, mais de, mesmo, apesar de*) under the heading of adverbs and conjunctions. Under the entry for *más* in the vocabulary section of the same work, the author also introduces the phrase *más qui* (*ainda que* 'even though') (1998[1941–42]: 175).

The evidence presented above illustrates the concessive value of the particle and the way it is used in the different Portuguese-based creoles of Eastern Asia. Whether the form came directly from Portuguese or was combined with Malay *meski/maski*, as some authors suggest, depends on how far into the past we are prepared to trace its history. Irrespective of how exactly it came about, the one thing we can say with certainty is that the form was borrowed into Malay from Portuguese.[11]

A Portuguese-based etymology has also been claimed in relation to the appearance of the form in Philippine Creole Spanish. Nevertheless, we believe that the notion of a Portuguese origin for Chabacano *maskin/masque* may have come about as a result of Whinnom's (1956: 38) failure to detect the occurrence of concessive *masque* in Spanish and Batalha's (1960: 301) assertion of the identity of the meaning of the word across both groups of creoles. In an article intended as a critical challenge against the supposed Portuguese origin of a number of aspects of Philippine Creole Spanish, Lipski (1988) furthermore chooses to exclude *maskin/masque* from his reappraisal, concluding instead, based on his assessment of the different *maski* forms ignored by Whinnom, that the item belonged to the Portuguese-based *lingua franca* that extended over many parts of Asia for several centuries:

> Variants of *maski(n)* are common in Asian and Oceanic creole Portuguese dialects, including Ceylon (Dalgado 1900:162), Macau (Ferreira 1978:31) and Malacca (Hancock 1973:30), but are not attested for African or Latin American Portuguese creoles. The form *maskee* was used in 19th-century Chinese Pidgin English (Leland 1876:12), which leads to the conclusion that it formed part of the Portuguese-based lingua franca in circulation in Asia during earlier centuries, regardless of whether similar or identical forms were used in Spanish at the same period.
>
> (Lipski 1988:35)[12]

It is hard to disagree with Lipski's conclusion in this respect. However, the fact that *maski* existed in the Portuguese *lingua franca* of Asia does not mean that Chabacano *masque* and *maskin* come from the same source. A detailed analysis of the meanings of the form in Chabacano shows significant differences between it and the *maski* particle found in other creoles. Moreover, all of these divergent meanings are traceable to the contact that took place between Spanish and the indigenous languages of the Philippines. Whinnom had it right the first time, therefore, in one respect, at least: *masque* does have a Spanish origin; however, in addition to its lexical derivation from *más*, which Whinnom acknowledges, the form also takes its concessive meaning from Spanish. Whinnom's claims regarding the influence of Tagalog *maski* or a possible origin in Cebuano are, therefore, mistaken. Whether it appears accented on the last or the penultimate syllable, ending in *-n* or without it, the *maski(n)* form present in many Philippine languages – from Ibanag in the north to Mandaya in the Davao region, southeast of Mindanao – is a borrowing from Spanish, not an indigenous word. It is worth noting that in no instance was *maski* ever used to replace a corresponding concessive conjunction in the indigenous language. Still in use, therefore, are Kapampangan *bista*, Tagalog *kahit*, Bikol *minsan*, Visaya *bisan* and others, to cite just one equivalent conjunction among many still found in each of these languages.

3. Concessive *mas que* in Spanish

Wofsy (1928) complains that scholarship has addressed only a fraction of the possible modal meanings of *mas que*, which occurs extensively in the literature of the Spanish Golden Age, with anger, indifference, certainty, doubt and desire representing just some of the meanings it is used to express.[13] Nevertheless, there is no shortage of references to Spanish *mas que* and its concessive meaning in works of lexicography or grammar. It is found, for example, in every single edition of the *Diccionario de la Real Academia Española* (or DRAE) of the 20th and 21st centuries, the only variation being the lexicographical entry in which it appears: sometimes the particle is grouped with *mas*, other times under *más* – see

Real Academia Española's *Diccionario de la lengua española* (2001a) and *Nuevo Tesoro Lexicográfico de la lengua española* (2001b). In the *Diccionario de la Real Academia Española*, *mas que* is classed as a conjunctive locution, together with the synonymic definition *aunque* 'although'; yet, in the illustration offered there, the phrase is used with an interjectional value: *más que nunca vuelva* (see entry for *mas*). This interjectional meaning also appears in the *Diccionario de Autoridades* of the Real Academia Española (1979[1726–1739]), where *mas que* is described as an "adversative interjection of anger" and attributed to the desire on the part of the speaker to mark his/her "low regard for the action taking place: hence, he/she says, *Fulano se ha ido, mas que nunca vuelva*" ['So-and-so has left, what matter it if he never comes back'] (see *mas*).

The grammars of Salvá (1988[1830–1847]), Bello (1988[1847–1860]) and Lenz (1920) also devote space to *mas que*. Salvá (1988[1830–1847]: 504), for example, points out that "cuando no enlaza los dos términos de una comparación, significa unas veces la indiferencia con que miramos las cosas, como *Se obstina en callarlo; más que nunca lo diga*, esto es, *poco importa que nunca lo diga*" ['when it does not link the two terms of a comparison, it can sometimes signify the indifference with which we look upon certain things: thus, *Se obstina en callarlo; más que nunca lo diga*, meaning "it matters little whether he says it or not"']. In chapter L of Bello's grammar, in reference to the uses of certain adverbs, prepositions and conjunctions, the author observes of *más que*:

> Ahora observaremos el sentido particular que se le suele dar a esta frase, haciéndola equivalente de *aun dado caso que*: 'No lo aceptaría *más que* me rogasen con ello'. Subentendiendo la proposición subordinante se dice: 'Mas que me maten' (cállese *no se me da nada, no importa*). (Bello 1847–1988[1860]: §1250)[14]

Lenz (1920) places *más que* in the category of concessive conjunctions. Significantly, *más que* is the only concessive he finds it necessary to illustrate with an example, specifically with one taken from *El Quijote* "*Mas que lo fuesen que me va a mi*": DQ, 1, 15, 107). The probable reason for this, we believe, is that the concessive use of the form was by this time becoming quite uncommon in certain parts of the Spanish-speaking world. At the end of the 19th century, in fact, Schuchardt (1883: 36) describes the concessive value as 'popular' and 'outdated', even though – as he himself acknowledges – Salvá and Bello still considered it in common usage.

Likewise, in Mexico, at the start of the 20th century, according to the account of Salado Álvarez, the use of concessive *mas que* struck an unfamiliar chord among educated speakers of the language; there is even a suggestion that the form might be a borrowing:

> Hay, por ejemplo, vulgarismos que tienen origen en cosas o sucesos tan distantes, pero tan legítimos, que sería error notorio desecharlos sin examen o condenarlos sin estudio. No hay ahora persona nacida que en Méjico no ría si oye decir *masque* en el sentido de 'no obstante', 'no importa', 'a pesar de todo', y sin embargo, *masque* es un lusitanismo o un hispanismo que probablemente recibimos de la China o de la India. (Salado Álvarez 1924:93)[15]

Nevertheless, in other parts of the Spanish-speaking world, the occurrence of *mas que* was not so uncommon, as work by Kany (1969[1945]) has shown. Kany's detailed analysis of the use of the particle as a concessive conjunction and as an interjection, with a meaning the author paraphrases as *no importa* 'what matter', describes a lower level of occurrence in Spain than in Latin America, where "equivocadamente se considera como un localismo, y se critica su uso" ['it is mistakenly viewed as a localism, and speakers are criticised for using it'] (Kany 1969[1945]: 442). He also presents evidence of the different uses of *mas que* in Chile, Costa Rica, Mexico, Ecuador, Peru, Venezuela and El Salvador (cf. Kany 1969[1945]: 442–443, 484–485).

The phrase also found its way into the Spanish of the United States, or at least into the Spanish of New Mexico, as studies by Espinosa show:

> *Aunque, manque, masque*, etc. AUNQUE > *aúnque, áunque, anque, onque, enque, unque*; MAS QUE > *masque, mahque, manque*. […] *Manque* is from *masque*, and the presence of the *n* is no doubt due to the influence of *anque* < AUNQUE, as Pietch has shown. (Espinosa 1911:281–282)

Among the glosses and notes included in the Spanish translations of Espinosa's work, published by Ángel Rosenblat in 1946, there is detailed analysis of the different meanings of *mas que* and the locutions in which it appears. *Más que nunca*, for example, appears in the senses of 'what matter, although, even if, however, and yet, despite': "*iré a la fiesta **más que nunca** llueva*" ['I'll go to the party *even if* it rains'] is just one illustration among many taken by Rosenblat from authors from different parts of the Spanish-speaking world (Chile, Murcia, Andalusia, etc.).

In light of all this evidence, it is hard to understand how concessive *mas que* in Spanish remains 'invisible' in the debate surrounding the origin of *maskin/masque* in the Spanish creoles of the Philippines. Since it is clear now that the particle not only existed in Spanish but spread to a large portion of the Hispanic world, where it survived for several centuries, the hypothesis of a possible Portuguese origin becomes superfluous and any additional consideration of its parts irrelevant. Nevertheless, if one could demonstrate that the Spanish who settled in the Philippines used the particle *in situ*, this would prove the hypothesis to be implausible as well.

We have identified examples of *más que* with concessive and/or modal meanings of indifference in a number of texts from the late 17th to the 19th century, published in the Philippines and written by Spaniards who had been living in the colony for many years. The books in question include several dictionary and grammar works by Spanish missionaries concerning the indigenous languages of the archipelago. The concessive and modal values of *mas que/masque* reappear time and again in these sources: as an equivalent in Spanish for some item in the indigenous dialect; or in relation to the explanation of certain nouns and adjectives. In *Arte de lengua pampanga*, in the section on disjunctive conjunctions, the Augustinian missionary Álvaro de Benavente (c. 1699[2007]) translates the phrase *bisa ya man, e yan bisa, pacayan*[16] *me queti* as "quiera o no quiera, hazlo venir aquí, o *mas que* quiera o *mas que* no quiera" ['whether he wants to or not, make him come here, or *what matter it if* he wants to or *what matter it if* he doesn't'] (our italics). A few decades later, in his *Vocabulario de la lengua pampanga en romance*, Diego de Bergaño (1732) uses *mas que* to give an equivalent meaning of the adverb *imburi(s)*[17] and as part of his explanations of the noun *tabug* and the adjective *tamasa*. Another Augustinian, Martínez de Zúñiga (1893[1803–1806]: vol. 1) offers a number of examples of *mas que* with concessive meaning in his study, *Estadismo de las Islas Filipinas*:

(6) Spanish (Martínez de Zúñiga (1893[1803–1806]: 265, 299, 534)

a. [...] *basta que no desprecie el culto Católico para que nadie se meta con él, á no ser que sea cristiano antiguo ó que se bautice,* **mas que** *sea por casarse* [...]
'it is enough that (he) does not despise the Catholic cult for no-one to disturb him, unless he is an old christian or receives baptism, even if it is only to get married'

b. *El Gobierno debía tomar en esto providencia y obligar á los indios con castigos al examen anual de la Doctrina,* **mas que** *no se les obligase con tanto rigor á confesarse, por no exponerlos á cometer un sacrilegio.*
'The Government should act in this regard and force the indians to do the annual exam of Doctrine, even if they were not so rigorously forced to confess, so that they were not exposed to sacrilege.'

c. *En llegando el Padre á casa del difunto, todos los del luto deben levantar el grito, y llorar,* **mas que** *no tengan gana.*
'When the Priest reaches the house of the deceased, everyone should shout and cry, even if they do not feel like it.'

In *Vocabulario de la lengua bicol*, the Franciscan missionary Marcos de Lisboa (1754) uses Spanish *masque* and *aunque* as semantic equivalents for the concessive conjunction *minsan* in Bikol. Similarly, Sánchez de la Rosa's (1895) *Diccionario hispano-bisaya para las provincias de Samar y Leyte* includes the adverbial locution *más que* under the entry for Spanish *mas*, with the form's equivalents in Visaya recorded as *cundi* and *bisan*. In the Visaya-Spanish section, the entry for *bisan* offers Spanish *más que* as one possible translation, in addition to other concessive expressions such as *aunque*, *á pesar de todo*, etc.

The evidence of these texts demonstrates beyond any doubt the Spanish provenance of the particle *maskin/masque*. As we will see in the next section, in Chabacano the form has not only preserved the functions it had originally in Spanish, but acquired new meanings through its assimilation into the local languages of the region.[18]

4. *Maskin*: from Spanish to Philippine Creole Spanish

In the course of its journey from Spanish to Chabacano via the languages of the Philippine Islands, the Spanish form *más que* appears to have retained its semantic quality of 'difficulty or inconvenience that can always be overcome', characteristic of constructions denoting concessivity. The use of *maskin* is associated with contexts in which the relationship between two parts of a discourse fails to produce the anticipated effect, with its introduction serving to increase the argumentative force of the utterance in which it appears. The particle is an indication that the information expressed by that sequence is unimportant or a matter of indifference. 'Inhibition' and 'indifference' thus represent two of the most common semantic-pragmatic features of the concessive expressions (Cortés Parazuelos 1993: 120).

The analysis of the examples in our corpus demonstrates two things: firstly, that *maskin* has retained the concessive and modal values of indifference exhibited by the original particle in Spanish in its conjunctive and interjectional forms; and, secondly, that it has acquired from the Philippine languages a new scalar or intensifying function, in addition to that of focal or indefinite quantifier. Equivalent meanings in Spanish include expressions such as *aunque, incluso, ni siquiera, cualquiera* and *no importa*.

As in Spanish, Chabacano uses *maskin* as a type of nexus in concessive constructions:

(7) Zamboanga Chabacano (*Serioso y Pendehadas*, 23 July, 2001)¹⁹
Alegre gat yo kay yan incuentro kita otravez, **maskin** aqui ya lang na internet.
'I am very happy to see you again, though it is only over the internet.'

(8) Zamboanga Chabacano (*Serioso y Pendehadas*, 15 December, 2001)
Na[,] el hombre dol ya perde man el camino? Aqui arriba na monte alegre lang came pirmi- **maskin** nuay relo tiene kalaw ta canta! **Maskin** nuay came camisa, nuay canamon quien bisya.
'It looks as if the man lost his way, eh? Up here in the mountains we're always happy, even if we don't have watches, we have the singing *kalaw* [a bird]! Even if we don't wear shirts, who is there to be looking at us?'

In both of these examples, a contrast or opposition is established between two clauses. The condition (or protasis) and the consequence (or apodosis) point to opposite conclusions. An apodosis is declared, in spite of the presence of implicit information that would seem to contradict its fulfilment. For instance, in (7) a contrast is established between the circumstance of meeting one another again and the fact that the encounter is a virtual one. The expectation is not fulfilled since, given how happy the visitor to the forum is about the meeting, one would have expected it to be a 'face to face' encounter, not a virtual one. The disappointment is minimised, however: it doesn't matter if the meeting is only by internet. The protasis, therefore, contains an obstacle that can be overcome. The same situation arises in (8), where the apodosis directly cancels out the information offered implicitly by the protasis: the speaker expresses happiness, even though it would be normal for him to be unhappy given his situation, living in the mountains with neither a watch nor clothes. Neither would one expect a person to connect to an internet forum if he or she had the chickenpox:

(9) Zamboanga Chabacano (*Serioso y Pendehadas*, 9 April, 2001)
Este Sypunin **maskin** enfermo de chicken pox, sigi pa siempre ta man SyP. Therapy daw, hehehe.
'Though he's sick with the chicken pox, this SyP-er [a participant in the SyP forum] is still SyP-ing. Like it's therapy, hehehe.'

The relationship between this kind of construction and a scalar concessive conditional is clear; indeed, a large number of grammar experts already look upon concessivity as a type of scalar relation. Observe in (7), for instance, how *maskin* is used to indicate that a virtual meeting is among the types of encounter least in keeping with the natural expectations of the situation. The substitution of *aunque* 'though' for *incluso si* 'even if' in the gloss would be just as acceptable. According to Flamenco García (1999: 3843), particles of this kind "sitúan la expresión sobre la que inciden en un punto o nivel determinado [de una escala] – concretamente, uno de los extremos y el menos previsible – y establecen implícitamente un contraste entre el nivel que describe dicha expresión y el de otras expresiones alternativas" ['place the sequence in which they occur at a particular point or level [on a scale] – specifically, at the most unexpected extreme of meaning – and establish an implicit contrast between the extreme circumstance described by the utterance and the alternative levels of meaning contained in the other clauses']. The concessive interpretation of constructions that begin with *incluso si* 'even if' is influenced by this 'counter-expectational' aspect of the meaning (Flamenco García 1999: 3843).

Associated with this concessive use of *maskin* is the occurrence of the form as an intensifying particle, where it functions as a focal or presuppositional quantifier. In (10) and (11), *maskin* has a gradational value and appears as a constituent part of the noun phrase. Its meaning is akin to a superlative, with the quantified element occupying the highest point on the scale (cf. Sánchez López 1999: 1109):

(10) Zamboanga Chabacano   (*Serioso y Pendehadas*, 20 November, 2000)
When we were into our final song, el Zamboanga Hermosa, I tell you **maskin** *maga classmate hombre ta pichi gayot el ojos […] para hende cay el lagrimas.*
'When we got to our final song, Zamboanga Hermosa, I tell you even the guys in the class were squeezing their eyes to stop the tears from falling.'

(11) Zamboanga Chabacano   (*Serioso y Pendehadas*, 4 October, 2001)
Ara, **maskin** *si Greggy Araneta, tiene ya ID clipped na su camisa, hehehe. Antes, hmmph! hende se ta usa ID.*
'Now, even Greggy Araneta has an ID tag clipped to his shirt, hehehe. Before – hmmph! – that guy never used to use an ID.'

In these two examples, the meaning of *maskin* has two semantic components: an 'inclusive' component and an 'elevating' one (cf. Santos Río 2003: see entry for *incluso*). In (10), the use of *maskin* places the male members of the class in the same category as those who had trouble holding back their tears. At the same time, it introduces the presupposition that the women in the class did cry or else made great efforts not to do so. It suggests that, as men, their presence on the scale of holding back tears in this context constitutes an unusual or uncommon and consequently unexpected circumstance. The situation in (11) is the same. Here, the use of *maskin* shows us that the fact that someone as famous as Greggy Araneta now wears an ID tag clipped to his shirt is not a normal or customary circumstance, and also that there are others besides him who wear identification. Note how in these examples the sense of 'indifference' is still present (i.e. it doesn't matter that the classmates were male, they too were moved; it doesn't matter if he is Greggy Araneta, he too wears an ID).

The additive value and increased argumentational force which derive from the concessive value of the particle occur in a number of different ways (addition of a time, place, subject, detail, etc.) in all of the Philippine languages where, as we have noted, *maski* exists side by side with its indigenous equivalents. For example, **bista man** /*maski ngeni* in Kapampangan, *kahit* /*maski ngayon* in Tagalog, *minsan*/*maski ngunian* in Bikol, and **bisan**/**maski** *karon* in Cebuano and other Spanish Visaya creoles translate as *incluso ahora* 'even now'. Sánchez de la Rosa's (1895) dictionary records the same intensifying value for *bisan pa* in Samareño, which he translates as part of the phrase "te daré los cien duros que me has pedido, y aun los doscientos, si los necesitas" ['I will give you the hundred *duros* you have asked me for, even two hundred, if you need them']. The adaptation of the Spanish particle to the concessive usages of the various Philippine dialects also extends to cases of negative addition in the presence of a quantifier: 'at least one', 'at least a few', 'not even one', 'not even a few', etc. The following example illustrates the use of Chabacano *maskin* in a context of negation, where its presence attaches a quantitative value to the element it is modifying:

(12) Zamboanga Chabacano   (*Serioso y Pendehadas*, 5 November, 2000)
No hay **maskin** uno zamboangueno!
'Not [even] one of them was from Zamboanga!'

The effect is the same in all the Philippine languages. Thus in Tagalog, for example, we find the construction (NEG) *kahit*/*maski* + quantifier; and in Cebuano, (NEG) *bisan*/*maskin* + quantifier, etc.

From its use as a focal or presuppositional quantifier, let us turn now to its occurrence as an indefinite quantifier, where it is used to denote an undifferentiated element within a series (see also Sippola, *this volume*). In this case, the form functions as what we might term a quantifier of indeterminacy (or, alternatively, of indifference – if we wish to highlight more clearly the semantic component of 'indifference' inherent in all the meanings of *maskin*):

(13) Zamboanga Chabacano   (*Serioso y Pendehadas*, 28 December, 2000)
Poreso ya busca kame dayun **maskin** cosa medicina para hace parra el sangre estaba na irida.
'That's why we immediately looked for any medicine that would stop the bleeding straight away.' [In reference to somebody who has had his head split open]

The use of the word *maskin* here in conjunction with *cosa* forms an indefinite syntagma signifying indeterminacy ('any medicine whatever'), with a meaning equivalent to 'some'. By contrast, in (14) *maskin* functions as a universal quantifier, denoting each and all of the things the person did to get to sleep:

(14) Zamboanga Chabacano (*Serioso y Pendehadas*, 11 January, 2001)
Dear Dr. Syp,
my problem is hende yo ta pwede dormi, **maskin** *qosa qosa yo ase, cant sleep there are times I tried to meditate but does not help at all.*
'Dear Dr Syp,
my problem is that I can't sleep, no matter what I do, I can't sleep. I have tried meditating but it does not help at all.'

Notice that *maskin* can also be translated in a generalising indefinite sense to form a concessive structure: 'whatever I do, I can't sleep'. The indefinite value that *maskin* acquires when it is followed by an interrogative particle is due to the influence of the indigenous languages of the Philippines; equivalent usages in Tagalog, for example, include: *kahit ano* or *maski ano* 'any'; *kahit sino* or *maski sino* 'whoever, anybody'; *kahit saan* or *maski saan* = 'wherever, in any place'; *kahit kailan* or *maski kailan* = 'at any time'; *kahit paano* or *maski paano* = 'in any way'; *kahit ilan* or *maski ilan* = 'any amount'. The same is also true of all the other Philippine variants.[20] In the following examples from Chabacano, *maskin* is combined with the Spanish pronoun *quien* 'who/whom' and with the adverbs *donde* 'where' and *cuando* 'when' – English translations of (15) and (16) consist of the corresponding verses in the *New King James Version* (1982):

(15) Zamboanga Chabacano (NTC 2001: John 5:22)
El Tata gendeh ta juzga ni con **maskin quien***, cay ya dale Le con el Anak todo el poder para juzga.*
'For the Father judges no one, but has committed all judgment to the Son.'

(16) Zamboanga Chabacano (NTC 2001: Acts 24:3)
Maskin cuando *y* **maskin donde** *ta acepta came este y ta dale gayot came gracias.*
'[W]e accept it always and in all places, […] with all thankfulness.'

(17) Zamboanga Chabacano (*Serioso y Pendehadas*, 4 May, 2001)
Maskin donde *ciudad o barrio ustedes anda, uno lang sila puede habla.*
'No matter what neighbourhood or city you go to / Whatever neighbourhood or city you go to, they always say the same thing.'

To finish, let us turn to the interjectional value of *maskin*, used to indicate an attitude of indifference on the part of the speaker. This meaning – which, as we have seen, was common in Spain in the past and which Kany (1969: 484) has documented more recently among Spanish speakers in Chile, Ecuador, Venezuela, Costa Rica, El Salvador and Mexico – is also present in the indigenous languages of the Philippines, in expressions such as *kahit na* or *maski na*, followed by a pause. It is also found in Chabacano:

(18) Zamboanga Chabacano [and English]
(*Serioso y Pendehadas*, 13 February, 2001)
*Everybody should believe in something. I believe I have to ask Kassandra this question: Are you man enough to be a woman? (**Maskin** rabia ya! Ay rayo ta prigunta lang!)*
'[…] (I don't care if the question makes you angry! / Don't bother getting angry! For heaven's sake, I'm only asking!).'

5. Conclusions

As this analysis has shown, whenever *maskin* is used, a concessive interpretation of the structure associated with the form is possible. The proximity between the concepts of concessivity, scalarity and quantification explains why the meanings they express can often overlap. Scalarity refers to the argumentative relationship between the elements of a discourse that creates meaning within certain concessive constructions. Moreover, because of the close link between scalarity and quantification, the presence of a quantified element can often be the determining factor in the argumentative structure of a sentence (cf. Sánchez López 1999: 1111).

Our analysis of the behaviour of *maskin* in Chabacano reveals significant differences from its counterparts in Asian Portuguese creoles, all of which may be traced back to the contact that occurred between Spanish and the native Philippine varieties. We have also identified evidence to show that these new meanings of *mas que* were also adopted by the Spaniards who had been living in the Philippines for a long period. At the archives of the Jesuit Province of Tarragona (now in Barcelona), a loose page was discovered inserted in the Tamontaca Register of Freedmen, containing a note written by one of the Jesuit missionaries in charge of the institution (all of whom were Spanish) concerning a freedman who had escaped and was subsequently found and returned: "Tomás [el muchacho fugado] dice que siguió á Bandar para ir á Bohayen – ó más que á donde. Que no tiene mas motivo que porque Bandar le convidó" ['Tomás [the boy who ran away] said that he followed Bandar to Bohayen – or wherever. For no more reason than that Bandar invited him'].[21]

It would appear, therefore, that the *maskin* form observed in the Spanish creole languages of the Philippines is not derived from Portuguese, despite the widely held view to the contrary among creole experts of the past and still to this day. The presence of *maski* in the Portuguese-based *lingua franca* spoken in parts of Asia over several centuries does not necessarily mean that the Chabacano *masque/masqué* or *maskin* forms originated from the same source. On the other hand, the concessive meaning of *maski* in Asian Portuguese creoles is traceable to the Portuguese origin of those varieties.

It is also clear from our study that the particle in question is a common feature of a large number of creole languages. As we mentioned earlier in the introduction, in addition to the Asian Portuguese creoles and Spanish-Philippine varieties examined in this study, the form is also present in other pidgin and creole languages of both the Atlantic and the Pacific regions: Papiamentu, Cape Dutch Pidgin, Rabaul Creole German, Negerhollands, Papua New Guinea Tok Pisin, Chinese Pidgin English, etc. The diversity of factors present in the formation of these languages is reflected in the variety of hypotheses regarding the provenance of the form, ranging from a superstratum of European languages (Portuguese, Spanish, Dutch, German) to an Austronesian substratum (Malay, Ramoaaina), and even Arabic being suggested as a possible source. The aim of most of these hypotheses is to account for the concessive value of *maskin* and the modal sense of indifference which, although not recorded in all the languages mentioned, may still be deduced from the semantic component of 'difficulty or inconvenience that can always be overcome' that is characteristic of all concessive constructions.

The particle also occurs in a number of non-creole languages. In this study, for example, we have observed how the Spanish expression *mas que* was introduced as a borrowing into four Philippine languages (Kapampangan, Tagalog, Bikol and Cebuano), but there are many more cases we could mention. In the course of our small investigation (a task made far easier thanks to the enormous advantage of being able to access millions of books, or fragments of them at least, via the internet), we have identified at least fourteen other Philippine languages in which *mas que* has been adopted: the form occurs in Ibanag, Yogad, Sambal, Baluga and other Aeta varieties in Luzon; in at least one of the Mangyan dialects in Mindoro; Aklanon, Hiligaynon, Waray and Kinaray-a in the Visayan Islands; Agutaynen, Tagbanwa, Batak and Palawano in the Palawan region; and Mandaya in Mindanao. The use of *mas que* is also documented in a great many other languages besides those of the Philippines. In fact, the phrase might arguably be classed alongside what Stolz (1996) terms 'circumpacific isoglosses': functional Spanish words present in at least one language each from Central America, South America and the Philippines and Oceania. Stolz actually only mentions four isoglosses of this type, identified from the 41 languages in his sample: (in alphabetical order) *antes, o, pero* and *porque*. He classes *mas que* as an isogloss of more limited range, albeit an impressive one, occurring (by his reckoning) in three of the seven South American languages in his study and ten out of the fifteen in the region of Austronesia, but none of the nineteen in Central America.[22] Extending Stolz's sample slightly, we have discovered additional occurrences of the particle, not only in Austronesia but also among the languages of South America. To Guaraní, Ayacucho Quechua and Inga, we can add, at a minimum: Cocama, from the Amazon region of Peru; Southern Quechua, spoken in Cuzco, Puno and Bolivia (Cusihuamán 1976); and Aymara, in Bolivia (Ayala Loaiza 1988; Ebbing 1965; Lucca 1987). In Central America, despite Stolz's failure to identify a single case, the use of concessive *maske/ maski* is widely recorded in Nahuatl, for example in the *Diccionario del Colegio de Lenguas y Literatura Indígenas* (1994) and in Tuggy (1991). It would appear, then, that we do have a fifth circumpacific isogloss after all.

Notes

1. The most commonly found use of the word is not with the purely concessive meaning mentioned here, but in the sense of 'never mind', where it usually occurs in the form of an independent clause: *maskee!*

2. See, for example, Hunter (1882), or Skeat (1900), who support the idea that the item entered Chinese Pidgin English through the creole of Macau. Alternative etymologies have also been proposed. One of these is the Malay word *meski* 'in spite of, although' (Clark 1979; Ferreira 1968: 120), documented as early as 1626, and in turn a derivation of the Portuguese form. The likelihood of a Malay origin becomes even stronger if we take into account that *meski* has also developed a sense of 'no matter', as the following example illustrates: *meski terang meski gelap* ('no matter how bright, no matter how dark'), a verse from a popular Malaysian song. The Arabic particle *ma'alish* has also been submitted as a possible origin (by Partridge & Simpson 1973, who regard as 'ingenious' Skeat's derivation of the form from Portuguese). For the *maski* form in Papua New Guinea Tok Pisin, the possibility of a German origin has been suggested: '[das/es] macht nicht' (Mihalic 1971); while Ross (1992: 372) proposes *maadeki* from the Ramoaaina dialect. In the case of Cape Dutch Pidgin *maskie*, which is sometimes used with the sense of 'maybe', the Dutch modal particle *misschien* 'maybe' or the older *machschien* form was proposed as one possible origin, with the Portuguese variant offering an alternative etymology that would account for the concessive value 'although' that it also contains (cf. Schuchardt 1883: 144, 1885: 485).

3. An exception to this is Roberge (2002), who devotes several pages to the subject of Cape Dutch Pidgin *maskie*.

4. The reference to McKaughan relates to the following fragment: *si kabáw ta pìdi konele maskin un fruta lang* 'the turtle was asking him for just one banana'. McKaughan's translation is accurate: *maskin* is not used here with a concessive value but in the sense it has when it appears before a quantifier, which we will look at later on. Whinnom took the mistaken view that his small collection of Zamboangueño texts represented a 'salutary correction' to the examples presented by McKaughan.

5. 'Contae, mas que me deixem congelado' and 'Por Deos, mas que me fundam; mas que me confundam, eu hei de tanger sempre a verdade'; from *Dialogos Apologaes*, by D. Francisco de Melo.

6. Batalha's example is taken from *Ásia Sínica e Japónica*, by Frei Jose de Jesus Maria (1950 [ca. 1745]): 'pello que atendendo o Senado ser aquela nau ou fragata de El-Rey (...) mandou se lhe dessem as seis peças de ferro: porém o capitão mal satisfeito e querendo as de bronze, *mas que* se tirasse das Fortalezas...'.

7. 'Because I will never defend that a Priest be on his own in the whole of christianity, even if he has little to do there, because of the many dangers and evils that may derive from it.'

8. '**Maisque, masque** (mais us.), por mais que, ainda que, mas se. Dial. mac. *masqui*, which, according to Marques Pereira, comes from Malay. However, David Haex (*Dictionarium Malaico-Latinum et Latino. Malaicum*) maintains the opposite to be the case: "*Quanvis ita sit*: mas que. *Quanto magis*: quanto mas".'

9. 'It is certain that there are many dark girls who are very attractive, so that (...) they beat the white ones, who, even though they have pleasant faces, are a little dull.'

10. 'The word **masquí** is very common in texts written in Macanese. It has a concessive value equivalent to 'even though, in spite of, even', undoubtedly the same as it has in texts from the Philippines.'

11. Professor Grant reminded us during the discussion that accompanied the presentation of this paper that the sequence /-sk-/ does not occur indigenously in Malay words of Austronesian origin.

12. Grant (2001, 2009) also mentions *maskín* as one of the forms in Zamboangueño that "may be relics of a Portuguese creole past" (2001: 104).

13. According to Brooks (1933: 29), *mas que* has been part of vernacular speech since the 16th and 17th centuries: "[w]hen the great flood of drama made literature out of popular speech and conversation, *mas que* came into its own".

14. 'Now we will examine the specific value that is usually attributed to this form, taking it as equivalent to the phrase *aun dado caso que* 'even if, even in the event that': *No lo aceptaría* más que *me rogasen con ello* 'I would not allow it *even if* they begged me to'. Keeping implicit the main clause, it is said: *mas que me maten* 'even if it kills me' (stop speaking, *it's a matter of indifference to me, I don't care*).'

15. 'There are, for example, certain vulgarisms which have their origin in some distant incident or object, but are nevertheless legitimate usages which it would clearly be a mistake to dispense with or condemn without prior examination. There is not a person alive in Mexico today who would not laugh to hear *masque* used in the sense of 'however', 'what matter', 'all the same', and yet the word is probably a derivation of Portuguese or Spanish that made its way to us from China or India.'

16. The 'c' represents a glottal stop; nowadays, the word is spelt *paayan*.

17. In Chapter XVIII of his *Arte de la lengua pampanga* (1729: 323), Bergaño also refers to *mas que* in the section dealing with the adversative adverb *imburis*.

18. A similar process has taken place in relation to other forms of Spanish origin: *basta*, for example, has developed new meanings in Zamboangueño (and other Philippine languages)

that are unheard of anywhere else, in any of the varieties spoken in Spain or the Americas (cf. Vázquez Veiga & Fernández Rodríguez 2008).

19. Most of the examples used in this section are taken from the now defunct internet forum, *Serioso y Pendehadas* (SyP), which the local people in Zamboanga used to keep in contact with emigrants around the world. We have maintained the original spelling in our examples, except for a few obvious mistakes, since many of the peculiarities are deliberate. Similarly, we have chosen not to discard examples written mainly in English, as these also shed light on the use of *maskin* in a colloquial context.

20. Thus, from Cebuano *bisansdiin* we get *maskin diin* 'in any place'; in Bikol, *minsan siisay* forms *maski siisay* 'anybody', and from *minsan anoman* comes *maski anoman* 'anything'; by the same process, Kapampangan saw the formation of *maski nanu* 'anything', *maski ninu* 'anybody', *maski nukarin* and *maski nu* 'anywhere', *maski kapilan* 'any amount', etc.

21. The note was found by Mauro Fernández inside *Origen y progreso del establecimiento de Tamontaca y registro de libertos* (E-II-b-72).

22. Ayacucho Quechua, Guaraní and Inga are the three South American languages Stolz refers to; Bikol, Hiligaynon, Tagalog, Tagbanwa, Chamorro, Sambal, Batak, Mansaka, Agta and Negrito are the ten in the Austronesian region (cf. Stolz 1996: 7–8).

References

Ayala Loaiza, J. L. 1988. *Diccionario Español-Aymara, Aymara-Español*. Lima: Juan Mejia Baca.
Baker, P., and P. Mühlhäusler. 1990. From business to pidgin. *Journal of Asian Pacific Communication* 1 (1): 87–115.
Batalha, G. N. 1960. Coincidências com o dialecto de Macau em dialectos espanhóis das Ilhas Filipinas. *Boletim de Filologia* 19: 295–303.
Batalha, G. N. 1977. *Glossário do Dialecto Macaense: Notas Linguísticas, Etnográficas e Folclóricas*. Coimbra: Instituto de Estudos Românicos da Universidade de Coimbra.
Baxter, A. N. 1988. *A Grammar of Kristang (Malacca Creole Portuguese)* [Pacific Linguistics. Series B; no. 95]. Canberra: Pacific Linguistics.
Baxter, A. N. 1996. Portuguese and Creole Portuguese in the Pacific and Western Pacific rim. In *Atlas of Languages of Intercultural Communication in the Pacific, Asia, and the Americas*, Vol. II.1, eds. S. A. Wurm, P. Mühlhäusler and D. T. Tryon, 299–338. Berlin: Mouton de Gruyter.
Bello, A. 1998 [1847–1860]. *Gramática de la Lengua Castellana Destinada al Uso de los Americanos*, 2 vols. Madrid: Arco/Libros.
de Benavente, A. 2007 [c. 1699]. *Arte de Lengua Pampanga*. Angeles City: Holy Angel University Press.
de Bergaño, D. 1860 [1732]. *Vocabulario de la Lengua Pampangan en Romance*. Manila: Imprenta de Ramírez y Giraudier.
de Bergaño, D. 1729. *Arte de la Lengua Pampanga*. Manila: Imprenta de la Compania de Jesus.
Bluteau, R. 1712–1728. *Vocabulario Portuguez & Latino: Aulico, Anatomico, Architectonico...*, 8 vols. Coimbra: Collegio das Artes da Companhia de Jesu.

Brooks, J. 1933. Más que, mas que and mas ¡qué! *Hispania* 16 (1): 23–34.
Callaway, J. 1820. *A Vocabulary in the Ceylon Portuguese and English Languages, with a Series of Familiar Phrases*. Colombo: Wesleyan Mission Press.
Clark, R. 1979. In search of Beach-la-Mar: Towards a history of Pacific Pidgin English. *Te Reo* 22: 3–64.
Colegio de Lenguas y Literatura Indígenas. 1994. *Diccionario Nahuatl-Español, Español-Nahuatl*. Toluca: Instituto Mexiquense de Cultura.
Cortés Parazuelos, M. H. 1993. 'Inhibición' o 'indiferencia': Rasgo común a expresiones de sentido concesivo. *Revista de Filología Románica* 10: 107–54.
Cusihuamán, A. 1976. *Diccionario Quechua, Cuzco-Collao*. Lima: Instituto de Estudios Peruanos.
Dalgado, S. R. 1913. *Influência do Vocabulário Português em Línguas Asiáticas*. Coimbra: Imprensa da Universidade.
Dalgado, S. R. 1998 [1900]. *Dialecto Indo-Português de Ceylão*. Lisbon: Comissão Nacional para as Commemorações dos Descobrimentos Portugueses.
Ebbing, J. E. 1965. *Gramática y Diccionario Aymara*. La Paz: Editorial Don Bosco.
Espinosa, A. M. 1911. Studies in New Mexican Spanish II. *Revue de Dialectologie Romane* 3: 251–286. (Translated into Spanish and annotated by Ángel Rosenblat. 1946. *Estudios sobre el Español de Nuevo Méjico*, Parte II: *Morfología* [Biblioteca de Dialectología Hispanoamericana]. Buenos Aires: Universidad de Buenos Aires).
Fernández, M. 2011. Chabacano en Tayabas: Implicaciones para la historia de los criollos hispano-filipinos. *Revista Internacional de Lingüística Iberoamericana* 17: 187–216.
Ferreira, J. S. 1968. *Macau sâ assi*. Macau: Published by the author.
Ferreira, J. S. 1978. *Papiá Cristâm di Macau: Epitome de Gramática Comparada e Vocabulário – Dialecto Macaense*. Macau: Tipografia da Missão (Reprinted Ferreira 1996).
Ferreira, J. S. 1996. *Papiaçám di Macau*. Macau: Fundação Macau.
Flamenco García, L. 1999. Las construcciones concesivas y adversativas. In *Gramática Descriptiva de la Lengua Española*, Vol. 3: *Entre la Oración y el Discurso. Morfología*, eds. I. Bosque and V. Demonte, 3805–3878. Madrid: Espasa Calpe.
Grant, A. P. 2001. Language intertwining: Its depiction in recent literature and its implications for theories of creolisation. In *Creolization and Contact* [Creole Language Library 23], eds. N. Smith and T. Veenstra, 91–111. Amsterdam: John Benjamins.
Grant, A. P. 2009. Contact, complexification and change in Mindanao Chabacano structure. In *Complex Processes in New Languages* [Creole Language Library 35], eds. E. O. Aboh and N. Smith, 223–241. Amsterdam: John Benjamins.
Hancock, I. F. 1973. Malacca Creole Portuguese: A brief transformational outline. *Te Reo* 16: 23–44.
Hunter, W. C. J. 1882. *The 'Fan Kwae' at Canton Before Treaty Days*. London: Kegan, Paul, Trench and Co.
Jacobs, H. ed. 1980. *Documenta Malucensia II (1577–1606)*. Roma: Jesuit Historical Institute.
de Jesus Maria, J. 1950 [ca. 1745]. *Azia Sinica e Japonica: Obra Postuma e Inedita do Frade Arrabido, Jose de Jesus Maria*, edited by C. R. Boxer, Vol. II. Macau: Escola Tip. do Oratorio de S. J. Bosco.
Kany, C. E. 1969 [1954]. *Sintaxis Hispanoamericana*. Madrid: Gredos.
Leland, C. 1876. *Pidgin English Sing-Song or Songs and Stories in the China-English Dialect*. Philadelphia, PA: Lippincott.

Lenz, R. 1920. *La Oración y sus Partes. Estudios de Gramática General y Castellana*, 3rd edn. Madrid: Publicaciones de la *Revista de Filología Española*.

Lipski, J. 1988. Philippine Creole Spanish: Assessing the Portuguese element. *Zeitschrift für Romanische Philologie* 104 (1/2): 25–45.

Lisboa, M. de. 1754. *Vocabulario de la Lengua Bicol*. Sampala: Convento de Nuestra Señora de Loreto.

Lucca, M. de. 1987. *Diccionario Práctico Aymara-Castellano, Castellano-Aymara*. La Paz/Cochabamba: Los Amigos del Libro.

Martínez de Zúñiga, J. 1893 [1803–1806]. *Estadismo de las Islas Filipinas. Mis Viajes por Este País*. Madrid: Imprenta de la Viuda de M. Minuesa de los Ros.

Mihalic, R. F. 1971. *The Jacaranda Dictionary and Grammar of Melanesian Pidgin*. Port Moresby: Jacaranda Press.

NKJV. 1982. *New King James Version (NKJV Bible)*. Nashville TE: Thomas Nelson. www.biblegateway.com/versions/New-King-James-Version-NKJV-Bible (accessed January 11, 2011).

NT. 1852. *O Novo Testamento de Nossa Senhor e Salvador Jesus Christo Traduzido ne Indo-Portugueza*. Colombo: Officina de Missão Wesleyano.

NTC. 2001. *El Nuevo Testamento na Chabacano*. Quezon City: Claretian Publications.

Partridge, E., and Simpson, J. 2000 [1973]. *The Routledge Dictionary of Historical Slang*. London: Routledge.

Real Academia Española. 1979 [1726–1739]. *Diccionario de Autoridades*. Madrid: Gredos.

Real Academia Española. 2001a. *Diccionario de la Lengua Española*, 22nd edn. Madrid: Espasa Calpe. Online version. http://www.rae.es/

Real Academia Española. 2001b. *Nuevo Tesoro Lexicográfico de la Lengua Española*. Madrid: Espasa Calpe. Online version.http://www.rae.es (accessed January 11, 2011).

Rêgo, A. S. 1998. *Dialecto Português de Malaca e Outros Escritos*. Lisbon: Comissão Nacional para as Comemorações dos Descobrimentos Portugueses (Includes 1941–1942. Apontamento para o estudo do dialecto português de Malaca. *Boletim Geral das Colónias* 17 (198): 3–78; 18 (203): 9–71; 18 (208): 3–88).

Roberge, P. 2002. The modal elements *mos* and *maskie* in Cape Dutch. *Language Sciences* 24: 397–408.

Ross, M. 1992. The sources of Austronesian lexical items in tok Pisin. In *The Language Game: Papers in Memory of Donald C. Laycock* [Pacific Linguistics. Series C; no. 110], eds. T. Dutton, M. Ross and D. Tryon, 361–384. Canberra: Australia National University.

Salado Álvarez, V. 1924. *Méjico Peregrino. Mejicanismos Supervivientes en el Inglés de Norteamética*. Méjico: Talleres gráficos del Museo Nacional de Arqueología, Historia y Etnografía.

Salvá, V. 1988 [1830–1847]. *Gramática de la Lengua Castellana Según Ahora se Habla*, study and edition by M. Lliteras, 2 vols. Madrid: Arco/Libros.

Sánchez de la Rosa, R. P. F. A., ed. 1895 [1886]. *Diccionario Hispano-Bisaya para las Provincias de Samar y Leyte*. Manila: Tipo-Litografía de Cofre y comp.

Sánchez López, C. 1999. Los cuantificadores: Clases de cuantificadores y estructuras cuantificativas. In *Gramática Descriptiva de la Lengua Española*, Vol. I: *Sintaxis Básica de las Clases de Palabra*, eds. I. Bosque and V. Demonte, 1025–1128. Madrid: Espasa Calpe.

Santos Río, L. 2003. *Diccionario de Partículas*. Salamanca: Luso-Española de Ediciones.

Schuchardt, H. 1883. Kreolischen Studien IV: Ueber das Malaiospanische der Philippines. *Sitzungsberichte der Kaiserlichen Akademie der Wissenschaften zu Wien* 105: 111–50.

Schuchardt, H. 1885. Einzage von: N. Mansvelt, *Proeve van een Kaapsch-Hollandch Idioticon*. *Literaturblatt für Germanische und Romanische Philology* 6: 464–70.

Silva, A. de M. 1789. *Diccionário da Lingua Portuguesa, Composto pelo Padre D. Rafael Bluteau, Reformado e Acrescentado por Antonio de Moraes Silva, Natural do Rio de Janeiro*. Lisboa: Officina de Thaddeo Ferreira.

Skeat, W. W. 1900. *Malay Magic: Being an Introduction to the Folklore and the Popular Religion of the Malay Peninsula*. Londres: MacMillan and Co.

Stolz, T. 1996. Grammatical hispanisms in Amerindian and Austronesian languages: The other kind of transpacific isoglosses. *Amerindia* 21: 137–58.

Thompson, R. W. 1957. Review of Whinnom (1956). *Spanish Contact Vernaculars in the Philippines Islands*. *Revista Portuguesa de Filologia* 8: 369–71.

Tuggy, D. H. 1991. *Lecciones para un Curso del Náhuatl Moderno*. Puebla: Universidad de las Américas.

Vázquez Veiga, N., and M. Fernández Rodríguez. 2008. Las aventuras de *basta* en las Islas Filipinas: huellas de un proceso de pragmaticalización. *Revista Internacional de Lingüística Iberoamericana* VI 2 (12): 157–74.

Whinnom, K. 1956. *Spanish Contact Vernaculars in the Philippine Islands*. Hong Kong, Hong Kong University Press/Oxford: OUP.

Wofsy, S. A. 1928. A note on *más que*. *Romanic Review* 19 (1): 41–48.

Nenang, nino, nem não, ni no
Similarities and differences*

Mauro A. Fernández

This article analyses the similarities and differences between four particles of negation in various Ibero-Asian creoles: *nenang* in Malacca's Kristang, *nem nun* in 19th-century Sri Lanka Indo-Portuguese, *nino* in Ternate Chabacano, and *ni no* in Zamboanga Chabacano. It also includes a study of the Portuguese *nem não* and Spanish *ni no* constructions, which subsist in Iberian and American dialectal varieties, and are in this article taken as direct sources of the above-mentioned creole constructions. Given that the meaning of Kristang *nenang* differs substantially from both the Portuguese construction proposed as the source and the other three creole particles, I analyse possible paths of semantic evolution which may have resulted in its particular characteristics.

1. Introduction

The Portuguese creole of Malacca, known as Kristang (*christão/christam*, or 'Christian'), contains a particle of negation – *nenang* [neˈnaŋ] – which may be translated as 'not yet' and, according to Baxter (1988: 139), functions in a manner similar to that of *belum* in Malay. While Baxter admits to be "uncertain of the origin of this negator" (1988: 148), he indicates as its possible provenance the Portuguese construction *ainda não*, a form also implicated in the derivation of the particle *indana* which Baxter documented in 1980 in the residual creole of Tugu, where it expresses the same meaning as *nenang*.

From a phonetic point of view, however, the derivation of *nenang* from *ainda não* raises a number of complex issues. Baxter (p.c. April 2011) argues that this path of origin could still be viable, based on a reduction along the lines of **nna + nang*. In my view, however, while it may be possible to make the vowel in the first syllable completely voiceless even when that syllable is stressed, as is the case in *nka* or *nda*, the syllable itself does not disappear, which means that *nka* and *nda* remain disyllabic.[1] In order to arrive at *nenang*, therefore, one would also have to account for the transformation of the disyllabic group [n#d] into the monosyllabic [nn], in contrast to the more usually conservative behaviour of this cluster: for *andá, mandá, prendé, undi* and the adverb of time in question, *nda/índa*, there is no monosyllabic variant [na]/[ne], or even a disyllabic [ína]/[íne].[2]

This paper proposes a different origin for *nenang*: the double-negative coordinate construction in Portuguese, *nem não*. It will demonstrate that the particle *nem não* was present in at least one other Asian Portuguese creole, that of Sri Lanka, as well as a number of varieties of Brazilian, African and European Portuguese. The probability of the hypothesis is supported by the existence of an analogous form in the Spanish-based creoles of the Philippines: *ni no / nino*, from the Spanish *ni no*, found in a number of varieties of Spanish, past and current.

While the phonetic derivation of *nenang* from *nem não* is a straightforward one, the semantic transformation is rather more complicated: nowhere among any of the varieties of Portuguese in which its occurrence is recorded is the particle *nem não* ever used with the meaning 'not yet', but rather as a synonym of *tampouco* 'neither' or *nem sequer* 'not even'. In order to justify my proposal, therefore, I will also need to offer some explanation to account for this change. A similar problem arises in relation to the Spanish creoles of the Philippines where, for example, the meaning of *nino* in Ternateño is different from its use in Zamboangueño and Spanish.

Working under the assumption that *nenang* and *nem não* are both derived from the same source, this analysis will investigate the functions performed by these constructions in the Portuguese creoles of Asia and the different varieties of Portuguese. I will then carry out a similar survey in relation to *ni no* in the Spanish creoles of the Philippines and in Spanish. Finally, I will examine the factors responsible for the semantic discrepancies between some of the derived creole forms and their originators in Portuguese and Spanish.

2. *Nenang/ nem não* in the Portuguese-based creoles of Asia

There are four particles of basic negation in Kristang (Malacca Creole Portuguese): *ńgka*, the general negator, used for past or present actions (< Ptg. *nunca* 'never'); *nádi*, a negator incorporating the future-irrealis (< Ptg. *não há-de* 'shall not'); imperative *nang* (Ptg. *não* 'not'); and the particle that concerns us here, *nenang*, containing a perfective aspect that indicates that an action has not taken place or has not been completed (Baxter 1988: 137–141). A broad translation in the context of the latter would be 'not yet'. As in the case of its counterpart *belum* in Malay, Baxter points out that *nenang* is "indifferent to time", and capable of combining with almost any type of predicate, with a few exceptions such as prepositional-phrase predicates of the type *eli di Trankera* ('she is from Trankera'; Baxter 1988:183). The most common occurrence of *nenang* is in combination with an active verb, as in Example (1):

(1) Malacca Creole Portuguese (Baxter 1988:140)
  nenáng kai   chua
  NEG.PFV fall rain
  'It hasn't/hadn't rained yet'

Nevertheless, the form is also combinable with stative predicates, as in (2a), with verbs denoting a change of state (2b), and with nominal predicates (2c, d):

(2) Malacca Creole Portuguese (Baxter 1988:140)
  a. *eli **nenáng** sabé   les   skribé*
      3SG NEG.PFV knows read write
      'He doesn't/didn't yet know how to read and write'
  b. *aké tempu, yo **nenáng** lembrá eli ladráng*
      that time   1SG NEG.PFV think   3SG thief
      'At that time I didn't yet think he was a thief'
  c. *aké tempu, pa   **nenáng** duénti*
      that time father NEG.PFV ill
      'At that time father wasn't ill yet'
  d. *eli **nenáng** mestri*
      3SG NEG.PFV teacher
      'He isn't/wasn't a teacher yet'

The only tense-aspect marker that combines with *nenang* is *ta*, as illustrated in (3):

(3) Malacca Creole Portuguese (Baxter 1988:140)
  *aké tempu, eli   **nenáng** ta   fai sibisu*
  that time   3SG NEG.PFV NPCT do work
  'At that time he wasn't working yet'

Occasionally, the particle can be found in combination with modal verbs (e.g. *podi* 'can': *ele nenang podi X* 'he cannot X yet'), but occurrences of this kind are rare. The most typical use is the combination of *nenang* with an active verb, as in the first example.

As mentioned in the introduction, the proposed derivation of *nenang* from the negative additive construction in Portuguese is supported to an extent by the evidence that *nem não* was also present in at least one other Portuguese-based creole in the region, that of Sri Lanka. The form occurs in a number of texts, including the New Testament translation by Newstead (revised version, NT

1852). The following verse is taken from that volume, and the translation is the corresponding verse in the 1611 King James Version (KJV):

(4) Sri Lanka Creole Portuguese (NT 1852: Romans 6:13)
Nem não presentá vossas membros per peccado como instrumentos de iniquidade.
'Neither yield ye your members as instruments of unrighteousness unto sin'

Newstead is thought to have modelled his version of the text on that of Almeida, who created the first Portuguese translation of the Bible in the last third of the 17th century. An edition of Almeida's work from the mid-19th century shows an almost perfect parallelism between the Portuguese version and its creole counterpart: *"nem tão pouco apresenteis os vossos membros ao pecado por instrumentos de iniquidade"* (Almeida (1848[1681])). Aside from the expected morphological differences and the change of preposition before the object, the only other deviation is in the use of *nem não* at the beginning of the verse, in place of *nem tão pouco*. This suggests that the use of *nem não* in the creole text was not pursuant to any literary model in Portuguese, nor simply an invention of Newstead's (or of those who revised his translation later on): the construction was extant in its own right at some level within the language, even though it disappeared from use subsequently. Dalgado (1900) claimed that, in comparison with the 1826 version, the 1852 edition of Newstead's translation

> representa o crioulo litterario actual [de 1900], não tendo havido necessidade, desde então para cá, de nova edição modificada, por não deixar nada a desejar sob qualquer aspecto que se encare [...] a syntaxe é inteiramente dialectal; o lexico muito vernaculo; a influencia do inglês quasi imperceptivel.
> (Dalgado 1900:87)[3]

All the evidence suggests that in the 19th century *nem não* was a proper, functional construction within Sri Lanka Creole, with the likely pronunciation being that denoted by the spelling *nem nun*, as found, for instance, in the following verse (translation taken from KJV 1611):

(5) Sri Lanka Creole Portuguese (NT 1852: Matthew 22:30)
parque ne o resurreiçao ellotros nunca caza, ***nem nun*** *tem dado ne cazamento* [...]
'For in the resurrection they neither marry, nor are given in marriage'

Overall, the form occurs with one of the two spellings in 12 separate instances. The meaning is always one of gently emphatic negative coordination – 'neither... nor', as in (5), or simply 'nor' – the obvious equivalent for which in modern-day

Portuguese would be the adverb *tampouco* or *nem tampouco*. Table 1 is a list of the verses in which *nem não* and *nem nun* occur, together with their equivalents in Portuguese as they appear in the 1848 edition of Ferreira de Almeida's work.

Table 1. Correspondence between NT (1852) and Almeida (1848[1681]) particles of negation

Verse	Spelling in NT (1852)	Corresponding version in Almeida (1848[1681])
Matthew 22:30	*nem nun*	*nem*
Matthew 23:10	*nem não*	*nem*
Luke 3:14	*nem não*	*nem*
Luke 12:24	*nem nun*	*nem*
Luke 12:29	*nem não*	*e não*
Luke 16:26	*nem nun*	*nem tão pouco*
Luke 20:8	*nem eu não*	*nem tão pouco*
Acts 17:25	*nem nun*	*nem tão pouco*
Romans 2:28	*nem nun*	*nem*
Romans 6:13	*nem não*	*nem tão pouco*
Hebrews 4:13	*nem nun*	*e não*
Revelations 9:20	*nem nun*	*nem*

Nowhere in the Wesleyan Bible is there the slightest indication that *nem não / nem nun* might have the same semantic value as the Malaccan particle *nenang* (i.e. 'not yet'). In Sri Lanka Creole, this 'not yet' meaning is expressed by the construction *ainda nun* or by merging this form with the word that follows it, as in the contractions *ainda nemiste*, *ainda nue*, etc. While in relation to other similarities between the two creoles (e.g. the occurrence in both of the future-irrealis marker *lo*), accounts have usually pointed to the existence of a common pidgin ancestor or the migration of speakers, such explanations are harder to justify in the case of *nem não / nem nun* and *nenang*. Despite their phonetic similarity, there is also a significant semantic disjunction that suggests the forms developed independently of one another.[4]

3. *Nem não* in Portuguese

Any speculation as to the possible etymology of *nem não* as a carry-over from some pre-creole pidgin is unnecessary, in any event, given that the form can be traced directly to Portuguese, where it still exists with the same meaning as that found in Sri Lanka Creole, i.e. 'neither... nor'. In addition, however, it also occurs in Portuguese as a synonym of *nem sequer* or *nem mesmo* 'not even'. As Olímpio (2005: 965) points out, the use of the connector *nem sequer* in a coordinate construction introduces a scalar presupposition in which the negated element occupies the highest point of a pragmatic scale (Fauconnier 1975), so that all elements lower down the scale are automatically negated, whether they are named explicitly or not. The same happens in Spanish in relation to the intensifying adverb *siquiera* which, according to Santos Río (2003: 604), fulfils the same function as *aun*, *hasta* or *incluso*, albeit in a necessarily negative sense (*ni...*, *sin...*, *no...*), even in the absence of any explicitly negative particle. Vázquez & Fernández (*this volume*) classify this structure as a focal quantifier.

Again, as in Spanish, the scalar focus meaning of *nem sequer* becomes even more apparent when the conjunction *nem* is not used in a coordinative sense (e.g. *a obra nem sequer foi entregue* 'the job was not even signed off on'); in such cases, the intensity of the construction is preserved even in the absence of the adverb: *a obra nem foi entregue*. The same principle applies in relation to the use of *nem não* in non-coordinate constructions, with one condition: whereas *nem sequer* (and its shortened form, *nem*) can take scope over both predicates and noun phrases, *nem não* (the contracted form of *nem não sequer* and *nem sequer não*, both still found in the language, albeit infrequently) only have scope over predicates. Thus, in the Portuguese varieties where the usage exists, a sentence like *João nem não foi à festa* would be possible, but not the structure **nem não João foi à festa* (contrast this with the situation in Spanish; see (25), below). In the case of *nem sequer* or the shorter *nem* form, on the other hand, both structures are valid, though the pragmatic scale created in each instance is different.

Brazilian Portuguese provides a number of examples of *nem não*. In the novels of Guimarães Rosa, for instance, the author makes frequent use of the construction as a feature of the vernacular of his native Minas Gerais. It also occurs in work by writers from other parts of Brazil: Ricardo Guilherme Dicke, from Mato Grosso; Mário de Andrade, from São Paulo; José Rezende, from Sergipe, and many more. For a genuine oral source, the *Corpus do Português* (Davies & Ferreira 2006) contains a number of samples, collected from the coastal city of Recife.

In Brazil, therefore, the occurrence of *nem não* in the everyday language of the people would appear to obtain across a very extensive area of the country, whether in the sense of *tampoco* 'neither', as in (6); or 'not even', as in (7) (although the author of the English version of the sentence in this instance has opted for an alternative translation, with the emphasis on *quase* rather than *nem não*):

(6) Brazilian Portuguese (Guimarães Rosa 1954: vol.1, 49)
[…] *porque estavam supeditando escondido na cachaça o pó de uma raiz, que era para ela enfarar de beber, então, sem saber, perdia o vício. Mas **nem não** valia.*
'[…] because they were sneaking root powder into her rum, to make it taste horrible and so, without her realising, get her out of the habit. But that did not work either.'[5]

(7) Brazilian Portuguese (Andrade 1937 [1928]: 27)
*Essa eu caço! êle fez. E perseguiu a viada. Esta escapuliu facil mas o herói poude pegar o filhinho dela que **nem não** andava quasi,* […]
'I'll hunt this one! he said to himself and chased the doe, which easily escaped; but the hero was able to pick up the fawn, which could as yet scarcely walk […]'[6]

Given the frequency with which the particle occurs, it could not fail to receive a mention in at least a few linguistic works, albeit only incidentally, as in the following example whose primary purpose was not to illustrate the use of *nem não* but to demonstrate the erratic nature of grammatical agreement in colloquial language:

(8) Brazilian Portuguese (Azevedo 1989: 867)
*aqueles um? – eu **nem não** sei – acho que é umas laranjas*
'those ones? those – I don't even know – I guess they are oranges'

In contrast to Azevedo's chance allusion to the construction, Moraes (1984: 124) refers explicitly to *nem não* as one of a large variety of negative constructions used in spoken Brazilian Portuguese to express the meaning 'not even', which she exemplifies with the following series of equivalent phrases: *ele nem não veio / ele nem veio / ele nem sequer veio / ele sequer veio* 'he did not even come'.

Although the possibility exists, the use of *nem não* in Brazil is unlikely to be the result of an independent development, considering the construction is also found in other Portuguese-speaking countries, including Portugal itself. In Standard European Portuguese today, the form is generally only used in a certain type of contrastive construction, such as *nem sim nem não* 'it is and it isn't' or *nem gosta nem não gosta* 'he likes and he doesn't', the effect of which is usually to indicate an attitude of indifference towards something. The evidence from literature, however, of novelists whose writing imitates or recreates the ordinary language of the people, shows the presence of values similar to those found in Brazil: for example, Ascencio de Freitas, in (9), borrowing from the popular speech of Mozambique; or Idalecio Cação with that of Gândara in Figueira da Foz (Portugal), in (10), in an example that incorporates both of the meanings discussed so far: first as a scalar focus particle, and then as an emphatic negative coordinate.

(9) Mozambican Portuguese (Freitas 1979: 73)
*Que ele agora já sabia outro coisa, mas **nem não** sabia em antes que sabia* [...]
'For he now knew something else but before he did not even know that he knew'

(10) European Portuguese (Cação 1991: 49)
*E o pátio e o caminho de carro que dava para o pátio **nem não** tinham as rodadas do carro, marcas imprimidas, **nem não** podiam, porque estavam forrados com mato e tojo para a cama do gado.*
'And in the yard and on the roadway up to it there were not even cart tracks, the imprint of a wheel, nor could there be, for yard and roadway were overgrown with weeds and furze for the animals to bed down in'

The form is also documented in the CORDIAL-SIN (*Corpus dialectal para o estudo da sintaxe*) with a meaning similar to 'not even', in an example from the village of Alte, situated in the municipality of Loulé in the Algarve region of Portugal. The source is a statement from a 42-year-old illiterate man explaining the various operations required to make coal, complete with practical demonstration. For some reason, however, the demonstration fails; the ground stove fills with earth and the fire goes out:

(11) European Portuguese (CORDIAL-SIN)
*É que **nem não** pode arder, pois ela afogou-se com a terra.*
'Thing is, it can't even burn, since it [= the furnace] got all choked up with earth'

Looking at these isolated pockets of use in Portugal, the residual status of the construction in the language nowadays would appear to be the legacy of a much more widespread presence in the past, either with its scalar focus meaning or as a negative coordinate. Neither was its use confined to colloquial language (though this context was the most relevant in terms of the emergence of creole varieties): the construction is also found among the higher registers of the language, even as late as the 19th century. We have, for example, the evidence of Midosi (1832), the author of a contrastive grammar of English and Portuguese. In rule 28 of his grammar, he contrasts the admissibility of the double negative in Portuguese with it inadmissibility in English, and uses *nem não* in its negative coordinate sense to illustrate his point:

Duas negativas, referindo-se ao mesmo objecto, destroem a sua força, ou sam equivalentes a uma affirmativa; vg.: *Never no imitator grew up to his author*, Nunca *nenhum* imitador chegou ao original: *I never did repent of doing good, nor shall not now*, Eu nunca me arrependo de ter feito bem, nem *não* o farei agora. Deve dizer-se *never did any*, &., *nor shall I now*. (Midosi 1832: 179)[7]

On the basis of what we have seen so far, there would seem to be a strong case to support a direct derivation from peninsular Portuguese of both Sri Lanka Creole *nem não* and the Malaccan particle *nenang*.

4. *Ni no* in the Spanish creole languages of the Philippines

As explained in the introduction, the etymology proposed here for the particle *nenang* is based on the existence in Chabacano of the negator *ni no*, a straightforward case of derivation from the Spanish construction *ni no*, which in Portuguese takes the form of *nem não*. *Ni no* or *nino* occurs both in the creole languages of Mindanao (Zamboangueño and its variant forms in Basilan and Cotabato[8]) and in Ternateño, spoken in the village of Ternate in the Manila Bay area of the island of Luzon.[9] The behaviour and meaning of the form in each case is not identical, however.

4.1 Zamboangueño

The expression of negation in Zamboangueño follows the model of the rest of the Visayan languages used in the Central Philippines (called after the collective name for the islands in that part of the archipelago). In the Visayan languages, the basic particle of negation varies depending on the aspect of the action: perfective aspect takes one negative particle, while imperfective aspect and contemplated (or anticipated) aspect (marking the irrealis mood) use a different one. In the case of perfective aspect, the form is *walâ* or *warâ*, depending on the language. The same particle is also used as a negator in existential and possessive clauses ('there is not', 'he does not have'), regardless of their aspectual value. The imperfective and contemplated aspects use the negator *dílì / dì*, or *índì / híndì*, depending on the variety. It is also used to express negative prohibition or exhortation (although, in Cebuano, the latter function can also be served by the negative auxiliary *ayaw*, instead of the more usual verbal negator, *dílì*). In negative clauses, the agent of the verb tends to move to a pre-verbal position from its more common location after the verb, repositioning it between the negator and the aspect marker.

The behaviour of Zamboangueño fits with this model for the most part, the only exception being that in expressions of negative prohibition and exhortation it uses the Spanish negative particle *no* instead of the negative marker for imperfective and contemplated aspect, *hende* [ˈhende / ˈhinde], sometimes pronounced with a glottal catch at the end and less commonly with the accent on the final syllable.

Table 2. Zamboangueño particles of negation

Irrealis mood	Realis mood		Existential negator	Negative prohibition, exhortation
Contemplated aspect	Imperfective aspect	Perfective aspect		
hende	hende (or no, with modal verbs)	nuay	nuay	no

The imperfective negator *hénde* may have originated in the Kinaray-a form *híndì*, or its variant in Hiligaynon, *índì*.[10] The perfective negator *nuay* [nu'aị] is the result of a relexification from Spanish of the negative existential construction *no hay*, motivated by its partial phonetic and structural resemblance to equivalent forms in the Visayan languages. The negator *walâ / warâ*, used in perfective-aspect and existential clauses in the Visayan languages, also occurs as the shortened variant *wa*. In colloquial language, it often acquires a type of ligature, *y*: *walay, waray, way*. It was most likely the shortest of these ligatured forms, namely *way*, that became identified with the Spanish existential negator *no hay*, based on the significant phonetic similarity between them; this, in turn, would be what gave rise to the existential negator present in Chabacano: *nuay*. As observed earlier, however, in the Visayan languages (in contrast to the varieties spoken in Luzon), the existential negator is the same as the perfective negator. As the process advanced, therefore, and *no hay* (> *nuay*) was established as the equivalent form in Spanish for the Visayan existential negator *way*, the new Chabacano form appropriated all the values corresponding to the indigenous particle, in what would appear to be a typical example of relexification, under the model proposed by Lefebvre (1998).

For the imperative mood and negative exhortation, Zamboangueño usually employs the Spanish negator *no*. This represents the only structural difference between it and the Visayan languages, which, as noted above, use the same negator for these functions as they do to mark the imperfective and contemplated aspects. Chabacano also tends to use *no* before modal verbs (*no puede, no quiere*) but not in any kind of systematic way, at least not in the modern form of the language.[11]

For negative coordination, Zamboangueño uses the Spanish copulative conjunction *ni*, the same for predicate clauses as for non-verbal phrases. If the coordination is between two predicate clauses, the *ni* form is followed directly by the corresponding positive aspect marker, as illustrated in (12) – the translation of which is from the 1982 New King James Version (NKJV):

(12) Zamboanga Chabacano   (NTC 2001: Matthew 6:26)
Mira ustedes con el maga pajaro na cielo: Gendeh[12] *sila ta siembra ni ta cosecha, ni ta pone maga grano na tambobo*
'Look at the birds of the air, for they neither sow nor reap nor gather into barns'

There is, in addition, the option of a double-negative form: *ni no / ni hende*, for imperfective and contemplated aspect, and *ni nuay*, for perfective aspect and existential negation. As in Portuguese, the effect of the repeated negative is to give extra emphasis to the negative additive marker in a coordinated structure ('neither'), or to produce a scalar focus meaning ('not even'), particularly when it is not used in a coordinating context.

The oldest evidence we have for any of these forms relates to the perfective aspect marker *ni nuay*. The particle occurs in the first known example of Mindanao Chabacano, written in the Polloc area (not far from Cotabato City) prior to 1884; the text was published in Fernández (2012).[13] The example found there reads as follows:

(13) Cotabato Chabacano   (ms., before 1884)
ni no hay [=*nwai*] *quitá   puede ensugá palay*
nor NEG.PFV 1PL.INCL puede secar   arroz
'We have not even been able to dry rice'

The most likely meaning here is the intensified scalar focus value 'not even', given that the information offered prior to this sentence is: 'there is nothing to eat for dinner, he already knows the kind of rain we've been having recently'.[14] In (14), on the other hand, where the particle appears as part of a coordinate series, the meaning expressed is 'neither… nor' – translation taken from NKJV (1982):

(14) Zamboanga Chabacano   (NTC 2001: Matthew 10:24)
Noay   discípulo mas importante pa   que   con
NEG.EXST disciple   more important   still than OBL
*su maestro, **ni   noay**   tamen muchacho*
his teacher   nor NEG.EXST   also   servant
mas   importante pa   que   con   su amo.
more important   still than OBL his master
'A disciple is not above his teacher, nor a servant above his master'

Unlike *nenang* in Kristang, the Zamboangueño variants *ni no* and *ni nuay* are regularly used before modal and stative verbs, which are precisely those that retain the Spanish negator *no* in their imperfective and contemplated aspects (as mentioned before). The sentence in (15) illustrates with an example from Zamboangueño folklore the frequent occurrence of *ni no* in combination with the verb *sabe* 'to know':

(15) Zamboanga Chabacano   (Cuartocruz 1992:68)
    Las   dalagas   de estos días [...] ***ni-no***
    DET   young-women of these days   not-even
    sabe man cociná
    know   also cook
    'Young women these days [...] do *not even* know yet how to cook'

In addition to its appearance in connection with modal verbs, examples have also been found of *ni no* combining with the verbs *considerá, llamá, juzgá* and others; in general, though, in their imperfective and contemplated aspects, the *ni hende* combination of the Spanish negative coordinator and the native negative particle is more common.

4.2 Ternateño

Just as the negation patterns in Zamboangueño correspond in general to the model of the Visayan languages, so in Ternateño negation takes its lead from the patterns in Tagalog. In Tagalog, the negator remains the same (*hindî*) irrespective of the grammatical aspect of the verb, and the same is true of Ternateño, which employs the Spanish negator *no*. Tagalog has a separate negator for existential and possessive clauses (*walâ*), and so does Ternateño: *nuay*, the same as in Zamboangueño. The correspondence of patterns is not a perfect one, nevertheless (see Sippola 2011a), with Ternateño diverging from Tagalog in relation to the expression of negative prohibition and exhortation, where it uses the general negator *no* in contrast to the auxiliary verb form *huwag* used in modern-day Tagalog.[15]

As in Zamboangueño, Ternateño also uses the double or reinforced negative particle *nino, ni nuay*; however, its meaning in Ternateño is different from those found in Zamboangueño. There is not a single recorded instance in Ternateño of the particle being used to express a negative additive value ('neither') or any obvious cases where the meaning could be interpreted in the sense of 'not even', though a few come close, as in (16d). The most common meaning appears to be that of an intensified *no* (Sippola 2011a, 2011b): a firmer, more resounding negative, frequently used in the context of establishing an opposition between a negative and the affirmative sentence that precedes or follows it.

In a recently published collection of legends and stories from Ternate and the surrounding area (Nigoza 2007), we find several examples of *nino* that provide a useful illustration of the different types of meaning and contexts of use exhibited by the particle:

(16) Ternate Chabacano (Nigoza 2007: 10, 11, 48, 47)
   a. *Ta   pensa eli   cung   di   sigui   eli*
      PFV think 3SG if [Tag. *kung*] CTPL follow 3SG
      cung   su   Tata   o   niño [= *ninó*]
      OBL[16] her father or NEG
      'She was wondering whether to obey her father or not [to]'[17]
   b. *Quel manga jente   ta   espanta como eli   mucho*
      DET   PL   person IPFV amaze   how   3SG a.lot.of
      ta   coge   pero quel lotro   pescador niño [= *ninó*]
      IPFV catch but   DET   others   fisher   NEG
      'The people were amazed for he caught great loads [of fish] and the others did not'
   c. *Bueno el   ugali   de este viejo.   Nino*
      good   DET character   of this old man   NEG
      ruing   y   pirme   abierto mano
      greedy and always   open   hand
      'He had a fine character, this old man. He was not at all greedy and always open-handed'
   d. *Ni   ung vez, nino lotru a   miedo cung*
      nor once   NEG   3SG   PFV fear   OBL
      quel manga pirata […]
      DET   PL   pirate
      'Not [even?] once did those pirates make them feel afraid'

The story in (16a) concerns a girl living under the strict control of her father. One day, as the girl is taking part in a traditional *karakol* dance procession, she is discovered by her father and ordered back to the house. The text refers to the girl's hesitation as to whether to obey him or not (*ninó*). This kind of contrastive disjunction is one of the contexts in which *nino* may be used in Ternateño. The sentence in (16b) also uses *nino* in a contrastive sense, but in a different way from the example before it: in this instance, a position of success is set up in contrast to one of failure. In (16c), an opposition is established between two adjectival predicates: the first, a negative statement; the second, a positive one. We gain a better sense of the meaning if the particle is translated using a strongly reinforced negative: 'he was *not at all* greedy *in the slightest*'. The last example is the only one in which a scalar focus value may be attributed to *nino*: 'not once, even', 'not even once'; nonetheless, it could also be interpreted as a case of emphatic negation. Sippola (2011b) points out that in absolute negative responses, a double-negative is commonly used in preference to a simple negative, which is in keeping with the particle's fundamental classification as an emphatic marker.

The same intensifying function is also performed by the existential negator, as in the following example:

(17) Ternate Chabacano (Sippola 2011a: 331)
Ninwáy   akí   landsláid
EMPH.NEG.EXST here   landslide
'No, there are no landslides here'

Overall, the use of *nino / ninuay* in Ternateño presents more differences than similarities from its occurrence in the creoles of Mindanao. It is worth asking, however, if the evidence upon which this finding is based is extensive enough to provide a comprehensive record of all the semantic and contextual variations possible in this regard. Diachronically speaking, the answer is clearly that it is not. Therefore we cannot discount the possibility that the similarities between these two varieties may have been greater in the past.

5. *Ni no* in Spanish

In parallel with the case of *nem não* in modern European Portuguese, today the particle *ni no* survives only residually in peninsular Spanish, in the form of the contrastive expression of indifference, *ni sí ni no* and other constructions akin to it. In various parts of Latin America, on the other hand (and, again, analogous to the situation in Portuguese), the use of the particle is still quite common. It occurs very frequently in Paraguay, for example, as in the case of (18):

(18) Paraguayan Spanish (<www.lanacion.com.py>: 6 October, 2010)
*Pai Ovispo **ni no** sabía manejar una pobre iglesia*
'Pai Ovispo couldn't even run a small church'

The example is taken from a comment left on a digital newspaper, in reference to the president of Paraguay, Fernando Lugo, who prior to becoming one of the country's leading political figures was once a bishop. The meaning suggested by the context has a clear scalar value, since what the writer is really contesting is the president's ability to run the country.

Ni no features abundantly in the spoken language of the country people depicted in the novels of the Paraguayan writer Casola, as in the extract below, where the construction is used in both its senses: 'not even' and, immediately after that, 'neither / nor':

(19) Paraguayan Spanish (Casola 1984: 134)
[…] *pero ese día, como te digo, uno se despertó asustado porque **ni no** cantaba los pájaro **ni no** se escucha ese ruido que siempre viene del bosque cuando está por amanecer y no había ni viento, nada*
'[…] but that day, I'll tell you now, it's a fright a man woke up with, for there wasn't [even] a bird to be heard singing nor that sound you do get coming out of the forest as the day is starting to break, and there was no wind, nothing'

Paraguay is not the only country where the particle is common: there are also documented examples of its use in texts from Mexico, Chile, Argentina, Peru, Cuba and Venezuela, though there may be further undiscovered cases from elsewhere in Latin America. The sentence in (20), taken from a Chilean website, is an unambiguous example of *ni no* used to express a scalar focus meaning. The comment refers to Pee Wee, an American singer of Hispanic origin, still relatively unknown in Chile:

(20) Chilean Spanish (<foro.univision.com>: 8 May, 2009)
Soy de Chile y aca su musica no llega, asiqe[18] ***ni no*** *sabia qien era*
'I'm from Chile and his music isn't played here, so I didn't even know who he was'

Also from Chile is the Facebook group whose title appears in (21), this time in a clear illustration of the negative additive function of *ni no*, as the founder of the group himself explains in his description of the online collective:

(21) Chilean Spanish
(<http://www.facebook.com/group.php?gid=2990842 2977>: 8 May, 2011)
*Si NO me acuerdo, no susedió **ni NO** lo hice.*
Description: *Exacto, tan simple como qe no me acuerdo quiere desir qe no sucedio ni tampoco lo hice, quedo claro?*
'If I don't remember, it didn't happen and I didn't do it.
Description: Precisely, simple fact being that since I don't remember means it didn't happen and I didn't do it either, got that?'

As in the case of its Portuguese counterpart, these uses of *ni no* were already present in peninsular Spanish prior to and during the period in which the language was being transplanted to America. It seems pointless, therefore, to try and speculate about the independent development of the particle in the New World, which in any case would necessitate a macro-explanation capable of encompassing multiple regions and the very different population histories of each. The most logical analysis is to assume that the construction arrived in America at the hands of the Spanish colonists and there in the Americas it remained, while back in

Spain it was gradually lost over time. The same process occurred in relation to *vos* and countless other features of the language which are now considered peculiar to American Spanish. This explanation is reinforced by the fact that the particle existed not only in Spanish, but in all the Romance languages of the Iberian Peninsula, including Portuguese, as discussed above. There are documented cases of the form from 1200 onwards in Leonese, Aragonese, Castilian and, also, Catalan (where it appears, for example, in the 13th-century works of Ramon Llull).

Up to now, all the examples of *ni no* as a scalar focus particle have been independent clauses, while examples of its use as a negative additive marker have tended to appear in the form of a coordinated construction. This is not to say, however, that a scalar focus meaning is incompatible with coordinated clauses, as the following example from the mid-16th century clearly illustrates:

> (22) Peninsular Spanish   (quoted in various sources: mid-16th century)
> [...] *y con todo esto, no halló gente en toda España para llevar, **ni no** pudo juntar 300 hombres*
> 'in spite of all this, in all of Spain he could not find people to bring, not even 300 men could he raise'

The author of the text is a member of the expedition headed by Álvaro de Bazán who, despite the temporary lifting of the restriction barring descendants of Jews and Arabs from making the journey to America, "could not even raise 300 men".

The form was still in use in Spain in the 17th century, as evidenced by Rojas Zorrilla, in whose play, *Peligrar en los Remedios*, it appears with a negative additive value.

No cases of the particle have been identified in peninsular Spanish for either the 18th or the 19th century, beyond the established contrastive case of *ni sí ni no*. Conversely, there is evidence of more recent usage. It may be that the form has been reincorporated into the language as a consequence of immigration from Latin America; or that in certain parts of the country it never actually disappeared, but simply failed to register in writing until the eruption of online social media and networking sites. The example in (23) is extracted from a notice published in Madrid, advertising an iPod for sale that has 'not even' been removed from its box:

> (23) Peninsular Spanish   (< madrid.campusanuncios.com >: 10 August, 2010)
> [...] *No a sido usado nunca, **ni no** a sido sacado de la caja*
> 'Never been used, never even been taken out of its box'

The advertisement in this instance could have been placed by an immigrant to the country from Latin America; in other cases, though, the evidence seems to indicate the survival and currency of the particle within Spain. In a blog based somewhere in the Canary Islands, one contributor issues the following warning in relation to a highly addictive computer game, available to download over the internet:

(24) Canarian Spanish
(<novelero.blogspot.com/2005/01/ni-no-lo-toques.html>: 3 January, 2011)
¡Ni no lo toques!
'Don't even touch it!' / 'Don't even think about touching it!'

The blog entry runs to several paragraphs, nowhere in the course of which is there the slightest indication that its author might be of Latin American extraction, either from the content of the entry or based on the linguistic markers present in the text. More than likely, therefore, the particle has simply always been a feature of the vernacular spoken in that part of the archipelago.

Yet this is not the only surprise my internet researches have uncovered. Earlier on in this study, in reference to Portuguese, it was observed that the use of *nem não* as a scalar focus construction is restricted to verbal predicates, in contrast to *nem sequer*, which can combine with any type of phrase. It seemed almost certain that the same would be true of Spanish; certain, that is, until the following text came to light on the website for the town council of Morón de la Frontera in the province of Seville. The sentence is taken from an enthusiastic report by the head of the publications department regarding the recent successes of the local basketball team:

(25) Peninsular Spanish   (<www.guiamoron.com>: 3 January, 2011)
Ni no los más optimistas esperaban una victoria de 25 puntos y un despliegue de juego tan brillante
'Not even the most optimistic supporters were expecting a victory margin of 25 points and such a brilliant sporting display'

One could dismiss the occurrence as some kind of unintended error, overlooked following a revision of the sentence at some point. However, it should be noted that the writing in the rest of the report shows great care and attention to detail, as well as being fluid in style and error-free. While there is no study on Morón de la Frontera vernacular to corroborate the hypothesis, by teasing out the thread of this initial example and thereby uncovering more examples of the particle on other pages and websites with links to Morón, it has become clear that the scalar focus use of *ni no* in combination with verbal predicates is still alive and well in the vernacular of this locality of southern Spain. Why, therefore, should the same not be true of noun phrases, as it is for *ni siquiera*?[19]

Evidence has also been found in a number of areas of fossilised uses of *ni no*, the meaning of which remains uncertain. Uruguayans use the phrase *¡que no ni* *no!* in the form of a cheer (in connection, for example, with a football team or a singer), or as an expression of satisfaction at accomplishing an important goal of some kind. In Spain, the work of the Santander writer, José María de Pereda (1833–1906), a novelist in the realist tradition typical of his generation, reproduces a usage peculiar to the native population of the mountains of Cantabria: after cursing something or somebody, the speaker adds the phrase *nunca ni no*, possibly as a way of attenuating the effect of the imprecation, or to guard against its coming true

6. Discussion

It is still difficult to understand how this construction can be present in all the Romance languages of the Iberian Peninsula (and in several beyond its borders, as we will see presently), considering that in Latin the construction *nec non / neque non* has an affirmative meaning. Any grammar or dictionary will tell us that in Latin the use of two negatives together transforms a negation into a positive statement: *non nemo* is equivalent to 'not nobody' and hence means 'somebody'; the same applies to *non nullus* 'some', *non nihil* 'something', *non nunquam* 'sometimes', etc. In this way, the phrase *nec non et* became a standard form of expressing positive addition, and not solely among the upper registers of the language. Take, for example, the account left by the 4th-century Spanish nun, Sr Egeria, of her pilgrimage to the Holy Places of Palestine. Egeria's narrative is written in Vulgar Latin and is otherwise quite devoid of any stylistic merit; throughout, though, *nec non et* and *nec non etiam et* are used systematically, with *atque* and other forms of positive addition all but completely absent.

It is likely, nevertheless, that, colloquially, *nec non* was also used to signify negative addition; alternatively, it may be that it was reinterpreted as such by the inhabitants of the Romanic world during the assimilation process. It was in this sense that it was sometimes used in Church Latin during the medieval period, as (26) illustrates with an example taken from the Council of Lerida in 1229. Following a lengthy catalogue of the clothing and ornaments that priests should not wear, the dictate adds:

(26) Latin (Tejada y Ramiro 1854: 333)[20]
[…] : **nec non** manicis, nec sotularibus consutitiis vel rostratis, […] non utantur
'neither bracelets wear, nor finely embroidered or pointed-toe shoes'

This negative value was the interpretation of the double-particle that prevailed in many of the Romanic countries. To my knowledge, nobody has ever conducted a comparative study of the construction across the different Romance varieties.

We do know for certain, though, that it was present in Provençal[21] and Tuscan,[22] in French, where it still forms part of the sequence *ni non plus* 'not either', and in all of the Iberian languages. The Spanish constructions *tampoco* and *ni siquiera* are actually relatively late grammaticalisations of complex expressions; while that process was being completed, and later on as the new forms started to become more prevalent, *ni no* and *nem não* were still commonly used to express these meanings. It is no surprise at all, therefore, to find them now present in some of the Ibero-Romance-based creole languages.

Evidence presented earlier on in this paper showed that *nem não* was still in use in Sri Lanka Creole around the middle of the 19th century, where its value was that of a negative additive particle. Additional testimony from the one-time Vicar-General of Ceylon, Monsignor Dalgado, shows that, in his view, the revised version of O Novo Testamento de Nosso Senhor (1852) from which this paper's examples are drawn is a faithful representation of the language as he knew it.

The case of Malacca Creole is less straightforward. Firstly, in present-day Malacca Creole, there is no conjunction to signify negative coordination, neither derivations of *nem* nor transformations from any other source. The idea of negative coordination is expressed by the repetition of the negation in both parts of the construction, linked by the connector particle *ku* or by their occurrence adjacent to one another, as in (27):

(27) Malacca Creole Portuguese   (Baxter, p.c. May 2011)
      agora ja   nus nté   mas   pesi, nté
      now   already we   NEG.have more fish NEG.have
      más   kambrang pun
      more   prawn   also
      'there are neither fish nor prawns left anymore'

It is very likely, nonetheless, that in the past the use of *nem* in Kristang would have been more prominent than it has since become. Indeed, residues of the particle can still be found in set phrases such as *neng abor neng sabor* 'tasteless' (Baxter & de Silva 2004: 45).

In Sri Lanka Creole, on the other hand, evidence of the use of *nem* abounds, not alone in O Novo Testamento (NT 1852), but also from other documentary sources and in the popular phraseology of the language: it is also found, for instance, in the samples presented by Dalgado (1900) and in the *cantigas* (traditional ballads) of Batticaloa, collected by Nevill (c. 1890). Furthermore, there is the possibility that forms such as *ninqueré*, *ninquería* are derivations of *nem*; and not, as Dalgado appears to suggest, of dialectal variants of *não*.

Beyond Sri Lanka, there is evidence of the presence of the conjunction *nem* in a number of other Asian Portuguese creoles, for example Norteiro (Dalgado

1906), Tugu Creole (Schuchardt 1890), etc. The fact that it does not exist in Kristang thus represents an exception to the overall pattern, an anomaly which may have been influenced by the absence of a conjunctive particle for this specific purpose in Malay as well, where the meaning is expressed using a positive coordinate construction combined with a single negator (Mintz 1994: 57).

The second difficulty, as mentioned in the introduction, is the difference in meaning between *nenang* ('not yet') and the various uses of *nem não* in Portuguese and Sri Lanka Creole. This discrepancy does not, however, seem a compelling enough reason to assume that *nenang* derived from *ainda/inda não*. In Baxter's own work (1988: 138), in fact, we find incidental data which could be interpreted as proof against the hypothesis of an origin in *inda não*, on the basis that sometimes *nenang* co-occurs with *ňda / inda*, as in (28) below:

(28) Malacca Creole Portuguese (Baxter 1988: 140)
 eli   **nenáng**   bai   kasa   (inda)
 3SG   NEG.PFV   go   house   yet
 'He hadn't/hasn't/won't have gone home yet'

The use of both forms simultaneously places an additional complication alongside the existing phonetic difficulty, for if *nenang* were a derivation of *ainda não*, representing the same 'not yet' meaning as its originator, it is unclear what purpose would be served by supplementing the sentence with a further *ainda* 'still'. The addition might make sense if, for instance, the *nenang* particle in (28) had a different meaning from 'not yet'. If there were some way to prove for certain that *nenang* sometimes has (or used to have, at least) a meaning comparable to 'not even', all the other difficulties would disappear: the phonetic issues, the semantic disjunction, and also the unexplained co-occurrence of the particle with *ňda/ inda*. The risk of pleonasm is avoided by virtue of the fact that 'ni siquiera' and 'todavía' are combinable components, since each construction contains its own distinct semantic value. The combinations *ainda nem sequer* and *nem sequer ainda* are commonly found across all registers of Portuguese.

Could it be, therefore, that the meaning of the example in (28) should be 'he had *not even* (= *nenang*) gone home *yet* (= *inda*)'? Without access to the full context of the sentence, it is impossible to say for certain; neither, however, can the possibility be dismissed. If my hypothesis is correct, it could account for one peculiarity pointed out to me by Baxter (p.c. May 2011): the first examples he recorded of *nenang* were collected from elderly women, in whose statements *nenang* is almost always used in combination with *inda*, the latter occurring at the end of the sentence. The question is: did they mean 'not yet' or 'not even... yet'? And, if not the latter, is it possible instead that the example in (28) might have been used in that sense in the past?

Baxter (1990, 1996) contended that a perfective negative marker evolved across all the Portuguese creole languages of the Pacific and Western Pacific Rim regions, evidence of which was to be found not alone in the Malacca Creole particle *nenang / nenang inda*, but also in *nunka inda* (Bidau), *inda nunka* (Macau) and *indana* (Tugu). This marker, he suggested, was "probably inspired by the functional parallel of Malay *belum*" (1996: 303). Even at that stage, however, he admitted that it was unclear to what extent the particle had been grammaticalised in Bidau creole (*nunka inda*) and in Macau (*inda nunka*). Today, he has also come to favour a more open classification for *nenang* than that of a 'perfective negator', in view of the adverbial values the form continues to exhibit in certain contexts (Baxter, p.c. June 2011).

A separate issue regarding *nenang* – assuming that it is derived from *nem não* – is whether the modification of its original meaning came about as result of the force of attraction exerted by the Malay particle *belum*. The degree of grammaticalisation of *belum* as a perfective verbal negator is itself a matter of debate: at times, its behaviour can make it seem more like an adverb than a grammaticalised perfective negator, as in the expression *saya belum yakin* 'I'm not sure yet'. Analyses of Malay usually depict the particle as the negative counterpart of the affirmative perfective form *sudah* 'already', yet even in the case of *sudah* it is uncertain to what extent the form has been grammaticalised as an aspect marker (the same doubt applies to the progressive markers *tengah* and *sedang*). This may be why when Goddard (2005) refers to the aspectual values of these adverbs, he prefaces his comments with the note of caution, "it is said that…".

There is also the possibility that, among the various other meanings expressed by Malay *belum*, the form may at some stage have been used in the sense of 'not even', which in certain contexts is not dissimilar to 'not yet'. Consider, for example, the following lines from the poem *Bidasari*, written around 1800 or a little earlier:

(29) Malay   (anonymous, *circa* 1800; English translation by Millie 2004: 64)
     Belum berapa hari lagi di sini / Dendamnya tiada tertahani
     'She has been here not even a few days / can he not bear her absence?'

If *nenang* were a derivation of the particle *nem não*, as this study claims, it follows that in the past *nenang* would have shared some of the semantic values of its originator form in Portuguese (as occurred in the case of Sri Lanka Creole). Although that situation might not have lasted (as the value of *nenang* changed, bringing it closer in meaning to *belum*), it is still conceivable that residual traces of earlier meaning may still persist in certain contexts. The example in (28) has been suggested as one instance of these vestigial uses, to which may be added any other co-occurrence of *nenang* and *inda* (a juxtaposition which would not be possible if the sole and unequivocal meaning of the former was 'not yet').

There are certain contexts in Portuguese (and also in Spanish) in which the difference in semantic value between *ainda não* and *nem sequer* is neutralised, transforming the forms into interchangeable equivalents of one another. The behaviour of the particles in such cases may be the key to understanding how speakers of Kristang came to assimilate one of the forms, having started off with the other. Consider the example below, featuring both possible constructions:

(30) Portuguese (own knowledge)
Ainda não / nem sequer tinham soado as 12 badaladas quando chegou o capitão
'It was not yet / not even 12 when the Captain arrived'

The above example is a slightly modified version of its counterpart in Kristang, collected by Baxter in the course of a *matá kantiga* session, recorded in 1981 and later transcribed by Jackson:

(31) Malacca Creole Portuguese (Jackson 2007: 323)
Nenang abri dozi ora / Kaptang ja chega pidi
NEG.PFV open twelve hour captain PFV arrive ask
'it was not yet / not even 12 / the Captain came to ask'

The lines are taken from an unfinished stanza, performed as part of a foreshortened rendition of the song.[23] It makes no difference in this instance whether we interpret *nenang* as 'not yet' or 'not even'; both are compatible with the context of the verse (Baxter, p.c. April 2011). That being the case, what we may be witnessing is a point of intersection between the Portuguese form *nem não*, *nenang* in Kristang and Malay *belum*, which, in turn, may reflect an early stage in the development of this particle and the moment in the evolution of *nenang* when it began to move closer to *belum*.

Regarding the occurrence of the form among the Spanish creole languages of the Philippines, the only question requiring further explanation is why the particle displays a different meaning in Ternateño from its variant in Zamboangueño. Both derived originally from the Spanish form *ni no*, albeit in their own different ways and at separate times. My analysis in this respect differs from the idea propagated by Whinnom (1956) that all the Philippine creoles are derived from a relexification into Spanish of an earlier Portuguese-based creole thought to have been used in the Moluccan island of Ternate. In a number of previous studies, I have discussed the difficulties involved, from both the linguistic and the historical points of view, in attempting to link all the Spanish-based creoles of the Philippines to a single source. The only case about which Whinnom may have been right is Ternateño, but even that is debatable.[24] In my opinion, therefore, it seems highly unlikely that *nino* should be relexification of *nem não*, rather than a continuation of the Spanish form *ni no*.

The case of *ni no / ni nuay* in Zamboangueño is straightforward, since both forms are used to express identical meanings to those documented in the peninsular and Latin American Spanish variants of the form. In Ternateño, on the other hand, those values appear to be absent, judging by the examples available and by the sole grammatical analysis of the language to date (Sippola 2011a, 2011b). The value of the particle in Ternateño would seem, instead, to be one of emphatic negation, whether used in a contrastive sense, as in (16a) and (16b); in single-clause constructions, as in (16c), (16d) and (17); or in negative response clauses.

In Spanish, the use of *ni no* in single-clause constructions (as in (18) and (24)) is not unusual. In the present survey, examples of this occurrence have been glossed with the construction 'not even'; equally, however, these sentences could be interpreted as cases of emphatic negation, bearing in mind the value of 'not even' as a negative intensifier: 'I had no idea at all', in (18); and 'Don't touch it in any way at all / under any circumstance!', in (24). This leads us quite easily to the use of *nino* as a form of emphatic negation, which I would argue is the meaning expressed by the construction in statements of negative response, as in (32):

(32) Ternate Chabacano (Sippola, p.c. September 2010)
Bo   ba   ay   mayor?
you   Q   DET   elder
Nino   pa,   kwatru   yo
EMPH.NEG   PRT   four   I
'Are you the eldest? – No, I'm the fourth'

This is not, in my opinion, a case of straightforward negation, but a resounding, intensified negative along the lines of 'no way!', 'no chance!', 'not at all!': not only is the respondent not the eldest, he is very far from it. The question we have to ask is: would the respondent still have used *nino* if he were a second son instead of a fourth? A more complete analysis of the particle will be necessary in order to reveal it in all its subtleties and variations of meaning.

The last remaining task in this analysis is to assess what role, if any, the indigenous languages of the Philippines have played in the formation of these values of *ni no* and *ni nuay* in Chabacano, considering that all the forms' uses in this respect are ultimately traceable to Spanish.

Unlike Malay, most, if not all the languages of the Philippines contain a conjunctive particle with a negative coordinate value; not indigenously, but as a result of the importation of *ni* from Spanish. This loan word is found in all the languages that came into close contact with Spanish, including those that became substrate and adstrate varieties of the new creole formations (Tagalog, Hiligaynon, Cebuano, according to what part of the region they were in). Tagalog most likely adopted the particle in the 18th century, on the basis that it appears in a dictionary from that period, though it is only referenced indirectly. Prior to this, the model used was similar to Malay, with the copulative conjunction *at* used to link the two negative clauses, the same as if two positive elements were being coordinated: 'not A and not B'. In order to give a phrase the additional sense of 'neither', with a slight emphasis on the negation of the second of the two negative clauses, the second negative element is supplemented by the adverb *din* 'as well'. To stress both negatives equally, the postpositional emphasizing particle *man* is added to both sides of the coordinate construction ([...] *man* [...] *man*); in the case of two predicative negative clauses, the resulting meaning is equivalent to the negative correlative construction 'neither... nor'.[25]

We do not know how quickly the borrowing took hold but its progress cannot have been very rapid, in view of one obvious complication obstructing its path: the fact that *ni* is also used as a genitive marker in relation to personal nouns, in addition to the positive coordinate value the particle has when it occurs between people's names or between a pronoun and a personal noun: *kami ni María* (Lit. 'we of María'), for example, translates as 'María and I'. Despite this difficulty, in their entry for the Spanish adverb *tampoco*, Noceda & Sanlúcar (1754) offer the following example: *Yaon man, po. Yaon pa man, po. Ni yaon man, po. Ni yaon pa man, po* (Lit. 'neither that as well also, Sir'). Abella (1869) features coordinated nominal phrases with the structure 'there is no X and no (*ni*) Y'. And, finally, Demond (1935: 136) includes *ni* among a list of adverbs of negation: "*ni ni, hindí hindí,* neither nor".

There are two formats in Tagalog for expressing the scalar value 'not even'. The first and possibly the older configuration consists of the addition of the particle *man* to the negator, followed by the particle *lang* ('only, just'): for example, "*hindí man lang tumawag si John* 'John didn't even call'" (De Vos 2010: 322). The second schema, described in the reference grammar compiled by Schachter & Otanes (1972), involves the loan particle *ni* from Spanish, stripped of all coordinate value and supplemented by a second negator. The examples supplied by Schachter & Otanes are all of the type ([NEG] ... *ni* [...]) or, alternatively, where the order of the elements in the construction is inverted and *ni* is found at the beginning instead: (*ni* ...*ay* [NEG] [...]). Neither of these is likely to have been the model from which *ni no* in Chabacano derived its 'not even' meaning, however. While the first of the two structures does exist in Chabacano in the form of *no... ni*, it is also common in Spanish, where there is no question of its frequency in constructions such as *no sale ni gota* 'there isn't even a drop out of it', *no quiero ni verte de-lan-te* 'I don't even want to look at you', etc. The fact that the form in Tagalog is only documented among more recent grammar indicates that here, too, the structure is most likely an import from the Spanish. The second type of construction – *ni*... [NEG] – does not exist in Chabacano.

Despite all this evidence in favour of a Spanish etymology, there is still a possibility that the model for *ni no / ni nuay* could have come from Tagalog or some one of the other Philippine languages. In Schachter & Otanes (1972), all the examples illustrating the use of negative constructions based on the particle *ni... ni* involve the coordination of the two noun phrases. However, *ni... ni* also occurs as a sentence coordinator, producing constructions along the lines of *ni hindi... ni hindi*, or *ni wala... ni wala* ('neither... nor'). These constructions are rarely featured in grammar books, with minor exceptions such as Bloomfield (1913) and L. English's *Tagalog-English Dictionary* (1986). Also possible are non-coordinate constructions involving the use of two consecutive negators, in which *ni* occurs initially; the meaning expressed is the scalar focus value 'not even'. This type of use is illustrated in (33), extracted from an interview between the president of the Philippines, Noynoy Aquino, and the author of a satirical blog. In response to criticism for posting a much younger photograph of himself on his Facebook page, the president proposes the following defence:

(33)   Tagalog [and English]
              (<professionalheckler.wordpress.com>: 9 September, 2010)
       *Besides, off the record huh..-**ni hindi** ko nga alam ang password sa Facebook account ko*
       'Besides, off the record, huh... I don't even know the password to my Facebook account'

Examples of the same double-negative structure are also found in relation to the other negative particles in Tagalog (*ni wala, ni huwag*), as well as their equivalents in Cebuano, Hiligaynon and Kinaray-a (the influence of Hiligaynon or Kinaray-a, or possibly both languages, was significant in the formation of the creole dialects of Mindanao). In Zamboangueño, in addition to *ni no*, the construction *ni hende* is also used. Of the two, *ni hende* is actually the more common, though this is hardly surprising considering that it is typically *hende* that combines with imperfective verb forms. In the following example, the construction appears with the *gendeh* spelling (translation from KJV 1611):

(34)   Zamboanga Chabacano   (NTC 2001: Mark 14: 68)
       No   conoce yo   con   ele   ni   **gendeh** yo   ta
       NEG   know   I   OBL   him   nor   NEG   I   IPFV
       entende   si   cosa   tu   ta   conversa
       understand PRT   what   you   IPFV   speak
       'I know not, neither understand I what thou sayest'

The form in this instance could also be translated in the sense of 'not even' (as, indeed, it has been in a number of Spanish versions of the text), even though this structure would have a coordinate value.

It is conceivable, therefore, that these constructions could have been introduced into Chabacano from other languages in the Philippines, though they in their turn would have acquired them as earlier borrowings from Spanish. Certainly, the hypothesis does not apply in the case of Ternateño, where the meaning of *nino / nuay* is distinct from that of *ni hindi / ni wala* in Tagalog. However, it also seems unlikely to prove to have been the case in relation to Zamboangueño, though the possibility cannot be discounted entirely. As the analysis of *hende* has shown, the provenance of the negator seems to be as a recent adoption from Hiligaynon or Kinaray-a, rather than a residue from some earlier layer of Tagalog as some authors have claimed (see, for example, Grant 2007: 175). The idea that *hende* is a recent introduction into Mindanao Chabacano, and that up to then *no* supplied the function of the imperfective aspect marker for all verbs, is also supported indirectly by the fact that nowadays *ni no* combines with ordinary verbs as well as modals (now virtually the only type of verb that still uses *no* as the basic negative imperfective aspect marker). The significance of this is uncertain, however: should it be interpreted as a sign of progress on the part of *ni no*, from modals to other verbs; or rather as a residue of a time when *no* was the standard negator for all verbs in the imperfective aspect? In the oldest recorded written use of Mindanao Chabacano, the verbal negator used is *no* (see note 10); *hende* appears only once in the text, as an adverbial negator. On balance, the evidence would seem to incline towards the second of the two explanations.

7. Conclusion

Vázquez & Fernández (*this volume*) show how the particle *maskí(n)*, though ultimately derived from Spanish *mas que*, in its Chabacano variant bears definite traces of its passage through the languages of the Philippines, in the form of the different uses presented by the indigenous concessive particles in those varieties. Although it does not answer definitively the question of how the particle arrived in Chabacano, it does strengthen the case for a Philippine origin: while the ultimate origin of *maski* is Spanish, the particle acquired at the creolisation stage was a modified version of the form, conditioned by the substrate languages that had incorporated it earlier. The case of *maski* thus presents a typical example of relexification, initiated not in Chabacano, but in the Philippine languages that adapted it first.

Could what happened in relation to *maski* also be true of *ni no*? The overall pattern of negation in Philippine Creole Spanish is structured along the same lines as the substrate languages (with a few negligible exceptions). However, in relation to the combination of *ni* in any of these contexts of negation, the behaviour of Zamboangueño seems to follow the model of Spanish *ni no*, with no trace of influence apparent from any of the Philippine varieties. Once again, it is difficult to say with certainty what path the double-negative form took: it is not impossible that the particle could have moved from Spanish to the Philippine languages, and from there on to Chabacano. It seems unlikely, nonetheless, given that the combined negative was not adopted until quite late among the languages of the Philippines and, particularly, in view of the fact that the traditional Philippine models of negative coordination and intensified scalar negation are not found in Chabacano.

The derivation path for the peculiar meaning of *nino* / *nuay* in Ternateño continues to defy any certain explanation: while a description in terms of a Spanish (or Portuguese) origin is not an impossibility, neither is there any obvious evidence pointing in that direction, much less to indicate the languages of the Philippines as the likely source. On the other hand, for those of us who do not hold with the idea of a single origin for all the Spanish creoles of the Philippines, here is one more piece of evidence in our favour.

My hypothesis regarding the provenance of *nenang* in Malacca creole identifies *nem não* as the origin, whether directly from colonial Portuguese or via some pidgin or creole ancestor variety. If this hypothesis were to prove correct, it would mean we were looking at an example of relexification from Malay. The critical question is whether the semantic possibilities contained in *nem não*, *nenang* and *belum* ever actually intersected. I have identified this point of intersection as the intensified scalar meaning of 'nem sequer', based on indications that at an earlier stage in their evolution both *belum* and *nenang* occurred with this meaning. The co-occurrence of *nenang* and *inda* (instances of which appear to decline in accordance with the decreasing ages of the sources) is one example of this earlier use.[26]

The use of *nem não* in Sri Lanka Creole is unproblematic, with the possible exception that there may have been additional uses of the particle in the past for which no evidence has been found. The function identified in the texts analysed ('neither') is well documented in Portuguese. The same structure is also found, in the senses of both 'neither' and 'not even', not alone in Portuguese and Spanish, but in all the Ibero-Romance languages and several others from the same family of Romanic languages.

Having encountered a substantial number of Spanish examples in the course of this survey, it is a source of perplexity to me that more attention has not been paid before now to this aspect of the language, absent even from some specific studies on the diachronic aspects of negation in Spanish. While the principal focus of this paper is creole languages, I hope it may also serve to throw some light into this small, unstudied corner of the history of Spanish and Portuguese.

Notes

*   I wish to express my thanks to the editors for all their helpful comments in relation to this paper. I especially wish to thank Alan Baxter, whose important data and even more significant support and discussions on the subject of *nenang* in Kristang, have been invaluable. Any remaining mistakes or errors are the fault of the author.

1.   This is clearly different from the clusters of nasals + plosives found in West African languages, which have traditionally been described as constituting a single phonological unit. The disyllabic status of these occasional sequences in Kristang is perceptible by ear, and could be easily confirmed with an acoustic analysis, such as suggested by one of the anonymous reviewers.

2.   One exception to the general rule of conservation in relation to the [nd] group is *grani*, a variant of *grandi* (Baxter & de Silva 2004: 26).

3.   'represents the literary creole of today [1900], no need having arisen between that time and this for a new, modified edition, since it is not wanting in any manner or respect [...] the syntax is wholly dialectal; the lexicon is strongly vernacular; the influence of English is almost imperceptible'.

4.   I thank one of the anonymous reviewers for reminding me of the possibility of an independent development (or reinforcement) of *nem não /nem nun* in Sri Lanka creole, as a consequence of the obligatory negative concord in the Indo-Portuguese creoles. From this perspective, the source for this construction could be purely local and syntactically motivated. This is, of course, a possibility, but one that I do not argue for. As I understand, in this creole there is no obligatory negative concord for the negative coordinator *nem* (in contrast with negative pronouns, which do require a verbal negator: *ninguem não* + V). *Nem* + V construction (like "*ellotros nunca bruffa nem sega*", Matthew 6:26) is much more frequently attested than *nem + não /num* + V (e.g. "[...] *nem não sega*"). In my opinion, a local development induced by the obligatory negative concord should have resulted in the progressive increase of the occurrence of *nem nun / nem não* but, in the present state of the language, this construction is no longer used (Ian Smith, pc. Octber 2010).

5.   The Spanish version of the text, published by Alfaguara, translates the last line here as "*pero no valía*" 'but that did not work'. This translation, however, fails to capture accurately the full meaning of *nem não* in the original where, for a whole page immediately prior to this, the subject has been the constant drunkenness of old Manitina. In my opinion, some kind of emphatic negation is needed, of the type *pero no valía de nada* 'but that did not work at all' or, better still, combining both aspects of the meaning: *pero tampoco valía de nada* 'but that did not work at all either'. Contrast this with the closing conversation of the novel:" – Uai, é duvida? – Nem não" (translated, correctly this time, using an emphatic negation: – "¡Uhé! ¿Hay discusión? – No, nada" ['– Well, anything else to say? – No, nothing']).

6.   English translation by Edward Arthur Goodland.

7.   'Two negatives, referring to the same object, destroy each other, or amount to an affirmative; e.g. *Never no imitator grew up to his author*, Nunca *nenhum* imitador chegou ao original:

I never did repent of doing good, nor shall not now, Eu nunca me arrependo de ter feito bem, nem *não* o farei agora. What it should say is *never did any*, &., *nor shall I now*.'

8. Or Cotabato, the variant featured systematically in 19th-century Spanish texts. This was also the variant available to Schuchardt, Pardo de Tavera, Blumentritt, and every other 19th-century scholar.

9. No evidence of the form's existence has been found in the Caviteño dialect or in the variant spoken at one time in Ermita and other parts of Manila.

10. The two languages are so closely related that they are not always thought of as separate varieties, with Kinaray-a treated as the variant of Hiligaynon spoken in the province of Antique and towns of Iloilo province, both in the island of Panay. Kinaray-a is not usually mentioned in connection with Chabacano, despite the very probable derivation from it of several aspects of the latter: not only the negative particle highlighted above, for example, but also its object and oblique personal pronoun forms *kanamon*, *kanaton* and *kaninyo*.

11. Similarly, in Kristang, the Portuguese negator *nang* (< *não*) is still used in imperative clauses (Baxter 1988:138). Modal verbs take a shortened form of the particle – *nté*, *mpodi*, etc. – in what may be a derivation of *ńgka* (Baxter 1988:139) or of *nang* (Baxter, p.c. June 2011).

12. *Gendeh* = *hende*. The spelling of the examples as they appear in the original sources has been maintained throughout.

13. Schuchardt had the text in his possession in January 1884 (see Fernández 2010b:269; 2012).

14. The same text contains another similar example: *ni no hay gane yo puede mirá* 'I could not even see him'.

15. The original meaning of *huwag* was 'to stop doing something because it is prohibited'. It was a full verb, with normal conjugated and derived forms. In San Buenaventura (1613), for instance, we find *hovagan*, *pahovagan*, *hinuhovagan*, *nahohovagan*, *pinahohovagan*, some of them with their respective arguments. Now that the grammaticalisation of *huwag* is all but complete, the form is generally classed as a particle of negation. For its treatment as an auxiliary verb, see Kroeger (1993:139ff).

16. This item is usually considered to be an ACC marker. The reasons for my disagreement have been explained elsewhere (see Fernández 2007, 2009 and 2010a).

17. Nigoza's book includes an English version of the legends collected there; however, they are not 'translations' as such from the Ternateño, but rather a retelling of the stories designed only to pass on their content. Nigoza's equivalents in English for the examples used here are as follows: (16a) "She had two things in mind – to obey or to disobey her father" (2007:20); (16b) "The natives were wondering of his luck in fishing for they could not catch many fish just like Esteban [= *eli*] did" (2007:23)'; (16c) "He was a kind-hearted old man. Because he was not greedy, he was open to all" (2007:50); (16d) "Indeed, the Mardicas were so brave and they showed their gallantry against the Moros not only once" (2007:54). There is no possibility of interpreting *niño* as the Spanish word for 'child'; this is but one of many typos that unfortunately plague the book, which was typewritten from the manuscript by someone with no knowledge of either Ternateño or Spanish.

18. As in the examples from Chabacano, the spelling in these Spanish examples has not been changed from their original sources.

19. Based on the clues offered by this first example, a number of analogous cases have since revealed themselves: *ni no los más peperos* ('not even the most convinced *Pepero* [supporter of the Partido Popular]'), taken from a message sent to a digital Spanish newspaper (*Libertad Digital*, 19 December, 2007); *ni no los más puristas* ('not even the greatest purists'), from a message sent from Catalunya to a blog based in Costa Rica ('El blog de Ramón Renacido', 18 April, 2011). Examples of noun phrases combining with the series *ni... ni no* have also been identified: in these instances, the two different meanings – 'neither' and 'not even' – seem to merge with one another, as in *ni el BCU ni no los Entes* ('neither the Uruguayan Central Bank nor [even] the smaller banks'), from a column by Jorge Jauri (<http://blogs.montevideo.com.uy/blognoticia_37286_1.html>: 3 January, 2011); and *ni los ilegales ni no los criminales* ('no illegal immigrants or [even] criminals either'), from a neo-Nazi website.

20. In the collection of canons compiled by Tejada y Ramiro (1854), the word *soturalibus* is used instead of *sotularibus*. Tejada y Ramiro translates the phrase as *ni gasten pulseras ni adornos con picos* ('neither bracelets nor pointed ornaments wear').

21. In Aimeric de Peguilhan, Peire Cardenal, Folquet de Marseille, etc.

22. In Dante, Bocaccio, Passavanti, etc.

23. In Jackson's partial transcription of Baxter's (1981) recording, the verses cited in (31) appear as part of the folk song *Jinggli Nona*. According to Baxter (p.c. May 2011), however, the lines are not found in any other version of the song, nor are they recorded in Rêgo (1941–1942). This performance was probably a mixture of different songs and even genres, therefore, Baxter adds, particularly in view of the fact that the performers involved were quite old and had not taken part in a singing competition of this type for many years. It would also account for why the stanza is incomplete.

24. Evidence to support this statement will be published shortly.

25. See, for example, Blake (1925:78). Today, this construction appears to have fallen into disuse, though it is possible that speakers may still understand its meaning.

26. Based on this discussion, Baxter (p.c. June 2011) suggests a timeline of relexification that begins with the co-existence of *nem não* 'not even' and *nem não + ainda* 'not even yet'. Later on, the meaning of *nem não + ainda* becomes restricted to 'not yet', owing to the convergence of meaning between Malay *belum* and the other particles mentioned above, brought about as a result of the situation of language contact obtaining at the time (Portuguese, Indo-Portuguese creole, Portuguese Pidigin, Malay as a first and a second language). Because *belum* occurs so frequently as 'not yet', it is this meaning that prevails. Finally, *inda* falls into disuse, leaving *nenang* as the predicate modifier, fulfilling the same function as *belum*.

References

Abella, V. M. 1869. *Vade-Mecum Filipino. Manual de la Conversación Familiar Español-Tagalog. Seguido de un Curioso Vocabulario de Modismos Manileños*. Manila: Imprenta de Amigos del País.

Almeida, J. F. 1848[1681]. *A Biblia Sagrada. Contendo o Velho e o Novo Testamento*. New York, NY: American Bible Society.

Andrade, M. 1937 [1928]. *Macunaíma: O Herói sem Nenhum Carácter*. 2nd ed. São Paulo: José Olympio.

Azevedo, M. M. 1989. Vernacular features in educated speech in Brazilian Portuguese. *Hispania* 72: 862–72.

Baxter, A. N. 1981. Kantiga: Tape sample of SE Asian Creole Portuguese songs and traditional story. Typescript.

Baxter, A. N. 1988. *A Grammar of Kristang (Malacca Creole Portuguese)* [Pacific Linguistics. Series B; no. 95]. Canberra: Pacific Linguistics.

Baxter, A. N. 1990. Notes on the creole Portuguese of Bidau, East Timor. *Journal of Pidgin and Creole Languages* 5 (1): 1–38.

Baxter, A. N. 1996. Portuguese and Creole Portuguese in the Pacific and Western Pacific rim. In *Atlas of Languages of Intercultural Communication in the Pacific, Asia, and the Americas*, II.1 Vol., eds. S. A. Wurm, P. Mühlhäusler and D. T. Tryon, 299–338. Berlin: Mouton de Gruyter.

Baxter, A. N., and P. de Silva, 2004. *A Dictionary of Kristang (Malacca Creole Portuguese), with an English-Kristang Finderlist*. Canberra: Pacific Linguistics/Australian National University.

Blake, F. R. 1925. *A Grammar of the Tagalog Language, the Chief Native Idiom of the Philippines*. New Haven, CT: American Oriental Society.

Bloomfield, L. 1913. *Tagalog Texts with Grammatical Analysis*. Urbana, IL: University of Illinois.

Cação, I. 1991. *Daqui Ouve-se o Mar*. Coimbra: Fora do Texto.

Casola, A. 1984. *La Catedral Sumergida*. Asunción: La República.

CORDIAL-SIN – Corpus dialectal para o estudo da sintaxe. http://www.clul.ul.pt/pt/recursos/225-description-cordial-sin-syntax-oriented-corpus-of-portuguese-dialects.

Cuartocruz, O. B., ed. 1992. *Zamboanga Chabacano Folk Literature*. Zamboanga City: Western Mindanao State University.

Dalgado, S. R. 1900. *Dialecto Indo-Português de Ceylão*. Lisboa: Imprensa Nacional.

Dalgado, S. R. 1906. Dialecto Indo-Português do Norte. *Revista Lusitana* 9: 142–66; 193–228.

Davies, M., and M. Ferreira. 2006. *Corpus do Português: 45 Million Words, 1300s–1900s*. http://www.corpusdoportugues.org.

Demond, H. V. S. D. 1935. *Elements of Tagalog Grammar*. Manila: Catholic Trade School.

De Vos, F. 2011. *Essential Tagalog Grammar: A Reference for Learners of Tagalog*. Brussels: Author's edition.

English, L. J. 1986. *Tagalog-English Dictionary*. Manila: National Book Store.

Fauconnier, G. 1975. Pragmatic scales and logical structure. *Linguistic Inquiry* 6 (3): 353–75.

Fernández, M. 2007. Sobre el origen de *con* en Chabacano. In *La Romania en Interacción: Entre Historia, Contacto y Política. Ensayos en Homenaje a Klaus Zimmermann*, eds. M. Schrader-Kniffki and L. Morgenthaler García, 457–478. Frankfurt: Vervuert & Madrid: Iberoamericana.

Fernández, M. 2009. La particula *con* y la organización de la transitividad en chabacano. In *La Lingüística como Reto Epistemológico y como Acción Social: Estudios Dedicados al Profesor Ángel López García con Ocasión de su Sexagésimo Aniversario*. 1 vols., eds. M. Veyrat et al., 423–436. Madrid: Arco Libros.

Fernández, M. 2010a. La partícula *con* en el chabacano, el español de Filipinas y el *taglish*. In *Actes du XXVe Congrès International de Linguistique et de Philologie Romanes*, eds. I. Tome, M. Iliescu, H. Siller-Runggaldier and P. Danler, 305–314. Berlin: de Gruyter.

Fernández, M. 2010b. Las cartas de Pardo de Tavera a Schuchardt sobre el "español de cocina" de las Islas Filipinas. *Grazer linguistische Studien* 74: 239–72.

Fernández, M. 2012. El Chabacano de Cotabato: el texto que Schuchardt no pudo utilizar. In *Cum Corde et in Nova Gramatica. Estudios Ofrecidos a Guillermo Rojo*, eds. T. Jimènez Juliá, Belén López Meirama, V. Vázguez Rozas and Alexandre Veiga, 295–313. Santiago de Compostela: Universidade de Santiago de Compostela.

Freitas, A. de. 1979. *E as Raiva Passa por Cima, Fica Engrossar um Silêncio*. Lisbon: Africa Editora.

Goddard, C. 2005. *The Languages of East and Southeast Asia. An Introduction*. Oxford: OUP.

Grant, A. 2007. Some aspects of NPs in Mindanao Chabacano. Structural and historical considerations. In *Noun Phrases in Creole Languages* [Creole Language Library 31], eds. M. Baptista and J. Guéron, 174–204. Amsterdam: John Benjamins.

Guimarães Rosa, J. 1954. *Corpo de Baile: Sete Novelas*. Rio de Janeiro: José Olympio.

Jackson, K. D. 2007. Singelle nona/Jinngli nona: A traveling Portuguese burgher muse. In *Re-exploring the Links: History and Constructed Histories Between Portugal and Sri Lanka*, ed. J. Flores, 299–323. Wiesbaden: Harrassowitz.

KJV. 1611. *King James Version (KJV Bible)*. London: Robert Barker. www.biblegateway.com/versions/King-James-Version-KJV-Bible.

Kroeger, P. 1993. *Phrase Structure and Grammatical Relations in Tagalog*. Stanford, CA: CSLI.

Lefebvre, C. 1998. *Creole Genesis and the Acquisition of Grammar: The case of Haitian Creole*. Cambridge: CUP.

Midosi, L. F. 1832. *A New Grammar of the Portuguese and English Languages*. London: A. A. de Beça.

Millie, J. 2004. *Bidasari: Jewel of Malay Muslim Culture*. Leiden: KITLV Press.

Mintz, M. W. 1994. *A Student's Grammar of Malay Indonesian*. Singapore: EPB Publishers.

Moraes, E. R. 1984. Alguns aspectos da variação sintática no português do Brasil. *Tempo Brasileiro* 78/79: 122–45.

Nevill, H. circa 1890. Manuscript of Sri Lanka Creole Portuguese Verses. British Library (London), Ms. 37538L.

Nigoza, E. 2007. *Bahra: The History, Legends, Customs and Traditions of Ternate, Cavite*. Cavite: Cavite Historical Society.

NKJV. 1982. *New King James Version (NKJV Bible)*. Nashville TE: Thomas Nelson. www.biblegateway.com/versions/New-King-James-Version-NKJV-Bible.

Noceda, J., and P. de Sanlúcar. 1754. *Vocabulario de la Lengua Tagala*. Manila: Imprenta de la Compañía de Jesús.

NT. 1852. *O Novo Testamento de Nossa Senhor e Salvador Jesus Christo Traduzido ne Indo-Portugueza*. Colombo: Officina de Missão Wesleyano.

NTC. 2001. *El Nuevo Testamento na Chabacano*. Quezon City: Claretian Publications.

Olímpio, A. M. 2005. O item *nem* no português brasileiro. *Estudos Lingüísticos* 34: 962–67.

Rêgo, A. S. 1941–1942. Apontamento para o estudo do dialecto português de Malaca. *Boletim Geral das Colónias* 17 (198): 3–78; 18 (203): 9–71; 18 (208): 3–88.

San Buenaventura, P. de Fr. 1613. *Vocabulario de Lengua Tagala*. Pila: Thomas Pinpin.

Santos Río, L. 2003. *Diccionario de Partículas*. Salamanca: Luso-Española de Ediciones.

Schachter, P., and Otanes, F. 1972. *Tagalog Reference Grammar*. Berkeley, CA: University of California.

Schuchardt, H. 1890. Kreolische Studien IX. Über das Malaioportugiesische von Batavia und Tugu. *Sitzungsberichte der Kaiserlichen Akademie der Wissenschaften zu Wien (philosophisch-historische Klasse)* 122 (9): 1–256.

Sippola, E. 2011a. Negation in Ternate Chabacano. In *Creoles, Their Substrates and Language Typology* [Typological Studies in Language 95], ed. C. Lefebvre, 325–336. Amsterdam: John Benjamins.

Sippola, E. 2011b. *Una Gramática Descriptiva del Chabacano de Ternate*. Helsinki: Unigrafia.

Tejada y Ramiro, J., ed. 1854. *Colección de Cánones y de Todos los Concilios de la Iglesia de España y de América*. Parte segunda (*Concilios del siglo IX en adelante*). 3 vols. Madrid: Santa Coloma y Peña, Impresores del Ministerio de comercio, Instrucción y Obras Públicas.

Whinnom, K. 1956. *Spanish Contact Vernaculars in the Philippine Islands*. Hong Kong: Hong Kong University Press/Oxford: OUP.

Bilug in Zamboangueño Chavacano
The genericization of a substrate numeral classifier*

Carl Rubino

This paper will report on a corpus-based study of the use of the numeral classifier *bilug* (*bilog*) in Zamboangueño Chavacano. Since *bilug* was borrowed as a numeral classifier from a neighboring indigenous Austronesian language Hiligaynon (Ilonggo), it is not present in other Ibero-Asian Creoles that do not share a Visayan substrate. I will offer a synchronic snapshot of the use of *bilug* in both Hiligaynon and Zamboangueño, showing that it has semantically evolved over time to disregard previous shape and animacy constraints. I will then introduce the Spanish equivalent, *pedaso*, which may be in the process of grammaticizing to take on the role of a second, more restricted numeral classifier in Zamboangueño.

1. Background on Zamboangueño Chavacano

Zamboangueño Chavacano is the most widely spoken of the Creole Spanish varieties spoken in the Philippines with 358,729 people claiming Zamboangueño Chavacano (ZAM) as their mother tongue in the 2000 Philippine census. This would make ZAM the largest Spanish Creole in the world. It is the dominant language of Zamboanga City and has a significant number of speakers on Basilan Island, as well as a community in Semporna (Sabah, Malaysia). Very closely related varieties of the language are also spoken in pockets on the island of Mindanao, most notably Cotabato and Davao. ZAM has a considerable presence in the media with regular radio and television programming from Zamboanga City.

Alternative theories have been posed to address the formative history of the Creole. Some scholars believe that Zamboangueño Creole developed from a military pidgin which evolved to meet the communicative needs of the residents of the Spanish military base at the tip of the Zamboanga Peninsula referred to as *Sambuwangan* by the local inhabitants (Whinnom 1956: 14). The base was established to protect the narrow strait between the Zamboanga Peninsula and Basilan

Island from the ravishing raids from hostile pirates and slave traders. Warren (1981:235) postulates the language evolved among fugitive slaves (*degradados*) who lived on the margins of the Spanish presidio as social outcasts (see also Worcester 1930:512). ZAM most likely creolized after 1719, when the Spanish reestablished a garrison composed of Mexican soldiers, and indigenous constituents speaking mostly Visayan languages and Tagalog where an earlier base, Fort Pilar, had been built in 1636 (Riego de Dios 1989). Cuatrocruz (1992:1) reports that among the workers who established Fort Pilar were 300 Spaniards and 1500 laborers from Iloilo who would have been speakers of Hiligaynon, a Visayan language spoken on the islands of Panay (Iloilo and Capiz provinces) and Negros (Negros Occidental province). This would explain why a substantial amount of lexical and grammatical substratal influence in ZAM hails from Hiligaynon, a language no longer spoken by the ZAM community.

There has been some speculation that ZAM did not develop as a true creole but as a natural common intersection of grammatically cognate Philippine languages which had already incorporated a substantial Spanish lexicon (Lipski 1992). It is undisputable that modern ZAM has not only incorporated many Visayan elements from the waves of Visayan immigration at the turn of the 20th century, but now continues to incorporate English and Tagalog structures, attributed to the increasing use of these two official languages in the school system and media.

Chavacano orthography has not been standardized, but many speakers prefer to write the language using Spanish-like conventions, and not with a phonemic alphabet. Santos (2010) spells Chavacano with either a Philippine phonemic or Spanish historic spelling depending on the etymology of the word, a model that is preferred by many Chavacano speakers.[1] However, this creates different phonetic values for letters like *j, h, g*. Moreover, since most speakers do not learn to speak, read or write standard Spanish, the inconsistencies in spelling are rampant, even in official publications. A council has been established to standardize the orthography, the *Consejo de Lenguaje Chabacano*, which will be invaluable for the latest Philippine program of mother tongue education (Barrios-Arnuco 2011). For purposes of this paper and to avoid the confusing use of the consonant symbols *c, f, j, q, v, x* and *z*, Chavacano examples will be rendered in a standardized fashion, following a phonetic model based on modern Tagalog orthography (Rubino 1998:8): *a, b, ch, d, e, g, h, i, k, l, m, n, ng* [ŋ], *o, p, r, s, t, u, w, y*. Word-medial glottal stop is sometimes written with a hyphen <-> or *h*. Word-final glottal stop is usually not represented orthographically, but when it is, the *h* is sometimes employed. For this paper, glottal stop in both these positions will be indicated by the apostrophe <'>.

2. Visayan numeral classifiers and *bilug*

Numeral classifiers are morphemes that appear next to a numeral or quantifier and usually serve to categorize the quantified noun in terms of animacy, shape, composition or another inherent property (for literature overview and examples, see Jones 1970, Aikhenvald 2000). They are relatively common in many languages of Southeast Asia, including some of the substrate languages of the Ibero-Asian Creoles, e.g. Malay, Hokkien and Cantonese.[2] The next three examples illustrate classifier use for Hokkien as spoken by the Malaysian diaspora, where the numeral classifier is determined for the most part by the semantic class of the referent noun and is used between the number and the quantified noun. Kao (1957) lists thirty two distinct numeral classifiers for Hokkien; we will exemplify here the classifiers *chiah* used for certain animals, *tè* used for tables, bowls and chairs, and *ki* used for lamps, umbrellas, and fans.

(1) Hokkien (Kao 1957: 3–6)
   a. *Chit chiah káu.*   *Chit chiah koe.*
      one CLF dog   one CLF chicken
      'one dog'   'one chicken'
   b. *Chit tè í.*   *Chit tè toh.*
      one CLF chair   one CLF table
      'one chair'   'one table'
   c. *Chit ki teng.*   *Chit ki khe sìn*
      one CLF lamp   one CLF fan
      'one lamp'   'one fan'

Unlike other Ibero-Asian Creoles such as Kristang and Macanese, ZAM developed from indigenous languages that had very impoverished or no numeral classifier system. However, ZAM is the only Ibero-Asian Creole that still productively employs a counting construction that was developed from a numeral classifier (*bilug*) at the time of contact.[3]

There is very little coverage of numeral classifiers in grammatical Philippine literature, perhaps because numeral classifiers do not exist in Tagalog, the most documented Philippine language, and their use in Hiligaynon is eroding and not mandatory. Spitz (2001) and Wolfenden (1971) offer no coverage of *bilug*. Zorc (1977: 100), in his ground breaking Visayan dialects monograph, does contain a section on the enumerative marker, but lists only one type: the particle *ka* that appears between numbers and some counted nouns in a majority of the Visayan languages in his study, and its counterpart *nak* which occurs in Bantuanon, Odionganon and Sibalenhon.

The best treatment of Visayan numeral classifiers appears in Kaufmann's Hiligaynon grammar (1916 [1939]: 80–87) where four are detailed by means of sentence translation exemplification. Kaufmann lists the following entries in his chapter on "Numerals and various other matters". They are not called classifiers, and the classifier *bóo* is missing from the discussion:

Isá ka bílug: one (a) (full piece, whole piece) piece of (bread, fruits, eggs, stones, cakes of soap, etc.)

Isá ka nahót: one (a) (full piece, whole piece) piece (of string, hair, wire, cable, rope, thread, etc.)

Isá ka pánid: one (a) (full piece, whole piece) piece (of cloth, paper, sheets, blankets, boards, planks or the like)

Isá ka báhin: one piece, share, part, division, section, portion (equal of or unequal of a whole number, amount, quantity, unit, etc.)

Further semantic analysis on the use of these classifiers is provided in Kaufmann's eighteen-thousand lemma 1934 Hiligaynon-English dictionary (*Kapulúngan Binisayá-Ininglís*), where three more classifiers can be found, *bóo* (with a variant *book*), *báto* (with a variant *bináto*), and *binángto* (with a variant *binántuk*). We will leave out the entry *bahin* here which does not serve to classify, but to divide:

bóo: a piece of anything roundish or cubical, applied to eggs, various kinds of fruit, stones, etc. (cf. *bílog, báto, bináto, book, binántuk, binángto*.)

binángto: A full grain; a piece or whole of something cubical in shape; full roast maize-grains that have not burst in the process of roasting.

báto: A complete thing, a whole, a piece of anything round or cubical in shape, as an egg, ball, coconut, brick, etc.

bílog: one piece or article, a whole, particularly applied to things that are roundish or cubical. (cf. *báto, bóo, book*)

nahót: Any oblong or lengthy piece of any material, that is comparatively slender for its length, as a pole, stick, bamboo, rope, fiber, ribbon, candle, etc.

pánid: Leaf, sheet, board (as of paper, cloth, wood, etc.).

Another semantic analysis of Visayan classifier use is given in Reyes et al. (1969) where three classifiers are discussed for the Aklanon language, another Visayan language spoken on the island of Panay. In their dictionary, Reyes et al. state that *bílog* was used as a unit of piece, e.g. *daywa-ng bílog nga manók* (TWO-LIG NCL LIG chicken) 'two chickens' and that *sambílog* 'one unit' was originally used for counting animate objects or people but now alternates with *sambato* 'one unit, piece'

(Reyes et al. 1969: 90, 95). Reyes et al. also cite a third classifier, *búo* which is used to count "food contained in breakable shells, like eggs or coconuts", e.g. *lima-ng búo-ng niyóg* (five-LIG NCL-LIG coconut) 'five coconuts'. The breakability analysis was not postulated by Kaufmann.

In Hiligaynon, classifiers are used after numbers and the enumerative linker *ka* which joins numerals, count interrogatives and count nouns:

(2) Hiligaynon (Rubino, field notes)
    a. *duhá ka bílog nga pahò*
       two NL NCL LIG mango
       'two mangoes'
    b. *Tátlo ka pánid nga sin*
       three NL sheet LIG galvanized iron
       'three sheets of galvanized iron'
    c. *isa ka nahot sang inyo buhok*
       one NL strand GEN 2PL.GEN hair
       'one strand of your hair.'
    d. *pila ka bulan*
       QNT NL moon/month
       'how many months; several months'

Hiligaynon classifiers can also be used in a nominal position to refer to previously mentioned or understood counted entities or with an interrogative:

(3) Hiligaynon (Rubino, field notes)
    a. *Bakal ka ánum ka bilog ánay.*
       buy 2SG six NL NCL please
       'Please buy six (pieces).'
    b. *Ang mga empleyado sádto lima lang ka bilog.*
       NOM PL employee formerly five only
       NL NCL
       'the employees formerly were only five.'
    c. *Indi' lámang isa ka bílog kundi lima gid.*
       NEG only one NL NCL but five in.fact
       'not just one but five.' (referent understood by addressee)
    d. *Pila ka bilog ang ímo upód?*
       how.many NL NCL NOM 2SG.GEN companion
       'How many people are you with?'

Of all the numeral classifiers in Hiligaynon, *bilog* is the most versatile. Aside from being used to refer to round objects, it can now be used for inanimate and animate objects, flat objects such as pictures, bread and beds, and long objects such as machine guns. A review of modern use will reveal that *bilog* may precede just about anything that can be individuated: decades, invitations, bombs, vehicles, cameras, trash cans, gowns, tables, walkers, bed sheets, chairs, televisions, stands, refrigerators, etc.

(4) Hiligaynon (Rubino, field notes)
    a. *Tatlo ka bilog nga íbos*
       three NL NCL LIG rolled.coconut.rice
       'three pieces of ibos rolls (rice and coconut milk rolls cooked in leaves)'
    b. *lima ka bilog nga maskara*
       five NL NCL LIG mask
       'five masks'
    c. *lima ka bilog nga litson.*
       five NL NCL LIG roast.pig
       'five roast pigs'
    d. *Isa lang ka bilog asawa ko pare.*
       one only NL NCL wife my buddy
       'I only have one wife, buddy.'

Motus (1971: 38), in her more modern dictionary of the language, characterizes the lexical entry *bílug* in Hiligaynon as a noun meaning 'piece' or 'part' and *bilúg* as a root for an adjective meaning 'round, circle'. No record of its use as a numeral classifier or quantifier is given in her dictionary. Her treatment of *batú* is similar, citing it as a noun meaning 'stone, rock, pebble'. Furthermore, no entries for the other classifiers *panid, nahút, binangto,* or *buo* appear in her dictionary.

Motus also neglects to mention another primary meaning of *bilúg* in her dictionary, that of entirety and solidity, an important meaning that may have contributed to the genericization of *bílug* in Hiligaynon.

(5) Hiligaynon (Rubino, field notes)
    a. *sa bilóg nga kapulo'an sang Pilipinas*
       LOC whole LIG islands GEN Philippines
       'in the entire Philippine archipelago'
    b. *sa bilóg nga kalibútan/pungsod*
       LOC whole LIG universe/nation
       'in the whole universe/nation'

3. *Bilug* in Modern ZAM

Numeral classifiers in Creole languages are quite rare. Aikhenvald (2000: 389) reports that most Creoles and pidgins have no numeral classifiers, even if they are surrounded by languages with numeral classifiers. A notable exception would be "classical" Chinese Pidgin English, or China Coast Pidgin, where the classifiers *pisi* 'piece' and *fɛlə* 'fellow' used to distinguish animate and inanimate counted nouns (Hall 1966: 109–110). Hall reports that this animacy distinction was lost in the modern pidgin, and *pisi* evolved into a meaningless numeral suffix, equivalent to the Chinese general numeral classifier *-ge*.

An exposition of a numeral classifier system in Chavacano has yet to appear in the literature. The only mentions of the word *bilug* available come from some dictionary entries in a subset of available Chavacano lexicons and a note in Camins (1989: 22) which specifies the origin of the word *bilug* to be Hiligaynon. Discussions of *bilug* do not appear in any grammatical descriptions of Chavacano.

Lexicographic coverage of *bilug* will reveal a variety of treatments. Riego de Dios (1989) specifies that *bilug* is a quantifier meaning 'piece' with the equivalents *pedaso* in Caviteño and *pedasu* in Ternateño Chavacano. This meaning carries over in Notre Dame University's (2002) Chabakano de Cotabato Dictionary. Chambers (2003: 131) cites *bilug* as a noun meaning 'article, item, piece' with no reference to its quantifier use. Likewise, Miravite et al. (2009) includes a 98 page glossary of ZAM in which *bilug* is treated as a noun meaning 'article, item or piece', followed by the subentry *por bilug* as an adverb meaning 'apiece'. The provenance of the term in this glossary is allegedly Visayan *bílug*. Santos (2010: 13) defines *bilug* in his dictionary as a noun meaning "a specified number of something, e.g. *dos bilug de mansanas* (two apples)." He also states in the definition that it is presently used for a specified number of people, but the examples he gives do not include the classifier *bilug*, e.g. *dos gente* (two people) or *dos kame* (we (exclusive) are two). *Bilug* does not appear at all in the 201 page dictionary of the *Komisyon sa Wikang Filipino* (2002).

Forman (1972) provides us with the most comprehensive grammatical description of ZAM to date but does not illustrate the use of *bilug* as a numeral classifier in his dissertation. This is unfortunate since there are dedicated sections on numbers, plurality and noun substitutes. He does, however, include the word in his glossary in three forms (*bíluk*, *bílug* and *bilog*) and gives it a nominal gloss as "(classifier) piece (or 'flock'?) used with birds". This definition should allude to its role as a counting lexeme. Lipski & Santoro (2007) also do not provide examples of *bilug* or numeral quantification in ZAM.

Camins (1989: 22) offers the most conclusive evidence that *bilug* is a numeral quantifier in ZAM. In his prescriptive handbook of ZAM, Camins states that *bilug* can be used when counting fruits and other objects, but not people. This would mirror its prescriptive, but not actual use in modern Hiligaynon. Camins provides an example of the use of *bilug* in a sentence counting two kinds of fruit. Since this is his only example illustrating the use of *bilug* in this way, the reader cannot assume that it is an optional particle.

The data used in this study originate from a corpus of Zamboangueño Chavacano compiled by the Ateneo de Zamboanga University in 2004 (henceforth *Ateneo de Zamboanga U. Corpus*). The corpus contains 3,357,714 words, derived from both printed and oral sources. Because ZAM orthography has yet to be standardized, the numeral classifier appeared in the corpus with five different spelling variants with the frequency of occurrence given in parentheses after each variant: *biluc* (46); *biluk* (284); *bilok* (134); *bilug* (500); and *bilog* (201). The variant *bilug* was chosen for the purposes of this paper because of its high occurrence in the corpus and also because it most closely matches the phonemic representation of the substrate languages.

The next two examples demonstrate how *bilug* may be used when counting coconuts, once with, and once without the genitive *de*. In the Ateneo de Zamboanga U. Corpus, *bilug* (with all its spelling variants) occurs 1165 times and *bilug de* occurs 29 times.

(6) Zamboangueño Chavacano (Camins 1989: 22)
Kompra dos bilug koko   pati un bilug kalabasa.
buy   two NCL coconut and one NCL   squash
'Buy two coconuts and one pumpkin.'

(7) Zamboangueño Chavacano (Ateneo de Zamboanga U. Corpus)
Si seko el malagkit raspa tu maga sinko
if dry ART sticky.rice scrape you PL   five
bilug de koko [...]
NCL of coconut
'If the sticky rice dries up, scrape five coconuts…'

The pre-nominal use of *bilug* is frequently attested in the corpus, but such a use is optional. Not all counted round objects are preceded by the classifier *bilug*.

(8) Zamboangueño Chavacano (Ateneo de Zamboanga U. Corpus)
 a. Un webos lang gad   kita nesesita.
    one egg   only EMPH INCL need
    'We only really need one egg.'
 b. ra ya usa kita dos webos, no?
    now PFV use INCL two egg   NEG
    'Wait, we use two eggs, right?'

c. *Aki ta usa kita dos bilug webos*
     here IPFV use INCL two NCL eggs
     'here we use two eggs.'
d. *[…] tres bilug duru kabesa*
           three NCL hard head
     '[…] three hard heads (stubborn people).'

Just as in Hiligaynon, *bilug* is often used after or in place of its nominal referent, relating back to a previously mentioned or understood entity.

(9) Zamboangueño Chavacano   (Ateneo de Zamboanga U. Corpus)
a. *ya chene yo butuy, tres bilug.*
     PFV have I boil three NCL
     'I had boils, three in total.'
b. *[…] el karabaw di amun kuatro bilug*
           NPM water buffalo GEN our four NCL
     '[…] (and) our water buffaloes (were) four in total.'
c. *Nuway man Neng, Mirinda lang un bilug.*
     not.have PRT Neng Mirinda only one NCL
     'There isn't any (7up), Neng, only Mirinda, one (bottle) left.'
d. *Manda dayun kon Aiza kaska dies bilug.*
     send immediately ACC Aiza shell ten NCL
     'Have Aiza shell ten (coconuts) right away.'
e. *Maskin aura gane' mira, tres bilug entohada pa.*
     though now even look three NCL desirous still
     'Even now, look, the three (women) are still obsessed.'
f. *Chene bilug chene, chene bilug nuway.*
     have NCL have have NCL NEG
     'There are some that have it and some that don't.'

Bilug is also commonly used following the quantitative interrogative *kuanto* 'how many, how much'. This use after the interrogative is not mandatory.

(10) Zamboangueño Chavacano   (Ateneo de Zamboanga U. Corpus)
a. *kuanto bilug ba ustedes man-ermana?*
     how.many NCL Q 2PL RECP-sister
     'How many sisters are you in total?'
b. *kuanto bilug baso, kuchara, […]?*
     how.many NCL glass fork
     'How many glasses, forks, […]?'

Bilug may be used in counting both singular and plural entities. Singular count entities may be expressed with or without the genitive *de*:

(11) Zamboangueño Chavacano   (Ateneo de Zamboanga U. Corpus)
   a. mas antes pa   gat   un   sen   un   bilug
       earlier more EMPH one cent one NCL
       biskocho antes   gayot.
       biscuit before EMPH
       'And even earlier one biscuit was one centavo.'
   b. Un   bilug de koko   chene siyete aguhero
       one NCL of coconut have seven holes
       'One coconut has seven holes.'

A cursory look at the uses of *bilug* in ZAM will immediately reveal that this classifier is not limited to counting only round objects such as fruit. It has been seen in the corpus to count a wide variety of objects such as tails, hotdogs, trees, cigarettes, nails, guns, candles, cans, glasses, rifles, 2x2 pieces of lumber, bamboo clips, books, M16 magazines and bananas:

(12) Zamboangueño Chavacano   (Ateneo de Zamboanga U. Corpus)
   a. el   un bilug saging tres peso
       ART one NCL banana three peso
       '(for) one banana, (it's) three pesos.'
   b. Maskin de un bilug de kandela sindi tu   kunel L.V.
       as.long of one NCL of candle light you ACC L.V
       'As long as you light one candle for La Virgen (the Virgen)'

Bilug can also be used with flat objects such as towels, books, pamphlets, bread, paper, prescriptions, articles of clothing, and blankets:

(13) Zamboangueño Chavacano   (Ateneo de Zamboanga U. Corpus)
   a. Chene kame kuanto bilug de papel
       have EXCL several NCL of paper
       para puede pone   nombre
       to   able.to put   name
       'We have several papers (you) can put (your) name on.'
   b. Bueno ya   puede yo ase nuebe bilug manta
       well PFV able I   make nine NCL   blanket
       'Well I was able to make nine blankets.'

It appears that, like in Hiligaynon, *bilug* is now used as a generic counting word that can apply to any item that needs to be individuated when counted. Examples from the corpus show how it may be used with machines, toilets, bakeries, viand, chamber pots, radios, baskets, padlocks, pillows, starfruit, corn cobs, carrots, houses, and vehicles (buses, jeeps, horse drawn carriages, etc.).

(14) Zamboangueño Chavacano　　　　(Ateneo de Zamboanga U. Corpus)
　a. *pati chene gad　kame mga makina de*
　　 also have EMPH EXCL PL machine of
　　 kusida, sa'is bilug
　　 sew　six　NCL
　　 'We also have sewing machines, six in all.'
　b. *Siempre　kasilyas un　bilug lang.*
　　 of.course toilet　one NCL only
　　 'Of course there was only one toilet (bathroom).'

Bilug also appears in the corpus as a seemingly legitimate classifier for both solids and liquids. However, with liquid referents, it generally refers to a single unit of quantity, typically to the container which is not always specified, e.g. bottles of milk, cans of beer:

(15) Zamboangueño Chavacano　　　　(Ateneo de Zamboanga U. Corpus)
　a. *[…] o　tres　bilug lang bir.*
　　 　 or　three　NCL　only beer
　　 '[…] or three beers.'
　b. *Kumpra kamo　dos dos　Tanduay dyutay*
　　 buy　　2PL　two two　Tanduay small
　　 ocho　dos bilug.
　　 eight　two NCL
　　 'Buy two, two small Tanduay (rum), two (cases?) of eight.'
　c. *Al maniana　aga　toma　tu　doble　dos*
　　 in morning　early drink 2SG double two
　　 bilug toma
　　 NCL　drink
　　 'In the morning, drink a double, drink two.'

Animacy is often a primary category for classifying nouns in languages with numeral classification systems. However, the ZAM classifier is also not limited to inanimate objects. There are numerous instances of *bilug* used with animals, both living and dead.

(16) Zamboangueño Chavacano　　　　(Ateneo de Zamboanga U. Corpus)
　a. *Ya　manda ba　　saka kabrito dos bilug*
　　 PFV　send EMPH　get goat　two NCL
　　 'He was already requested to get goats, two in total.'
　b. *Ase　sila mata sila singko bilug puerko.*
　　 make 3PL kill 3PL five　　NCL　pig
　　 'They had them kill five pigs.'

(16) c. Pehro lang chene, dos bilug pehro
       dog   only have two NCL dog
       '(I) only have dogs, two dogs.'
    d. Ta   dale komigo peskaw maskin dos bilug,
       IPFV give to.me   fish   though two NCL
       tres bilug gulay   na alegre tamen yo.
       three NCL   vegetable SUB happy also 1SG
       '(he) gives me fish, even only two (and) three vegetables and I'm happy.'
    e. Para sabroso tamen, na   meskla tu   na mongo
       for tasty   also   well mix   2SG   in mung
       krisido depe   itcha un bilug kamaron grande
       growth after throw one NCL   prawn   big
       'And to make it tasty, mix in the mung bean sprouts then throw in a large prawn.'

Additionally, humans, most notably kin terms and other common nouns referring to humans are also quantified with *bilug*. The kinterm *anak* 'child (offspring)' was immediately preposed by *bilug* 73 times in the corpus.

(17) Zamboangueño Chavacano   (Ateneo de Zamboanga U. Corpus)
    a. Dimiyo subrina tamen dos bilug, unu ombre,
       my   niece   also two NCL   one man
       unu muher.
       one woman
       'Also I have two 'nieces', one man and one woman.'
    b. El dimiyo maga ermana, tres bilug talya
       ART my   PL   sister three NCL   EXST
       na Manila sila.
       in Manila 3PL
       'Of my sisters, three are in Manila.'
    c. El   mi trabaho ta   kuida   bata' dos bilug
       ART my work   IPFV care.for child two NCL
       diamon   anak.
       EXCL.GEN child
       'My work is caring for children, two of our children.'
    d. Ta   dale pa   yo   pari, na este mes
       IPFV give still 1SG birth in this month
       de agosto dos bilug pa   yo ya   dale pari
       of August two NCL   still 1SG PFV give birth
       'I still deliver (babies as a midwife), in this month of August I even delivered two (babies).'

Since the use of *bilug* is not restricted by animacy or human vs. non-human constraints, the classifier may now also be used with pronouns:

(18) Zamboangueño Chavacano (Ateneo de Zamboanga U. Corpus)
    a. *Singko bilug sila man-ermano puru sila*
        five   NCL 3PL RECP-brother pure 3PL
        kwan maga military
        FIL   PL   military
        'They are five siblings, they are all… um… soldiers (military personnel).'
    b. *Hinde', el anak dituyu muher kuanto*
        no,   ART child 2SG.GEN female how.many
        bilug sila?
        NCL 3PL
        'No, how many daughters do you have?'
    c. *Maga kuanto bilug ustedes ta puede*
        PL   how.many NCL 2PL   IPFV can
        munta li?
        ride   there
        'How many of you can ride there?'
    d. *Katorse bilug lang kame ya gradua de*
        fourteen NCL only EXCL PFV graduate of
        diamon kurso gat
        our   course EMPH
        'Only fourteen of us (excl) graduated our course of study.'
    e. *Na, kuanto bilug ustedes ta resibi*
        well how.many NCL 2PL IPFV receive
        tres-sientos?
        three-hundred
        'Well, how many of you are receiving three hundred?'

Newell (2006: 129) reports in his dictionary entry of *bilug* in Romblomanon Visayan, that it is a measure noun used to indicate a specific or nonspecific number of individuals or units. He adds that it is commonly used for counting between one and ten, and uncommonly used for eleven and above. A restriction he places on this classifier in Romblomanon is that it is not used for things which are in pairs such as shoes, eyeglasses or slippers. However, in ZAM, *bilug* can be used for nouns that are inherently dual. In these cases, it serves to individualize the two entities making up the whole, or to treat each dual noun as one unit in counting.

(19) Zamboangueño Chavacano (Ateneo de Zamboanga U. Corpus)
    a. *Dos bilug gat sapatos dituyu?*
       two NCL EMPH shoes 2SG.GEN
       'You really have two (sets of) shoes?'
    b. [...] *ya tene anak dos bilug kambal*
       already have child two NCL twin
       '[...] he had twins (two twin children).'
    c. *kay chene pa yo dos bilug pantaloon*
       because have still I two NCL pants
       'because I still have two (pairs of) pants.'

One will notice the classifier *bilug* used with inherently non-singular entities. In this case, *bilug* is a mechanism to disassemble these entities into smaller components. With mass nouns, it may refer to single quantities:

(20) Zamboangueño Chavacano (Ateneo de Zamboanga U. Corpus)
    a. *Ni un bilug ropa nuay gat puede*
       NEG one NCL clothes NEG.PFV EMPH can
      liba aki
       bring here
       'she wasn't able to bring a single (article of) clothing here.'
    b. [...] *kay kuanto bilug lang el*
       because how.much NCL only ART
      pelo diila.
       hair 3SG.GEN
       '[...] (they wear wigs) because they have only a few (strands of) hair.'
    c. *ya kumpra dos bilug karne*
       PFV buy two NCL meat
       'he already bought two (chunks? of) meat.'

As the use of *bilug* genericized to encompass a wider semantic domain, it now can be used with abstract, non-tangible nouns to emphasize either individuation or completeness:

(21) Zamboangueño Chavacano (Ateneo de Zamboanga U. Corpus)
    a. [...] *y imbuelto el uno na singko*
       and involved ART one LOC five
      bilug insidente de lansiada na Baliwasan
       NCL incident of stabbing LOC Baliwasan
       '[...] and one was involved in five (separate) stabbing incidents in Baliwasan.'
    b. *un bilug istoria*
       one NCL story
       'one (complete) story.'

One seemingly restrictive environment where *bilug* does not occur in the corpus is with other measure words. The word *kilo* appears in the corpus 442 times, but never with the classifier *bilug*. It also does not appear with the quantifiers *manada*, *mucho* or *muchos* 'many, much':

(22) Zamboangueño Chavacano (Ateneo de Zamboanga U. Corpus)
   a. Manada del maga hoben-es ya tene
      many of PL young-PL PFV have
      el oportunidad experiensia mucho-s kosa.
      ART opportunity experience many-PL thing
      'Many young people had the opportunity to experience many things.'
   b. Basta chene lang kita maga un kilo
      as.long have just INCL PL one kilo
      sotanghon, chene un bilug manok o dos kilo karne
      noodles have one NCL chicken or two kilo meat
      'as long as we have one kilo of bean thread noodles, one chicken or two kilos of meat (for the birthday).'
   c. Nuway pa ase klaro si porke mucho
      NEG.EXST still CAUS clear SUB why many
      maga bata' ta sale na Sabah
      PL child IPFV leave LOC Sabah
      'It still has not been explained why many youth are leaving for Sabah.'

There was only one instance in the corpus where *bilug* co-occurs with the pluralizer *maga*. It was in a news report where a list of confiscated items formerly belonging to an alleged drug pusher was detailed. No instances of *maga* preceding the number and *bilug* were found, probably since *maga* before numbers expresses an approximate count:

(23) Zamboangueño Chavacano (Ateneo de Zamboanga U. Corpus)
      180 bilug maga bala del M16 rifle
      180 NCL PL bullet GEN M16 rifle
      '180 M16 rifle bullets'

There may be some resistance also to the use of *bilug* with some high frequency inherently plural nouns. The word *grupo* 'group' which occurred 1,100 times in the corpus was never quantified with *bilug*. Likewise, temporal nouns such as *semana(s)* 'week(s)', *mes(es)* 'month(s)', and *anyo(s)* 'year(s)' did not occur with *bilug*. In their plural form, *meses* occurred 633 times in the corpus and *anyos/años* occurred 508 times, all without *bilug*. Likewise, *beses* (or *veces*) 'times' occurred 523 times in the corpus and never quantified with *bilug*.

(24) Zamboangueño Chavacano (Ateneo de Zamboanga U. Corpus)
  a. *tres rebelde grupo ke ta   opera*
     three rebel   group SUB IPFV operate
     na Mindanao
     LOC Mindanao
     'three rebel groups operating in Mindanao'
  b. *maga tres   meses kaha' kame huntu   konel*
     PL   three months maybe EXCL together ACC
     disuyu nana
     3SG.GEN mother
     'We were with his mother probably for about three months.'
  c. *Muchos anyos ke ya   pasa, chene ta*
     many   years SUB PFV pass have IPFV
     keda un rey Mohametano. Chene le un
     stay one King Muslim   have 3SG one
     hija   si Barbara.
     daughter PA Barbara
     'Many years ago there was a Muslim King. He had a daughter Barbara.'
  d. *Dos beses le ya pari kambal*
     two times 3SG PFV birth twin
     'She gave birth to twins twice.'

Bilug also did not appear with the quantifier *kada* 'each'. The phrases *kada kada* or *kada unu* is used to further individuate, *kada unu persona* 'each person'.

(25) Zamboangueño Chavacano (Ateneo de Zamboanga U. Corpus)
  a. *Kada baun   chene sen*
     each provision have money
     'Each packed lunch had money.'
  b. *Singkuenta peso ya   kel kada hente*
     fifty   peso already DIST each person
     'The (entrance fee) is already fifty pesos each person.'

4. *Pedaso* in Modern ZAM

It is important to draw attention to another ZAM word *pedaso* ([*pidaso*] in Caviteño and Ermiteño), from the Spanish *pedazo* meaning 'piece.' This would be the closest Spanish-based equivalent to the Hiligaynon borrowing *bilug*. There were 204 uses of *pedaso* in the ZAM corpus which include eleven uses of the spelling variant *pedazo* and 193 uses of *pedaso*. As one would expect, *pedaso* most commonly occurs as a noun in the corpus meaning 'piece' or 'part'. This same meaning would carry over in the Tagalog-influenced varieties of Spanish Creole languages spoken in Luzon. No instances of *pedaso* as a numeral classifier appear in the literature for Caviteño or Ternateño, but the following two examples from Caviteño show how the word *pedaso* may both refer to a piece and a whole unit. The first is a Caviteño proverb with notable Tagalog syntax and lexicon, and the second is a transcription of a Caviteño conversation as posted on a blog:

(26) Caviteño Chavacano (<filipinokastila.tripod.com> (5 July, 2011))
Un   pedaso de kulpa bida ay   kapalit
one   piece   of fault life PRED exchange
'One little fault (piece of fault) merits a lifetime in exchange.'

(27) Caviteño Chavacano (<hablachabacano.blogspot.com> (5 July, 2011))
Kuanto   pedaso lang esi? Kunta tu.
how.many   piece just MED   count 2SG
'How many (lamp posts) are there? Count (them).'

The use of *pedaso/pidaso* to refer to both a piece and a unit or a whole entity in Caviteño mirrors not only the use of *bilug* in ZAM, but also the use of the Spanish loanword *piraso* in Tagalog, the major substrate for Caviteño.

(28) Tagalog (<austronauta.com> (5 July, 2011))
a. *Ilang   piraso ng pinggan ang   hinuhugasan*
   how.many:LIG   piece of plate   NOM   wash
   sa   Jollibee kada araw?
   LOC   Jollibee each day
   'How many plates are washed at Jollibee per day?'
b. *Apat na   piraso=ng galunggong   ang*
   four LIG piece=LIG mackerel.scad NOM
   kinain ko.
   ate   1SG.GEN
   'I ate four mackerel scad fish'

In the ZAM corpus, the majority of *pedaso* tokens represent the nominal meaning of 'piece'. A few common lexicalized collocations with this meaning are also prevalent, e.g. *pedaso-pedaso* 'in pieces' and *por pedaso* 'by the piece':

(29) Zamboangueño Chavacano (Ateneo de Zamboanga U. Corpus)
a. *Nuway   gayot ni   un   pedaso*
   NEG.EXST   EMPH neither one piece
   'There wasn't even one piece left.'

(29) b. *Kasa   dimiyo   este pedaso medya, el   medya*
house 1SG.GEN this piece half ART half
dimi   ermana.
1SG.GEN sister
'My house is this half (half piece), the other half belongs to my sister.'

c. *Ta   bende yo   pedaso-pedaso si   puede*
IPFV sell 1SG piece-piece if can
kel   paga.
DIST pay
'I'm selling (my land) piecemeal (by the piece) if he can pay.'

However, of the 204 uses of *pedaso* in the ZAM corpus, 26 of them appear to refer to entities in their entirety, not parts thereof. Counted nouns represented by *pedaso* in the corpus included soap, cows, meat, pistols, 100 peso bills, handheld radios, agricultural machinery, watches, pots, articles of clothing, donuts, blouses, computers, eggs, forms, and sticks. The difference in form between *bilug* and *pedaso* is that *pedaso* prefers to be followed by the genitive *de* 'of', while *bilug* can immediately precede the counted noun phrase:

(30) Zamboangueño Chavacano   (Ateneo de Zamboanga U. Corpus)

a. *ta   plania pa   sila omenta dos o   kuatro*
IPFV plan still 3PL increase two or four
pedaso de makina   para chekia el   umo
piece of machinery to check ART smoke(s)
'They are still planning to add two or four machines to check the smoke.'

b. *Incluido   na   perdision maga 50 pedaso de*
included LOC loss PL 50 piece of
relo   Rolex
watch Rolex
'Included in the loss (robbery) were fifty Rolex watches'

c. *Kabar chene tamen kita   tres   pedaso de webos*
then have also INCL three piece of eggs
'then we also have three eggs.'

d. *Chene era aunke un   pedaso de proyekto*
have CF even one piece of project
'there should be at least one project.'

e. *Maga pulis   ya   kompiska maga 90 pedaso de palo*
PL police PFV confiscate PL 90 piece of stick
'The police confiscated around 90 batons [...]'

Like its Austronesian equivalent *bilug*, the use of *pedaso* representing whole entities may be used anaphorically, referring to a previously mentioned or understood referent:

(31) Zamboangueño Chavacano (Ateneo de Zamboanga U. Corpus)
 a. El diila target de kada meses amo el
  ART their target of each months PRED ART
  kambiada de maga 200 pedaso.
  changing of PL 200 piece
  'Their monthly target was to change about 200 units (water pipes)'
 b. Kuanto pedaso tu ya kusi, amo kel
  how.many piece 2SG PFV sew PRED DIST
  kuntigo paga? Kuanto lang man akel
  2SG.ACC pay how.many just PRT DIST
  el pedaso?
  ART piece
  'How many pieces (costumes) did you sew, the ones you were paid for? How much was it per piece?'

The major distinguishing factor in the ZAM corpus between the use of *pedaso* and *bilug* when referring to whole entities is that the use of *pedaso* is more constrained. While *bilug* in modern ZAM can be used to refer to both animate and inanimate objects in their entirety, *pedaso* prefers inanimate entities, which include previously animate food sources, e.g. *pedaso de karne* 'piece/unit of meat'.

It can be argued that the concept of the classifier in ZAM now used to express individuation is so engrained in the minds of ZAM speakers that it is also observed in code-switching. The next three textual news examples from the corpus show how the English word "unit" is employed as a substitute loan filling the slot for the numeral classifier. Unlike *pedaso*, ZAM speakers using, reading or hearing the word "unit" will know that it is a borrowed word, from a language with which most speakers will have attained a certain level of fluency.

(32) Zamboangueño Chavacano (Ateneo de Zamboanga U. Corpus)
 a. [...] *parte del 40 units de computers ke ya*
   part of 40 units of computers that PFV
  promete dale el Kongresista Llobregat.
  promise give ART Congressperson Llobregat
  '[...] part of the 40 computers that Congresswoman Lobregat promised to give.'

(32) b. Ya   habla un opisyal ke   una bes ya
       PFV   speak one official that one time PFV
       anda estos maga soldao na   pueblo y
       went these PL   soldier LOC town   and
       ya   kompra na   un tienda lang sien units
       PFV   buy   LOC a store only 100 unit
       de cellular phone
       of cellular phone
       'An official said that these soldiers once went to town and bought just in a store one hundred cell phones.'

   c. El   report ta   dale mira ke   ilegal maga
      ART   report IPFV give see that illegal PL
      ocho nuebo tricycle units ke chene el prangkisa
      eight new   tricycle units that have ART franchise
      'The report shows that the eight new tricycles the franchise has are illegal.'

The innovative use of *pedaso* could be due to an ongoing decreolization process in ZAM, where a Spanish equivalent takes on the role of a substratal word or pattern of language use (Rubino 2008). Spanish is generally considered to be the prestige language, which is often reflected in written ZAM where Spanish patterns not present in the spoken Creole appear in formal textual representations of the language. Nevertheless, substratal phenomena continue to shape ZAM revealing well-defined Austronesian roots.

A corpus-based look at the second person singular nominative pronouns will reveal these forces at play. The second person singular Austronesian enclitic =ka is gaining ground over the more generally accepted 'standard Chavacano' pronouns. *Ka* is not included in the pronoun discussions of Forman (1972), Riego de Dios (1989), Chambers (2003) or Lipski & Santoro (2007). In the ZAM corpus, however, it is the third most widely used of six second person forms, with over one thousand counts. Second person pronouns used in the corpus in order of frequency were: *tu, bo, ka, vos/bos, uste(d)*, and *ebos*.

5. Conclusion

The modern corpus of ZAM demonstrates that the Visayan numeral noun classifier system has eroded in ZAM, mirroring its history in its substrate Visayan language Hiligaynon. The traditional use of *bilug* as a numeral classifier in ZAM is more often practiced by grammarians than linguistically naive speakers. However, this does not necessarily mean that numeral classification in ZAM has been completely lost. If *pedaso* grammaticizes into a bona-fide numeral classifier, it will undoubtedly compete with *bilug* and the role of each classifier will be negotiated functionally as the language evolves.

The modern synchronic ZAM corpus attests that the selectional restrictions of *pedaso* and *bilug* are already different. When used in counting, the substrate classifier *bilug* is the generic choice, while the Spanish loan *pedaso*, and most likely the English borrowing *unit* as well, are more restricted in their use. When representing single entities, *pedaso* and *unit* maintain their primary nominal meaning of 'piece' and are constrained to inanimate objects.

If ZAM continues to flourish as a vibrant language, time will tell whether the historic classifier *bilug* will be completely lost in a process of decreolization, or further refined to carry a classificatory function like at the time of its original borrowing.

Notes

*   Special thanks to Dr. Aireen Barrios, Hsiu-chuan Liao and Hugo Cardoso for comments on an earlier version of this paper and to Dr. Ike Escalante for his input on Caviteño. None of them are responsible for any mistakes herein.

1.   For the most part, a few exceptions will occur in Santos (2010), e.g. *selos* 'jealousy', *sampaloc* 'tamarind', *bené* 'come', *haquéca* 'fuss/headache', *güevos* 'testicles', *bucug* 'bone', *cuguítah* 'octopus', etc. Also the vowels *o* vs. *u* and *i* vs. *e* occur in the dictionary as phonetic renditions, not always following original Spanish spelling, e.g. *urgúllo* 'pride', *iscují* 'choose', *sipíllo* 'brush', etc.

2.   Hopper (1986: 310) mentions that for Malay, although dozens of classifiers might be listed in grammatical descriptions, only a few are used in practice. Only two classifiers *orang* (for people) and *buah* (for solid inanimate objects) make up 75% of the textual occurrences of classifiers in his written corpus.

3.   Classifiers may have played a role in other construction types for these languages. Baxter (2009: 287) and Pinharanda Nunes (2008: 17) assert that the incorporation of the indefinite article/number *unga* 'one' in the Macanese demonstrative *estunga* (that) may derive from substrate influence where a classifier is required in an analogous context, e.g. Macanese *est-unga linguazi* (this-one language), cf. Cantonese *g ó2-dī7 yàhn haih6* (that CLF person) 'those people' (data from Baxter 2009).

References

Aikhenvald, A. Y. 2000. *Classifiers: A Typology of Noun Categorization Devices*. Oxford: OUP.
Barrios-Arnuco, A. 2011. Zamboanga City goes multilingual. *Philippine Daily Inquirer*, 2 November 2011.
Baxter, A. N. 2009. O português em Macau: contacto e assimilação. In *Português em Contato*, ed. A. M. Carvalho, 277–312. Madrid-Frankfurt: Vervuert-Iberoamericana.
Camins, B. S. 1989. *Chabacano de Zamboanga Handbook*. Zamboanga City: First United Broadcasting Corporation.
Chambers, J. 2003. *English-Chabacano Dictionary*. Zamboanga: Ateneo de Zamboanga University.
Cuatrocruz, O. B. 1992. *Zamboanga Chabacano Folk Literature*. Zamboanga: Western Mindanao State University.
Forman, M. L. 1972. Zamboangueño Texts with Grammatical Analysis: A Study of Philippine Creole Spanish. PhD dissertation, Cornell University.
Hall, R. A. 1966. *Pidgin and Creole Languages*. Ithaca, NY: Cornell University Press.
Hopper, P. J. 1986. Discourse functions of classifiers in Malay. In *Noun Classes and Categorization* [Typological Studies in Language 7], ed. C. D. Craig, 309–325. Amsterdam: John Benjamins.
Jones, R. B. 1970. Classifier constructions in Southeast Asia. *Journal of the American Oriental Society* 90 (1): 1–12.
Kao, L. 1957. *The Comprehensive Book on Hokkien Dialect*. Singapore: Marican and Sons.
Kaufmann, J. 1916. *Principles of Visayan Grammar*. [Reprinted 1939]. Manila: Catholic Trade School.
Kaufmann, J. 1934. *Visayan-English Dictionary*. Iloilo, Philippines: LA Editorial.
Komisyon Sa Wikang Filipino. 2002. *Diksyunaryong Chabacano-Filipino-Ingles*. Manila: Komisyon sa Wikang Filipino.
Lipski, J. 1992. New thoughts on the origins of Zamboangueño (Philippine Creole Spanish). *Language Sciences* 14 (3): 197–231.
Lipski, J., and M. Santoro. 2007. Zamboangueño Creole Spanish. In *Comparative Creole Syntax* [Westminster Creolistics Series 7], eds. J. Holm and P. Patrick, 373–398. London: Battlebridge Press.
Miravite, R. M., U. C. N. Sanchez, D. S. Tardo, S. J. B. Viloria, and Fr. D. J. M. De Los Reyes. 2009. *Chavacano Reader*. ed. by R. David Zorc. Hyattsville MD: Dunwoody Press.
Motus, C. 1971. *Hiligaynon Dictionary*. Honolulu HI: University of Hawaii Press.
Newell, L. E. 2006. *Romblomanon Dictionary*. Manila: Linguistic Society of the Philippines.
Notre Dame University. 2002. *Chabakano de Cotabato Diksyonaryo*. Cotabato City, Philippines: Notre Dame University.
Pinharanda Nunes, M. 2008. Os demonstrativos em Maquista: Uma análise morfosintáctica contrastiva. *Papia* 18: 7–21.
Reyes, V., N. L. P. Prado, and R. D. P. Zorc. 1969. *A Study of the Aklanon Dialect*, Vol. 2: Dictionary. Kalibo, Aklan, Philippines: Public Domain.
Riego de Dios, M. I. O. 1989. *A Composite Dictionary of Philippine Creole Spanish (PCS)*. Manila: Linguistic Society of the Philippines and Summer Institute of Linguistics.
Rubino, C. 1998. *Tagalog (Pilipino) Standard Dictionary*. New York, NY: Hippocrene Books.

Rubino, C. 2008. Zamboangueño Chavacano and the potentive mode. In *Roots of Creole Structures: Weighing the Contribution of Substrates and Superstrates* [Creole Language Library 33], ed. S. Michaelis, 278–299. Amsterdam: John Benjamins.
Santos, R. A. 2010. *Chavacano de Zamboanga Compendio y Diccionario*. Zamboanga: Ateneo de Zamboanga University Press.
Spitz, W. L. 2001. *Hiligaynon/Ilonggo*. Munich: Lincom Europa.
Warren, J. F. 1981. *The Sulu Zone 1768–1898*. Singapore: Singapore University Press.
Whinnom, K. 1956. *Spanish Contact Vernaculars in the Philippine Islands*. Hong Kong: Hong Kong University Press.
Wolfenden, E. P. 1971. *Hiligaynon Reference Grammar*. Honolulu, HI: University of Hawaii Press.
Worcester, D. 1930. *The Philippines Past and Present*. New York, NY: Macmillan.
Zorc, R. D. P. 1977. *The Bisayan Dialects of the Philippines: Subgrouping and Reconstruction* [Pacific Linguistics Monograph Series C, Number 44.]. Canberra: Australian National University.

Portuguese pidgin and Chinese Pidgin English in the Canton trade*

Stephen Matthews and Michelle Li

While the role of Chinese Pidgin English in the Canton trade is relatively well-understood, the role of pidgin Portuguese has remained less clear. We review the evidence for the use of pidgin Portuguese and for its influence on the development of Chinese Pidgin English. There is evidence of gradual replacement of certain Portuguese lexical items by English ones. In addition, we propose that two puzzling grammatical properties of Chinese Pidgin English may be explained in terms of pidgin Portuguese influence: the use of *have* as locative copula, and the use of *for* as complementizer. Taken together, the lexical replacement and grammatical influence provide evidence for the role of pidgin Portuguese in the development of Chinese Pidgin English.

1. Introduction

In the course of European exploration and colonization in Africa, Asia, the Indian Ocean, the Atlantic and the Pacific Oceans, a considerable number of contact languages developed as means of interethnic communication. The Portuguese were the first Europeans to discover trade routes to the East and were among the first to trade slaves from West Africa to the Atlantic, and the large number of Portuguese-based contact languages around the world is testimony of the Portuguese seaborne empire. On account of the substantial similarities between European-lexified pidgins and creoles, historical relationships involving Portuguese have often been assumed. However, the extent of these links remains insufficiently understood. A case in point is the relationship of Chinese Pidgin English (CPE) and (pidgin) Portuguese. The Portuguese came into contact with the Chinese as early as the 16th century, while the close trade connections between Canton and Macau before the opening of Hong Kong as treaty port already entail considerable social and linguistic interactions between people of these two places (Coates 1966).

The China trade refers to trade between China and various European and American powers from the 16th century to the early 20th century. Canton (today's provincial capital Guangzhou) was the main port for the trade in its heyday. Macau, a small Portuguese enclave between 1555 and 1999, stands at the entrance to the Pearl River. It played an important role in the Canton trade. Canton and Macau remained closely connected before the opening of Hong Kong as a major entrepot. According to Van Dyke's (2005) detailed study on the Canton Trade during the period 1700–1845, upon arrival at the Pearl River, a foreign ship had to hire a pilot who probably spoke 'broken' Portuguese to lead her way from Macau to upriver Whampoa. The *línguas* ('linguists' or interpreters) also played an important role in the China trade. They were licensed middlemen between foreigners and Chinese officials, appointed by the Chinese authorities who regulated trade (Van Dyke 2005: 77). In the early 18th century these linguists mainly came from Macau, so they naturally spoke some form of Portuguese. Van Dyke (2005: 80–81) mentions accounts documenting the use of Portuguese as well as (pidgin) English in the early 18th century. However, most narratives from the 1730s onwards only mentioned use of 'English'. Therefore, Van Dyke speculates that pidgin English had replaced Portuguese as the lingua franca by the 1730s.

While CPE words such as *mandarin, savvy, pickenini*, etc. are well-known examples of Portuguese derived vocabulary, this paper aims to investigate a less explored area – the extent of Portuguese influence on CPE grammar. Two grammatical features from early CPE texts will be examined: (1) the use of *have* as copula and (2) the use of *for* as complementizer. A characteristic of these features is that they were attested primarily in early CPE sources. These functions of *have* and *for* were either replaced by other morphemes or disappeared. It will be shown that the copula *have* and the complementizer *for* have sources in Portuguese *ter* 'have' and *para* 'for' respectively, and that parallel structures are found in other Portuguese-lexified creoles.

2. The role of Portuguese in the China trade

The Portuguese were the first European power to establish a regular trading relationship with China. In the 16th century, Portuguese traders were allowed to anchor at Macau and subsequently they obtained the right to settle permanently in Macau by paying an annual rent of 500 taels to the Qing government. Effectively Macau became a Portuguese colony, although the situation was not recognized by treaty until 1887 (Cheng 1999: 1). Because of the strong economic interests of the Portuguese in Asia, Portuguese and some forms of pidgin Portuguese became the lingua franca for foreign trade.

The role of CPE in the China trade is well documented (see e.g. Baker & Mühlhäusler 1990, Bolton 2003, Ansaldo et al. 2010). Much less well understood is the role of Portuguese, including Macau Creole Portuguese and pidgin Portuguese. However it is clear that Portuguese, or Portuguese-lexified contact languages, played a role in the early development of CPE. The evidence includes:

a. reports of Portuguese (often qualified as 'broken') being used in the China trade;
b. Portuguese-derived elements in CPE, especially in the earlier years.

Many accounts note the need for knowledge of Portuguese in the context of the Canton Trade. For example, Morse says:

> The first requirement for a supercargo on English ships trading to China was a knowledge of Portuguese. For over a century from 1517, the only European ships to visit China were Portuguese, and their language became, to some extent, the lingua franca of the coast. ... The English, coming first in 1637, could have no communication with the Chinese except through an interpreter who knew both Portuguese and Chinese. This was sometimes an untrustworthy Chinese who could speak Portuguese; sometimes a low-class Portuguese who could speak Chinese; more commonly a half-breed, who had acquired the one tongue from his father, and the other from his mother. ... From about 1715 the Chinese merchants themselves learned the curious patois known as 'pidgin English', which thereafter became the lingua franca of the China trade. (Morse 1926, I: 66–67)

Van Dyke's study of the Canton trade also notes the role of Portuguese in the early Canton trade:

> [...] foreigners depended on the Chinese... In the early years of trade, many of these lower-level Chinese came from Macao, where they had learned enough Portuguese to communicate with foreigners... The Chinese in Macao... often worked their lives there and, if they learned any foreign language at all, it was Portuguese. Thus, when going to Canton to trade, all foreigners needed to do was to make sure they had a Portuguese speaker aboard [...]   (Van Dyke 2005: 9)

While CPE is quite widely attested, the use of pidgin Portuguese is mostly inferred from contemporary accounts such as the following:

> [...] a *Chinese* Pilot put on board us, and told us, in broken *Portuguese* he would carry us to *Macao* [...]   (Anson 1748: 467)

Several of these accounts mention 'broken' (pidgin) Portuguese and English in the same context, which implies that the two were in contact and even used by the same speakers:

> [...] there are few of the merchants but have a person who can speak *broken English and Portuguese*. So that French, Dutch and Danes, are obliged to speak either the one or the other when they traffick with them.
>
> (Noble 1762: 210, emphasis added)

> [...] they gave me many answers in broken and mixed dialect of English and Portuguese, which I could not understand. (Noble 1762: 244)

> The dialect the Chinese use in common with us, is a mixture of European languages, but mostly, as we formerly hinted, of English and Portuguese, together with some words of their own. (Noble 1762: 262)

> They generally converse with the *Swedes* in broken *English*; and sometimes in broken *Portuguese, French, and Dutch*: and some of them speak a few words of Swedish. (Toreen 1771: 237–238)

From such evidence, Tryon et al. (1996) draw the following inferences:

> [...] we think it likely that [in Macau], in addition to some speakers of Metropolitan Portuguese, there would also have been a distinctive language with a predominantly Portuguese-based lexicon spoken by the locally-born population not of pure Chinese descent (i.e. probably a creole and probably the ancestor of modern Macanese) while the Cantonese Chinese who worked with or for Portuguese-(Creole-) speakers in and around Macao probably also spoke pidginized varieties of Portuguese (Creole). (Tryon et al. 1996: 489–490)

That is, at least two Portuguese-based contact languages may be assumed, which must have interacted:

1. the creole used in Macau itself (Macanese or Makista)
2. a pidgin used for trade between Macau and Mainland China or between European trading powers and the Chinese (the 'broken Portuguese' of the historical accounts)

Following the work of João Feliciano Marques Pereira, Cabreros (2003: 140–141) hypothesizes that these contact varieties formed part of a continuum from Portuguese to pidgin as follows:

Portuguese	Macanese *Patois*	(Pidgin) Macanese
←——————————————————————————————————→		
as spoken by Portuguese-born or Portuguese- educated residents	spoken by the Macau population of mixed ancestry	as spoken by the Chinese

Of these varieties, Macanese is fairly well documented and understood (see e.g. Holm 1989, Ferreira 1996, Ansaldo & Matthews 2004, Fernandes & Baxter 2004, Pinharanda Nunes & Baxter 2004, Pinharanda Nunes 2008, Baxter 2009), whereas the pidgin remains poorly attested and therefore has not been subjected to substantial analysis. The investigation of this 'likely' pidgin, which Tryon et al. (1996) call "Macao Pidgin Portuguese" (MPP), is hampered by the lack of texts from the first half of the 19th century.

3. Phrasebooks as sources

CPE data comes from various sources. English language sources, assembled by Philip Baker, are divided into two sub-corpora: CPE1 (1721–1842) contains texts from early China-West contact to the close of the First Opium War (Baker 2003a) and CPE2 (1843–1990) covers the period from the opening of five treaty ports to the last decade of the 20th century (Baker 2003b). The Chinese language sources are phrasebooks for the teaching and learning of pidgin. The use of phrasebooks in the context of China trade is also a unique method for transmission of a pidgin (Shi 1993: 460). Whereas for western traders it was assumed that familiarity with pidgin would develop after a short time in the China trade, for the Chinese there was a thriving market for phrasebooks teaching vocabulary and phrases needed for trading purposes. These books used Chinese characters (intended to be pronounced as in Cantonese) to represent the pronunciation of pidgin words (see Li et al. 2005, Ansaldo et al. 2010).

Williams (1837) discussed two pidgin phrasebooks in use in Canton during the 1830s. The first represented a variety of pidgin Portuguese used among Chinese traders and Europeans. The book was named *Gaoumun fan yu tsă tsze tesuen taou* (澳門番語雜字全套) (hereafter *Gaoumun fan yu*) which was translated as 'A complete collection of the miscellaneous words used in the foreign language of Macao'.

> The collection of Portuguese and Chinese words is designed for natives residing at Macao and its vicinity; and in the compass of thirty-four pages contains upwards of 1200 examples. They are arranged under sixteen heads; as eatables, social relations, natural objects, buying and selling, furniture, weights, &c.; and under each division there are found words sufficient for the common intercourse of life. The examples are placed in columns, and the translation is given in Chinese sounds immediately beneath each one, but in a smaller type.
>
> (Williams 1837: 277)

In the title of this work, *fan yu* (番語 *faan¹jyu⁵* in Cantonese) clearly designates a pidgin, as in the well-known CPE phrasebook 紅毛通用番話 *Hung⁴mou⁴ tung¹jung⁶ faan¹waa²* 'The Common Foreign Language of the Redhaired People' (hereafter *Redhaired*, see e.g. Bolton 2003:169).[1] Another important phrasebook, *The Chinese and English Instructor* (Tong 1862) clearly distinguishes between standard English and 廣東番話 *Gwong²dung¹ faan¹waa²* 'Canton pidgin' which designates the pidgin (CPE) equivalents given in the margins of the text (Li et al. 2005:81, Ansaldo et al. 2010:77).[2]

The second pidgin phrasebook mentioned in Williams (1837) was a CPE chapbook called *Hungmaou mae mae tung yung kwei hwa* (紅毛買賣通用鬼話) (hereafter *Hungmaou*), translated rather literally by Williams as 'those words of the devilish language of the red-haired people commonly used in buying and selling'. According to Williams the work had only sixteen pages with less than 400 words. Both the pidgin Portuguese and CPE phrasebooks described by Williams were anonymous and were printed at Foshan (佛山), a city near Canton. In addition, both depicted on their covers the same Portuguese gentleman who also appears on the glossary of *Aomen Jilüe* (澳門記略), translated as *The Monograph of Macao* of 1751 (see Bawden 1954, Thompson 1959, Bolton 2003:166).

That both Portuguese and English pidgin phrasebooks were available in the market around the 1830s is good evidence that the two pidgins were considered distinct and coexisted for a certain period in Canton. Williams (1837:278) even suggests that the two phrasebooks were works of the same author; and since the coverage of *Gaoumun fan yu* was more extensive than the *Hungmaou* phrasebook, the author evidently "knew much less English than he did of Portuguese." Accounts by travelers and traders show that some form of 'broken' Portuguese was used (see Section 2) and Williams' own account of the two phrasebooks also points to the existence of a Portuguese pidgin text being used until at least the 1830s. In addition, given that the number of pidgin items in *Gaoumun fan yu* was almost three times that of the *Hungmaou* phrasebook, it is likely that the lexicon and grammar of pidgin Portuguese had also expanded substantially.

4. Macau Pidgin Portuguese and Chinese Pidgin English

In view of the above historical evidence that Portuguese or some forms of 'broken' Portuguese were used as a lingua franca in the early period of China trade, discussions on the origin of Chinese Pidgin English often associate it with the preexisting use of pidgin Portuguese, as in the following statements by Van Dyke and Holm:

> By the early 1730s, pidgin English had replaced Portuguese as the medium of communication with foreigners.
> (Van Dyke 2005: 77)

> There is evidence that Chinese Pidgin English grew out of the pidginized Portuguese brought to the ports of China in the sixteenth century.
> (Holm 1989: 512)

Given this scenario, one hypothesis is that CPE arose through relexification of (pidgin) Portuguese. As Tryon et al. (1996: 489) note, this idea goes back as far as Hunter (1882) who said that CPE:

> [...] was undoubtedly an invention of the Chinese, and long anterior to the appearance of the English at Canton in its origin, as may be proved by the admixture of Portuguese and Indian words still to be found in it... The English came more than a hundred years after; words from their language were then gradually incorporated, and increased with the disappearance of the Portuguese, who confined themselves to their own colony of Macao, until, finally, the former became the principal traders, and thus this language became known as Pigeon-English.
> (Hunter 1882: 61)

Two lines of argument support this view:

a. historically, the role of Macau in the China Trade, especially before the establishment of Hong Kong, provides the opportunity. The contemporary accounts cited above testify to the use of 'broken' Portuguese, presumably MPP, in the Canton Trade;
b. as has often been observed, the earlier attestations of CPE contain several lexical items from Portuguese (Tryon et al. 1996)

Baker & Mühlhäusler (1990) and Tryon et al. (1996) are pessimistic about the prospects for establishing the relexification hypothesis, or more generally, the nature of the (pidgin) Portuguese influence on CPE, in the absence of texts from pidgin Portuguese. But they acknowledge a possible role of such a language:

> While the opportunity for Macao Pidgin Portuguese to have influenced CPE in the first half of the 19th century does not appear to be reflected more than marginally in CPE's lexicon, the possibility that MPP may have played some role in some of the rapid changes which took place in CPE in that period should not be dismissed. But this can only be determined if and when MPP data of that period come to light.
> (Tryon et al. 1996: 490)

Baker & Mühlhäusler (1990: 107) and Tryon et al. (1996: 490) suggest that the use of pidgin phrasebooks in Canton and Macau may have been one source of relexification (see Section 3 for discussion of these phrasebooks). They speculate that calquing from pidgin Portuguese to CPE may have taken place, especially if the phrasebooks were the work of the same hand (as suggested by Williams 1837).

Bolton (2003: 168) argues that phrasebooks such as *Aomen Jilüe* could be seen as an important "missing link" to connect the contact situations between Macau and Canton. Bolton's speculation is not implausible, since subsequent publications of pidgin Portuguese and pidgin English phrasebooks seem to rely upon *Aomen Jilüe* as a model.

5. Portuguese elements in the Chinese Pidgin English lexicon

The earliest source for the China trade is *The Travels of Peter Mundy* in which the English trader recounted contacts between Britain and China in 1637. In his diary, Mundy provided a glossary of some 88 words which include:

(1) Early Asian words in English (Mundy 1637, quoted in Bolton 2003: 140–143)
  mandareene 'Chinese official' (< Ptg. *mandarim*)
  muster 'sample'   (< Ptg. *amostra*)
  tay 'tael'   (< Ptg./Mal.)
  cattee 'catty'   (< Mal./Jav.)

Many of the words in the glossary were derived either from Portuguese or from Asian languages in contact with it. Bolton (2003: 139) argues that the significance of Mundy's word list lies not only in the presentation of early "Asian-English" but also in its implication for later developments such as Portuguese influence on English in Canton, Macau and Hong Kong. At the vocabulary level it is apparent that Portuguese has had an influence on CPE. Other lexical items which were derived from Asian languages such as Malay *picul* may have reached CPE via Indo-Portuguese or Malayo-Portuguese. The same may also be true of the CPE expression *maskee* 'never mind', often said to be derived from a Portuguese expression *mas que* (Holm 1989: 515) but an alternative etymology involving the Malay conjunction *meski(pun)* meaning 'although' seems semantically more plausible (Clark 1979: 59; see Vázquez Veiga & Fernández Rodríguez, *this volume*). A multiple etymology for this item is also possible. At any rate, this expression is found in Papia Kristang as *maski* (Baxter 1988), *masqui* in Macanese, whence it appears to have entered CPE, and *maski* in Tok Pisin (Steinbauer 1969).

While most vocabulary in CPE is of English origin, Hall (1944: 95) notes that the presence of Portuguese vocabulary is a characteristic of early CPE. Certain lexical items such as the ones in (1), *savvy* 'to know' (< Ptg. *saber*) and *joss* 'god' (< Ptg. *deus*) left a permanent mark in CPE. Others were gradually replaced by English, for example *padre* 'priest', *grande* 'great' and *pikinini* 'small' which were later replaced by pidgin English *joss pidgin man, big* or *largee* and *smalla* respectively (Hall 1944:95). In one CPE phrasebook the Chinese term 大 *daai⁶* 'large' was given three pidgin renderings as shown in (2).³

(2) Chinese Pidgin English   (夷音輯要, quoted in Uchida & Shin 2009:367)
    大   喇治   忌烈   架攔地
    daai⁶   laa¹zi⁶   gi⁶lit⁶   gaa³laan⁴di⁶
    large   large   great   grande

The fact that three pidgin equivalents were given, two derived from English and one from Portuguese, suggests that Portuguese and English lexical items coexisted for some time in the China trade.

Accounts by traders and travellers that mentioned words of Portuguese origin were also plenty. For example, the sentence in (3) contains three words from Portuguese, one *(hola)* either from English *(whore)* or Swedish *(hora)*.

(3) Chinese Pidgin English and/or Pidgin Portuguese (1747–; Noble 1762:240)
    Carei grandi hola, pickenini hola?
    want   old/big whore young/small whore
    'Do you want an older whore or a younger one?'⁴

Indeed, while this is often presented as an early example of CPE, Baxter (2009) suggests that it might rather represent a rare attestation of pidgin Portuguese. Alternatively, it may be an example of the "broken and mixed dialect of English and Portuguese" described by Noble (1762) as discussed in Section 2.

The verb *carei* 'want' (< Ptg. *querer*) as seen in (3) above was attested in early CPE, but was gradually replaced by *wantchee*. Forms of English *want* were first attested in an early 19th-century text:

(4) Chinese Pidgin English   (Morrison 1807–8)
    If no wanty catch profit what for come?
    'If you don't want to get profit, why did you come?'

While CPE phrasebooks of the 1830s such as 紅毛通用番話 (the *Redhaired*) transcribed in Bolton (2003, Appendix 4) still retained the use of *carei* meaning 'want', the English-derived *wantchee* had taken over by the time of *The Chinese and English Instructor* (Tong 1862):

(5) Chinese Pidgin English
                (紅毛通用番話 c.1835 璧経堂; quoted in Bolton 2003:281)
    (口奴)⁵   加利
    nou⁴   gaa¹li⁶
    2SG   want
    'you want (it)'

(6) Chinese Pidgin English   (Tong 1862: IV.42)[6]
     my   wantchee thisee
     1SG   want   this
     'I want this'

In Tong (1862) two alternative words are used for 'account': 干打 *gon¹daa²* (< Ptg. *conta*) and the English 交吾打 *gaau¹ng⁴daa²* (< *account*, see Li et al. 2005: 102–3).[7] Since the former term 干打 *gon¹daa²* is used in the earlier phrasebooks, we again have a prima facie case of replacement of a Portuguese term by an English one.

6. Portuguese elements in Chinese Pidgin English grammar

While it is well documented that a portion of the CPE lexicon consists of words of Portuguese origin, whether or how Portuguese grammar left its mark in CPE grammar is a largely unexplored subject. If relexification took place at all, it should have left traces in the grammar of CPE. Many of the distinctive grammatical features of CPE can be attributed to the Cantonese substrate (Ansaldo et al. 2011, Matthews & Li, *forthc.*). Among those that cannot be so attributed, some may show Portuguese influence. We will examine two such features: the copula *have* and the complementizer *for* in CPE, which may have been influenced by Portuguese.

6.1 *Have* as copula

It has long been noted that, in early CPE texts, apart from functioning as a possessive verb, *have* (sometimes spelt *hab*) can also be used as a copula (Hall 1944, Baker 1987, Holm 1989). However, no studies have attempted to trace the origins of this copula. Holm (1989: 298) briefly suggests an influence from the Indo-Portuguese creoles, but does not exclude the possibility of Cantonese or Bazaar Malay influence. We will first look at the various functions that *have* takes on at an earlier period of CPE and then examine possible influence from the contributing languages.

The marking of possessive, existential and copula constructions underwent several changes in various phases of CPE. Using a CPE corpus comprising English language sources, Baker (1987) shows that *have* is used primarily as a possessive verb as in (7), a copula as in (8)–(11) and a perfective aspect marker as in (12) before the first half of the 19th century. These functions persisted until the mid-19th century, when the form *have* remained only as an aspect marker.

1. *Have* as a possessive verb:

    (7) Chinese Pidgin English   (1769; Spencer 1925: I.199)
    Hi yaaw, no have eyes, how can see.
    'Hi ya, if it has no eyes, how can it see?'

2. *Have* as a copula:

    (8) Chinese Pidgin English   (1743; Anson 1748: 524)
    Chinese man very great rogue truly, but have fashion, no can help.
    'Chinese people are really great rogues, but this is the way they are. There is nothing we can do.'

    (9) Chinese Pidgin English   (1769; Spencer 1925: 1, 226)
    Hy you, truly that man have too muchee great fool.
    'Hi ya, that man is truly a great fool.'

    (10) Chinese Pidgin English   (1783; Keate 1788: 97)
    this have very poor place, and very poor people
    'This place is very poor and has many poor people'

    (11) Chinese Pidgin English   (1813; Grant 1988: 254)
    I have very trouble because all that money American gentlemen owe for me.
    'I am very troubled because of the money that the American gentleman owed me.'

3. *Have* as a perfective marker:

    (12) Chinese Pidgin English   (1817–; Connolly 1942: 104)
    Me think have go Pekin.
    'I think (he) has gone to Peking.'

In the CPE phrasebook 紅毛通用番話 (*Redhaired* glossary) assumed to have circulated around the 1830s, *have* is represented by the character 哈 (pronounced *haa¹* in Cantonese). As in the English sources, *have* functions as a possessive verb (13a–b) as well as a locative copula (13c).

(13) Chinese Pidgin English
           (紅毛通用番話, c.1835 璧経堂; quoted in Bolton 2003: 282)
  a. 有事   哈   卑賤
       have business
    'I've got business/I'm busy'
  b. 得閒   哈   点
       have time
    'to have free time'
  c. 唔在   哪   哈
      NEG   have
    '(He is) not here'

However, by 1860s the possessive and copula meanings of *have* had been replaced by *hap got* 'have got'. This is confirmed in another Chinese source, *The Chinese and English Instructor* (Tong 1862):

(14) Chinese Pidgin English (Tong 1862: VI.1, VI.37)
    a. *my hap got alla color*
        'I have all sorts of colors'
    b. *what placee my hat hap got*
        'Where is my hat?'

This Chinese source also confirms Baker's (1987) observation that by this time *hap* alone was only used as an aspectual marker as in (15).

(15) Chinese Pidgin English (Tong 1862: IV.32)
    my hap go court one time
    'I have been to Court once'

The possessive and existential uses of *hap got* parallel the uses of Cantonese *jau⁵* 'to have, to exist'. As for the copula construction, based on English sources Baker (1987: 173) notes that the last attestations of *have* in [N = N] and [N = ADJ] constructions are 1857 and 1870 respectively. In the *Instructor*, zero copula predominates, as in (16).

(16) Chinese Pidgin English (Tong 1862: IV: 32)
    court expensee too muchee
    'The Court fees are very heavy'

(17) Chinese Pidgin English (Tong 1862: VI: 14)
    The tea belong first crop
    'This is first crop tea.'

(18) Chinese Pidgin English (1860; Anon 1860)
    You belong tailorman?
    'Are you the tailor?'

The rise of *belong* as copula as in (17)–(18) may be attributed to the use of *suk⁶jyu¹* 'belong' in Cantonese (Ansaldo et al. 2011).⁸

The presence of Portuguese is evident in the CPE lexicon (see Section 5). Historical accounts presented in Section 2 also point to the use of a Portuguese pidgin preceding the emergence of CPE. The copula function of *have* would be an interesting case to see how the three languages affect the development of copula construction in CPE.

First, we look at the lexifier – English. CPE *have* or *hap* is derived from English *have* which is itself a possessive verb (19). As in CPE, in addition to being a lexical verb, *have* is an auxiliary verb to mark perfect aspect as in CPE (12). English *have* however is not a copula. Various forms of the verb *be* are used in copula constructions as in (20). English *have* therefore is unlikely to provide the copula function of *have* in CPE.

1. Possessive *have*:

    (19) English
    I have some books

2. Copula *be*:

    (20) English
    a. *Dogs are mammals.*
    b. *Some books are on the table.*

Similar to English, possessive verb and copula are formally differentiated in Cantonese, as seen in Examples (21)–(23). Note that Cantonese has two copulas: *hai⁶* for equative sentences as in (22) and *hai²* for locatives as in (23). So, again, Cantonese does not seem to be the model for the copula function of *have* in early CPE.

1. Possessive *jau⁵*:

    (21) Cantonese
    Ngo⁵   jau⁵   hou²do¹   haai⁴.
    1SG   have   many   shoes
    'I have many shoes.'

2. Copula *hai⁶* 'to be':

    (22) Cantonese
    Keoi⁵   hai⁶   jam¹ngok⁶gaa¹.
    3SG   COP   musician
    'He is a musician.'

3. Locative copula *hai²* 'to be at':

    (23) Cantonese
    Zi¹   bat¹   hai²   toi²   dou⁶
    CLF   pen   COP   table there
    'The pen is on the table.'

However, the influence of Cantonese became more apparent in later phases of CPE. With respect to the functions of *hap got* (a form replacing the former *have/ hap*), by mid-19th century besides the possessive meaning, *hap got* was attested in existential sentences, which can be attributed to the possessive and existential uses of *jau⁵*, as in (24).

(24) Cantonese
Jau⁵ go³ jan⁴ kei⁵ hai² go² dou⁶
exist CLF man stand COP DEM there
'There is a man standing over there.'

Having examined the possessive and copula constructions in the two major contributing languages: English and Cantonese, it seems that neither language can adequately explain how *have* came to be used as a copula in CPE (see Examples (8)–(11) and (14b)). Portuguese may provide an explanation for this peculiar usage in CPE. The main possessive verb in Portuguese is *ter* 'to have':

(25) Portuguese
Ele   tem   um cachorro.
3SG.M have.PRS.3SG ART dog
'He has a dog.'

In contemporary usage, existential sentences are often indicated by *haver* as in (26).

(26) Portuguese
Há   um banco aqui perto.
EXST ART bank here near
'There is a bank nearby.'

However, diachronically there are periods in which both *haver* and *ter* can be used impersonally with an existential function. Sampaio (1973) shows that, beginning from the 16th century, *ter* is used in existential construction alongside *haver*.

(27) Portuguese   (Sampaio 1973: 21)
Na   frontaria deste   patio... **tinha hum**
LOC.ART front   of.DEM patio   EXST one
grande arco lavrado...
big   arch carved
'In front of the patio…there was a large carved arch'

Enedino dos Santos (2010: 209) links the rise of *ter* as an existential verb in the 16th century to the Portuguese maritime expansion. Although in continental Portugal the existential construction remains expressed by *haver*, the existential meaning of *ter* as in (28) is found in other varieties of European Portuguese, such as in the Azores.[9]

(28) Portuguese   (Carrilho 2010)
Mas tinha   muitos   moinhos por aqui fora.
but EXST.PST many.PL mills   by here out
'But there were many mills out here.'

From the above examples, it can be seen that *ter* can take on various functions: as a possessive and existential verb, and as a copula. This multifunctionality is also evident in various forms of *ter* in Portuguese-based creoles, such as Macau Creole Portuguese and Papia Kristang.

1. Macau Creole Portuguese *têm*:
   a. Possessive

   (29) Macau Creole Portuguese (Fernandes & Baxter 2004: 160)
   Iou têm dôs gato marilo
   1SG have two cat yellow
   'I have two tawny cats.'

   b. Existential

   (30) Macau Creole Portuguese (Fernandes & Baxter 2004: 160)
   Têm tánto lorcha na mar
   COP so.many boat LOC sea
   'There are so many boats out at sea.'

   c. Locative copula 'to be at'

   (31) Macau Creole Portuguese (Fernandes & Baxter 2004: 160)
   Iou têm na casa
   1SG COP LOC house
   'I'm home.'

2. Papia Kristang *teng*:
   a. Possessive

   (32) Papia Kristang (Baxter 1988: 181)
   eli teng dos prau
   3SG have two boat
   'He has two boats.'

   b. Existential

   (33) Papia Kristang (Baxter 1988: 173)
   mai, teng ńgua omi na fora!
   mother COP one man LOC outside
   'Mother, there's a man outside!'

   c. Locative 'to be at'

   (34) Papia Kristang (Baxter 1988: 173)
   mai, John teng na fora!
   mother John COP LOC outside
   'Mother, John is outside!'

The similarities of function between *have* in early CPE, *têm* in Macau Creole Portuguese and *teng* in Papia Kristang are suggestive of an influence of Portuguese on CPE. They also point to the important role of Papia Kristang in the transmission of features to Macau Creole Portuguese and thence to CPE (see Cardoso, this volume).

Apart from the Asian varieties of Portuguese above, existential *ter* is also evident in varieties of (Creole) Portuguese in Africa (35) and Brazil (36).

(35) Cape Verdean Creole (Baptista, Mello & Suzuki 2007:71)
Ten   un   mudjer   ki   ten   un   fidju-fema
COP   one   woman   COMP have one   child-female
'There is a woman who has a daughter'

(36) Brazilian Portuguese (Baptista, Mello & Suzuki 2007:71)
Tem   alguém   aqui
COP   somebody   here
'There is somebody here'

A close parallel here is offered by Hawaii Creole English (HCE), where the verb *get* is used in both possessive and existential sentences. Interestingly, the alternative forms *have* and *had* are also attested:

(37) Hawaii Creole English (Siegel 2000:215)
a. *By this tree have some golds buried.*
'By this tree, there's some gold buried.'
b. *Had dis old gree house…*
'There was this old green house…'

Following Knowlton (1967:234–5), Siegel (2000) suggests that the existential function of *have/had* in HCE may be influenced by Portuguese *ter*. If so, this would be parallel to the influence we have suggested in early CPE. Alternatively, Siegel suggests, the usage may have been imported from CPE itself. Thus Portuguese could have influenced HCE both indirectly (through CPE) and directly (through the Portuguese presence in Hawaii).

6.2 *For* as complementizer

A second feature in CPE which may have been influenced by Portuguese is complementation using *for*.[10] While complement clauses are zero marked in the majority of cases, overt complementizers are attested, including *for* and *so* (Li 2011, Matthews & Li, *forthc.*). *For* has three functions in CPE: as a preposition, as in (38); marginally as a conjunction, as in (39); and as a complementizer, as in (40)–(41).

(38) Chinese Pidgin English (Tong 1862: IV.32)
My can settle that pidgin for you
'I will get the matter arranged for you.'

(39) Chinese Pidgin English (1769; Spencer 1925: I.227)
Here can make handsome face, for too muchee handsome face have got.
'Now I can paint a beautiful portrait of him because he has got a handsome face.'

(40) Chinese Pidgin English (1819; Jenkins 1944: 13)
Now my flinde, Misser Tillen, you must go long my for catche chow chow tiffin (get something to eat) and den (then) can make see My No.1 Book loom (library).
'Now my friend, Mr Tilden, you must go with me to get something to eat and then visit my big library.'

(41) Chinese Pidgin English (1839; Read 1840: II.275)
He old custom for tshin tshin jos
'It is an old custom to worship god.'

Hawaii Creole English also uses a form *for/fo* as complementizer:

(42) Hawaii Creole English (Kearns 2000: 13, quoted in Siegel 2008: 101)
He ask me for cheer you up.
'He asked me to cheer you up.'

(43) Hawaii Creole English (Yamanaka 1993: 155, quoted in Siegel 2008: 101)
I neva have money for buy some more.
'I didn't have money to buy some more.'

(44) Hawaii Creole English (Roberts 1998: 30, quoted in Siegel 2000: 223)
I think more better for I write that answer.
'I think it's better for me to write that answer.'

Siegel (2000: 224) argues that while the prepositional function of *for* and the introduction of a VP complement can be partly attributed to English, *for* introducing a finite complement as in (44) is not a feature of English. He thus proposes that this usage is influenced by Portuguese *para* which can be found in all syntactic contexts in which *for* is found in HCE:

1. *Para* as preposition:

(45) Portuguese (Siegel 2007: 75)
Isto é para si
this COP for 2SG.OBL
'This is for you.'

2. *Para* as complementizer:

(46) Portuguese (Siegel 2007:75)
 Eles pediram   para eu   voltar.
 3PL ask.PST.3PL for 1SG return.INF
 'They asked me to return.' [lit. 'They asked for I to-return.']

In Macau Creole Portuguese there are also instances where forms of *para* 'for' are used in these functions. In (47), *p'ra* functions as complementizer and *para* as preposition:

(47) Macau Creole Portuguese (Coelho 1880–86:190, quoted in Holm 1989:298)
 Eu fazê este carta p'ra dizê a vôs se
 1SG make this letter for tell to 2 if
 ácaso   mandá dinhêro para mi [...]
 by.chance send money for 1SG.OBL
 'I write this letter to tell you that if by chance you sent money to me...'

Here the uses of *p'ra/para* in Macau Creole are similar to Portuguese *para*. (47) shows that the use of *p(a)ra* 'for' as complementizer was present in Macau Creole. Since this function is not available in English, the influence of Portuguese (via Macau Creole and pidgin Portuguese) provides a plausible explanation for *for*-complementation in CPE.[11]

6.3   Pidgin Portuguese influence on the grammar of Chinese Pidgin English

We have looked at two grammatical features in CPE (*have* as copula and *for* as complementizer) which cannot be readily explained on the basis of English or Cantonese, but can plausibly be attributed to Portuguese influence via pidgin Portuguese and/or Macau Creole. In both cases, parallel developments are seen in HCE, which can be attributed either directly to influence from Portuguese (in which case they constitute typological parallels to the CPE cases) or to influence from CPE itself (in which case the ultimate source could be Portuguese). It may well be that further features of CPE can be explained with reference to pidgin Portuguese.

It is noteworthy that both copula *have* and *for* complementizer were attested in early CPE texts, i.e. pre-1842 sources, and later disappeared. These changes can be seen as a linguistic reflection of changes in China trade history; the opening of Hong Kong and other treaty ports in addition to Canton resulted in decreasing influence of Portuguese. Post-1842 sources show increasing use of *belong* as copula, thus taking over the role of *have* as copula. The near disappearance of *for* as complementizer after 1842 also indicates a strong preference for zero marked complement clauses in CPE, consistent with the influence of Cantonese. Lexically, although there were still some Portuguese words retained in CPE phrasebooks, these items were apparently gradually replaced by English items by the middle of the 19th century.

7. Relexification revisited

Different versions of relexification have been put forward. One theory that involves relexification is the monogenesis hypothesis of pidgin and creole formation. Proponents of the monogenetic view believe that European-based pidgins and creoles originate from a 15th-century Portuguese-based pidgin spoken in West Africa, possibly a relexified version of Mediterranean Lingua Franca. An essential component that makes monogenesis possible is relexification, which assumes that there is a wholesale replacement of vocabulary of the proto-Portuguese pidgin by another language, but the grammar of the proto-pidgin was kept intact. The creoles of the Philippines and Papiamentu have been said to result from an earlier Portuguese pidgin being replaced with Spanish lexicon (Whinnom 1956, Taylor 1957). For Whinnom, Chinese Pidgin English would represent an extreme form of relexification:

> [...] if China Coast Pidgin *is* a relexification of a Portuguese creole, this relexification is almost total, and the usual kind of linguistic evidence necessary to prove the affiliation is lacking.'   (Whinnom 1965: 520)

Baker & Mühlhäusler (1990: 90) note a more moderate version of relexification assumed in Bauer (1974), who acknowledges the role of pidgin Portuguese in the crystallization of CPE at earlier stages, while noting strong influence from Chinese and English in its subsequent development.

In reconsidering this hypothesis of the emergence of CPE, some caveats should be borne in mind:

1. the relexification hypothesis does not entail the theoretical sense of relexification as used by Lefebvre (1998). At a more descriptive level, it means replacement of lexical items while retaining the grammar of the earlier language.
2. the relexification hypothesis does not necessarily entail a monogenetic view of pidgins and creoles, although such a view is often associated with relexification. In this context, then, the relexification hypothesis means only that English replaced Portuguese as the principal lexifier during the history of the China trade.

We have reviewed part of the linguistic evidence which may be recapitulated as follows:

1. Lexical items, principally trade-related terms such as *compradore*, which survived relexification;
2. Lexical items which underwent replacement by English terms during the course of the China trade period, such as *conta* 'account' replaced by *account* and *carei* 'want' replaced by *wantchee*;
3. Grammatical usages of function words such as *have* as copula and *for* as complementizer, which cannot be attributed to the Cantonese substrate but are plausibly explained in terms of pidgin Portuguese influence. The phonological form of the words is English, while the syntax is that of Portuguese *ter* and *para* respectively (or more precisely, that of the pidgin variants of these, which we assume to be derived from the Macau Creole *têm* [teŋ] and *pa* [pa]/*pra* [pra]/*para* [para] respectively) (Fernandes & Baxter 2004: 123, 160).

While the relexification model may be applicable to certain lexical items, it should be noted that the scenario differs from the paradigm cases of relexification as discussed by Lefebvre (1998). Her model assumes that native speakers of a language A replace the lexical items of A with corresponding items from language B. In the case of CPE, relexification would mean that native speakers of Chinese acquired pidgin Portuguese as an auxiliary language for trading purposes and replaced Portuguese lexical items with English ones as English speakers came to dominate the China trade.

8. Conclusion

In this article, we have reconsidered the role of pidgin Portuguese in the Canton trade and its influence on Chinese Pidgin English. Although, as in other European-based contact languages the presence of Portuguese vocabulary in CPE does not necessarily imply a monogenetic account of the origin of CPE, the routes by which Portuguese expanded in Asia might provide clues to the historical linkages and influence of different Portuguese-based contact varieties in Asia. Alternatively, a relexification account that invokes only the replacement of lexical items from one source language to another, in this case English supplanting Portuguese, could explain remnant Portuguese features in early CPE. This is particularly plausible when CPE grammatical features have parallels in neither Cantonese nor English grammars. The uses of *have* as copula and *for* as complementizer in early CPE texts are good evidence of Portuguese influence.

Several pidgin phrasebooks with English and Portuguese as lexifiers were discussed. The importance of these phrasebooks for the relationship between pidgin Portuguese and pidgin English is that they could act as a medium for transmitting pidgin Portuguese features to CPE, via calquing as one possibility (Baker & Mühlhäusler 1990). Pidgin in these phrasebooks often seems to represent older usage even though some such phrasebooks continued to circulate until the 1830s. For example, the English sources show that *large* is first attested in 1807 (Morrison 1807–8); while the last attestation of *grande*, apart from the *Redhaired* phrasebooks, is 1769 (Spencer 1925). From the 1830s onwards, only the word *large* is found in English sources. It is likely that changes took place more rapidly in the spoken language than the phrasebooks could capture. Therefore pidgin expressions in these phrasebooks are likely to represent older usage.

Furthermore, there is evidence that pidgin Portuguese and pidgin English interacted for a considerable period of time in Canton and Macau. CPE is said to have arisen around 1715, and from the 1730s onwards it gradually supplanted pidgin Portuguese as the dominant lingua franca in the China trade (Morse 1926, Van Dyke 2005). As a result of English domination in the China trade and the frequent encounters between the Chinese and the English, the more obscure features in early CPE that we discussed above were subjected to influence from both Cantonese and English.

In this article, we have added some grammatical evidence to the pool of lexical evidence of Portuguese influence on CPE. This evidence helps to provide a more complete account of the grammatical development of CPE. It may be that other grammatical features of CPE can be accounted for along similar lines. The nature and extent of interactions between Macau Creole/MPP and CPE call for further research.

Notes

* We thank Hugo Cardoso, Alan Baxter, Mário Pinharanda Nunes and two anonymous reviewers for helpful commentaries on this paper.

1. In Chinese 話 *waa²* means 'speech' and is used to refer to the spoken language, for example *Gwong²dung¹waa²* 廣東話 'Cantonese', while 語 *jyu⁵* means 'language' as *Jing¹jyu⁵* 英語 'English'. The crucial term is the modifier 番 *faan¹*, literally 'foreign'.

2. Unless references are made to other authors' work, Romanization of Cantonese follows the conventions of *Jyut⁶ping³* as developed by the Linguistic Society of Hong Kong.

3. This entry appeared in a CPE phrasebook called 夷音輯要 'A summary of foreign sounds'. The Chinese characters are provided by Uchida & Shin (2009:367) while we have added Romanized Cantonese and glosses. The date of publication is unknown; however since the characters used to represent the pidgin are clearly to be pronounced in Cantonese, the phrasebook can be assumed to have circulated in Canton.

4. This sentence is also translated 'Do you prefer a big or a small prostitute?' Based on the Cantonese terms *daai* and *sai*, the distinction could refer to either physical size or age.

5. Parentheses indicate that the two characters □ and 奴 should be read as a single character.

6. Examples from Tong (1862) are based on the transcription of *The Chinese and English Instructor* in Li et al. (2005).

7. This reading is confirmed by the Standard English phrase given in the phrasebook, where *account* is rendered by the characters 押交吾 (aat^3 gaaau^1 ng^4). Here the first character represents the first syllable (missing in the pidgin form), the second two characters represent *count* just as in the pidgin form. In the pidgin form 交吾打 the last character (missing in the Cantonese rendering for English *account*) evidently represents an epenthetic vowel.

8. Ansaldo (2009:201–202) notes the similarities between CPE *belong* and Bazaar Malay *punya* and speculates that if Bazaar Malay was available in Canton, it might have been used instead of Portuguese pidgin for interethnic communication.

9. We are grateful to an anonymous reviewer for referring us to relevant studies on the historical functions of *ter* and *haver* and the existence of an existential *ter* in other varieties of European Portuguese.

10. We thank Jeff Siegel (p.c. September 2010) for suggesting the possibility of a role for Portuguese in *for*-complementation.

11. An anonymous reviewer points to a possible role for the archaic English construction in which *for to* functions as a complementizer. To the extent that this construction was used in the varieties which provided input to CPE, it could have contributed to the development of *for* as a complementizer. It is difficult to evaluate this possibility since only a single instance of *for to* is attested in the entire CPE corpus (Li 2011:145):

> (i) Chinese Pidgin English   (1798; Fanning 1924:191)
> *Oh! that be for to take care and guard Josh, and see no man hurt him.*
> 'Oh! This is used for the purpose of taking care and guarding the god, and to make sure that nobody hurts him.'

References

Anon. 1860. *The Englishman in China*. London: Saunders, Otley & Co.
Ansaldo, U. 2009. *Contact Languages: Ecology and Evolution in Asia*. Cambridge: CUP.
Ansaldo, U., and S. Matthews. 2004. The origins of Macanese reduplication. In *Creoles, Contact and Language Change: Linguistic and Social Implications* [Creole Language Library 27], eds. G. Escure and A. Schwegler, 1–19. Amsterdam: John Benjamins.

Ansaldo, U., S. Matthews, and G. Smith. 2010. China Coast Pidgin: Texts and contexts. *Journal of Pidgin and Creole Languages* 25 (1): 63–94.

Ansaldo, U., S. Matthews, and G. Smith. 2011. The Cantonese substrate in China Coast Pidgin. In *Creoles, Their Substrates and Language Typology*, ed. C. Lefebvre, 289–301. Amsterdam: John Benjamins.

Anson, G. 1748. *A Voyage Round the World in the Years MDCCXL, I, II, III, IV.* London: Printed for John and Paul Knapton.

Baker, P. 1987. Historical developments in Chinese Pidgin English and the nature of the relationships between the various pidgin Englishes of the Pacific region. *Journal of Pidgin and Creole Languages* 2 (2): 163–207.

Baker, P. 2003a. CPE1: Corpus of Chinese Pidgin English as attested in English language sources (1721–1842). Ms.

Baker, P. 2003b. CPE2: Corpus of Chinese Pidgin English as attested in English language sources (1843–1990). Ms.

Baker, P., and P. Mühlhäusler. 1990. From business to pidgin. *Journal of Asian-Pacific Communication* 1: 87–115.

Baptista, M., H. Mello, and M. Suzuki. 2007. Cape Verdean, or Kabuverdianu, and Guinea-Bissau, or Kriyol (Creole Portuguese). In *Comparative Creole Syntax*, eds. J. Holms and P. L. Patrick, 53–82. London: Battlebridge.

Bauer, A. 1974. *Das Kanton-Englisch*. Frankfurt: Peter Lang.

Bawden, C. R. 1954. An eighteenth century Chinese source for the Portuguese dialect of Macao. In *Silver Jubilee Volume of the Zinbun-Kagaku-Kenkyusyo*, 12–33. Kyoto: Kyoto University.

Baxter, A. N. 1988. *A Grammar of Kristang (Malacca Creole Portuguese)*. Canberra: Pacific Linguistics.

Baxter, A. N. 2009. O português em Macau: Contacto e assimilação. In *Português em Contato*, ed. A. M. Carvalho, 277–312. Madrid-Frankfurt: Vervuert-Iberoamericana.

Bolton, K. 2003. *Chinese Englishes: A Sociolinguistic History*. Cambridge: CUP.

Cabreros, P. 2003. Macao Patois words in English. *Review of Culture* 5: 126–51.

Carrilho, E. 2010. Sintaxe dialectal Portuguesa: aspectos da distribuição geográfica de construções sintácticas não-padrão. Conference series of the Centro de Estudos Humanísticos da Universidade de Minho, Braga, Portugal, December.

Cheng, C. M.-B. 1999. *Macau: A Cultural Janus*. Hong Kong: Hong Kong University Press.

Clark, R. 1979. In search of Beach-la-Mar: Towards a history of Pacific Pidgin English. *Te Reo* 22: 3–64.

Coates, A. 1966. *Macao and the British 1637–1842: Prelude to Hongkong*. Oxford: OUP.

Coelho, F. A. 1880–86. Os dialectos românicos ou neolatinos na África, Ásia e América. *Boletim da Sociedade de Geografia de Lisbon*. (Republished in J. Morais-Barbosa (ed.) 1967. *Estudos Linguísticos Crioulos*. Lisbon: Academia International de Cultura Portuguesa).

Connolly, J. B. 1942. *Canton Captain*. New York NY: Doubleday, Doran.

Enedino dos Santos, R. 2010. Flagrantes de variação no Português escrito de Macau no século XVII: Um breve exame dos verbos *haver* e *ter*. In *A China, Macau e os Países de Língua Portuguesa – XX Encontro da Associação das Universidades de Língua Portuguesa*, 205–214. Macau: AULP.

Fanning, E. 1924. *Voyages and discoveries in the* South Seas, *1792–1832*. Salem, MA: Marine Research Society.

Fernandes, M. S., and A. N. Baxter. 2004. *Maquista Chapado: Vocabulary and Expressions in Macao's Portuguese Creole*. Macau: Instituto Cultural.

Ferreira, J. S. 1996. *Papiaçám di Macau*, 2 Vol. Macau: Fundação Oriente.

Grant, F. D. 1988. The failure of the Li-ch'uan Hong: Litigation as a hazard of nineteenth century foreign trade. *American Neptune* 48 (4): 243–260.

Hall, R. A. Jr. 1944. Chinese Pidgin English grammar and texts. *Journal of the American Oriental Society* 64: 95–113.

Holm, J. 1989. *Pidgins and Creoles*, 2 Vol. Cambridge: CUP.

Hunter, W. C. J. 1882. *The 'Fan Kwae' at Canton Before Treaty Days*. London: Kegan, Paul, Trench and Co.

Jenkins, L. W., ed. 1944. *Bryant Parrott Tilden of Salem, at a Chinese Dinner Party*, Canton, 1819. Princeton, NJ: Princeton University Press.

Kearns, Y. 2000. *Pidg Latin and How Kitty got her Pidgin Back*. Honolulu HI: Honolulu Theatre for Youth & Kumu Kahua Theatre.

Keate, G. 1788. *An Account of the Pelew Islands (…)*. London: G. Nicol.

Knowlton, E. C. Jr. 1967. Pidgin English and Portuguese. In *Proceedings of the Symposium on Historical, Archeological and Linguistic Studies on Southern China, Southeast Asia and the Hong Kong Regions*, ed. F. S. Drake, 228–237. Hong Kong: University of Hong Kong.

Lefebvre, C. 1998. *Creole Genesis and the Acquisition of Grammar*. Cambridge: CUP.

Li, M. 2011. Chinese Pidgin English and the Origins of Grammar. PhD dissertation, University of Hong Kong.

Li, M., S. Matthews, and G. P. Smith. 2005. Pidgin English texts from *The Chinese and English Instructor*. Special issue of the *Hong Kong Journal of Applied Linguistics* 10 (1): 79–167.

Matthews, S., and M. Li. Forthcoming. Chinese Pidgin English. In *Atlas of Pidgin and Creole structures*, eds. S. Michaelis, P. Maurer, M. Haspelmath and M. Huber. Oxford: OUP.

Morrison, R. 1807–8. Journal. Unpublished journal in Council for World Mission archives, South China – Journals, Box 1. London Missionary Society. SOAS, London.

Morse, H. B. 1926. *The Chronicles of the East India Company Trading to China, 1635–1834*. Oxford: Clarendon Press.

Mundy, P. 1637. *The travels of Peter Mundy, in Europe and Asia, in 1608–1667*, ed. by R. C. Temple. Cambridge: Hakluyt Society.

Noble, C. F. 1762. *A Voyage to the East Indies in 1747 and 1748*. London: T. Becket and P. A. Dehondt.

Pinharanda Nunes, M. 2008. Os Demonstrativos em Maquista: Uma análise morfosintáctica contrastiva. *Papia* 18: 7–21.

Pinharanda Nunes, M., and A. N. Baxter. 2004. Os marcadores pré-verbais no crioulo de base lexical portuguesa de Macau. *Papia* 14: 31–46.

Read, G. 1840. *Around the World: A Narrative of a Voyage in the East India Squadron Under Commodore George C. Read*. New York, NY: Charles S. Francis.

Roberts, S. J. 1998. The role of diffusion in the genesis of Hawaiian Creole. *Language* 74: 1–39.

Sampaio, M. L. P. 1973. *Estudo Diacrónico dos Verbos TER e HAVER, Duas Formas em Concorrência*. São Paulo: Assis.

Shi, D.-X. 1993. Learning pidgin English through Chinese characters. In *Atlantic Meets Pacific: A Global View of Pidginization and Creolization* [Creole Language Library 11], eds. F. Byrne and J. Holm, 459–465. Amsterdam: John Benjamins.

Siegel, J. 2000. Substrate influence in Hawai'i Creole English. *Language in Society* 29: 197–236.

Siegel, J. 2007. Recent evidence against the Language Bioprogram Hypothesis: The pivotal case of Hawai'i Creole. *Studies in Language* 31 (1): 51–88.

Siegel, J. 2008. *The Emergence of Pidgin and Creole Languages*. Oxford: OUP.

Spencer, A., ed. 1925. *Memoirs of William Hickey*, 4 Vols. London: Hurst & Blackett.
Steinbauer, F. 1969. *Concise Dictionary of New Guinea Pidgin (Neo-Melanesian)*. Madang, New Guinea: Kristen Pres.
Taylor, D. R. 1957. Review of Whinnom (1956), *Spanish Contact Vernaculars in the Philippine Islands*. Word 13: 489–99.
Thompson, R. W. 1959. Two synchronic cross-sections in the Portuguese dialect of Macao. *Orbis* 8: 29–53.
Tong, T.-K. 1862. *The Chinese and English Instructor*. Guangzhou.
Toreen, O. 1771. *A Voyage to Suratte*. London: printed for Benjamin White.
Tryon, D. T., P. Mühlhäusler, and P. Baker. 1996. English-derived contact languages in the Pacific in the 19th century (excluding Australia). In *Atlas of Languages of Intercultural Communication in the Pacific, Asia, and the Americas*, Vol. II.1, eds. S. A. Wurm, P. Mühlhäusler and D. T. Tryon, 471–495. Berlin: Mouton de Gruyter.
Uchida, K., and K. H. Shin. (内田慶市. 沈國威) 2009. 言語接触とピジン：19世紀の東アジア. Tōkyō: Hakuteisha.
Van Dyke, P. A. 2005. *The Canton Trade: Life and Enterprise on the China Coast, 1700–1845*. Hong Kong: Hong Kong University Press.
Whinnom, K. 1956. *Spanish Contact Vernaculars in the Philippine Islands*. Hong Kong: Hong Kong University Press.
Whinnom, K. 1965. Contacts de langues et emprunts lexicaux: The origin of the European-based creoles and pidgins. *Orbis* 14: 509–27.
Williams, S. W. 1837. Gaoumun fan yu tsa tsze tsuen taou, or A complete collection of the miscellaneous words used in the foreign language of Macao. 2. Hungmaou mae mae tung yung kwei hwa, or those words of the devilish language of the red-bristled people commonly used in buying and selling. *Chinese Repository* 6: 276–79.
Yamanaka, L.-A. 1993. *Saturday Night at the Pahala Theatre*. Honolulu HI: Bamboo Ridge Press.

Traces of superstrate verb inflection in Makista and other Asian-Portuguese creoles

Mário Pinharanda Nunes

The Makista (Macau Creole Portuguese) verb paradigm contains two types of verbs derived from the indicative mood of the superstrate: those which do not represent superstrate functions and those which bear functional superstrate inflectional morphology of the simple present, the past perfective and the past imperfective. The distribution of inflection with superstrate functions, however, is inconsistent throughout the three existent corpora of Makista. Such inflectional morphology is not found in Makista's immediate predecessor – Kristang, or Malacca Creole Portuguese. However it is found among the Indo-Portuguese creoles of Diu, Daman and Korlai. The chapter argues that diachronic differences in the Makista verb paradigm indicate the incorporation of inflectional morphology through a late-stage second language acquisition process occurring during decreolization. This view contrasts with the account proposed by Luís (2008) to explain the presence of inflectional morphology in the Indo-Portuguese Creoles via an early stage second language acquisition process based on a Post-basic Variety.

1. Introduction

The earlier descriptions of the Makista (MAC) verb paradigm, in Coelho (1880–86), Schuchardt (1889), Batalha (1974[1958]) and Ferreira (1996[1978]),[1] present various morphological forms derived from the superstrate that, nevertheless, do not maintain the functions they have in the superstrate:

1. a form derived from the infinitive of the superstrate (<INF), wherein the word-final consonant is deleted, but the syllable-final stress is preserved: [mo 'ra] < Ptg. INF [mo 'rar] 'to reside'; [be 'be] < Ptg. INF [be 'ber] 'to drink'; [su 'bi] < Ptg. INF [be 'ber] 'to climb/rise/raise';

2. the 3SG inflection for the superstrate present indicative (PRS) on the restricted group of verbs (3sGr): *vai* < Ptg. 3SG for PRS of *ir* 'to go'; *vem* < Ptg. 3SG for PRS of *ir* 'to come'; *cai* < Ptg. for PRS of cair 'to fall'; *sai* < Ptg. 3SG of *sair* 'to exit'; [2]
3. *sang* < Ptg. *são*, the 3PL for the PRS of *ser* 'be';
4. 1SG PRS inflection on *quero* < Ptg. 1SG for PRS of *querer* 'to want' and *gosto* < Ptg. 3SG for PRS of *gostar* 'to like', both occurring only after negation.

In summary, the previous descriptions on verb forms in MAC, based on the earliest corpus available for this creole, the 19th-century texts, reported one predominant form, <INF; a restricted group of high frequency verbs deriving from irregular conjugation patterns of the lexifier, exhibiting the superstrate 3SG inflection for the PRS; and an even more restricted use of the superstrate 1SG. For the purposes of this study, we consider these forms to be basilectal, as their superstrate derived morphological forms do not represent any of their original tense-aspect functions. Such forms would have entered the language at an early stage of development and typify the variety of MAC most removed from Portuguese. They contrast with the forms of superstrate indicative (IND) inflection that maintain their original tense-aspect functions. These few cases of superstrate-derived PRS forms occur both in contexts of simultaneousness and anteriority in relation to the moment of speaking. Furthermore, they do not present a corresponding non-finite form in those two written corpora. Such forms are also found in Kristang, or Malacca Creole Portuguese (MALC) with the same typology as in MAC. On the other hand, the Indo-Portuguese Creoles (IPC) considered in this study – those of Korlai (KOR), Diu (DIU) and Daman (DAM) –, present different forms for reference to a point in time prior to the moment of speaking, i.e. past reference, and for reference to a point in time simultaneous with the moment of speaking.[3]

Contrasting with the classically described paradigm of MAC verb forms, Pinharanda Nunes (2011), working with both written and oral corpora, found forms derived from the 3SG of the PRS, and observed that this form was also extended to verbs other than the restricted group mentioned in point (3) above. This additional group is referred to as 3sGe (Pinharanda Nunes 2011). Furthermore, evidence was found of a much wider range of forms displaying lexifier morphology for the IND, namely, past perfective (PST.PFV) and past imperfective (PST.IPFV) inflection for the 3SG, yet occurring in variation with the basilectal verb forms.

The existence of inflectional verb morphology in Portuguese-based KOR, DIU and DAM was recently analyzed in terms of naturalistic L2 acquisition by adults at the early stage of their formation (Luís 2008), as well as within the framework of an evolutionary model of language change based on Croft (2000) and Mufwene (2001), by Clements (2009a). These studies serve as a starting point for the current chapter, which is a comparative survey of the similarities and differences of the presence and use of IND superstrate verb morphology between MAC and the three Indo-Portuguese creoles considered by Luís (2008) and Clements (2009a).

The MAC data to be discussed are from the three corpora studied in Pinharanda Nunes (2011):[4] (a) a written corpus from Barreiros' (1943–44) anthology of late 19th-century texts – lyrics, poems, letters, anecdotes, theatre scripts;[5] (b) a written corpus from Ferreira's (1996) anthology of narratives, produced between the 1950s to the early 1990s; (c) an oral corpus of semi-guided interviews of 16 elderly L1 speakers of MAC, born in Macau, Hong Kong and Shanghai.[6] Information presented here for the other creoles are taken from existing studies, viz. Baxter (1988) for MALC; Clements (2009a, 2009b), Clements & Koontz-Garboden (2002) and Luís (2008) for DAM, KOR and DIU; Cardoso (2006, 2009) for DIU.

We will start by introducing the hypotheses of Luís (2008) and Clements (2009a) in relation to the IPCs. We then present criteria differentiating superstrate and non-superstrate functions evident in the inflection forms, prior to considering the diachronic distribution and variation in use patterns of verbal morphology in MAC. This discussion is followed by a comparison of superstrate forms in the IPCs considered by Luís (2008) and Clements (2009a). A final section outlines the early sociodemographic context of Macau. On the basis of the linguistic and sociodemographic evidence, we develop the hypothesis that the superstrate verbal morphology in this creole is a consequence of its gradual modification in the direction of its lexifier, amounting to decreolization. However, we do not rule out the possible existence of variation between basilect and non-basilect verb forms in MAC from its very inception.

2. Theoretical framework

The study of creole morphology by Luís (2008) emphasizes the socio-cultural and attitudinal factors of substrate speakers towards the target language (i.e. Portuguese) as a reason for the retention of superstrate verbal morphology at an early stage. Luís argues in favor of the early acquisition of verb morphology for IPCs. Her case is based on the fact that "verbal suffixes have preserved both the form and function of their superstrate counterparts and that superstrate functions have been extended to newly developed affixes" (Luís 2008: 84). She considers this as evidence that these creoles derived from a post-basic variety.

Approaches to creolization based on Second language acquisition (SLA) stress the similarities between the L2 variety acquired by adult learners in naturalistic environments, restricted pidgins and pre-pidgins, in what concerns morphological simplicity (see e.g. Givón 1979; Bardovi-Harlig 2000; Mufwene 2001; Clements 2003). This L2 variety is referred to by Klein & Perdue (1997) as the Basic Variety, and described as "simple, versatile and highly efficient for most communicative purposes" (1997: 303). As Siegel (2004: 149) points out, this assumption implies "some learners felt no communicative reason to acquire a more native-like version of the target language". For the IPCs, however, Luís (2008) proposes that they derived from L2 varieties where inflectional paradigms were already present. She supports her proposal by drawing on Klein & Perdue's (1992, 1997) findings on adult naturalistic SLA, according to which inflectional morphology can be found in more elaborate L2 varieties or "Post-Basic L2 varieties" (Becker & Veenstra 2003; Veenstra 2003; Siegel 2004).

As justification for an early presence of inflectional morphology in the three IPCs in question, Luís (2008) stresses the role socio-cultural factors may have played in the formation of adult L2 varieties spoken by substrate speakers in the settings in which they arose. Such a proposition is based on the notion developed by e.g. Thomason & Kaufmann (1988), Clements (1992) and Siegel (2004) that a higher complexity of the interlanguage of adult language learners reveals a receptive attitude towards the target language (TL) among substrate speakers in the mentioned settings. Drawing on Clements (1996), Luís proposes that the plausible isolation of the IPC communities "from their native Hindu community, as a result of conversion to Catholicism, seems to have provided the necessary motivation for converted Indians to prefer the TL comparatively to their native language and to show a favorable attitude towards the target language" (Luís 2008: 88).

Thus, the preservation of superstrate suffixes, according to Luís (2008: 107), was achieved at an early stage in the development of these creoles, when access to the TL was still readily available, as they maintain not only the form but also the function of their superstrate counterparts. Luís (2008: 88) further supports this proposition based on the very limited Portuguese presence in Korlai the absence of Portuguese rule and presence in Korlai from the very beginning of the community, and its isolation from Portuguese influence since 1740. As for Diu and Daman, despite the continued Portuguese presence until 1961 (the year the Indian government took the Portuguese colonies of Goa, Daman and Diu), it diminished progressively from 1850, in Diu, and the late 19th century, in the case of Daman (Clements 2009a: 29).

Despite the much longer presence of the Portuguese in Diu and Daman, Luís (2008) does not consider the possibility of the overt verbal inflection in these IPC as having resulted from decreolization. Furthermore, she rejects the idea that structural similarities between substrate and superstrate languages may enhance retention of common linguistic features, contra e.g. Clements (1992, 1996), Siegel

(2004) and Plag (2008). In the case under survey, this means that the Gujarati and Marathi tense-aspect suffixation system is not seen as having been retained or relexified with the existing superstrate suffixes used in the IPC, based on moderate structural similarities shared by both substrates and the superstrate. To make her case, Luís (2008: 111) stresses that "the shape of tense and aspect suffixes in Indo-Portuguese are of Portuguese origin (…)". She further supports her view on this issue by comparing the IPC case with that of the Batticaloa Creole Portuguese (BATT) of Sri Lanka. Based on Smith (1979), Luís points out that whereas KOR, DAM and DIU have a few superstrate affixes, "Batticaloa Creole Portuguese has retained hardly any (…)" (Luís 2008: 112). She stresses that this is even more surprising given that one of the substrate languages of BATT, Sinhala, contains theme vowels and stem allomorphs, as does Portuguese, whereas neither Gujarati nor Marathi have conjugation classes and both possess very few allomorphic alternations.[7] Thus, she asserts, unlike KOR, DAM and DIU, BATT must have "developed from a Basic Variety" (Luís 2008: 112). Although she proposes the socio-linguistic factors of isolation resulting from religious conversion to have affected the IPC communities' attitude toward the superstrate as a TL, she does not consider the possible influence from speakers of other more acrolectal varieties of Indo-Portuguese who may have shifted to these communities. Nor does Luís mention the possibility of gradual decreolization as a result of a prolonged presence of Portuguese rule (in the cases of Daman and Diu).

The study by Clements (2009a), which accounts for the similarities and differences among the same three Indo-Portuguese Creoles, covers the lexicon as well as several grammatical categories, including verb morphology. In the evolutionary model considered, the size of each community, their respective social structures and the degree of contact maintained with Portuguese are proposed as factors capable of having shaped the similarities and differences between the TAM systems of these IPCs. The study looks into how the frequency and perceptual salience (factors inherent to naturalistic SLA approaches) may account for their morphology. Clements' comparison of the similarities and differences among these three IPC considers the evolutionary model of language change. In this model, which considers a language to be analogous to a biological species, the study of the social, cultural and political contexts surrounding it are crucial to explain its ultimate form. Clements' (2009a) looks at the three IPCs from the viewpoint of a social organizational typology, taking the following non-linguistic factors into consideration: population size, presence of Portuguese culture, government, language and the community's social stratification. Thus Korlai's smaller population size and homogenous blue-collar typology, as well as its much briefer period of contact with Portuguese is claimed to account for the differences in relation to DIU and DAM regarding lexicon, question words, pronoun systems, consonants, direct object order relative to verb, and adposition order. Such differences amount to less acrolectal forms overall: "The large degree of differences between Korlai, on the one hand, and Daman and Diu, on the other, follow from, not only the nature and size of each community, as mentioned above, but also from the variable presence of Portuguese language and its linguistic features"(Clements 2009a: 44).

The evolutionary approach in Clements's study also encompasses two notions related to naturalistic language acquisition and language processing, viz. frequency of use and perceptual saliency (Siegel 2008). The first of these "refers to the number of times in a given corpus that a certain item or form appears" (Clements 2009a: 40). It follows that an item with a high rate of frequency of occurrence in the superstrate or TL has a greater margin of probability of being transferred to the emerging L2 variety – in our study, to the creole. The frequency factor also encompasses the notion of retention of a particular item (not originating in the superstrate or not maintaining the exact superstrate phonological and morphological shape) used by a large number of speakers in the initial dialect mixing stages in the formation of a creole. This frequency of use provides a higher probability of retention of such an item once the creole reaches a more stable stage. The similarities among these creoles, as presented by Clements, are agued as resulting from such factors: "This is most apparent in the verbal forms that found their way into the three creoles: the base forms of the verbs, both present- and preterit-tense, are all either the most frequent occurring form of the finite verb paradigm or the most frequently occurring non-finite form" (Clements 2009a: 45).

As for MAC, data in the three corpora under study provide evidence that the IND superstrate inflectional morphology is absent from the 19th-century corpus but begins to appear in the speech of Makista L1 speakers born in the 1920 and the 1930s. Given the absence of data prior to the 19th-century texts, we cannot attest the presence of such morphology in MAC at the very earliest stages of its formation. Yet, nor can we argue against its possible existence in varying degrees along this creole's continuum. However, in the earliest available corpus from the 19th century, MAC shows scant superstrate inflectional morphology and presents a verb form paradigm identical to that of MALC. Therefore, we may hypothesize that, contrary to what Luís (2008) finds for IPC, MAC and its Southeast Asian predecessor appear to have been formed from basic varieties lacking any overt functional verb inflection acquired from the lexifier.

Socio-political factors reviewed in Section 6 illustrate that the elderly MAC speakers from the early 20th century are the first batch of L1 speakers of this creole to increasingly receive a formal education in Portuguese (mainly in Macau and marginally in Hong Kong) and in English. Therefore, certain factors analyzed in

Clements (2009) with regard to the IPCs, namely population size, the nature and duration of the Portuguese presence and the frequency of occurrence of forms, also seem relevant to the study of superstrate morphology in MAC. The progressive exposure of MAC speakers to the lexifier language suggests the existence of appropriate conditions for what is known as decreolization.

We assume decreolization as a phase in a creole's continuum in the same terms as summarized by Siegel (2008: 236): a "gradual modification of a creole in the direction of the lexifier. It is usually thought of in terms of the adoption of particular features for example, in TAM marking (…)". This gradual modification is produced by natural SLA processes, as well as explicit learning of the superstrate. The main difference in an SLA process involving the lexifier at an early formation stage and one involving the lexifier in the decreolization stage is the amount, nature and quality of exposure to that same lexifier. In the formation stage there would be (a) some amount of restriction on the creole speaking community's access to the lexifier (i.e. TL); (b) there would be a pool of varying degrees of approximations to the lexifier; (c) the number of L1 speakers of the lexifier would decrease just as the number of creole speakers increased. On the contrary, and basing ourselves on evidence from the case of MAC in the decreolization phase (cf. Section 6): (a) the access to the lexifier becomes increasingly easy and frequent; (b) it is continuous; and, (c) it includes naturalistic acquisition opportunities as well as monitored formal learning situations. On the one hand, the SLA creole formation processes within the proposal by Luís (2008) are also applicable to the creolization phase. However, the socio-demographic factors listed above in (a), (b) and (c) may better account for the differences between the scope of the superstrate IND morphology and its functions in MAC and the IPCs SLA creole formation processes, as proposed in Luís (2008) for the latter group. Such factors are also applicable to the decreolization phase. In Sections 4 and 5, we shall try to find an answer to this by looking in detail at the distribution of this morphology in those creoles.

3. Defining verbs from three different Portuguese TAM inflections

Before discussing the use of Portuguese verb morphology for the IND (present, perfective and imperfective past) in MAC and the IPCs, a brief definition of the aspectual and tense values and their use in European Portuguese is called for.[8] This will provide a base for assessing the use of the respective verb forms in the Creoles under observation.

3.1 The Portuguese present indicative

In Portuguese, only with verbs representing states does the PRS strictly convey present tense information, i.e., it provides reference to the moment of speaking (Mateus et al. 2003:154).[9] With verbs representing events, it is limited to direct reports and to performative enunciations. When used with other lexical classes, the PRS marks habitual aspect rather than strictly tense. When used together with appropriate adverbials, the PRS may also express reference to a moment subsequent to that of the enunciation (Mateus et al. 2003). The PRS inflections can be used for the delivery of instructions that imply a virtual deontic modal value (Mateus et al. 2003:154–155). Finally, the 'historical present', i.e. reference to past events by way of the present, is yet another possible reference expressed by PRS verb morphology in Portuguese. It should be noted that no example of the use of PRS inflection on MAC verbs in reference to the historical past was found in all three corpora for this creole. Table 1 presents the inflectional paradigm of PRS for the declension of regular -*a* and -*e* theme vowel verbs and one of an irregular declension in the lexifier.[10]

Table 1. Inflectional paradigm of PRS†

Person	Regular declension		Irregular declension	
	a-theme vowel *gostar* 'to like'	*e*-theme vowel *morrer* 'to die'	*estar* 'to be'	*ser* 'to be'
1SG	gost-o	morr-o	est-ou	s-ou
2SG	gost-a-s	morr-e-s	est-á-s	és
3SG	gost-a	morr-e	est-á	é
1PL	gost-a-mos	morr-e-mos	est-a-mos	s-omos
2PL	gost-ai-s	morr-ei-s	estai-s	s-oi-s
3PL	gost-a-m	morr-e-m	est-ão	s-ão

† In European Portuguese, the 2SG may take two inflections: an informal form of address (*tu*) a formal one (*você*). The formal takes the 3SG marking; the informal takes the suffix /s/ after the theme vowel. The 2PL also has two possible inflections. One inflection follows the more commonly used personal pronoun for the person (*vocês*), taking the 3PL marking. The other corresponds to an old form of address (hardly used today), (*vós*), which has specific person-number markings (cf. Tables 1, 2, and 3).

3.2 The Portuguese past perfective

In Portuguese linguistic descriptions, this inflection is referred to as the *pretérito perfeito simples* 'simple preterite perfect'. As defined by Mateus et al. (2003:139), the simple preterite perfective (henceforth past perfective) PST.PFV inflection in

Portuguese confers the notion of termination in the past on accomplishments and achievement-type verbs. In the case of states, PST.PFV may also convey this same notion, i.e., the end point (or termination) of a state, in the sense that it implies a previous state in opposition to the one in reference. Again, the effect of termination and end point is expressed by PST.PFV on an activity-type verb. Table 2 presents the PST.PFV inflectional paradigm for the declension of regular -*a* and -*e* theme vowel verbs and one of irregular declension in the lexifier.

Table 2. The Perfective Past Indicative Paradigm in Portuguese

Person	Regular declension		Irregular declension
	a- theme vowel *gostar* 'to like'	*e*- theme vowel *morrer* 'to die'	*ir* 'to go'
1SG	gost-ei	morr-i	f-ui
2SG	gost-a-ste	morr-e-ste	f-oste
3SG	gost-ou	morr-eu	f-oi
1PL	gost-á-mos	morr-e-mos	f-o-mos
2PL	gost-a-stes	morr-e-stes	f-o-stes
3PL	gost-a-ram	morr-e-ram	f-o-ram

3.3 The Portuguese imperfective past[11]

In traditional Portuguese linguistic descriptions, this inflection is referred to as the *pretérito imperfeito* 'imperfect preterite'. As is the case of the PST.PFV, the Imperfective Past (PST.IPFV) is equally a tense that refers to states and events occurring prior to that of the enunciation, i.e. past. Its grammatical aspectual value of imperfectivity represented by its inflection expresses the absence of finiteness/temporal end, opposed to what we observed for the PST.PFV. As such, the PST.IPFV may transform telic into atelic events that do not carry the notion of temporal end. The aspectual value conferred onto originally telic events may transform them into habitual states (Mateus et al. 2003: 140).[12] The use of the PST.IPFV demands some sort of temporal framing, a subordinating temporal phrase or a temporal adverbial phrase, in association to it. As it is a broad tense, it is able to change telic events into limitless atelic predicates, as well as changing them into states, be they habitual or other (Mateus et al. 2003: 140). Table 3 describes the PST.IPFV inflectional paradigm for the declension of the same regular *a*- and *e*- theme vowel verbs and one of irregular declension in Portuguese.

Table 3. The Perfective Past Indicative Paradigm in Portuguese

Person	Regular declension		Irregular declension
	a- theme vowel	*e*- theme vowel	
	gostar 'to like'	*morrer* 'to die'	*ter* 'to have, to exist'
1sg	gost-a-va	morr-ia	tinh-a
2sg	gost-a-vas	morr-ia-s	tinh-a-s
3sg	gost-a-va	morr-ia	tinh-a
1pl	gost-á-va-mos	morr-ia-mos	tính-a-mos
2pl	gost-á-vei-s	morr-íei-s	tinh-ei-s
3pl	gost-a-va-m	morr-ia-m	tinh-a-m

4. Criteria for distinguishing superstrate and non-superstrate functions of inflections

In the MAC corpora, the use of PRS inflection covers both tense and aspectual contexts in conformity with their superstrate value, as well as others where such values are violated. Therefore, in this section we present criteria to distinguish these two types of uses of PRS inflection in MAC, which are essential in order to understand the role and pattern of its use in this creole.

4.1 The Present Indicative: identification criteria

Based on the definition of the PRS in Portuguese, we consider it to be used in varieties of Asian Creole Portuguese (ACP) with functions similar to the lexifier when it refers to contexts of:

1. present-tense and imperfective grammatical aspect;
2. future-tense, with the appropriate adverbials.

On the contrary, it is considered not to exhibit superstrate Portuguese functions if:

1. it is used in past-tense contexts;
2. it is used in present tense contexts of imperfective aspect but where the verb is preceded by an aspectual marker;
3. it is used in the perfect aspect, in the present or in the past, with or without preverbal aspect markers.

4.2 The Perfective Past: identification criteria[13]

Based on the definition of the value of PST.PFV morphology in Portuguese, we consider such morphology to be used in ACP with functions similar to the superstrate when it refers to contexts of:

1. past-tense and perfective grammatical aspect.

On the contrary, it is considered not to exhibit superstrate functions if:

1. it is used in present-tense contexts;
2. it is used in past-tense contexts of perfective aspect but where the predicate is preceded by an aspectual marker;
3. it is used in the past-tense contexts of imperfective aspect.

4.3 The Imperfective Past: identification criteria

Based on the definition of the PST.IPFV in Portuguese, we consider that it is being used in ACP with functions similar to the lexifier when it refers to contexts of:

1. past-tense and imperfective grammatical aspect.

On the contrary, it is considered not to exhibit superstrate functions if:

1. it is used in present-tense contexts;
2. it is used in past-tense contexts of imperfective aspect but where the predicate is preceded by an aspectual marker;
3. it is used in the past-tense contexts of perfective aspect.

5. Verb forms in Makista: their distribution in the corpora

This section presents the distribution and functional range of IND inflection forms in MAC. Figure 1 is a graph summarizing the distribution of the IND inflection throughout the three MAC corpora individually, and helps to visualize its increase from the earliest known corpus of this creole until the stage spoken by the last L1 speakers from the first half of the 20th century. The values in the columns correspond to the percentage that each form represents among all the MAC forms in each individual corpus.

As for the two written corpora, the chart illustrates the close similarity of the distribution of verb forms. The <INF is the predominant form used in both these corpora: 54% for the 19th-century and 59% for the 20th-century texts. The

3sGr represents 23.3% of the verb forms in the 19th-century written corpus and 16.1% for the 20th-century texts. The remaining forms display a drastic drop in frequency in these two corpora. As may be observed, 3sGe represents only 8.6% of the verb forms in the 19th-century texts and 9.2% of those in the 20th-century written corpus. As for the 1sG, a total of 5 cases were counted among all the data quantified for these two corpora: 3 in the 19th-century texts (0.8%) and 2 in the 20th-century texts (0.4%). In both written corpora this inflection is exclusively used with *quero* < Ptg. 1sG of *querer* 'to want' and *gusto* < Ptg. 1sG of *gostar* 'to like' when preceded by negation: *nang quero* and *nang gusto*. As per the numbers in that study, only one case of PST.PFV and one of PST.IPFV were found among these two corpora. For that reason, and for practical purposes, we have chosen to represent these two forms as inexistent in the written data considered.

Figure 1 also illustrates how the 20th-century oral corpus is the one to present the least frequency of <INF (14.6%). This same corpus presents the highest frequency of 3sGr (30.6%). It also displays the highest frequency of 3sGr, which is its most frequent verb form overall (37.8%). As for the other IND form in the PRS, 1sG, it represents 2.7% (249 tokens) of the verb forms in the 20th-century oral corpus. The IND forms for the PST in this corpus are mainly used in the PST.PFV form (3.4%), followed by 2.1 % of PST.IPFV forms.

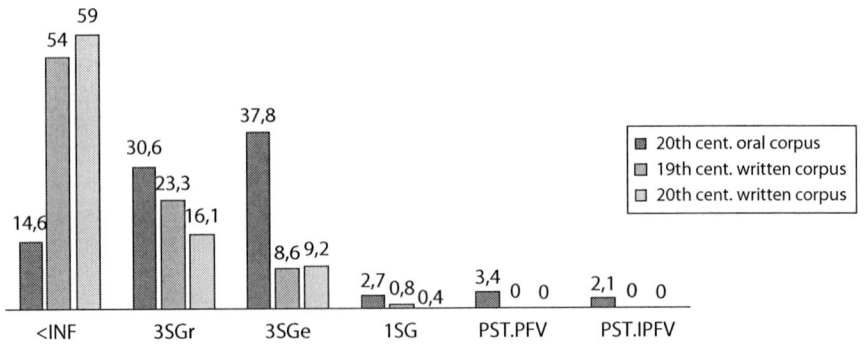

Figure 1. The distribution of the verbal forms in the 3 MAC corpora

In sum, the 3sGe is the most frequent verb form in the oral corpus of MAC, whereas the <INF is the predominant form of the earlier records of this creole, namely the 19th- and 20th-century written corpora.

5.1 3SGe in the MAC oral corpus

The following examples illustrate the superstrate and non-superstrate use of the 3SGe form in the main corpus considered for MAC. In the examples relating to past tense contexts, Examples (1), (2) and (3), 3SGe corresponds to its non-superstrate values, whereas in Examples (4), (5) and (6), in present and future tense contexts, it corresponds to its superstrate values.

PAST CONTEXTS

a. **Perfective**

(1) Makista (Pinharanda Nunes, fieldwork)
Nãong essi pai mãe ensina eli.
NEG DEM father mother teach 3SG
'No, the parents taught him.'

b. **Habitual**

(2) Makista (Pinharanda Nunes, fieldwork)
Dó,14 velha uza. Nova nunca usa
dó elderly use young NEG use
'The dó is/was used by elderly women. Young women do/did not use it'

c. **Progressive**

(3) Makista (Pinharanda Nunes, fieldwork)
Esse gajo Americano namora na quarto.
DEM guy american court LOC bedroom
'That American guy was courting in his bedroom.'

PRESENT CONTEXTS

a. **Habitual**

(4) Makista (Pinharanda Nunes, fieldwork)
Ieu qana aniversário manda cartãong.
1SG when birthday send card
'When it is my birthday, she sends me a card.'

b. **Progressive**

(5) Makista (Pinharanda Nunes, fieldwork)
Você atrapalha iô.
2SG interrupt 1SG
'You are interrupting me.'

FUTURE CONTEXTS

(6) Makista (Pinharanda Nunes, fieldwork)
   Sábado nos encontra.
   saturday 1PL meet
   'We shall meet up on Saturday.'

The examples provided in (1) to (6) are all cases of the use of Ø + 3SGe inflection for the aspect and tense contexts indicated. However, 3SGe is not restricted by the aspectual preverbal marker *ja* for the perfective, in Example (7) below, or *ta* for the progressive, in Example (8) below, nor by the irrealis marker *logo*, in Examples (9) and (10), in the respective aspectual and modal contexts with which these two markers are most frequently used, according to Pinharanda Nunes & Baxter (2004) and Pinharanda Nunes (2011).

(7) Makista (Pinharanda Nunes, fieldwork)
   já encontra iloutro tudo
   PRF meet-f them all
   'I have met all of them.'

(8) Makista (Pinharanda Nunes, fieldwork)
   Larga sarongong nós... ta corta unga corta outro
   fly-f kite 1PL HAB cut-f one cut-f another
   'When flying our kites, we would cut one (string) after another.'

(9) Makista (Pinharanda Nunes, fieldwork)
   Nos logo ri
   1PL IRR laugh
   'We would laugh.'

(10) Makista (Pinharanda Nunes, fieldwork)
   Você lo conversa com ôloutro, você logo convers
   2SG IRR talk-f with 3PL 2SG IRR talk-f
   como criada
   like maid
   'If you were to talk to them, you would (end up) talking like a maid.'

In spite of the predominance of 3SGe in the oral corpus, which is the only corpus where other superstrate inflectional morphology is used (i.e. 1SG, PST.PFV and PST.IPFV), its evenly balanced distribution between present tense and past tense reference contexts, as well as among cases of person-number agreement and non-agreement, proves that the speakers are not yet entirely conscious of its superstrate functions.

5.2 1SG in the MAC oral corpus

In addition to the restricted and non-functional use of 1SG in *quero* and *gusto* when preceded by NEG, the oral corpus displays examples of this form on other verbs, regardless of the presence of or absence of NEG. The extended use of the 1SG inflection has been exclusively observed in the oral corpus and in present tense contexts. This is particularly interesting, as it presents a scenario of juxtaposition of tense and aspectual values relatively to those exerted by this inflection in the lexifier. Further proof of the level of conscious use of this inflection by the speakers in the oral corpus is the fact that among the 597 tokens of 1SG, 334 (84%) correspond to cases of person-number agreement. These figures relate to the use of 1SG in superstrate tense-aspect functions. However, the 16% margin in the agreement variation shows that the integration of this inflection is not yet complete.

Contrary to 3SGE, judging by the absence of the sequence [Preverbal marker + V.1SG], 1SG in the oral corpus is highly restricted by the presence of the preverbal particles. In this corpus, 1SG only appears in present and future tense contexts – i.e., in contexts where it maintains its superstrate aspectual and tense marking functions, and thus rules out the possibility of occurrence with the perfective preverbal marker *ja*. The fact that, in such contexts, *ta* and *logo* are not found marking verbs with 1SG morphology stresses the superstrate use of this form, found exclusively in the oral corpus. This is yet further confirmed by the absence of this form in progressive contexts.

In the oral corpus used by Pinharanda Nunes (2011), the cases of 1SG forms are lexically diverse. Among a total of 132 tokens for 1SG, the most frequent form found is the irregular form *sei* (from the Ptg. verb *saber* 'to know'), as in Example (11a). Another irregular conjugation form found for 1SG forms in the oral corpus is *vou*, from the Portuguese verb *ir* 'to go' (12b). The remaining tokens all display the regular final allomorph for 1SG of the PRS, /o/, as may be observed in (13c), (14d) and (15e).

(11) Makista　　　　　　　　　　　　　　　(Pinharanda Nunes, fieldwork)
 a. *Eu   nang   sei   agora.*
    1SG NEG   know-f   now
    'I do not know now.'
 b. *Eu   vou   aqui.*
    1SG go-f   here
    'I am going here.'
 c. *nang   posso   dá   nada.*
    NEG   can-AUX   give-INF   nothing
    'I cannot give anything.'

(11) d. *Eu muito gosto chouriço.*[15]
   1SG much like chouriço
   'I like chouriço very much.'
   e. *Ainda lembro.*
   still remember-f
   '[I] still remember.'

Lastly, the 1SG forms *sei* 'know' and *quero* 'want', the two most common instances of this inflection in the oral corpus (from Ptg. *saber* 'to know' and *querer* 'to want', respectively) proved to be the most frequent forms for their PRS paradigms in Portuguese, among a sample count based on the Davies & Ferreira (2006) online corpus of Portuguese. The high person-number agreement produced by the 1SG forms as well as the 3SG forms on the copulas *é* and *está* (cf. previous section) indicates that these forms are more recent in MAC than the remaining 3SGe verbs and present a greater resemblance to their value in the superstrate.

5.3 The Past Perfective in the MAC oral corpus

As observed in Figure 1, the superstrate IND inflection morphology in MAC used for references prior to the enunciation act (i.e. past tense), occurs only in the oral corpus.

The 312 tokens of PST.PFV forms in the oral corpus considered in Pinharanda Nunes (2011) overwhelmingly occur in past perfective contexts (93.3%). Only 21 tokens (6.7%) appear with other aspectual contexts. Those 93.3% of PST.PFV equally exhibit superstrate person-number agreement with 3SG subjects of the sentences in which they are used. Such a distribution makes it clear that the speakers of MAC are conscious of the superstrate tense-aspect and person-number agreement functions of the 3SG inflection for the PST.PFV. In Portuguese, there is a high degree of fusion between the tense-aspect and person-number morphology in PST.PFV, and therefore agreement may aid the acquisition of this tense-aspect superstrate inflection. The PST.PFV form in MAC is mainly applied on regular *-a*, *-e* and *-i* theme vowel verbs in the superstrate. The remaining cases of the PST.PFV inflection refer to specific forms of verbs with an irregular conjugation paradigm in the superstrate, applied in varying small frequencies (Pinharanda Nunes 2011: 200): (a) 61 tokens for *foi* < Ptg. 3SG of the PST.PFV of both *ir* 'to go' and *ser* 'to be'; (b) 23 tokens for other irregular superstrate verbs: (c) 10 tokens of *veio* < Ptg. 3SG of the PST.PFV of *vir* 'to come'; (d) 6 tokens of *teve* < Ptg. 3SG of the PST.PFV of *ter* 'to have / there to be'; (e) 3 tokens of *disse* < Ptg. 3SG of the PST.PFV of *dizer* 'to say'; (f) 1 token each of the following forms: *esteve* < Ptg. 3SG of the

PST.PFV of *estar* 'to be' (see note 12): *fez* < Ptg. 3SG of the PST.PFV of *fazer* 'to do'; *trouxe* < Ptg. 3SG of the PST.PFV of *trazer* 'to bring'; *pus* < Ptg. 3SG of the PST.PFV of *pôr* 'to put'; *viu* < Ptg. 3SG of the PST.PFV of *ver* 'to see'. Besides these, a mere 4 tokens presenting inflection other than 3SG, specifically 1PL, were found: *tivemos* < Ptg. 1PL of the PST.PFV of *ter* 'to have' and *fomos* < Ptg. 1PL of the PST.PFV of both *ser* 'to be' and *ir* 'to go'.

A probabilistic trinomial analysis of the distribution of this form in MAC according to the lexical classes concludes that PST.PFV is mainly favored by the combined set of telic verbs (cf. note 9) – <achievements> and <accomplishments> (pr. 64), e.g. *matou* < Ptg. 3SG for PST.PFV of *matar* 'to kill' as an <achievement> and *morreu* < Ptg. 3SG for PST.PFV of *morrer* 'to die' as an <accomplishment>.[16] Secondly, this form is favored by the atelic class <states> (pr. 37), e.g. *gostou* < Ptg. 3SG for PST.PFV of *gostar* 'to like' (Pinharanda Nunes 2011:221).

The PST.PFV superstrate inflection is disfavored by the remaining atelic class <activities>, e.g. *corrê* < Ptg. INF *correr* 'to run'. On the contrary, the non-superstrate forms <INF, <3SGr and 3SGe (for this specific tense/aspect context) are favored by <state> and <activity> predicates and disfavored by <accomplishments> and <achievements> – precisely the two lexical classes that favored PST.PFV (Pinharanda Nunes 2011:200). This distribution is in agreement with Andersen & Shirai (1996) and Andersen's (2002) prediction concerning the acquisition of past verb morphology in naturalistic L2 contexts, based on the Primacy of Aspect Hypothesis, which proposes that L2 and L1 learner/acquirers select morphological tense-aspect inflection based on the lexical aspect of the verbs associated to those same elements. Andersen & Shirai (1996) state that the acquisition of verbal morphology in languages with an overt PFV/IPFV distinction first achieves PFV inflection and only later IPFV. In the acquisition of the PFV morphology, it begins with <achievements> and <accomplishments> (i.e. [+telic]) and only later extends to <activities> and <states> (i.e. [–telic] verbs). In the case of the acquisition of IPFV inflection, the authors predict the inverse, i.e. that speakers will begin by applying them on <states> and <activities>, only later extending to <achievements> and <accomplishments>.

The consonance of the use of PST.PFV inflection in the MAC oral corpus with this Hypothesis gains even greater plausibility when we consider that the probabilistic trinomial analysis in Pinharanda Nunes (2011:220) revealed that the only speakers of MAC who favor this superstrate inflectional morphology PST.PFV are those who have had a high degree of contact with Portuguese.

Examples of PST.PFV inflection from the MAC oral corpus for verbs with regular and irregular conjugation patterns in the superstrate follow:

(12) Makista (Pinharanda Nunes, fieldwork)
   a. *Eu   sa   mae   qui ja naceu   na Macau.*
      1SG POSS mother who PRF be.born-f LOC Macau
      'My mother, who was born in Macau.'
   b. *Dipois um ano, ja cá chegou, encontrou marido.*
      after one year PRF LOC arrive-f find-f husband
      'One year after I arrived, I found a husband.'

With regard to the co-occurrence of the PST.PFV with preverbal markers, only 14 tokens in the MAC oral corpus display such a sequence, with the marker *ja*. These cases correspond to either of two possibilities: (a) an ungrammatical redundancy in the marking of the perfective by maintaining the creole marker in the presence of the superstrate inflection, as in Examples (13a,b); (b) the use of *ja* according to its superstrate adverbial value 'already', as in Examples (14a,b).

(13) Makista (Pinharanda Nunes, fieldwork)
   a. *Eu sa marido ganha bem. Cava eli ja morreu.*
      1SG POSS husband earn-f well then 3SG PRF die-f
      'My husband earned well. Then he died.'
   b. *Doutor aprinta eu: Como ja caiu?*[17]
      doctor ask-f 1SG how PRF fall-f
      'The doctor asked me: "How did you fall?"'

(14) Makista (Pinharanda Nunes, fieldwork)
   a. *Agora all my friends ja morreu.*
      now - - - PRF/ADV die-f
      'Now, all my friends have already died.'
   b. *Pedro falou eli busca ôcê. Eu ja preguntei eli.*
      Pedro say-f 3SG fetch-nf 2SG 1SG PRF/ADV Ask-g 3SG
      'Pedro said he would fetch you. I (already) asked him.'

The absence of any instance of preverbal marking of PST.PFV verbs by means of *ta* indicates a possible restriction by this marker on the mentioned inflection. This matches the distribution of *ta* observed in Pinharanda Nunes & Baxter (2004) and Pinharanda Nunes (2011), who treat *ta* as an imperfective marker of the progressive aspect, contra earlier descriptions of MAC which considered it a present tense marker. Bearing in mind that the TAM marker *ta* derived from the Portuguese COP *estar* 'to be', it is relevant to note that the oral corpus of MAC does reveal instances of this COP bearing the 3PS inflection, i.e. *está*. Furthermore, it marks the superstrate person-number agreement in 85.7% of the cases for tokens used in tense/aspect contexts where it maintains its superstrate functions.[18] The use of *está* in the oral corpus thus indicates the re-installation of inflection, corresponding to yet another step in the decreolization process of the MAC TAM system. The conscious use of *está* (very often abbreviated to /ta/ in superstrate informal speech) seems to be a very plausible motive for the absence of co-occurrence of *ta* and verbs bearing PST.PRV inflection.

5.4 The Past Imperfective in the MAC oral corpus

Similarly to the case of PST.PFV, verbs inflected for PST.IPFV in the MAC oral corpus strictly occur in tense and aspect contexts where their superstrate values are maintained. This means the inflection applies to verbs in past tense contexts which entail an imperfective grammatical aspect. The oral corpus used for this study records a total of 199 verbs with PST.IPFV morphology in MAC. Of these, 97 correspond to verbs of regular conjugation in the lexifier with *-a* and *-e* theme vowels. The remaining cases correspond to irregular superstrate verbs: (a) *tinha* > Ptg. 1SG/3SG for PST.IPFV of *ter* 'to have' – 55 tokens; (b) estava > Ptg. 1SG/3SG for PST.IPFV of *estar* 'to be' – 23 tokens; (c) *era* > Ptg. 1SG/3SG for PST.IPFV of ser 'to be' – 14 tokens. The person-number combination for the cases of PST.IPFV in MAC is exclusively that of the shared 1SG/3SG forms. Below, we provide examples for each of the two regular conjugation groups in the lexifier, and for each of the irregular verbs used with PST.IPFV morphology in MAC.

(15) Makista (Pinharanda Nunes, fieldwork)
    a. *porque mae de ela tambem nang trabalhava.*
       because mother POSS 3SG.F also NEG work-f
       'Because her mother also did not use to work'
    b. *eu havia vai Austrália.*
       1SG AUX go-f Australia
       'I was to have gone to Australia.'
    c. *Nos tinha panha barco vai Kowloon.*
       1PL AUX catch-f boat go-f Kowloon
       'We had to catch the boat to [go to] Kowloon.'
    d. *Dos ilouto estava na essi campo.*
       two 3PL be-f LOC that camp
       'The other two were in that prisoner camp.'
    e. *Era mais animado qui agora.*
       be-f more lively than now
       'It was livelier than now.'

Following Clements' (2009a) analysis of the frequency of use of certain superstrate verb forms as one of the factors behind their transfer to the three IPCs (cf. Section 2), Pinharanda Nunes (2011) applies the notion to the case of superstrate IND morphology in MAC. The frequency counts of the occurrence of verbs bearing the IND inflectional morphology for 3sGe, 1sG, 3sG for PST.PFV and 3sG for IPFV reveal that all these forms correspond to the verb inflections that most frequently occur in their respective verb paradigms in the superstrate, compared with other person-number combinations for those inflectional paradigms (Pinharanda Nunes 2011: 222).[19]

6. Superstrate-derived IND forms in Indo-Portuguese Creoles

Table 4 presents the distribution of the verb forms under study among the three Indo-Portuguese Creoles considered. All exhibit the default form <INF. We have considered the 3sGr group of forms as non-applicable to the three Indo-Portuguese creoles under survey, the reason being that in IPC the forms *tem, vem, vai, sai,* and *cai* (belonging to 3sGr in MALC and 19th-century MAC), are exclusively used for present tense reference. In these three IPCs, these verbs have corresponding forms with superstrate-derived morphology specifically for past reference contexts (cf. distribution paradigm in Tables 5 and 6 in the following section). On the one hand, the 3sGe group in these Indian creoles, when compared with MAC, is only partially represented in KOR and DAM, yet fully represented in DIU (cf. distribution paradigm in Table 6 and related discussion in 6.1). On the other hand, PST.PFV morphology is found in all three creoles currently under discussion. However, the three only partially exhibit PST.IPFV, since this inflection is restricted to a limited set of verbs, as will be discussed in Section 6.3.

Table 4. Distribution of verb forms in the Indo-Portuguese Creoles

	INF	3sGr	3sGe	PST.PFV	PST.IPFV
KOR	+	−	±[†]	+	±
DIU	+	−	+	+	±
DAM	+	−	±	+	±

[†] ± indicates that a particular group of verb forms is applied to smaller range of verbs comparatively to MAC.

6.1 Vestiges of present indicative morphology

As explained in the previous section, the 3sGr in the Indo-Portuguese Creoles defy our classification criteria for those verbs when applied to the written corpora of MAC and to MALC (cf. Section 1). The nature of these verbs is exemplified in Table 5. Both in this paradigm as well as that in Table 6, we have included the forms for 19th-century MAC and MALC to demonstrate the similarity between these two creoles and their distance from the IPC paradigms.[20]

Looking at Table 5, we observe that *tem* appears only with present tense contexts, whereas in past reference contexts the Indo-Portuguese group of creoles uses superstrate derived past forms: *ti* (in KOR) and *tiŋ* (in DIU and DAM), for example. The same paradigm also shows the corresponding past tense morphology for each of the remaining forms of the 3sGr, i.e.: *vai, vem, cai, sai*.[21] These superstrate-derived past forms in the Indo-Portuguese creoles, however, cannot be fully equated with those in the MAC oral corpus as they are only tense-sensitive and not aspect-sensitive.

In KOR and DAM, the past marker *ja* is prefixed to the superstrate PST.PFV 3sG morphology of *vai* and *vem*, producing the lexicalized forms highlighted on the right-hand side of Table 5. KOR exhibits a similar case for the superstrate verb *dar* 'give', producing *jade* (Clements, p.c. July 2011).

Table 5. Correspondence of the MALC and MAC 3sGr paradigm in the Asian-Portuguese creole

MAC		MALC		KOR		DAM		DIU	
PRS†	PST	PRS	PST	PRS	PST	PRS	PST	PRS	PST
vai	*vai*	*vai*	*vai*	*vai*	*yafoy*	*vai*	*jafoy*	*vai*	*foy*
vem	*vem*	*vem*	*vem*	*vem*	*yawe*	*vem*	*jayo*	*vem*	*vey*
cai	*cai*	*cai*	*cai*	*cai*	*kaiw*	*cai*	*kaiw*	*cai*	*kaiw*
sai	*sai*	*sai*	*sai*	*sai*	*saiw*	*sai*	*saiw*	*sai*	*saiw*
tem	*tem*	*tem*	*tem*	*tə*	*ti*	*te*	*tiŋ*	*te*	*tiŋ*

† For practical reasons, we have extended the orthography used for these 3sGr verb forms in Pinharanda Nunes (2011) to their use in the present-tense of the three Indo-Portuguese Creoles.

In the case of *tem*, in parallel with the common function it shares among all Asian Portuguese creoles, as a possessive, existential, and copular verb,[22] in KOR and DAM it also presents the function of preverbal tense marker (Clements & Koontz-Garboden 2002), or an auxiliary according to the terminology applied in Cardoso (2009: 146) in the case of DIU. In the following paradigm for non-past contexts these instances are signaled in bold.[23]

Table 6. Superstrate-derived present tense inflection

	MAC	MALC	KOR	DAM	DIU
Simple Present	fala/ falə	fala	fala	fala	fal
Progressive Present	(ta) fala	ta fala	(tɛ) fala-n	te fala-n	te fala
Habitual Present	(ta) fala	fala	(tə) fala	fala-n	fal
Completive Present	fala	fala	fala-d	(te) fala-d	te fala-d

The contrastive paradigm in Table 6 further serves the purpose of exemplifying the distribution of the 3sGE in the Indo-Portuguese Creoles. As Clements notes:

> In Daman, and Korlai, the base form of the verb is based on the infinitival form (…). However in DIU, for the simple and habitual present, at least, the default form *fal*, is not derived from the infinitival form, but rather on the 3sG form (…), i.e. the most frequently-occurring form of the present-tense superstrate paradigm.
> (Clements 2009: 42)

Clements accounts for the difference of the base form in DIU (3sG of the PRS), compared to that of KOR and DAM (<INF) based on the typology of the DIU community: small, homogeneous and historically white-collar. There, "[b]etween the forms *falá* and *fal*, as a base form, the latter, present-tense form would be closer to an acrolectal form referring to present situations" (Clements 2009a: 42).

Nevertheless, 3sGE is not applied in DIU completely free of constraints. Cardoso (2009: 151) mentions the case of *kere* < Ptg. *querer* 'to want', which in its use as the volitive 'to want', takes on the 3sG inflection for PRS in non-anterior contexts, *kɛr*. For past contexts it assumes an innovative morphological form, probably derived from an approximation to the 3sG inflection of the PST.PFV for regular -*e* or -*i* theme verbs in the lexifier: *keriw*. However, when used as an auxiliary expressing deontic modality, it exhibits the infinitive form *kere*. Whether the use of 3sGE in DIU is a question of maintenance – following the analysis of Luís (2008) –, or of acquisition due to the prolonged presence of contact with the lexifier, is a relevant matter for discussion, which however, transcends the aims of this paper.

6.2 Vestiges of perfective past morphology

The forms *tem, vai, vem, cai, sai,* classified as 3sGr for the MAC written corpora, and in MALC and Tugu Creole Portuguese (TUG), display a different morphology in Indo-Portuguese Creoles for past-tense contexts. This morphology is derived from superstrate forms inflected for this tense and suffixed to *ja: jafoy, yawe, jayo, saiw, kaiw*. Clements & Koontz-Garboden (2002: 213) classify *vai* and *vem* for KOR and DAM as instances of a possible variation in the use of the PST.

PFV morphology in these two creoles, whereby the erstwhile past marker *ja* has been lexicalized, resulting in a fossilized form.[24] Despite the fossilization of the lexicalized marker *ja*, the forms *jafoy, yawe, jayo* are used only in past tense contexts. The morphological variations of *vai, vem, cai, sai*, specifically for past-tense contexts, leads to the exclusion of these verbs in IPC from our classification of the 3SGr group found in MALC and in the earlier descriptions and corpora of MAC. It thus follows that the PST.PFV derived inflection is broadly used on all other verbs, of both regular and irregular conjugations of the superstrate among the IPCs. As Luís points out, the presence of genuine theme vowels from the superstrate verbs in the IPCs accounts for the conjugation class distinction that is generally applied with the superstrate inflection in these creoles. Therefore, the 3SG inflection of the PST.PFV, used in Indo-Portuguese Creoles for regular verbs in the superstrate, displays "allomorphic shape alterations that are triggered solely by conjugation class distinctions" (Luís 2008: 83). This implies that for verbs with the *-a* theme vowel the final vowel is replaced with *-o*, while with the *-e* and *-i* theme vowels the glide *-w* is added (cf. Table 7 below). In MAC, such forms are only found in the oral corpus (cf. Figure 1, and Section 5.1.). Furthermore, in the IPCs as well as in MAC, the PST.PFV form is used to mark past perfective aspect, thus matching its value in the superstrate. MALC does not exhibit the PST.PFV form.

Table 7. Superstrate-derived past perfective inflection

	MAC†	MALC	TUG	KOR	DAM	DIU
-*a* (falar)	*falo*	–	–	*falo*	*falo*	*falo*
-*e* (comer)	*kumew*	–	–	*kumew*	*kumew*	*kumew*
-*i* (subir)	*subiw*	–	–	*subiw*	*subiw*	*subiw*

† Only the oral corpus of MAC is being considered.

6.3 Vestiges of imperfective past morphology

In the IPCs, *tem* may function as a possessive, copula and existential verb. In past-tense contexts, in all three IPCs considered, *tem* displays a form derived from the superstrate's common inflection for 1SG/3SG of the PST.IPFV in Portuguese *tinha*, with deletion of the final vowel (*tiŋ*). The fact that this form is common to two person-number markings in the superstrate increases its frequency in the pool of variants the creole speakers were exposed to. Moreover, the initial syllable of the PST.PFV of *ter* (*ti-*) is present throughout the entire mentioned tense-aspect paradigm. Bybee (1985) refers to strong phonological representations within a paradigm as 'lexical density'. Thus, in the case if *ti* and *tiŋ* in the three IPCs, lexical density may be an additional contributing factor in increasing the probability of retention of derived forms of the superstrate PST.PFV for *ter*.[25] In KOR, in past tense contexts, *tem* takes on the form of *ti*. This too suggests that the latter may also derive from the superstrate *tinha*, although we should not disregard the possibility of it deriving from the superstrate 1SG inflection of PST.PFV *tive*. As a preverbal tense marker, *ti* precedes predicates in imperfective contexts (i.e. progressive and habitual), as well the completive past. In these cases, *ti/tiŋ* merely mark the past, irrespective of the aspect in question. Considering that both *tiŋ/ti* could derive from the superstrate imperfective form *tinha,* the use of *ti / tiŋ* with the completive past broadens its functional scope beyond that which the superstrate form *tinha* covers when used as an existential or a possessive. The specific inflection for the aspects at issue is realized then by suffixation on the main verb: *-n* for progressive and habitual, and *-d* for the perfective aspect implicit in the completive past. When used as the auxiliary of a periphrastic expression of the past perfect, *ti/tiŋ* maintains the superstrate value for similar tense-aspect contexts – the Ptg. *pretérito mais-que-perfeito composto* (past anterior).[26]

Table 8. Superstrate-derived past imperfective inflection

	MAC†	MALC	KOR	DAM	DIU
Progressive Past	*falava*	–	*ti fala-n*	*tiŋ falan*	*tiŋ fala*
Habitual Past	*falava*	–	*ti fala*	*tiŋ falan*	*tiŋ fala*
Completive Past (past perfect)	–	–	*ti fala-d*	*tiŋ fala-d*	*tiŋ falad*

† Only the oral corpus of MAC is being considered.

Clements & Koontz-Garboden (2002: 217–218) draw attention to two other cases of PST.PFV derived morphology found in DAM, and which maintain their past habitual inflection function: [*avidi/aydi* + V][27] and [*er* + *də*]. In the first instance *avidi* and its reduced form *aydi* derives from the superstrate *havia de* < Ptg. 1SG/3SG for PST.IPFV of *haver* 'there to be' followed by the preposition *de*, rendering the periphrastic expression of future intension equivalent to 'shall'. As for *er də*, it derives from the superstrate *era*[28] < 3SG for PST.PFV of *ser* 'to be' followed by the preposition *de*. In both instances, the forms are used to mark the past habitual, thus partially matching their superstrate values. The authors admit the need for further study to establish whether these alternate means of marking the past habitual may be based on lectal variants. DIU also has a cognate form, *vidi*, which is the past equivalent of the irrealis marker *ad* < Ptg. 3SG *haver* + *de* (*há-de*), with the same volitive meaning as its cognate forms in DAM.

The form *er* is similarly found in DIU as the past tense variant of *é* – a copular verb alternating with *tə* and *tiŋ*. Cardoso notes that in highly acrolectal speech, DIU registers a marginal use of PST.IPFV as the morphological inflection of the past habitual, where the "corresponding suffix *-v* is equivalent to the standard Portuguese imperfective marker *-va-*" (Cardoso 2009: 143) for *-a* theme vowel verbs. One of the two examples provided in Cardoso to show this acrolectal use of PST.IPFV refers to the copular *estar*, realized as *ista-v*. As was the case with PST.PFV, neither of these two superstrate verb forms are found in MALC.

In this section we have observed several differences between MAC and the three IPCs as far as the distribution of superstrate IND morphology is concerned. In the three IPCs, the verbs included in the 3SGr group for MALC and the traditional verb form paradigm of MAC are used according to their superstrate tense-aspect functions and have corresponding past forms. Still with regard PRS forms, only in Diu is the 3SGe applied as widely as in MAC. As for the PST indicative forms, only PST.PFV matches the use in MAC, in all three IPCs. On the other hand, PST.IPFV is only applied to a restricted group of verbs in the IPCs. Among them, the one that reveals a more significant role in past contexts in all three creoles is *ti/tiŋ*. Its superstrate imperfective function is partially lost and gains a function it does not hold in MAC, that of a marker of past tense with progressive and habitual aspect.

7. The sociohistorical context of Makista in Macau and Hong Kong[29]

In this section we outline aspects of the socio-historical and demographic context in which MAC developed. The circumstances described suggest a scenario for the acquisition of superstrate inflectional verb morphology which is rather different from one proposed by Luís (2008) for the IPCs.

The Portuguese formed a permanent settlement in Macau from 1557 onwards. This was almost 50 years after the occupation of Goa and 45 years after the conquest of Malacca, ample time for the IPCs and MALC to be well into their second or even third generation of speakers. In 1557, the Christian population numbered roughly 500 inhabitants.[30] Another significant section of the population was comprised of Fujian traders, whose presence in the maritime trading points of greater Canton long preceded the Portuguese presence. As in other trading ports occupied by the Portuguese in South and Southeast Asia, peoples of numerous diverse linguistic and ethnic origins gathered in Macau:

> Na primeira década após a sua fundação em 1557, a população de Macau contava principalmente com estrangeiros: o contingente português, politicamente dominante, e um maior contingente subordinante de marinheiros, soldados e outros auxiliares, todos de diversas origens. (Conim & Teixeira 1998:109)[31]

Baxter (2009) notes that the 'Portuguese' element comprised *reinóis* (European-born Portuguese), Portuguese born in Asia and *mestiços* (Eurasians) from diverse origins. The latter were in many cases the offspring of *casados* – Portuguese officially married to Asian women, a significant sub-group. Interracial marriage was common practice in all the Portuguese Asian colonies, and resulted in the creation of loyal Luso-Asian bilingual communities. By the end of the 16th century, this Luso-Asian component was a very significant sub-group in Macau; Conim & Teixeira note that "em 1600 havia 600 famílias indo-portuguesas" ('in 1600 there were 600 Indo-Portuguese families'; Conim & Teixeira 1998: 109).

In our opinion, the term Indo-Portuguese in the previous reference should not be taken as meaning literally of direct origin from the Indian sub-continent. Rather, the term should be taken as signifying both Asian-born Portuguese and Luso-Asians, the latter naturally having some Indian stock, but potentially originating in any of the enclaves between India and Macau, owing to the easterly development of the Portuguese empire. These Indo-Portuguese families would have originated in Portuguese ports more relevant to the Macau endeavor. Malacca would have been especially relevant, yet there would have been a presence too of elements from further afield, in India, where the Portuguese colonial administration had its power-base. This would mean that, in the 16th century, the population under Portuguese jurisdiction comprised a good number of linguistic imports, many of which, we will argue below, would have spoken Malay.

At a later date, however, towards the mid-17th century, Chinese Christians become evident in the Macau population. A 1635 account by the Portuguese chronicler António Bocarro describes Macau as having 850 Portuguese residents and their children, with slaves from Africa and other origins: "Alem deste número de cazados portuguezes tem mais esta cidade outros tantos cazados entre naturais da terra, chinas christãos, que chamão Jurubassas, de que são os mais, e outras nações, todos christãos" (Bocarro 1992[1635]).[32] There is no mention of non-Christian Chinese living within the Christian quarter of the city.

Malacca was the nearest official Portuguese port city to Macau. It was from there that the Portuguese exploratory expeditions of the Macau coastline set out. Naturally, the initial Portuguese and Luso-Asian influx to Macau came mainly from Malacca and secondly from the remaining Southeast Asian ports under Portuguese control – all within the geo-political and economic region where varieties of Malay were used. With the rapid increase in the control of these routes by the Portuguese, and the emergence of Luso-Asian communities spread out along this Southeast Asian network, we assume that pidgin Portuguese (and creolized varieties thereof, including MALC) were used in parallel to vehicular Malay varieties. The continuous population movements within this sea route network very likely opened way to the currency of pidginized varieties of Portuguese in Southeast Asia, influenced by vehicular Malay – the substratum of MALC itself. Thus MALC and varieties of Southeast Asian Portuguese-based pidgins would have continued to be the means of common linguistic interactions among these groups in the newly founded Macau. In such a scenario, MALC (and closely related Southeast Asian Portuguese pidgin varieties) would have been used as L1 and L2 in different degrees of proficiency by the groups of Portuguese, Eurasians and Asians.

The census data in Conim & Teixeira (1998) points to an influx of peoples from Malacca, Batavia and other ports in the Malay Archipelago well into the 19th century. The combination of these factors may explain the many affinities between MAC and MALC, distinguishing these two creoles from the IPCs. The influence of MALC and Malay on MAC is visible both in the lexicon (Batalha 1988; Senna Fernandes & Baxter 2004; Cardoso, *this volume*), as well at the morphosyntactic levels.[33] In relation to the latter, Pinharanda Nunes & Baxter (2004) and Pinharanda Nunes (2011) point out significant similarities between the TAM system of MALC, MAC and Malay, regarding use and functions of preverbal markers. Pinharanda Nunes (2008) too presents overlapping values between the demonstratives in MAC and those in MALC and in Malay. The composition of the migrated population at the early setting of Macau suggests the creation of a strong linguistic and cultural identity and support network between Southeast Asian Luso-Asians and Asians from the same region and from South Asia, diminishing the effect of the attitudinal factor which led the northern IPC speakers to strive for a less basic variety of Portuguese, as proposed by Luís (2008). Historical documentation of the socio-political development of this port city indicates that the process of interaction and mutual integration (via marriage, for instance) between the Portuguese, the *mestiços* and other Asian Christians who came to Macau began at a much earlier stage and at a more rapid pace than their integration with the local Chinese communities. According to Amaro (1988:7), at Liampó, the first Portuguese settlement on the South China Coast before moving to Macau, there were 300 *casados* with their Portuguese and *mestiço* wives. There is no record of Chinese wives for that period. The first Christian residents of Macau did not mix with the Chinese population. The women with whom they lived were of Japanese, Malay, Indonesian and Indian stock many of whom were slaves Boxer 1997:48). Also in support of a mainly South and Southeast Asian influx of women to Macau, Seabra (2006/2007: 198) makes reference to a description by Father Francisco de Sousa in 1563 of young maidens and orphans participating in a procession and performing exactly as was customary in Goa and other Portuguese ports in Asia. She interprets this as an indication that the women who came with the first Portuguese to Macau included Portuguese-Eurasian orphans, and slaves bought in Asian markets. Given the strong Southeast Asian and Indian Eurasian network in the Christian households of early Macau, this community would appear to have been less affected by the attitudinal factor that Luís (2008) claims as essential to the acquisitional outcome she observes in the northern IPCs. Thus, in Macau, two factors may have combined to produce MAC: (a) the habitual inaccessibility, in similar contexts, of the substrate speakers to the ruling European minority's language; (b) bilingualism in MALC, other Portuguese-based Asian creoles or pidgins, and Malay and other Southeast Asian or Indian languages in the early stages, which allowed for local in-group models to emerge as the TL instead of Portuguese.

The Chinese ascendency of Macanese families throughout the centuries was, to a large extent, the result of the presence of the *muitsai* within the Portuguese and Eurasians households in Macau (Boxer 1997: 48).[34] Many wills entrusted to the *Santa Casa da Misericórdia* (Holy House of Mercy) in Macau by Portuguese and Macanese men and widows stand as evidence of this (Seabra 2007). The sale of these children to residents in Macau began early on and continued for two more centuries, despite prohibitions from both the Portuguese and the Chinese authorities (Seabra 2007: 201–202). Given the very young age at which these *muitsai* – also referred to in Portuguese documentation as *bichas* and *criações* – were brought into the Portuguese and Eurasian households, they would not have contributed with much of their parents' mother tongue to the MAC feature pool, as it is.

Besides the demographic factor and cultural practices mentioned, another possible reason for the slow integration of the Chinese into the Macanese community, and thus of Cantonese elements into MAC, was the overall segregation between the two groups, imposed by the layout of the city itself, as well as administrative regulations within the city and on land travel by the Portuguese beyond the boundaries of Macau. The Chinese 18th-century (1751) monograph *Ou-Mun-Kei-Leok* (Yin & Zhang 2009[1751]) on Macau reports that in 1574 a barrier was built by the Chinese three *li*[35] from the city of Macau, where soldiers and officers were stationed:[36]

> Abria-se às segundas-feiras e sábados, deixando passar um determinado número de dan de arroz. Abria-se ao todo seis vezes por mês (…) as autoridades civis e militares deixavam a porta selada após uma inspecção conjunta.
> (Yin & Zhang 2009[1751]: 335)[37]

As for the existence of separate resident areas for the Portuguese and Christian communities and the non-Christian Chinese, this same source provides evidence of an effort by the Chinese, early on, to restrain the spread of the foreigners and their mixing with Chinese:

> (…) foram levantadas umas cercas nas quatro ruas principais, onde se concentravam as casas (…). Nas altas paliçadas afixaram-se cartazes com os seguintes dizeres: "Temama nossa grandeza e reconheçam a nossa virtude.
> (Yin & Zhang 2009[1751]: 335)[38]

In Bocarro's description, we read that:

> Os muros que tem esta cidade estavão quazy acabados por Dom Francisco Mascarenhas, o primeiro capitão-geral que teve (…) porem, os chinas, como são tão desconfiados, fizeram derrubar grão parte deles (…)
> (Bocarro 1992[1635]: 264)[39]

This is confirmed in the 18th-century Chinese monograph:

> Em Macau havia uma muralha que cercava a cidade bárbara que foi destruída durante a anterior dinastia Ming (…). Agora só exite um pequeno muro. (…) Os bárbaros residem dentro do muro, onde chineses vivem misturados com eles. (…)
> (Yin & Zhang 2009[1751]: 363)[40]

These reports in the monograph to the Chinese authorities testify to the initial segregation and to the later (18th-century) gradual mixing of the Chinese into the Portuguese (Christian) quarters. Nevertheless we should not be led to believe that the gradual intersection of the living quarters of these two communities was synonymous with an effective integration of the Chinese on a large scale. 19th-century accounts still talk of a city divided into Portuguese and Chinese areas, despite the confirmation of the ongoing incursion of Chinese into the predominantly Portuguese areas:

> A cidade de Macau (..) dividindo-se em cidade christã e basar (a parte chineza). (..) O basar é exclusivamente habitado por chinas. (..) O basar é o centro commercial dos chinas em Macau. (..) A antiga povoação de S. Lazaro, hoje encorporada na cidade, esta na continuação da parte christã, e é o recinto habitado pelos chins que teem abraçado a nossa religião. (..) A cidade christa propriamente dita abrange a parte mais pitoresca de Macau. (..) A cidade christã tem sido invadida por habiantes chinezes: nos bairros chins é que raro moram christãos. Alem dísto, na maior parte das casas de moradores portuguezes, ou estrangeiros, há creados chinezes.
> (da França 1897: 44–47)[41]

This is not to say that there was no integration of Chinese individuals into the Christian community (both European and Luso-Asian). However, it did not commence as early, nor was it as widespread, as miscegenation in other Asian port cities under Portuguese rule. This breaches the usual practice of early racial mixing of the newly arrived Portuguese and camp-followers with the local inhabitants in Portuguese settlements in Asia. Thus, in the case of Macau, one should stress the very likely central role that MALC (and various pidginized versions of it) apparently played from 1557 onwards and for a considerable amount of time in the linguistic reality of Macau.

The late 19th century and early 20th century brought political, economic and social changes which directly affected the course of the Macanese community and the MAC continuum. New opportunities brought by the establishment of the British colony of Hong Kong in the mid-19th century made the MAC-speaking community conscious of the possibility of social and economic promotion, both in Macau and in Hong Kong. Consequently, the need for better education of their youth to prepare them for the emerging socio-economic changes became a priority. The migration of many families to Hong Kong, and later to the European concessions established along the Chinese coast (especially Shanghai), awakened the spirit of identity among the MAC-speaking families, and the need to preserve that identity. In the Hong Kong community, the wealthy and educated members promoted the learning of Portuguese as a means of reinforcing the Portuguese half of their heritage, differentiating themselves, at the eyes of the British, from the local Chinese community (Braga 1997).

At the same time, in Macau, the first Portuguese-medium public schools were opened, providing the MAC speakers with access to regular schooling. The new generation of Portuguese- and English-literate MAC speakers gained access to the civil service, exposing them further to close and continued contact with Portuguese (Braga 1997; Pinharanda Nunes 2011). This new era introduced modern European lifestyle and ideology to the region. Families grew smaller, more freedom was given to young women, who, with the abolition of the dowry practice, gained more freedom in marriage affairs, thus increasing the possibility of marrying into the Chinese community as well (Seabra 2007: 203).

Table 9 summarizes the socio-linguistic context of MAC, in the way data is presented in Clements (2009) for DIU, DAM and KOR.

Table 9. Sociolinguistic context of the MAC-speaking community

Languages in contact	Presence of Portuguese	Principal means of employment
– Portuguese, Malacca Creole Portuguese and Malay (in the early stages); – Chinese (Cantonese and Hokkien).	– Strong governmental presence until 1999; – Schooling: very irregular and only for a minority; – General public schooling of MAC speakers from the late 19th century onwards; – Continued contact with Portuguese after the Handover of Macau to China in 1999 through schooling, television and radio.	– Extensively stratified society in social, economic and racial terms; – No religious or caste-like discrimination; – Semi-skilled and skilled labor (clerks, lawyers, doctors, teachers), especially form the mid-20th century onwards.

8. Conclusion

This chapter examined the superstrate morphology for PRS, PST.PFV and PST.IPFV found in MAC comparing its profile with superstrate morphology found in three IPCs: DIU, KOR and DAM. Earlier descriptions of verbal forms in MAC presented a verb form paradigm comprised of <INF and 3SGr, identifying it as a near-perfect copy of its principal antecessor, MALC. However, the verb form paradigm of MAC presents a wider range of superstrate morphology than previously reported, exceeding both in range and function its equivalents in the three IPCs. The emergence of superstrate inflection in MAC shows the following patterns: (a) the progressive increase in the use of 3SGe between the written corpora and the oral corpus; (b) inversely, the progressive decrease of the frequency of the use of <INF; (c) the use of PST.PFV and PST.IPFV solely in the oral corpus; (d) the favored use of PST.PFV and PST.IPFV exclusively by speakers with an intense contact with the lexifier. Similarly to what Luís (2008) claims for the superstrate inflectional morphology in the three IPCs, the verb morphology considered in MAC shows evidence of superstrate distinctions of tense and aspect – partially in the case of 3SGe, and fully in the case of PST.PFV and PST.IPFV for the 3SG. These high frequency forms in the superstrate coincide with the perceptive salience of the ubiquitous CV and VCV sequences (cf. e.g. *falou* < Ptg. 3SG for PST.PFV of *falar* 'to speak'; *comeu* < Ptg. 3SG for PST.PFV of *comer* 'to eat'; *havia* < Ptg. PST.PFV of *haver* 'there to be'; *gostava* < Ptg. 1SG/3SG for *gostar* 'to like'). This observation indicates the correlation between the approaches that consider the frequency of use of an item in the TL as a significant factor for its transfer to the L2 variety in naturalistic SLA and processes of creole formation (e.g. Lefebvre 2004; Lefebvre et al. 2006; Sprouse 2006; Siegel 2006).

The diachronic analysis of the MAC data strongly suggests that these inflectional paradigms are the result of L2 acquisition of the target language (the lexifier, Portuguese). However, this has not occurred in the same terms as in the IPCs wherein such morphology has been claimed to be the result of early L2 acquisition of a non-basic variety during their formative stage (Luís 2008). In MAC, the linguistic and socio-linguistic evidence indicates that the superstrate-like verb morphology emerged as L2 acquisition at a later stage in this creole's evolution, which we have identified as its decreolization phase. The gradual shift of the MAC verb paradigm towards that of the superstrate was motivated by external sociolinguistic factors to the L1 MAC-speaking community, which in turn created the need for a closer identification of these speakers with the L1 European Portuguese elite in Macau, for social and professional promotion. Those socio-linguistic factors relate to political and administrative changes brought about in Macau from the turn of the 20th century onwards which resulted in the increase of formal and informal exposure of MAC speakers to Portuguese, both through social and work-related networks as well as through schooling. This eventually lead to a situation of increasing bilingualism and the progressive decline in the number of basilect speakers, thus resulting in the variation of basilect and superstrate verb forms, as studied in this paper for the case of the IND inflectional morphology. This scenario coincides with the arguments Clements (2009a) presents for naturalistic SLA processes in the IPCs. Picking up from Romaine's argument with regard to the Anglicization of Tok Pisin (1992: 171), we too claim that the increasing use of Portuguese signals the decreolization of MAC.

Notes

1. Ferreira's (1978) brief grammar of MAC was included in a later publication (1996) which collected many of Santos Ferreira's poems, short stories and short plays. It is this reedited version we have used in our references to his description of the MAC grammar.

2. In Portuguese, the inflectional morphology of the present indicative expresses the present nature of an action and, at times, may be used to express non-present action (cf. Section 3). In terms of grammatical tense it coincides with the simple present in English, with the exception that in Portuguese it may also refer to actions that in English, for instance, are expressed by the present progressive tense and thus marked accordingly. To simplify cross-language terminology, we shall refer to the Portuguese Present Indicative as the simple present (PRS).

3. Cf. Baxter & Bastos (*this volume*) for reference to Clement's (2000) Malabar coast pidgin hypothesis, referring to the 16th century.

4. The distribution of MAC tokens in Pinharanda Nunes' (2011) quantitative study is as follows: 9258 tokens for the oral corpus, 465 for the 20th-century written corpus and 536 for the 19th-century written corpus.

5. The data used in Pinharanda Nunes (2011) were extracted exclusively from letters.

6. In the oral corpus, 3 interviews were done by Prof. Michelle Charpentier in Macau and Hong Kong in 1984. The remaining 13 were collected by myself in Macau, Vancouver and San Francisco with L1 speakers born between the 1920's and the 1930's. Unfortunately, no other oral recordings are known. Graciete Batalha was the only Portuguese researcher to have collected oral recordings throughout the mid 20th Century. Tragically, and ironically, these recordings disappeared after her death. It is absolutely critical that the remaining elderly speakers be recorded to provide a more solid database for further research and language preservation purposes. There is no longer any generational transmission. The language is under dire threat of extinction.

7. Tamil appears to be, however, the most important of the two substrates of BATT. In fact, Smith & Paauw (2006:176) categorically single Tamil out as the substrate of BATT, stating that "even if Sinhala were admitted to have an influence, the fact that its TAM categories are similar to those of Tamil means that the two languages would have acted in concert rather than in competition".

8. The superstrate inflectional morphology marks both tense and grammatical aspect. We consider tense as 'absolute tense' in the terms defined by Comrie (1993:36): "the traditional term absolute tense, (…) should be interpreted to mean a tense which includes as part of its meaning the present moment as deitic center (…)". With regard to grammatical aspect (also marked by this morphology), we again follow Comrie (1993:3) who, based on Holt (1943:6), considers this category as expressing "different ways of viewing the internal temporal constituency of a situation". There are two types of internal constituency of a situation: situations that are mere end points (i.e. perfective), and others that involve moments or processes, with duration and possibly several stages (i.e. imperfective). The perfective expresses the completed stage of events; for a brief description of the imperfective aspect, see note 11.

9. The lexical classification adopted here is that of Vendler (1967) as used in Smith (1991). This classification considers five lexico-semantic classes of verbs: (a) states [–dynamic]; (b) activities [+durative atelic events]; (c) accomplishments [+telic durative events]; (d) achievements [+telic durative events]. Telicity implies finiteness (both special and temporal). The two [+telic] classes listed are also [+resultative], as they express a change of state; and (e) points [+instantaneous, +atelic].

10. The verbs chosen for this sample paradigm correspond to the regular and irregular conjugation verbs in the superstrate that most frequently occur with this tense-aspect morphology inflection in MAC. Evidence of *-i-* and *-o-* theme verbs with PRS in the MAC corpora were too scarce to be considered. The same applies for the PST.PFV sample paradigm in Table 2.

11. The imperfective aspect expresses the internal structure of the duration of a situation. In this sense an imperfective aspect situation may be habitual. This implies it comprises duration and iterativity at intervals, interrupted by other situations. An imperfective aspect situation may also be continuous in nature. The continuous expresses the duration, or the iteration of verbs denoting a state, a change of that state, or existence. Lastly, imperfectivity also comprises the notion of progressive aspect. The progressive encompasses both the notion of progression and non-stativity, i.e., of movement and action (Comrie 1993:24–35).

12. In European Portuguese, the latter aspect is most commonly rendered periphrastically with the auxiliary verb *estar*: AUX-PST.IPFV + V-INF. In the current study, this case shall not be

considered, since this would imply a separate analysis of the various forms of *estar* as an auxiliary. Its forms do have marginal occurrence in the oral and the 19th-century written corpora of MAC. It would also imply a detailed study of the preverbal particle *ta*, as it coincides with the frequent phonological reduction of the 3SG PRS form of that auxiliary in informal speech in Portuguese: /ta/.

13. The functional superstrate inflectional morphology on verbs in MAC for references to events or states prior to the enunciation act (i.e. past) implies grammatical aspect marking. According to Comrie (1993:3), grammatical aspects "are different ways of viewing the internal temporal constituency of a situation", and "[t]he internal temporal contour of a situation provides the conceptual basis for the notion of aspect, which refers to the grammaticalization of expression of internal temporal constituency". The two grammatical aspects involved in the superstrate morphology in MAC are the perfective and the imperfective. The former expresses both actions and events completed within a definite timeframe and considered in their entirety (Comrie 1993:18). The imperfective, on the other hand, expresses the internal temporal structure of a situation, and is thus subdivided into the habitual, progressive and continuous aspects (Comrie 1993:24).

14. *Dó* is the designation given to the long headscarf worn traditionally worn by Macanese women.

15. *Chouriço* is a smoked Portuguese sausage.

16. In a trinomial probabilistic analysis, the favoring value is established from pr. 33 upwards, given that the sum of pr. 33 x 3 (one for each of the three independent variables) is pr. 100.

17. Given the pragmatic context of (14a) and (14b), the use of *ja* with a verb inflected for PST.PFV allows an overlapping of its creole value as a preverbal marker of aspect as well as its superstrate value as the adverb 'already'.

18. Conversely, in the written corpora, the 7 tokens in the 20th-century texts and the 9 tokens in the 19th-century material were too scarce to be considered for a quantitative analysis (Pinharanda Nunes 2011:192–93).

19. The frequency counts in Clements (2009a) and in Pinharanda Nunes (2011) are based on the online corpus of Portuguese of Davies & Ferreira (2006).

20. The MALC paradigm here refers exclusively to the traditional earlier descriptions of this creole and its written corpora.

21. These two paradigms were drawn up based on Clements & Koontz-Garboden (2002:213–214), Clements (1996:230) and Cardoso (2009:141).

22. In the case of the latter two, in place of the superstrate *haver* and the copulatives *ser* and *estar*.

23. Based on Clements & Koontz-Garboden (2002:213–214), Clements (2009a:230; 2009b), Cardoso (2009:141) and Luís (2008). These same studies were also used to build the verb paradigm maps in Tables 6, 7 and 8.

24. I thank an anonymous reviewer for pointing out this fossilization trait to me.

25. I thank an anonymous reviewer for calling my attention to this relevant fact.

26. The past anterior in Portuguese is composed of AUX-PST.IPFV (*tinha*) + Past Participle of the V-f.

27. Also used in the expression of counterfactuality (Clements & Koontz-Garboden (2002:217).

28. Regarding the forms *er* and *é* < Ptg. 3SG (PST.IPFV and PRS) of the copulative *ser* 'to be', Clements (2009a:44) claims that such 3SG forms in the IPCs considered "follows directly from the frequency argument (…): *é* and *era* are the most frequently used [forms] in their paradigms".

29. I thank Alan Baxter for discussion regarding the ethnic and linguistic mapping of early Macau society.

30. Archival source: <Carta do Pe. Gregório Gonzalez a D. Juan de Borja> s.l., s.d., AGI, Philippines, 27, fl.1v.

31. 'In the first decade after its establishment in 1557, the population of Macau was comprised mainly of foreigners: the politically dominant Portuguese contingent, and a larger subordinate contingent of sailors, soldiers and other helpers, all of diverse origins'.

32. 'Besides this number of Portuguese *cazados*, this city has an equal number of local *cazados*, Christian Chinese, who are the majority, and other nations, all Christians'. Bocarro's manuscript *O livro das plantas de todas as fortalezas, cidades e povoações do Estado da Índia*, complied between 1633 and 1665, gives details on all the fortresses, cities and settlements held by the Portuguese in Asia at the time.

33. Batalha (1988:127), in reference to the Luso-Malay ethnic and linguistic component of the MAC-speaking community claims that "(..) grande parte dos vocábulos malaios do velho macaísta denunciam indubitávelmente a mulher e indicam que deviam ter sido malaias ou malaio-portuguesas as companheiras e esposas dos mais antigos 'moradores' de Macau." ('many of the Malay terms in old Makista clearly reveal the women's contribution and indicate that the first residents of Macau must have taken Malay and Luso-Malay women as their wives and companions'). She exemplifies this claim by selecting some lexical items from her extensive glossary related to culinary terms, household and clothing items and superstitions as evidence of the Malay/Luso-Malay female influence in MAC.

34. *Muitsai* is the Cantonese term given to female babies and children rejected by their parents and sold for the purpose of becoming household servants, for a certain number of years or for life.

35. A traditional Chinese measurement for distance, equivalent to around 500 meters.

36. This barrier was kept all through the Portuguese colonial rule of Macau. In the 19th century, the Macau government substituted it with a neoclassic arched passageway, which still stands at the present day border between the Special Administrative Region of Macau and mainland China.

37. 'It was opened on Fridays and Saturdays to allow a certain *dan* [Traditional Chinese mass and weight measurement] of rice into the city. It was opened six times a month. (…) the civil and military authorities would seal the gateway after each joint inspection'; translated from the Portuguese edition.

38. '(…) fences were erected on the four main streets where the houses were concentrated (…) On the high palisades posters were put up with the following warnings: "Fear our greatness and acknowledge our virtue"'.

39. 'The walls that this city has were almost completed by Dom Francisco Mascarenhas, its first captain-general (…), however, as the Chinese are very suspicious, they had most of them pulled down (…)'.

40. 'In Macau there was a centenary wall surrounding the barbarians'city, which was destroyed during the previous Ming Dynasty (..). Now only a small wall is left. (…) The barbarians live within the wall, where Chinese live among them'.

41. 'The city of Macau (…) is divided into the Christian city and the Chinese bazaar (the Chinese sector). The bazaar is exclusively inhabited by Chinese. The bazaar is the commercial hub of the Chinese in Macau. (…) The old village of São Lazaro, which nowadays falls within the city walls, is the continuation of the Christian half of the city. It is inhabited by the Chinese who have converted to our religion. (…) The Christian half of the city lies on the most picturesque part of Macau (…) The Christian city has been invaded by Chinese inhabitants. However, very seldom does a Christian live in the Chinese quarters. Besides this, most of the Portuguese and foreigners' homes have Chinese servants'.

References

Amaro, A. M. 1988. *Filhos da Terra*. Macau: Instituto Cultural de Macau.
Andersen, R. W., and Y. Shirai. 1996. The primacy of aspect in first and second language acquisition: The pidgin-creole connection. In *Handbook of Second Language Acquisition*, eds. W. C. Ritchie and T. K. Bhatia, 527–570. San Diego, CA: Academic Press.
Andersen, R. W. 2002. The dimensions of pastness. In *The L2 Acquisition of Tense-Aspect Morphology* [Language Acquisition and Language Disorders 27], eds. R. Salaberry and Y. Shirai, 79–107. Amsterdam: John Benjamins.
Bardovi-Harlig, K. 2000. *Tense and Aspect in Second Language Acquisition: Form, Meaning, and Use*. Oxford: Blackwell.
Barreiros, D. L. 1943–44. *O Dialecto Português de Macau: Antologia*. Macau: Renascimento.
Batalha, G. N. 1974 [1958]. *Língua de Macau – o que foi e o que é*. Macau: Centro de Informação e Turismo.
Batalha, G. N. 1988. *Glossário do Dialecto Macaense. Notas Linguísticas, Etnográficas e Folclóricas* and *Suplemento ao Glossário do Dialecto Macaense. Notas Linguísticas, Etnográficas e Folclóricas*. Macau: Instituto Cultural de Macau.
Baxter, A. N. 1988. *A Grammar of Kristang (Malacca Creole Portuguese)* [Pacific Linguistics. Series B; no. 95]. Canberra: Pacific Linguistics.
Baxter, A. N. 2009. O português em Macau: Contacto e assimilação. In *Português em Contato*, ed. A. M. Carvalho, 277–312. Madrid-Frankfurt: Vervuert-Iberoamericana.
Becker, A., and T. Veenstra. 2003. The survival of inflectional morphology in French related Creoles. *Studies in Second Language Acquisition* 25: 283–306.
Bocarro, A. 1992 [1635]. *O Livro das Plantas de Todas as Fortalezas, Cidades e Povoações do Estado da Índia Oriental*, II Vol. Lisbon: Imprensa Nacional – Casa da Moeda.
Boxer, C. R. 1997. *O Senado da Câmara de Macau*. Macau: Leal Senado de Macau.
Braga, J. M. 1997. O Ensino da Língua Portuguesa em Hong Kong. In *Ensino da Língua Portuguesa em Hong Kong* [Colecção Educação Memórias 5], eds. A. S. Silva, A. Aresta and A. Barata, 15–51, Macau: Direcção dos Serviços de Ensino.

Bybee, J. L. 1985. *Morphology: A Study of the Relation Between Meaning and Form* [Typological Studies in Language 9]. Amsterdam: John Benjamins.
Cardoso, H. C. 2006. Linguistic traces of colonial structure. *Trans: Internet Journal for Cultural Sciences* 16. www.inst.at/trans
Cardoso, H. C. 2009. The Indo-Portuguese Language of Diu. PhD dissertation, University of Amsterdam.
Clements, J. C. 1992. Elements of resistance in contact-induced language change. In *Explanation in Historical Linguistics* [Current Issues in Linguistic Theory 84], eds. G. W. Davis and G. K. Iverson, 41–58. Amsterdam: John Benjamins.
Clements, J. C. 1996. *The Genesis of a Language: The Formation and Development of Korlai Portuguese* [Creole Language Library 16]. Amsterdam: John Benjamins.
Clements, J. C. 2000. Evidência para a existência de um pidgin português asiático. In *Crioulos de Base Portuguesa*, eds. E. d'Andrade, M. A. Mota and D. Pereira, 185–200. Braga: Associação Portuguesa de Linguística.
Clements, J. C. 2003. The tense-aspect system in pidgins and naturalistically learned L2. *Studies in Second Language Acquisition* 25 (2): 245–81.
Clements, J. C. 2009a. Accounting for some similarities and differences among the Indo-Portuguese creoles. *Journal of Portuguese Linguistics* 8 (2): 23–47.
Clements, J. C. 2009b. *The Linguistic Legacy of Spanish and Portuguese; Colonial Expansion and Language Change* [Cambridge Approaches to Language Contact series]. Cambridge: CUP.
Clements, J. C., and A. J. Koontz-Garboden. 2002. Two Indo-Portuguese creoles in contrast. *Journal of Pidgin and Creole Languages* 17 (2): 191–236.
Coelho, F. A. 1880–86. *Os Dialectos Românicos ou Neo-Latinos na África, Ásia e América*. Lisbon: Sociedade de Geographia de Lisboa.
Comrie, B. 1993. *Aspect* [Cambridge Textbooks in Linguistics series]. Cambridge: CUP.
Conim, C. N. P. S., and M. F. B. Teixeira. 1998. *Macau e a sua População, 1500–2000: Aspectos Sociais, Demográficos e Económicos*. Macau: Direcção dos Serviços de Estatística e Censos.
Croft, W. 2000. *Explaining Language Change. An Evolutionary Approach*. London: Longman.
Davies, M., and M. Ferreira. 2006. *Corpus do Português: 45 Million Words, 1300s–1900s*. http://www.corpusdoportugues.org
Givón, T. 1979. *On Understanding Grammar*. New York, NY: Academic Press.
Ferreira, J. S. 1978. *Papiá Cristâm di Macau: Epitome de Gramática Comparada e Vocabulário – Dialecto Macaense*. Macau: Tipografia da Missão.
Ferreira, J. S. 1996. *Papiacam di Macau*, 2 Vol. Macau: Fundação Oriente.
da França, B. 1897. *Macau e os Seus Habitantes: Relações com Timor*. Lisbon: Imprensa Nacional.
Holt, J. 1943. Études d'aspect. *Acta Jutlandica* 15 (2): 1–94.
Klein, W., and C. Perdue. 1992. *Utterance Structure: Developing Grammars Again* [Studies in Bilingualism 5]. Amsterdam: John Benjamins.
Klein, W., and C. Perdue. 1997. The basic variety (or: Couldn't natural languages be simpler?). *Second Language Research* 13 (4): 301–47.
Lefebvre, C. 2004. *Issues in the study of Pidgin and Creole languages* [Studies in Language Companion Series 70]. Amsterdam: John Benjamins.
Lefebvre, C., L. White, and C. Jourdan. 2006. Introduction. In *L2 Acquisition and Creole Genesis* [Language Acquisition and Language Disorders 42], eds. C. Lefebvre, L. White and C. Jourdan, Amsterdam: John Benjamins.
Luís, A. R. 2008. Tense marking and inflectional morphology in Indo-Portuguese creoles. In *Roots of Creole structures: Weighing the Contribution of Substrates And Superstrates* [Creole Language Library 33], ed. S. Michaelis, 83–121. Amsterdam: John Benjamins.

Mateus, M. H. M., A. M. Brito, I. Duarte, and I. H. Faria, et al. 2003. *Gramática da Língua Portuguesa*. Lisbon: Caminho.

Mufwene, S. 2001. *The Ecology of Language Evolution*. Cambridge: CUP.

Pinharanda Nunes, M. 2008. Os demonstrativos em maquista: uma análise morfossintáctica contrastiva. *PAPIA – Revista Brasileira de Estudos Crioulos e Similares* 18: 7–22.

Pinharanda Nunes, M. 2011. Estudo da Expressão Morfo-Sintáctica das Categorias de Tempo, Modo e Aspecto em Maquista. PhD dissertation, University of Macau.

Pinharanda Nunes, M., and A. N. Baxter. 2004. Os marcadores pré-verbais no crioulo de base lexical portuguesa de Macau. *PAPIA – Revista Brasileira de Estudos Crioulos e Similares* 13: 31–46.

Plag, I. 2008. Creoles as interlanguages: Syntactic structures. *Journal of Pidgin and Creole Languages* 23 (2): 307–28.

Romaine, S. 1992. The evolution of complexity in a creole language. The acquisition of relative clauses in Tok Pisin. *Studies in Language* 16: 139–82.

Schuchardt, H. 1889. Beiträge zur Kenntnis des creolischen Romanisich. V. Allgemeineres über das Indoportugiesische (Asioportugiesische). *Zeitschrift für Romanische Philologie* 13: 476–516.

Seabra, L. 2006/2007. Traços da presença feminina em Macau. *Campus Social* 3–4: 197–208.

Senna Fernandes, M., and A. N. Baxter. 2004. *Maquista Chapado: Vocabulary and Expressions in Macau's Portuguese Creole*. Macau: Macau International Institute.

Siegel, J. 2004. Morphological simplicity in pidgins and creoles. *Journal of Pidgin and Creole Languages* 19: 139–62.

Siegel, J. 2006. Links between SLA and creole studies: Past and present. In *L2 Acquisition and Creole Genesis* [Language Acquisition and Language Disorders 42], eds. C. Lefebvre, L. White and C. Jourdan. Amsterdam: John Benjamins.

Siegel, J. 2008. *The Emergence of Pidgin and Creole Languages*. Oxford: OUP.

Smith, C. S. 1991. *The Parameter of Aspect*. Kluwer.

Smith, I. R. 1979. *Substrata vs. universals* in the formation of Sri Lanka Portuguese. In *Papers in Pidgin and Creole linguistics* 2, ed. P. Mühlhäusler, 183–200. Canberra: Pacific Linguistics.

Smith, I. R., and S. Paauw. 2006. Sri Lanka Malay: Creole or convert? In *Structure and Variation in Language Contact* [Creole Language Library 29], eds. A. Deumert and S. Durrleman. Amsterdam: John Benjamins.

Sprouse, R. A. 2006. Full transfer and relexification: Second language acquisition and creole genesis. In *L2 Acquisition and Creole Genesis*, C. Lefebvre [Language Acquisition and Language Disorders 42], eds. L. White and C. Jourdan, 169–181. Amsterdam: John Benjamins.

Thomason, S., and T. Kaufman. 1988. *Language Contact, Creolization, and Genetic Linguistics*. Berkeley, CA: University of California Press.

Veenstra, T. 2003. What verbal morphology can tell us about creole genesis. In *Phonology and Morphology of Creole Languages* [Linguisticshe Arbeiten 478], ed. I. Plag, 293–313. Tübingen: Niemeyer.

Vendler, Z. 1967. *Linguistics in Philosophy*. Ithaca, NY: Cornell University Press.

Yin, G., and R. Zhang. 2009 [1751]. *Breve Monografia de Macau*. Macau: Instituto Cultural.

Mindanao Chabacano and other 'mixed creoles'

Sourcing the morphemic components*

Anthony P. Grant

Mindanao Chabacano owes many of its features (including over 10% of its basic and more of its non-basic lexicon) to the influence of Philippine languages, and some of its typological features, such as the basic VSO constituent order, typify Philippine languages but atypical of Ibero-Asian creoles as a whole. Its sizeable component of basic Philippine-derived vocabulary and its incorporation of structural features which cannot be traced back simply to Spanish, allow us to classify it as a mixed creole. In this paper I examine the extent to which various structural features of Mindanao Creole Spanish and other mixed and sometimes less mixed creoles (including Saramaccan, Angolar, Korlai Portuguese, and also the recently extinct Berbice Dutch, most with a sizeable Iberoromance lexical component) parallel one another as to the derivation of sets of features from sources other than their chief lexifier language. I also examine the degree to which structural transfers in these creoles coexist with typically 'creole' features and with etymologically mixed lexica, and compare some aspects of mixing in mixed or intertwined languages and mixed creoles.

1. What is a 'mixed lexicon (or lexifier) creole'?

For the purposes of this paper, a mixed-lexifier creole is defined as one for which at least 10% of the Swadesh list derives from languages other than the chief lexifier. A number of these mixed-lexifier creoles contain large amounts of vocabulary which derive from Iberoromance languages, while also containing non-Iberoromance lexical material; Mindanao Creole Spanish [MIN] (this label includes varieties spoken in Zamboanga City [ZAM] and Cotabato City [COT]) is one such. Not all Ibero-Asian creoles fit the above criterion, although Korlai Creole Portuguese [KOR] just meets it with its tranche of basic loans from

Marathi. Diu Creole Portuguese (Cardoso 2009), Sri Lanka Creole Portuguese and Papia Kristang or Malacca Creole Portuguese [MALC] do not. Nor for that matter does a Luso-African creole such as Guinea-Bissau Creole Portuguese (Scantamburlo 1999). Data on languages profiled here come from Alleyne (1987), Baxter (1988), Clements (1996), Forman (1972), Good (2009), Grant (2009), Holm & Patrick (2007), Kouwenberg (1994), Lorenzino (1998), Maurer (1995), and Riego de Dios (1989).

Angolar [ANG] is the most lexically diverse Gulf of Guinea Portuguese creole. Smaller proportions of material from substratal languages, which the creators of these creoles once spoke, occur in Principense (Maurer 2009), Fa d'Ambu of Annobon (de Granda 1984), and Sãotomense or Forro [STM], an earlier form of which is the source of all these; Lorenzino (1998: 100) puts the proportion of substrate-origin words in Sãotomense's 100-item Swadesh list as 11% (see Fontes 2007).

We do not have lexica as full as we would like for the creoles of interest here. Tables 1 and 2 give details on the main lexical sources in the respective creoles, addressing the contents of the creole as a whole and of the Swadesh list, while a partial breakdown of etyma in Mindanao Creole Spanish is given in Table 3.

One mixed-lexifier creole of note is a mixed-lexifier Iberoromance creole as both major components use Iberoromance lexicon; this is Papiamentu [PAP] of the ABC Islands (see recently Jacobs 2009; also Grant 2008a, 2008b), where an early form of Guinea-Bissau Creole Portuguese provides most functional elements and some basic vocabulary, and Spanish most general vocabulary.[1] The similarity of these two lexica means it is often impossible to establish if a Papiamentu word is ultimately of Portuguese or Spanish origin (if it cannot be both), so I do not discuss this creole here much further. Two other mixed-lexifier creoles which are not discussed further here are Grand Ronde Chinook Jargon/Chinuk Wawa (lexicon documented in Zenk, Johnson & Hamilton 2010), which was a community language in Grand Ronde, Oregon, but which was the only language of very few people (most speakers knowing also English and/or a Native American language and/or Canadian French), and creolised forms of Sango of the Central African Republic (Bouquiaux et al. 1978), which is the everyday language of many but is still the sole language of few, and which like Chinuk Wawa coexists with more widespread pidginised varieties of the language.

Among the creoles addressed here, Korlai Creole Portuguese and Berbice Dutch [BER] are *primordial* creoles, as they do not appear to descend from a pre-existing creole which underwent later absorption of features from other languages and has split off from its original creole source. Saramaccan [SAR] is a development of Sranan, from which it derives some of its Dutch and maybe some

African elements, while being partially relexified by Portuguese (possibly pidginised or creolised forms of this, though we cannot be sure) and adlexified with further material from Loango Bantu, Gbe languages and modern Sranan, the last being the source of Dutch items. Mindanao Creole Spanish is apparently an offshoot of certain Manila Bay Creole Spanish varieties such as Caviteño, whence some elements from Tagalog and Portuguese in addition to Spanish ones, and Angolar is clearly a development from an earlier form of Sãotomense, whence it derives its Kikongo and Bini elements, and possibly some from Ịjọid languages (Hagemeijer & Ogie 2011). It later took many words from the Kimbundu language of the ancestors of its speakers and from unknown sources which are not shared with other Gulf of Guinea creoles.

Like Angolar, Korlai Creole Portuguese is an *endogenous* creole – according to Clements' work, it appears to have arisen near where it is now spoken, at the fortress in Chaul – while speakers of Saramaccan and Berbice Dutch have developed their creoles some distance away from the areas where their source creoles arose (coastal Surinam and the Berbice River of Guyana respectively, to be spoken in eastern Surinam and near Wiruni Creek in Guyana). This relocation is especially the case of Mindanao Creole Spanish (within which Cotabato Creole Spanish has probably moved away from its possible source in Zamboanga del Sur province, as has the underdocumented Davaueño Creole Spanish). These three can be regarded as *exogenous* creoles. Speakers of Berbice Dutch are mostly of Amerindian or of mixed Amerindian, African and European origin rather than being primarily of Ịjọid origin; it appears their ancestors adopted Berbice Dutch from the ancestors of some people living by the Berbice River who now speak Guyanese Creole English (or Creolese).

From what our sources suggest, Korlai Creole Portuguese seems to have formed in the mid-16th century, Angolar apparently developed in the 17th century from a form of Sãotomense. Berbice Dutch apparently also formed some time in the 17th century, while Saramaccan developed from an earlier form of Sranan in the final decades of the 17th century. Mindanao Creole Spanish may have formed around 1719 with the permanent establishment of the Spanish garrison of Fort Pilar in Zamboanga City. Dates of first attestation of data for the creoles range from the late 1770s for Saramaccan, 1793 for Berbice Dutch, 1895 for Angolar, 1929 (if not before) for Mindanao Creole Spanish, to the mid 1970s for Korlai Creole Portuguese. General structural and lexical change from earliest attested records to modern times is, however, slight in all these languages: the lexica of Mindanao Creole Spanish, Berbice Dutch, Saramaccan and the others were as mixed in the past as now.

One further issue, namely whether these creoles are *prototypical* or not (see McWhorter 2003 for discussions of this theory) also arises. Prototypical creoles have arisen as the result of the expansion of prior pidgins and they are not themselves derived from a currently or previously-existing creole. The three features which are supposed to constitute this prototype are:

a. the possession in the language of non-compositional derivation only;
b. the absence of lexical tone;
c. the absence of bound inflectional morphology.

It is claimed that the concatenation of these three features within a single language increases the distribution in these languages of what could be considered 'less complex' single morphemic forms (rather than forms with morphemic irregularity or extensive allomorphy) to encode structural and other ideas, and proves that the language derives from a pidgin. McWhorter claims that no language which is of non-pidgin origin shares all three features. The Creole Prototype is an ontological explanation: prototypical creole languages share these prototypical features because they do not continue the morphology of the source language of their lexicon. The language systems from which they developed never had that morphology. Not all creoles are perfectly prototypical creoles in the McWhorterian sense. Berbice Dutch certainly is not, because it has a battery of productively-used bound morphology needed to indicate aspect, tense or (on nouns) plurality. Angolar and Saramaccan both use lexical tone (and both use tone for grammatical purposes), and Mindanao Creole Spanish has a fairly rich and productively used derivational morphological system of Philippine origin, buttressed by the occurrence in Mindanao Creole Spanish of a number of word families of Spanish origin using Spanish stems and elements of Spanish affixal derivational morphology.

The use of terms such as *substrate*, *superstrate* and *adstrate* has varied from one creolist to another; there was a long period in the 1970s to 1990s when the term *adstrate* (which had been used in earlier creolistic writing) almost fell into disuse. In this paper substrate languages are those which the speakers of the pidgins which underlie creoles spoke (and sometimes passed onto their creole-speaking children), the superstrate is the language of the European exploiters and is the source of most of the lexicon of the creole, while adstrate languages are those which supply further lexicon to creole languages which have consolidated their structure and core lexicon. The same language can discharge more than one of these roles in the history of a creole (see Table 10 below).

Table 1. Etymological composition of attested morphs in the sample creoles†

Language	Recorded items	Etymological strata
MIN	c. 8000 (estimate)	Spanish 80%+, **Philippine languages** c. 15%, English and others < 5%; see Table 3 for more details on a more limited lexical sample
ANG	c. 1450	Portuguese 76.4%, *Kimbundu* 10%, **Kikongo** 1.6%, **Bini** (or **Ẹdo**) 1.2%, unknown 10.8%
SAR	1100‡	English c. 56%, **Portuguese** 16%, Sranan 11%, Dutch 3.5%, *various African languages* 5.3%, Kari'na 1.4%, unknown 7%
KOR	c. 800 available to me	Portuguese 67%, 32% *Marathi*, <1% unknown
BER	1090 (morphemes; lexical items c. 1400)	Dutch 40%, *Guyanese Creole English* (*Creolese*) 20%+, **Eastern Ịjọ** 16%, *Arawak* 15%, other lgs 2%, unknown c. 5%

† The superstrate language is the chief lexifier. (Probable) substrate languages are emboldened, adstrate languages are italicised. Those names which are both emboldened and italicised show that these categories are not mutually exclusive in all these creoles.

‡ This refers to the lexical sample in Good (2009), where the material is etymologised as fully as is possible in the stare of our present knowledge. 79 forms are of unknown origin, though about a dozen of these seem to be confined to secret languages used by some groups within the Saramaccan community. More extensive lexical material (< 2200 morphemes) is available for Saramaccan and data on some but not all etymological strata therein are available.

Table 2. Composition of the Swadesh 100+ 200-item lists in the sample mixed-lexifier creoles

Language	100 + 200-item Swadesh list components aggregated in percentages
MIN	Spanish 85.5, **Philippine languages** 12.5, others 2 (100-list loans 9%)
ANG	Portuguese 74, *Kimbundu* 17+, **Kikongo** 2+, **Bini** 2, unknown 3+, *Bailundu* (Bantu) 0.5. (100-list loans 15% in all)
SAR	English 59, *Portuguese* (or creole Portuguese?) 30, *Dutch* 5, *Sranan* 3†, *African lgs* 3 (some overlap in terms of labelling of concepts due to much partial synonymy; 100-list loans 37% overall)
KOR	Portuguese 88, *Marathi* 11, unknown <1 (100-list loans 5%)
BER	Dutch 66, **Eastern Ịjọ** 30, *Arawak* 1, *Guyanese Creole English* 1, unknown 2. (38/99 items on the 100-item list are Eastern Ịjọ)

† Most of the words marked as Sranan are Dutch elements found both in Sranan and Saramaccan.

Table 3. Etymological strata in Cotabateño Creole Spanish (Riego de Dios 1989:188)

Spanish	5396	82.49%
'Local' (Maranaw, etc.)	318	4.86%
Tagalog	308	4.7%
English	164	2.5%
Cebuano	139	2.12%
Others	85	1.3%
Hiligaynon	83	1.3%
Incomplete data	49	0.75%
Total	6542	100%

Some language identifications in Table 3 cannot be taken at face value. Even during a cursory check of forms in Riego de Dios (1989) I have come across forms which she labels 'Local', which are not exclusively from Sinama, or Tausug, or Yakan, or (in the case of Cotabato Creole Spanish) from Magindanaw or Tiruray, two other languages which donated vocabulary to this subvariety, but also occur in Tagalog and/or Cebuano and/or Hiligaynon. 'Others' refers to words of various origins which have come into the creole, almost always indirectly and by way of other listed languages – for example Malay loans which have entered via Tagalog, Nahuatl loans which came in via Spanish, and so on. Apart from any Portuguese-derived elements which may have come in through a Manila Bay Creole ancestor, the only possible exception, of which I have found no good examples, may be Japanese words acquired during Japanese occupation of the Philippines between 1942 and 1945. It is certainly true that many of the Philippine elements in the language can be found in both Hiligaynon and Cebuano, as often also in non-Bisayan Tagalog and other languages, but the demarcations of Riego's table do not allow for this. The statistics are broadly informative but they need to be taken carefully.

2. Transfer of fabric and transfer of pattern

There are two kinds of transfer: *transfer of fabric* and *transfer of pattern* (adumbrated in Grant 1999, 2002). They are not mutually exclusive, but rather can coexist in the same example. Extensive reshaping of the structure of one language by aping or copying of patterns of another language is *metatypy* (Ross 1996), and the structures of many creoles show numerous examples of this, with structural copies being taken from substrate or adstrate languages. For instance, in Mindanao Creole Spanish, in addition to considerable mixture of cultural elements in the lexicon, we may note:

1. borrowing from Philippine languages and use with personal names of a 'personal article', in singular subject form *si* and in plural form *kanda*, which can be distinguished from the definite and indefinite articles (*el* and *un* respectively);
2. marking of plural noun groups with preposed Philippine-derived *manga* used with or without definite articles (*el manga gato* 'the cats' = 'the various kinds of cats');
3. complexity of the personal pronominal system, which has absorbed borrowed material from Hiligaynon for most plural pronouns (plus the occasional use of a 2SG pronoun *ka* in addition to several Spanish-derived pronouns) and which makes mostly Central Philippine-type case and status distinctions, using the forms from Hiligaynon paradigms. Following this, a reconstrual on Philippine lines of the semantics of some Spanish personal pronouns occurs in respect of degrees of politeness and formality;
4. use of three negators, *hindi'* (borrowed from a Central Philippine language), and Spanish-source *nway* (< Sp. *no hay* 'there is not', used with past-tense verbs and as a negative existential) and imperative *no*, employed under different syntactic circumstances, just as found in Philippine languages, but Spanish only uses one (*no*);
5. use of a large number of Philippine particles, both singly and in Spanish-Philippine blends, for instance postposed emphatic *gayot* 'very' (*bweno gayot* 'very good'), post-head *lang* 'only' (*dos lang* 'only two'), the interrogative particle *ba*, the emphatic *pa*, and the blend *nway pa* 'not yet';
6. borrowing of a sizeable proportion (10%+) of everyday lexicon from Central Philippine languages despite the fact that the concepts which these terms express were already perfectly adequately expressible by pre-existing Spanish words;
7. despite the presence of numerous derived forms of Spanish origin in these languages, the bulk of productive items of derivational morphology in Mindanao Creole Spanish are also of Central Philippine origin, from the reciprocal verbal affix *-han* to the ordinal numeral marker *ika-/aka-*. Meanwhile, Central Philippine languages are also the inspiration for the verbal prefix *man-* which does not correspond simply to any one Philippine prefix of that form and meaning but which is used to assimilate most verbs of non-Spanish origin into the creoles' particle- and pronoun-driven verbal structure;
8. transfers of pattern without concomitant transfers of fabric, for instance the use of *kon* (literally 'with') or *konel* (literally 'with the') to indicate direct object in the manner of a Philippine-style object marker, and a usage which is not restricted to human nouns as Spanish personal *a* is;

9. similar remarks could be made about the greater or lesser philipinisation of the structure of numerous semantic fields, such as food terminology, kin terminology and temporal adverbials, even when most of the forms in these fields are of Spanish etymological origin (Frake 1971: 232–3).

Overt direct object-marking is not the only feature of Philippine syntax which is sometimes transferred into Mindanao Creole Spanish; for instance, as the general constituent order in Mindanao Creole Spanish is VSO, as usual in Philippine languages (and which also occurs but much less often in Spanish), this provides further reasons for overtly marking direct objects. Many of these features make Mindanao Creole Spanish structure increasingly isomorphic with those of Central Philippine languages.

Metatypy is not confined to Mindanao Creole Spanish, of course: for instance Clements (2007: 172) gives a list of metatypised features in Korlai Creole Portuguese (such as paired echoic words) which have their origins in Marathi but which are constructed in Korlai Creole Portuguese using morphs of Portuguese origin.

3. Overlap of transferred fabric features among mixed-lexifier creoles: a view from Swadesh lists

Some of the Swadesh-list items which mixed-lexifier creoles absorb from other lexifiers (*allolexical items*) are borrowed more often than others and they are found across most form-classes. 53 elements out of the 100-item list are borrowed into at least one of Mindanao Creole Spanish, Angolar, Saramaccan and Korlai Creole Portuguese. This is also true of 127 of the 207 items, and of 10 out of the 16 supplementary items. Of the 100-item list, 12 of them, namely 'cloud, to fly, louse, rain, sand, small, tail, tree, woman, horn, moon, round' are allolexical in origin in two or more languages. Items in the rest of the 223-item list which are allolexical in more than one of these four creoles refer to: 'and, child, to count, dull, father, to float, to flow, flower, fog, to hold/take, ice, in, lake, left side, to push, river, rotten, to rub, to scratch, sea, to squeeze, to stab, to suck, they, thin, to vomit, woods, ye, spear, six, nine', that is at least 31 items; this is a greater proportion of loans than that on the 100-item list. The borrowed forms are provided in the Appendix.

Historical continuity between these creoles can often be seen in the perpetuation of some elements which are shared with other creoles of similar origin and which are exclusively shared innovations or synapomorphies, for instance the use of Igbo-derived *unu* to express 'you.PL' in many Atlantic English Creoles, including Sranan and also in its early lusitanised and reafricanised offshoot Saramaccan, which looks like a form of Sranan (itself a creole which has a tranche of forms of Portuguese origin) which has replaced a high proportion of its lexicon with elements of Portuguese origin, a process which was essentially complete by the end of the 18th century (Smith & Cardoso 2004). This includes borrowed forms such as *akí, alá* 'here, there' (Ptg. *aquí, alá*) which as deictics are hardly ever borrowed (Matras 1998).

Berbice Dutch material has been left out of this list as its status, and the way in which its components combine, is unique. 38 of the items on the Berbice Dutch 100-item Swadesh list come from Eastern Ịjọ, compared with 57 whose origin is Dutch, and 1 each from Arawak/Lokono, Guyanese Creole English and an unknown source. On the longer Swadesh list the number of new Eastern Ịjọ elements declines to 16 against 64 fresh ones from Dutch, and the proportion of Eastern Ịjọ elements declines still further in the attested Berbice Dutch lexicon as a whole, to 111 fresh morphemes out of a little under 900 fresh non-Swadesh items (compare 179 fresh morphemes in the category of non-Swadesh items from Arawak). Words of Eastern Ịjọ origin feature in every stratum in Berbice Dutch apart from the numerals, which are taken from Dutch (or in the case of some higher numerals, from Creolese). All bound inflectional morphemes in Berbice Dutch come from Eastern Ịjọ (Berbice Dutch has few morphemes which are distinctively or solely bound derivational elements), but some less frequently-used free inflectional morphemes in the Berbice Dutch verbal system are taken from Dutch (*sa* 'irrealis') or Guyanese Creole English (*justu* 'used to', *dasn* 'negative continuous'). The number of non-nominal elements (verbs, stative verbs/adjectives, pronouns etc.) of Eastern Ịjọ origin in Berbice Dutch is greater than that of the number of nouns (112 such forms versus 65 nouns). Mikael Parkvall (p.c. 2011) has suggested that Berbice Dutch may originate in a pidginised form of Dutch combined with other components, which was later partly reshaped as a mixed language with the addition of morphological and lexical elements from Ịjọid languages (I have wondered if this was maybe an Ịjọid koine with Kalabạri Eastern Ịjọ at its heart). The forms of Ịjọid or Kikongo origin in Angolar can be shown, by the application for instance of Venn diagrams, to be a subset of those occurring in Sãotomense.

Zamboangueño and Cotabateño contain far more Philippine lexical and other elements than other forms of Creole Spanish spoken in the Philippines do, as an examination of the Riego de Dios (1989) indexes shows. Ternateño is the most aberrant as, in addition to elements from Spanish and Tagalog which Caviteño also contains, it includes small bodies of items from Portuguese, Moluccan Malay and the non-Austronesian language Bahasa Ternate. The record of this creole furnished in Tirona (1923) shows a greater proportion of such forms than are found in present-day speech.[2] This suggests that the two creoles still spoken in Manila Bay have separate origins; both of them, though, show far less than 10% borrowed items on their Swadesh lists, although some of the Philippinisms are common to Mindanao Creole Spanish, Caviteño and Ternateño (eg. *puno'* 'tree'; Sp. *árbol*).

Details of the actual borrowed forms on the Swadesh lists for the mixed-lexifier creoles reviewed here, or of forms of other origins (including those items of unknown origins) which do not trace back to the chief lexifier, are found in the Appendix.

Table 4. Stratification of elements in the sample mixed mixed-lexifier creoles, inspired by Smith (1999)†

	Mindanao Creole Spanish
Basic lexicon (fabric)	Spanish, 10% Philippine (= Hiligaynon and Tagalog)
Peripheral lexicon (fabric)	Spanish, 10% Philippine
Cultural lexicon (fabric)	Philippine (and Spanish)
Derivational morph. (fabric)	Philippine (for the most part), Spanish
Function words (fabric)	Spanish, Philippine
Inflectional morph. (fabric)	(Philippine, TAM markers mostly shared with Caviteño)
Syntax (pattern)	Philippine in terms of element and constituent order
Suprasegmental phon. (pattern)	Philippine (and Spanish?)
Segmental phonology (pattern)	Philippine + Spanish + increasingly English
Allophonic system (pattern)	Philippine
	Angolar
Basic lexicon	Sãotomense, Kimbundu (Kikongo, Ẹ̀dó)
Peripheral lexicon	Sãotomense + Kimbundu
Cultural lexicon	Kimbundu, Sãotomense
Derivational morphology	Sãotomense (one morpheme)
Function words	Sãotomense (Kimbundu)
Inflectional morphology	Sãotomense
Syntax	modified Sãotomense (more use of zero-marking)
Suprasegmental phonology	Kimbundu (Angolar is 'tonal')
Segmental phonology	Kimbundu features (especially interdental fricatives /èð/ replacing STM /sz/) on a base of Sãotomense
Allophonic system	Sãotomense + Kimbundu?
	Saramaccan
Basic lexicon	English (as elsewhere, via Sranan), Portuguese, Dutch
Peripheral lexicon	English, Dutch, Portuguese
Cultural lexicon	Gbe and Kikongo; Dutch
Derivational morphology	(there is no distinctive derivational morphology)
Function words	English, Gbe, Portuguese, Dutch
Inflectional morphology	English via Sranan
Syntax	English and universals (SVO, etc.)
Suprasegmental phonology	Gbe and Kikongo (Saramaccan is 'tonal')
Segmental phonology	Gbe and Kikongo
Allophonic system	Gbe and Kikongo segments (e.g some alternation between /m/ and /mb/, or between /n/ and /nd/)

	Korlai Creole Portuguese
Basic lexicon	Portuguese (10% Marathi)
Peripheral lexicon	Portuguese (c. 30% Marathi or unknown)
Cultural lexicon	Marathi and Portuguese
Derivational morphology	Portuguese?
Function words	Portuguese (few Marathi)
Inflectional morphology	Portuguese
Syntax	Increasingly Marathi
Suprasegmental phonology	Marathi?
Segmental phonology	Portuguese and Marathi shared features
Allophonic system	Marathi (for instance use of [dz] for /z/)
	Berbice Dutch
Basic lexicon	65% Dutch + 35% Eastern Ijọ
Peripheral lexicon	Dutch, Creolese (+ Eastern Ijọ)
Cultural lexicon	Arawak local, Eurocultural = Dutch + Creolese
Derivational morphology	(there are no distinctive derivational morphs)
Function words	Dutch + Eastern Ijọ + Creolese
Inflectional morphology	Eastern Ijọ (but reduced from the system found in any Eastern Ijọ variety)
Syntax	'universals' (eg. SVO word order) + Eastern Ijọ
Suprasegmental phonology	More Dutch than Eastern Ijọ (no phonemic tone but some traces of vowel harmony)
Segmental phonology	Eastern Ijọ modified (plus /h/ and a postalveolar sibilant)
Allophonic system	Some Eastern Ijọ features (e.g. incipient vowel harmony)

† The most frequent source language for a particular kind of feature is separated from less frequent ones by a comma. Plus-signs placed between the names of languages indicate that both languages have made more or less equally significant (if not equally numerous) contributions, while brackets around a language name indicates that its contribution to this particular stratum is present but very small. Here the use of the term 'Philippine' means that the features are common to Tagalog, Hiligaynon and Cebuano.

4. The typically creole structural features of mixed creoles: some comparative observations

We may ask how typical of creoles and how 'creole' mixed-lexifier creoles are. Both Philip Baker and Mikael Parkvall have developed metrics which enlighten us on the presence of distinctively creole features in a range of languages. Parkvall (2001) examines seventeen speech varieties for the occurrence of 45 features, ending with a list of 7 phonetic and phonological features as well as 38 morpho-syntactic ones which are typically found in Atlantic creoles (Parkvall also examines Mauritian; I have added Korlai Creole Portuguese, Mindanao Creole Spanish and Berbice Dutch).

A clear majority of these features, which mostly deal with aspects of morphosyntactic typology, can be argued as representing somehow the simplification of an element or a construction from the lexifier language, either by replacing it with a less marked feature, or with an exponent made up of elements which occur in other parts of the structure of the language, or by the use of a zero-marker. I have examined the five mixed creoles in my set for the presence or otherwise of such features. The scores are in Table 5, which builds upon the information in Parkvall (2001: 188). The lowest score for any language surveyed by Parkvall was –24 for St Thomas French. 6 of Parkvall's features represent element reduction, 23 represent element extension, and 5 represent zero-marking. Parkvall scores two points for each positive feature and deducts one point for each negative one, so an optimal score would be 90. We see that Mindanao Creole Spanish is at the lower end of the table but that Korlai scores 0.

Table 5. Features denoting restructuring in some pidgins, creoles and other languages†

Language	Score	Language	Score
Sranan, **Saramaccan**	68	Martiniquais	38
Sãotomense, **Angolar**	63	Mauritian, *Papiamentu*	35
Kittitian	51	Cape Verdean	23
Jamaican	48	Barbadian	20
Haitian	42	African American Vernacular English	16
Gullah	42	**Berbice Dutch**	13
Negerhollands	41	**Mindanao Chabacano**	9
Guadeloupean	41	**Korlai Portuguese**	0
Guyanais	41	Brazilian Portuguese, Dominican Spanish	–5
Louisianais	39	Bermudan English	–23

† Statistics slightly expanded from Parkvall (2001: 188), mixed creoles emboldened.

Philip Baker's purpose (developed in Baker 2001 and presented in Table 6) is to see how far features typical of pidgin languages are also found in some stage of the recorded history of creole languages. All 24 features relate to simplicity (mostly zero-marking and element extension). Most features are also given in Parkvall's inventory above. Mindanao Creole Spanish and Angolar were among the 16 languages examined in Baker's study. I reproduce Baker's table of the number of pidgin features found in the languages he consulted (indicated here with an asterisk) with comparable data for other creole languages discussed in Holm & Patrick (2007), for Papia Kristang (Baxter 1988), for Sri Lanka Creole Portuguese (Smith 1977) and for Saramaccan The structures of the mixed creoles in the sample show a range from 12 to 22 pidgin features out of a possible 24. The scores for

Saramaccan and Ndyuka and/or Sranan in these tables are almost identical and bespeak the fact that these languages are close to being identical in terms of morphosyntactic typology. Asterisked forms in the table belong to the original set of creoles which Baker surveyed in his paper.

Table 6. Number of pidgin features (out of 24) attested in the creoles listed above

Language	Number of pidgin features attested
Berbice Dutch	12
*Réunionnais	12
Sotavento Cape Verdean	13
*Pitcairnese	13
*Korlai Creole Portuguese	14
Palenquero	14
Sri Lanka Malay	15
Sri Lanka Portuguese	15
*Zamboangueño	15
*Hawai'ian Creole English	16
Angolar	16
*Tayo	17
*Louisianais	18
Nubi	18
Negerhollands	19
*Guyanais	20
*Papiamentu	20
*Sãotomense	20
Nagamese	20
*Caribbean English Creoles (incl. Jamaican)	23
Saramaccan	22
*Haitian	23
*Mindanao Creole Spanish	23
*Sranan	23
Papia Kristang	23
Ndyuka	23
Krio	23
Seselwa	23
*Antillean Creole French	24
*Tok Pisin	24
Average for Creoles surveyed	18.8

5. On the need for caution when examining potential cases of transfer of pattern

When transfer of fabric and transfer of pattern are invoked in an attempt to understand the history of languages, the great power and advantage of transfer of fabric is that it involves the sharing of forms which have actual phonological shapes, and is not merely the transmission of the means of putting elements (of whatever origin) into new orders or sequences. An example of the potentially misleading use of information from examining transfer of patterns can be found with serial verb constructions. All five creoles under examination have strings of conjoined verbs which help to refine or narrow the sense of the complex verb group (see Alleyne 1987 for accounts of verb serialisation in Saramaccan, and the sketches of the creoles in Holm & Patrick 2007 for information on serialisation in the other creoles).

One might be tempted *prima facie* to assume that this is the kind of feature which characterises mixed-lexifier creoles. This view is erroneous. Mindanao Creole verb strings (Forman 1993) show few if any of the properties of the kinds of serial verbs which are found in Saramaccan, Angolar and other Atlantic creoles, which themselves differ from those in Berbice Dutch, and the system of serial verbs in Korlai is both different from and more limited in the range of verbs which can be used as serial verbs than that found in Mindanao Creole Spanish. Furthermore, many creoles without heavily mixed core lexica, such as Antillean Creole French, may also use serial verbs. The presence of serial verbs in creoles generally relates to their prior presence in relevant substrate languages, not to their role as a typical creole feature (Mikael Parkvall, p.c. October 2011).

Table 7 lists borrowed structural morphemes in creole language structures, and demonstrates that most of the categories exhibit at least one case of a borrowed morph; Mindanao Creole Spanish shows non-Spanish forms in 10 out of 29 features.

Table 7. Some structural morphemes in the sample of mixed-lexifier creoles (and other creoles, data given in brackets) which are not taken from the chief lexifier language

NP plural marker	Zam. *manga* from Tagalog/Hiligaynon; Ber. *-apu* from Eastern Ijọ (Pap. *nan* from Bini)
Locative marker	Zam. and Sar. *na* from Creole Portuguese; Ber. *-angga* from Eastern Ijọ (Pap. *na* from Portuguese)
(In)definite articles	Zam. *si* 'personal article', plural *kanda*, from Hiligaynon
Adjectival comparison	Sar. *pasá* from Portuguese
Anterior marker	Ber. *-tɛ* from Eastern Ijọ (Pointe Coupee Louisianais *bin* from English)

Irrealis marker	Ber. *ma* from Eastern Ịjọ (Negerhollands *lo* from Pap. ?)
Punctual marker	Ber. *-a* from Eastern Ịjọ
Copula	latterly Zam. *amó* from Hiligaynon (Sango *yɛkɛ* from Kikongo)
'to be at'	(Guyanais *fika* from Portuguese)
'to have'	(Sango uses a 'be with' construction with a loaned *yɛkɛ*)
1SG *personal pronoun*	(Cape Verdean *n* from West Atlantic languages?)
2SG	(possibly Skepi Dutch *ashu* from sources unknown; Pap. *bo* from Portuguese)
3SG	Ber. *ori* from Eastern Ịjọ
1PL	Zam. *kitá* and *kamí* from Hiligaynon, including Hiligaynon oblique case forms (true also of the other Zam. plural pronouns)
2PL	Atlantic Creole Englishes, including Sar., *unu* from Igbo; Zam. *kamó* from Hiligaynon
3PL	Zam. *silá* from Hiligaynon; Ber. *eni* from Eastern Ịjọ (Pap. *Nan* from Bini)
possessive marker	(none are borrowed per se)
reflexive pronouns	(other strategies, e.g. 'my head/body' for 'myself', are used)
'this'	Kor. *ye* from Marathi
'that'	(none are borrowed)
'here'	Sar. *akí* from Portuguese
'there'	Sar. *alá* from Portuguese
'as, like, so'	Ber. *kɛkɛ* from Eastern Ịjọ; Zam. *ansina* (and Pap. *asina*) from Portuguese (Chinuk Wawa *kakwa* from Nuuchahnulth)
'who?'	Sar. *ambè* from Fon
'what?'	Sar. *andí* from Fon
'where?'	Ber. *(w)angga* from Eastern Ịjọ
'how?'	Zam. *kiláya* from Creole Portuguese
locative adpositions	Sar. *dendu* 'inside' from Portuguese
general negator(s)	Zam. *hende'* from Hiligaynon or Tagalog; Ber. *ka*(*nå*) and *furi* 'it is not' from Eastern Ịjọ (Sango *pèpè* from Ngombe; Chinuk Wawa *wik* from Nuuchahnulth and *hilu* from Haida)

Table 8 looks at a different aspect of structural change, as it discusses the fate of different kinds of lexifier-language grammatical morphemes in creoles generally, drawing on ideas in Romaine (1994) and Muysken (2003).

This table is based on a general picture of what Atlantic creoles usually do in terms of expressing these concepts, and on the whole the picture fits Angolar and Saramaccan quite well, and less so Berbice Dutch, with its battery of productively used inflectional morphology and its handful of function words of Guyanese Creole English, Ịjọid or Arawak origin. Korlai Creole Portuguese draws almost all these elements from Portuguese; like Réunionnais (Baker & Corne 1982) it keeps (simplified) verb conjugations.

Table 8. A classification of morphological items which tend to be generally reconstituted, non-reconstituted and retained in European-lexifier creoles†

Morphemes not reconstituted	Reconstituted morphemes	Retained morphs
gender agreement	tense, aspect, modality forms	(often) articles
number agreement	interrogative pronouns	some adpositions
bound verbal morphology	noun group pluraliser	cardinal numerals
derivational morphology	personal pronoun systems	some copular forms
pronoun case and gender forms	oblique case-markers	some conjunctions
most adpositions	general locative prepositions	time adverbs
	irrealis complementiser	place adverbs
	relativising particle	discourse particles
	reflexives and reciprocals	many quantifiers
	many comparative markers	most auxiliaries
	(often) possessive marking	major negators
	purposive markers	'to have'

† Adapted and expanded from Romaine (1996: 590); see also Muysken (2003).

Actually, despite what Romaine suggests, the idea that derivational morphology from the chief lexifier language is not perpetuated in creoles is a matter for debate. The matter is complex. Certain affixes in a number of creoles, which are transmitted as part of batches of lexemes from the chief lexifier language which are retained in the creole lexicon, remain as affixes in the creole and may become increasingly productive. Many other affixes in the lexifier language cease to be productive and remain attached to just a few stems, and are synchronically unanalysable, having entered the lexicon of the creole as part of a word which is regarded within the creole lexicon and morphological system as being monomorphemic or at best part of an irregular derivational cycle. Yet again, some original non-affixes which entered the creole's lexicon as full contentive stems are reconstrued and regrammaticalised as affixes, and then become productive within the lexicon of a creole (Sranan *-man* 'agentive' from English 'man', also used as an independent contentive, is an example of this; the same form also occurs in Saramaccan as *-ma*, where it is solely an agentive suffix and is unrelated to *womi*, the Portuguese-derived word for 'man').

Mindanao Creole Spanish was not in the minds of the people who evolved these analyses of morphological tenacity, and they may serve as instances of the validity of these assumptions from the standpoint of a non-European substrate creole. In the case of Mindanao Creole, the forms which are perpetuated are some adpositions, singular personal pronoun case (but not gender) forms, some derivational morphology, the relativising particle and complementiser *ke*, the comparative and superlative markers, the purposive marker *para*, some articles, the numerals, some conjunctions and time/place adverbs, the NP-NP Possessum-Possessor marking mechanism with *de*, some quantifiers and most auxiliaries (including modal auxiliaries), two of the three negators, and 'to have'. Gender and number agreement, bound verbal morphology (including TAM markers and the semantic system which underlies them) and some derivational morphology and adpositions are not reconstituted. TAM forms, some question words, the oblique case marker, reflexives and reciprocals are reconstituted as their forms are made anew from the lexical resources of the creole. What has not been allowed for is the process of borrowing or absorbing elements from substrate languages, but this accounts in Mindanao Creole Spanish for plural personal pronouns in their various case forms, the personal definite singular and plural articles, the noun pluraliser, the major copula, one of the three negators (the distinction between which is a Philippine semantic pattern), most derivational morphology, some coordinating and subordinating conjunctions, and many discourse particles.

6. Looking a little beyond creoles: sources of elements in mixed-lexifier creoles contrasted with those in mixed languages

Some languages which earlier investigators of creolistics took to be pidgins and creoles turn out to belong to another rather loosely-defined class of languages distinguished by having two different source-languages: one providing most of the basic lexicon, the other most of the inflectional morphology, in a set of structural subsystems which may be regularised and generalised somewhat but which is largely a carryover or transmission of the productive parts of the other source language's bound inflectional morphology. These are known as *intertwined languages* or *mixed languages* (Bakker and Mous 1994; Grant 1999, 2001; Matras 2003). They are regarded as stable languages because most basic structural and lexical features in these languages are consistently expressed by forms from one and only one language. There are different patterns of combination of elements in mixed languages. Data on sources of some major features of the four best-attested stable mixed languages (out of dozens) are presented in Table 9.

Table 9. Source languages of major components in a range of mixed languages

	Ma'á	Media Lengua	Mednyj Aleut	Michif
Overall lexicon	mixed: Bantu, West Rift and Easter Cushitic, Maasai	85–90% Spanish; rest Ecuadorian Quichua	predominantly Attuan Aleut; some Russian	French and Plains Cree; Eng. loans
Swadesh-list lexicon	mixed: mostly West Rift Cushitic	predominantly Spanish	almost all Aleut	52% Cree; 47% French, 1% English
Segmental phonology	Tanzanian Bantu with 'exotic' /x ɬ ʔ/	Quichua with some Spanish phones	Aleut; Russian sounds in Rus. words	Cree for Cree component, Fr. in Fr.
Canonical phonology	Bantu; only open syllables	Hispanised Quichua (CC-, etc.)	Aleut and Russian elements largely intact	Cree and French components intact
Nouns	etymologically mixed	mostly Spanish	Aleut (many less basic Rus. nouns)	overwhelmingly French
Nominal morphology	Pare Bantu	Quichua	Aleut	French
Verbs	etymologically mixed	mostly Spanish	Aleut, some Russian stems	Cree
Finite verbal morphology	Pare Bantu	Quichua	Russian	Cree
Non-finite vb. morphology	Pare Bantu	Spanish	Aleut	Cree
Adjectives	etymologically mixed	mostly Spanish	Aleut	French; Cree stative verbs also used
Adjectival morphology	Pare Bantu	Quichua	Aleut	French or Cree, as to stem origin
Personal pronouns	West Rift Cushitic	Spanish with Quichua typology	Aleut, increasingly Russian	Cree
Interrogative pronouns	West Rift Cushitic	Spanish with Quichua typology	Aleut; increasingly Russian	Cree
Demonstratives	West Rift Cushitic	Sp. (Quichua typology)	Aleut	Cree
Reflexives	Bantu	? (no data)	Aleut	Cree
Adpositions	West Rift Cushitic	(Qui case suffixes)	Aleut	Cree, some from Fr.
Possessive marking	Bantu	Quichua	Aleut	French
Lower numerals	Southern Cushitic	Spanish	Aleut	French ('1' is Cree)

	Ma'á	Media Lengua	Mednyj Aleut	Michif
Copula	Bantu	Quichua postclitic	Aleut	Cree; French
'To be at'	Bantu	Quichua postclitic	Aleut	Cree
'To have'	Bantu 'be with' replacing Cushitic verb for 'have'	Spanish stem	Aleut 'be' verb in Russian pronominal construction	Cree; mostly French
Predicate negator	Pare Bantu	Spanish free morph, Quichua clitic	Russian proclitic	Cree
Conjunctions	Increasingly Swahili	Quichua clitics	Russian	Cree; French
'as, like'	Bantu	? (no data)	Russian	Cree

The forms listed in Table 9 are marked up as instances of the transfer of fabric rather than of pattern. I have surveyed the origins of these forms in some of the best-attested mixed languages, though I recognise that the size, scope, range and kinds of data and historical range of attestation of these various mixed languages vary wildly: for Ma'á of Tanzania (Mous 2003) the main elements are West Rift Cushitic, to a lesser extent the Nilo-Saharan language Maasai, and Pare Bantu; for Mednyj Aleut of Copper Island, Siberia (Golovko & Vakhtin 1990), the mixture is a two-language one of Attuan Aleut and Siberian Russian; for Media Lengua of Ecuador (Muysken 1997; Gómez Rendón 2008), another two-language mixture, that of Andean Spanish with Ecuadorean Quichua; and for Michif of Manitoba and North Dakota (Bakker 1995), it is Northern Plains Cree and Metis Canadian French. Van Gijn (2009) discusses the phonological systems of several mixed languages.

Accounts of the structure and development of mixed languages, such as those listed in the previous paragraph, make it clear that these languages have developed among social groups whose identity is separate from those whose languages have provided the material for the mixed languages. For example, the Métis are not regarded as French or as Indian either by the French-Canadians or by members of Native American groups, although they derive their physical inheritance from French and Native American (and also English and Scottish) ancestors. Speakers of Media Lengua were regarded as urbanised Runa (Quichua-speakers) rather than as an new ethnic group; speakers of Ma'á are phenotypically different from other groups in northern Tanzania, and the speakers of Mednyj Aleut, which was originally spoken on the ethnically very diverse Copper Island until the speakers' migration to Bering Island in 1969, combined Russian and Aleut heritage, but often with family connections to several other Siberian ethnic groups, such as Itelmens and Komis.

Overall, there are some similarities in what these creoles retain and in the kinds of features which many of these creoles borrow (for example, they often borrow subordinating and coordinating conjunctions). But there is not a series of exception-proof parallels, nor is there a Guttman-scaled implicational hierarchy among the kinds of features which are transferred within the mixed-lexicon creoles, let alone among the mixed languages.

Morphologically, especially regarding inflectional morphology, there is a basic difference between creoles and mixed languages: mixed languages use (somewhat regularised, less allomorph-heavy and scaled-down) versions of sets of their contributory languages' inflectional (and often derivational) morphology.[3]

In contrast, as the contents of Table 8 showed, creators of creole languages construct new morphological systems over time (new features may emerge centuries after the rise of a creole), largely by drawing on typological blueprints provided by their substrate languages for the concepts and functional categories (and often the syntagms) which are overtly expressed by these emerging creole morphosyntactic systems. They gather material for this by applying, reapplying or recycling elements, often originally lexical (and some may remain as lexical items in the language), mostly taken from their pidginised chief lexifiers which are their superstrate components. It is less easy to attribute substrates and superstrates in the development of mixed languages, although they too can be said to have adstrates if they have been strongly influenced by a language which is neither of the two languages from which they have originally been built. Indeed Baker (2000), using a constructivist approach which fully recognises the importance of grammatical restructuring in the evolution and expansion of newer languages, has dispensed with the old pidgin/creole distinction and sees a Medium for Interethnic Communication being expanded in role and range until it is adopted as the major medium of a speech community and becomes a Medium for Community Solidarity.

Table 10 details substrate, superstrate and adstrate languages for the mixed-lexifier creoles in the sample according to the definitions of these terms which I gave in Section 1. Given the nature of mixed languages, which possess batteries of inflectional morphological forms that mixed-lexifier creoles generally do not have, it is not easy or feasible to list their superstrate and substrate languages. However, adstrate languages which especially provide lexicon but which also still exert other influences on mixed languages are Shambala and Swahili for Ma'á, French and, increasingly, English for Michif, Russian for Mednyj Aleut, and predominantly Spanish for Media Lengua.

We can get a more finely-grained picture of the origins of certain subsets of structural elements from Table 11, which deals with the etymological sources of various kinds of function words in several mixed languages and creoles. Its

Table 10. Substrate, superstrate and adstrate languages in the mixed-lexifier creoles surveyed

Language	Substrate	Superstrate	Adstrate
MIN	Hiligaynon; Sinama and Yakan; Manila Bay Creole Spanish	(Creole) Spanish (and Tagalog?)	Spanish, Tagalog, Cebuano, English
SAR	Gbe languages and Loango Bantu, probably Portuguese-lexifier language	Sranan, Portuguese-lexifier language	Dutch, Portuguese, African lgs, Wayana, Kari'na
ANG	Kimbundu	Sãotomense	Sãotomense, later Portuguese
KOR	Marathi	Portuguese	Marathi, some Portuguese
BER	Eastern Ịjọid languages, others? (Arawak?)	Dutch	Guyanese Creole English, Arawak

original source of inspiration was Smith (1987), with his comparison of the origins of functions words in Saramaccan and St. Lucian Creole French, but his original 20 categories have been enlarged upon and some further ones have been added, based on my three decades of creole research. Having more historical information for Saramaccan than for some other creoles, I have provided data for the Saramaccan column as to how far the forms on the list below indicate the restructuring or redeployment of elements (from whichever source they may come) in Saramaccan structure.

Table 11. Expression of certain linguistic features in some mixed languages and mixed-lexifier creoles†

		Ma'á	MdA	MdL	Mich	Min	Sar	Ang	Ber	Kor
1a	personal pronouns	Cush	Rus;Al	Sp(Qui)	Cr	Sp;Hil	Eng;Gb	Stm	Du;EI	Ptg
1b	possessive pronouns	Cush	(Al)	Sp	Fr(Cr)	Sp;Hil	Eng;Gb	Stm	Du;EI	Ptg
1c	possession: 'NP of NP'	Cush	Al	Qui	Fr	Sp	Eng	Ø	Du	Ptg
2	Numerals	Cush	Al	Sp	Fr	Sp	Eng;Du	Stm;Kb	Du	Ptg
3	other prenominal quants	Cush	Rus;Al	Qui	Fr;Cr	Sp	Eng;Du	Stm	Du;EI	Ptg
4	quantifier nouns	Cush	Al	Sp	Fr;Cr	Sp	Eng	Stm	Du	Ptg
5	relative pronouns	Ban?	Rus	Qui	Fr;Cr	Sp	Eng*	Stm	Du	Ptg
6a	Reflexives	Ban?	Al	?	Cr	Sp	Eng	Stm	Du	Ptg
6b	Reciprocals	?	Al	?	Cr	Sp	Du	?	Du	Ptg
6c	indefinite pronouns	?	Rus	?	?	Sp	Eng	Stm;Kb	Du	Ptg
7	interrogative pronouns	Cush	Al	Sp	Cr	Sp	Eng;Gb	Stm;Kb	Du	Ptg
8	'quantifying' adverbs	?	Rus;Al	Sp;Qui	Cr;Fr	Sp;Hil	Eng;Ptg	Stm	Du	Ptg
9	place adverbs	Unk	Al	Sp	Cr	Sp	Ptg*	Stm	Du;EI	Ptg
10a	time adverbs	Unk	Rus;Al	Sp	Cr(Fr)	Sp	Eng;Ptg*	Stm	Du;EI	Ptg

Table 11. (continued)

		Ma'á	MdA	MdL	Mich	Min	Sar	Ang	Ber	Kor
10b	phasal adverbs	Unk	Al	Sp	Cr	Sp	Eng*	Stm	Du	Ptg
11a	'abstract' adpositions	Ban	Rus	Qui	Cr;Fr	Sp	Ptg	Stm	Du;EI	Ptg
11b	place adpositions	Ban	Al	Qui(Sp)	Cr;Fr	Sp	Eng;Ptg*	Stm	Du	Ptg
11c	time adpositions	Ban?	?	Qui	Cr;Fr	Sp	Eng;Ptg*	Stm	Du	Ptg
12	dative word	Ban?	Rus	Qui	Fr	Sp	Eng	Stm	Du	Ptg
13a	instrumental word	Ban	Rus	Qui	Fr	Sp	Eng	Stm	Du	Ptg
13b	'and' linking NPs	Ban	Rus	Sp;Qui	Fr	Hil	Eng*	Stm	Du	Ptg
14a	'and' linking VPs	Ban	Rus	Sp;Qui	Cr;Fr	Sp;Hil	Eng	Stm	Du	Mar
14b	'or'	Cush?	Rus	?	Fr	Sp	Eng	Stm	Du	Ptg
14c	'but'	Cush	Rus	?	Cr	Sp	Du	Stm	Du	Ptg
14d	other coordinators	Ban	Rus	Sp;Qui	Cr;(Fr)	Sp	Eng	Stm	Du	Ptg
15a	most complementisers	Ban?	Rus	Sp	Cr	Hil	Eng*	Stm	EI	Ptg
15b	'if'	Cush	Rus;Al	Sp	Cr	Sp;Hil	Eng	Stm	Du	Ptg
15c	'because'	Ban	Rus	Sp;Qui	Fr	Sp;Hil	Eng	Kb	Du	Mar
15d	'in order to'	?	Rus	?	Cr	Sp	Eng*	Stm	Du;EI	Ptg
15e	'when' (temporal)	?	Rus	?	Cr	Sp	Eng*	Stm	Du	Ptg
15f	other subordinators	?	Rus	Sp	Cr;Fr	Sp	Du?	Stm	Du	Ptg
16a	Copulas	Ban	Al	Qui	Cr;Fr	Sp;Hil	Eng*	Stm	Du	Ptg
16b	'to have'	Cush-Ban	Al	Sp	Cr	Sp	Eng	Stm	Du	Ptg
17a	INFL morphemes	Ban	Rus	Qui	Cr	Ø	Ø	Stm	Du;EI	Ptg
17b	modal verbs	Ban?	Rus	?	Cr;Fr	Sp	Du	Stm	Du;EI	Ptg
18	negative particles	Ban	Rus;Al	Sp;Qui	Cr;Fr	Sp;Hil	Eng	Stm;Kb	Du;EI	Ptg
19a	definite articles	Ø	Ø	Ø	Fr	Sp;Hil	Eng	Ø	Du	Ø
19b	indefinite article	Ø	Ø	Sp	Fr	Sp	Eng	Ø	Du	Ø
19c	demonstratives	Cush	Al(Rus)	Sp	Cr	Sp	Eng	Stm	Du	MP
19d	other determiners	Cush	Al	Sp	Cr;Fr	Sp;Hil	Eng	Stm	Du	Ptg
20	plural NP markers	Ban	Al	Qui	Cr;Fr	Hil	Ø	Stm	EI	Ø
21	question particle	Ø	Rus	Ø	Cr(<Fr)	Ø	Ø	Ø	Ø	Ø
22	deictic adverbs	Unk	Rus	Sp	Cr	Sp	Ptg	Stm	EI+Du	Ptg
23	manner adverbs	Unk	Rus	Sp	Cr	Sp	Eng	Stm	EI	Ptg
24	focus particle	?	Rus	Qui	?	Ø	Gb	?	EI	Ø

† Abbreviations in the table: Al (Aleut), Ang (Angolar), Ban (Bantu), Ber (Berbice Dutch), Cr (Cree), Cush (Cushitic), Du (Dutch), EI (Eastern Ijọ), Eng (English), Fr (French), Gb (Gbe languages), Hil (Hiligaynon), Kb (Kimbundu), Kor (Korlai Creole Portuguese), Mar (Marathi), MdA (Mednyj Aleut), MdL (Media Lengua), Mich (Michif), Min (Mindanao Chabacano), Ptg (Portuguese), Qui (Quichua), Rus (Russian), Sar (Saramaccan), Stm (Sãotomense), Sp (Spanish), Unk (Unknown). The rubrics are as follows: A(B): A with some forms of B; A + B: blended form using elements of A and B. * indicates that the form in question is used in SAR in ways differing from those in which the form is employed in the source language. ? means my sources, listed elsewhere in this paper, lack data for this particular structural point.

The sense of most of the elements discussed in Table 11 is clear. Items 1–20 are from Smith (1987) and bear his numbers; the other entries are my own additions. However, item 1c relates to the means of expressing possession between a possessum noun and a possessor noun, 3 refers to items such as 'both', 4 refers to such things as 'a lot of x', 8 refers to items such as 'very X or quite X', 10b to 'soon, now, already' and the like, and 11a 'abstract' adpositions are those, such as Pap. *na*, which have little semantic content. 12 and 13a refer to /to, for' and 'with, using' respectively. Forms found in 14d would include 'and then, and so', and category 19d includes forms such as 'such an X, what an X'. 15a includes the complementiser corresponding to the English noun clause marker 'that', while 15f includes forms such as 'although'. The forms 21–24 have been added by me to the list of forms which Smith (1987) offered as 1–20; 21 refers to interrogative particles in yes/no questions, 22 to 'here, there' and the like, 23 to forms such as 'thus', and 24 refers to the focus particle which some creoles have as a highlighter (for instance *se* in current Mauritian Creole).

Here again the kinds of forms which are transferred from one language to another differ markedly between individual creoles, between individual mixed languages, and also between these groups as a whole. A glimpse at personal pronouns makes this clear. Perusal of the Appendix shows us that Angolar uses non-Portuguese forms for 2PL and 3PL, Mindanao Creole Spanish for all plural forms (even transferring case-marking bodily from Hiligaynon), Berbice Dutch for 3SG and 3PL, Saramaccan for 2PL only while Korlai Creole Portuguese's pronouns all derive from Portuguese, although their forms represent Korlai-internal grammaticalisations of combinations of Portuguese morphs. Similarly, other subsets of function words may embrace both lexical heterogeneity and the transmission or replication of semantic structures for a substrate language. This is certainly the case with the patterning of the various negators in Mindanao Creole Spanish (Frake 1971) and in Berbice Dutch (Kouwenberg 2000), both of which use sets of negators derived from more than one language. The sources of function words of various kinds in a mixed-lexifier creole may tell us certain things about the origins of a language, but an examination of the semantic distribution of such forms within the language would enlighten us more about the effects of different languages upon the development of such a language, and especially about the languages to which it is typologically closest.

7. A note on sources of mixed-lexifier creole phonology: inventories of segments and syllabic canons

In the past few years several comparative accounts of contact language phonology have appeared: we may mention van Gijn (2009) for the phonology of several stable mixed languages, Klein (2011) for creole phonologies, and Bakker (2009) for phonological systems of pidgins. We can briefly assess what kinds of influences substrate and adstrate languages have had on the phonologies of mixed-lexifier creoles.

For the record, van Gijn makes a distinction between mixed languages which divide their components with different sources for nouns and verbs (such as Michif and Mednyj Aleut), and those which divide with different sources for stems and morphology (such as Ma'á and Media Lengua). The former preserve the essentials of the different source language segmental and canonical phonological systems for verbs and for nouns, while in the latter cases both stems and morphology used one phonological system which derives from that of the morphological source language.

The mixed-lexifier creoles surveyed take different approaches to the assembly of both segmental and canonical inventories in their systems. Angolar segmental and canonical phonology resembles that of its ancestor Sãotomense in its lack of distinction between /l/ and /r/ and its use only of open syllables, although Sãotomense /s z/ are often replaced in Angolar by /θ ð/ respectively (a sound change which also typifies the Angolan Bantu language Ndingi) and, unlike Sãotomense, Angolar does not tolerate complex onsets (Lorenzino 1998). Both languages are tonal.

Mindanao Creole Spanish phonology (Ing 1967) incorporates segments and canons from both Central Philippine languages (including typically Philippine /ʔ/ and /ŋ/) and from a variety of creolised Spanish which keeps /j/ and /ʎ/ distinct. It has apparently added some segments from Philippine English which have passed into pre-English strata of the Mindanao Creole lexicon, such as /ʃ/ and /dʒ/ (e.g. /ʃete/ 'seven', Sp. *siete*; /dʒente/ 'tooth', Sp. *diente*), while many speakers replace Spanish and English /f/ with /p/; /v/ is exclusive to loans from English. Although CC-onset syllables typify Mindanao Creole forms of English or especially Spanish origin, the flexibility and wide range of syllable-final and especially word-final consonants is something which typifies words of Philippine (and English) origin.

Saramaccan phonology resembles that of its Gbe substrates as it contains implosive and non-implosive forms of /b d/ (Smith & Haabo 2007), the use of lexical and grammatical tone, a lack of distinction between /r/ and /l/, and it uses only syllables which are either open or which are checked with nasalised vowels. Unlike in Sranan, complex onsets are not tolerated.[4]

Korlai Creole Portuguese segmental phonology is very close to that of Marathi – for instance /h/, used in Marathi, is favoured over Portuguese /f/ (a loan phoneme in Marathi) in many Portuguese stems commencing in /f-/ –, but there is far less use of aspirated plosives, which occur in Marathi loans but not in most Portuguese elements. Its canonical phonology resembles that of Marathi but also uses CC- onsets, which are less frequent in Marathi than in Portuguese.

Finally, Berbice Dutch phonology lacks the tonal system and most of the features of the tongue-root harmony of Ijoid languages (indeed the functional yield between /e/ and /ɛ/ in Berbice Dutch is minimal), and uses (C)CC- onsets and –C(C) codas, which are permissible in Dutch but not in Ijoid languages. It has innovated slightly with the addition of /ʃ/ from an earlier /si/, which is found in words of all origins although it is neither Ijoid nor Dutch in origin (but occurs in Guyanese Creole English). /h/ is confined to non-Ijoid words.

8. Extensive contact-induced change without basic lexical borrowing: the cases of Sri Lanka Creole Portuguese and of Papia Kristang of Malacca and Singapore

Contact-induced change upon a language can also be indirect. Although inflectional and derivational morphological elements are rarely borrowed into creole languages, the process of metatypy of substrate language structures in creoles (usually occurring without the transfer of structural morphemes from these sources) is especially typical of some of the Luso-Asian creoles in our sample, which typify many metatypised languages in that they have often borrowed plentiful cultural lexicon but less basic lexicon.

Smith (1979a) discusses the effects of the interaction of a Portuguese lexicon with structural features of Sri Lanka Tamil in the case of Sri Lanka Creole Portuguese. At 2.5% (a proportion of borrowings which is comparable to those found in the Daman and Diu Creole Portuguese languages but which is far lower than that in Korlai Creole Portuguese), Sri Lanka Creole Portuguese does not have enough borrowings in its Swadesh list to merit classification as a mixed lexicon creole here, although its overall lexicon does contain elements from Tamil, Dutch, English and marginally Sinhala. Confining our gaze to morphosyntax, some Sri Lanka Creole features which can probably or certainly be traced to influence from local forms of Tamil include the use of an indefinite particle *o~wo* (which may be taken from Tamil *wo*, the sole example of an actual particle which may have been borrowed, both fabric and pattern, from Tamil into Sri Lanka Creole Portuguese), and also several forms whose fabric derives from Portuguese but whose uses come from Tamil: a quotative particle, noun case-marking patterns using bound postpositons (themselves a Tamil feature) developed from Portuguese prepositions, reduplication, noun-adjective order, a reportative particle, and the means of expressing the comparison of adjectives, to name but a few.

Smith (1977) discusses Sri Lanka Creole Portuguese phonology and much more besides, with especial interest in the effects of contact-induced change. Smith (1977: 151) points out the strong structural and typological similarities between Sri Lanka Creole Portuguese and the Tamil spoken in Batticaloa, while stating that Sri Lanka Creole Portuguese is far more than simply Batticaloa Tamil structures which are replicated (or as we would now say, metatypised) with Portuguese words. The question of the role of substrate influences against creole universals in the development of Sri Lanka Creole Portuguese is explored in Smith (1979b). Nonetheless, the degree of metatypy of Sri Lanka Creole Portuguese towards Tamil is immense, though this is not paralleled by the tiny proportion of lexical elements in it that originate in Tamil, and the even smaller number from Sinhala and Dutch. There is no recent modern dictionary of Sri Lanka Creole (Callaway 1820 being the last published dictionary of this language which reflects the spoken language rather than a lusitanised idealization) or indeed for any Indo-Portuguese creole, but the long Swadesh list for the language (Smith, Cardoso & Clements, ms.) shows a loan proportion of 2%, equally divided between Tamil and Dutch. Similarly low figures for the amount of borrowed basic lexicon can be cited for the creoles of Daman and Diu, which have been influenced by Gujarati, and I have no evidence that Luso-Asian varieties spoken in Dravidian areas of India exhibited a greater amount of replacement of basic lexicon with words from local languages. Korlai Creole Portuguese, with its high proportion of Marathi loans, is the anomaly here, though the profusion of Marathi loans can be explained by intense societal bilingualism (Clements 1996).

One should also mention the effects of metatypy and borrowing on Papia Kristang. Hancock (1970, 1973, 1975), Marbeck (1995, 2004), Scully & Zuzarte (2002) and Baxter (1983, 1988, 2005) and Baxter & de Silva (2004) are major sources on Papia Kristang as it is used in Malacca (in the case of the works of Hancock and Baxter, and the native speakers Marbeck and de Silva) and in Singapore (the very similar variety which is represented in the works of the other authors). In Papia Kristang, there are not many basic-level or Swadesh list loans from Malay, Hokkien, Dutch or English in the lexicon, although cultural loans there are plentiful. Simplex Kristang words in Baxter & de Silva (2004; see Baxter 2005) number 2429. Of these, 139 are from Malay, 13 from Dutch, 11 from English, 1 from Malayalam, 5 from Konkani or Marathi, and 6 from Chinese languages (Hokkien, Hakka, Cantonese) – in all, fewer than 6% of the forms in the dictionary are borrowings from any language.[5] But the language features lots of metatypy and transfer of pattern from Malay and often indirectly from Hokkien, and there is lots of borrowed cultural vocabulary too from both these languages, though certainly more derive from Malay. Hancock (1975:228–230) provides eighteen structural parallels which are in most cases typologically unusual, including features such as reduplication (involving verbs to indicate iteration and interrogatives to create indefinite forms), serial verb constructions, and extraposed possession. These connect Papia Kristang, Bazaar Malay and Afrikaans but not their chief lexifiers Portuguese, Malay and Dutch. One example of structural metatypy towards Malay in Papia Kristang, which is not given in Hancock's collection, will suffice. The enforced passive ('to get X-ed') in colloquial Malay using the auxiliary verb *kena* 'to touch, to hit' echoes the similar use as a passive auxiliary of Malc. *toká* 'to touch; to have to, to be obliged to; to be, to get, to suffer'.[6] A sentence such as (1) in Papia Kristang, could be expressed in Malay as (2) – see also Chung (2005) on the use of *kena* in passivisation in Malay.

(1) Malacca Creole Portuguese   (Baxter & de Silva 2004)
Eli   ja   tokah pegah di Japang
3SG PST PASS take   by Japan
'He was captured by the Japanese.'

(2) Malay   (own knowledge)
Dia kena berkas   oleh orang Japan
3SG PASS capture by   person Japan
'He was captured by the Japanese.'

The impact of Tamil on Sri Lanka Creole Portuguese is as profound as that of Philippine languages on Mindanao Creole Spanish, but it manifests itself differently, and in ways which suggest that Sri Lanka Creole speakers have over the past several generations gained increasing fluency in (and have made increasing use of) Tamil. It exhibits metatypy as described by Ross (1996) in great abundance. Indeed Bakker (2000) has classified Sri Lanka Creole Portuguese, together with Sri Lanka Malay, as a 'converted language'. The same is true, *ceteris paribus*, for speakers of Papia Kristang in regard to Malay.

We can take Smith's observations about Sri Lanka Creole Portuguese and apply them to our mixed creoles with varying degrees of success. If Sri Lanka Creole Portuguese is more than just Batticaloa Tamil recreated using Portuguese words, as Smith rightly observes (though many Sri Lanka Creole features copy those of Tamil), then Mindanao Creole Spanish comes closest of the group of five creoles to being a case of metatypy as it is a closer approximation to a metatypised form of Hiligaynon using mostly Spanish or Caviteño morphemes. But there are exceptions to this openness to borrowing of features into Mindanao Creole Spanish and to its degree of isomorphism with Philippine languages. Up till now, as Nolasco (2005) points out, Mindanao and other varieties of Philippine Creole Spanish have not developed an ergative model of syntax despite the fact that Austronesian Philippine languages (in which many Mindanao Creole speakers are fully bilingual) customarily use ergative syntactic models which are more complex than the nominative-accusative syntax of Spanish and Mindanao Creole Spanish. Only recently have they developed Philippine-style ligatures to be used between nominal heads and their modifiers of the sort which is found in Tagalog *matandang bahay* 'old house' (*matanda* 'old', *bahay* 'house'); see Rubino (*this volume*) for a developing Mindanao Creole Spanish numeral classifier of Hiligaynon origin. But even that development may occur some time in the future. We cannot predict that such a change is going to happen in a later decade. We can at best restrain our surprise (or lack of it) if and when it does.

9. Conclusion

From an examination of the data above, what strikes us is the fact that major substrate lexifiers are not always the closest typological fits to the mixed creoles in question. Angolar is typologically closer in terms of its phonology and morphosyntax to non-Bantu Niger-Congo languages such as the Ẹ̀dóid languages (just as its ancestor Sãotomense is) than it is to either the Kimbundu of its speakers' ancestors (which has supplied more than a tenth of its lexicon) or Portuguese. Saramaccan is typologically quite close to Fongbe and the other Gbe languages (though Loango Bantu is the single biggest African lexical source for Saramaccan), and it is of course very close to Sranan and Ndyuka. But Berbice Dutch's syntactic similarities to Ijoid languages or the possible semi-creole Ijo variety which underlies its morphological structure are not close enough for us to regard it as an example of metatypy. Meanwhile, Korlai Creole Portuguese shares a number of unusual structural features with Marathi (such as the possession of paired echoic words, a typically South Asian feature) but is not simply Marathi metatypised with Creole Portuguese lexicon. Zamboanga Creole Spanish and Cotabato Creole Spanish share many lexical, semantic and morphosyntactic structures with Philippine languages but have not carried over the infixal topic-focus system which is the very heart of every Philippine-language declarative and interrogative sentence. Given the nature of the formation of intertwined languages, the degree of metatypy which these mixed creoles share with their morphosyntactic source languages is likely to be greater than what we find in other creole languages, although this topic has yet to receive the detailed attention it deserves.

Forty years ago, Frake (1971) showed the importance of inspecting semantic subsets of a language in order to examine the degree and nature of contact-induced change. Since the amount of contact-induced change on a language consists not only of transfer of fabric (morphs with phonological shapes) but also transfer of patterns (be they phonological, semantic, morphosyntactic or otherwise), it is important to recognize the contribution of several levels of language, including abstract typological features (as we can see in Tables 5 and 6, and some aspects of Table 4), in order to understand how some languages developed. A fertile field of study is the examination of the morphosyntactic and semantic structure of subsets of function words in regard to their origin, and also with respect to the roles they discharge in each language compared with parallel forms in each creole's substrate, superstrate and adstrate languages – see Baxter & Bastos (*this volume*), Veiga & Fernández (*this volume*), and Fernández (*this volume*).

A number of conclusions arise from the comparative study of mixed-lexifier creoles, and from comparing these with structural phenomena which are found in a number of better-recorded stable mixed languages:

1. Different mixed-lexifier creoles each draw different sets of features, or perpetuate different sets of structural features from their substrate languages;
2. The area where there is the greatest degree of conformity in diffusion is in the kinds of Swadesh-list items (and the concepts themselves) for which labels are borrowed, but even here the correlation is not very great. The degree of correlation is also weak in regard to the sources of function words of various classes;
3. There is only a rather weak correlation between the amount of borrowed basic lexicon in a mixed-lexifier creole and the proportion of borrowed structural features and function words which it exhibits. This may be a consequence of the fact that some mixed lexica in non-primordial creoles are inherited from the major source creole (this is true of Angolar, which derives much of its non-Portuguese material from Sãotomense). Meanwhile in other mixed creoles the lexical macaronicity or mixedness which we find results from borrowing from substrate or adstrate languages (or both) into a previously less lexically diverse creole (Mindanao Creole Spanish, maybe Korlai Creole Portuguese and, to a lesser extent, Saramaccan). What early records we have of these languages suggest that the mixture of elements had pretty much stabilized by the time of the first records;
4. Berbice Dutch shows the impact of other languages upon it in a much more basic (and much more base-centred) way than the other creoles do. Of especial interest are the greater number of non-nominal (verbal, adjectival, pronominal etc.) than nominal forms taken over from Eastern Ijọ and the set of productive bound inflectional morphemes;

5. It is principally the case of partial relexification which distinguishes Angolar from other Gulf of Guinea Creoles and which distinguishes Saramaccan from other Surinamese creoles, as the broad typological differences (illustrated in Tables 5 and 6) are minimal;
6. This study incidentally supports the idea that the Swadesh 100-item list is more resistant to borrowed material than the 200- or 215-item lists, and the data available to us suggests that the longer lists are more resistant to borrowed material than is the lexicon as a whole;
7. Mixed lexifier creoles do not constitute anything more than a weakly defined class per se (at best) as opposed to less mixed lexifier creoles, but in their very diversity of content they allow us to get a better sense of how creoles develop and acquire (and change, and increase their sets of) lexical and structural features;
8. This study also raises questions about how far high proportions of pattern transfer are paralleled or are in lockstep with high proportions of fabric transfer, and the overall predictability of these kinds of borrowing operating in concert in the same language.

Notes

* This paper was presented at the Ibero-Asian Creoles Workshop, University of Macau, October 2010. Many thanks to Hugo Cardoso, Alan Baxter, Mário Pinharanda Nunes, J. Clancy Clements, Eeva Sippola, Ian Smith and Patrick Steinkrüger for their assistance, and especially to Aireen L. Barrios for guidance about Chabacano. All errors are mine. This paper is dedicated to the memory of Martin French.

1. Apart from the large Dutch lexical component there are further important elements in PAP. In regard to its African connection it is noteworthy that a number of the few African-derived elements in PAP lexicon not found in other creoles are of Gbe origin and come from Gbe varieties spoken in modern-day Benin or Ghana, while some other forms seem to go back more readily to Upper Guinea Creole languages or to Luso-Asian languages.

2. I thank Eeva Sippola for Tirona (1923) and Patrick Steinkrüger for information on the modern creole.

3. Most languages which have contributed to mixed languages are agglutinative – Bantu languages, Plains Cree, Ecuadorean Quichua, Attuan Aleut – but some, such as Russian, are fusional; Golovko & Vakhtin (1990) show that, for instance, Mednyj Aleut has taken over only one of Russian's two inflectional paradigms for finite verbs, and only one of the two subsets of that conjugation, meaning that all Mednyj Aleut verbs are regular; it may be noted that the structure of Mednyj Aleut combines the Aleut case system and most of its non-finite verbal system, all of which are simpler than that of Russian, with the Russian finite verbal system, which is simpler than that of Aleut.

4. Incidentally, one feature which Angolar and Saramaccan have in common if compared with their chief lexifiers and with Sãotomense and Sranan respectively is that both creoles quite independently replaced earlier cases of /-VlV-/ by /-VV-/ sequences.

5. I have insufficient information on Macanese to make similar observations, though the material in Senna Fernandes & Baxter (2004) shows a low percentage of loans in Swadesh-list vocabulary from other languages.

6. See the entry in Baxter & de Silva (2004: 87), spelt as <to<u>kah</u>>, where the entries expressing obligation or passivity are separated from the meaning 'to touch'.

References

Alleyne, M. C. ed. 1987. *Studies in Saramaccan Language Structures.* Amsterdam: ATW, Universiteit van Amsterdam.
Baker, P. 2000. Theories of creolization and the degree and nature of restructuring. In *Degrees of Restructuring in Creole Languages* [Creole Language Library 22], eds. I. Neumann-Holzschuh and E. W. Schneider, 41–63. Amsterdam: John Benjamins.
Baker, P. 2001. No creolization without prior pidginization? *Te Reo* 44: 31–50.
Baker, P., and C. Corne. 1982. *Isle de France Creole: Affinities and Origins.* Ann Arbor MI: Karoma.
Bakker, P. 1995. *A language of our own: The Genesis of Michif, the Cree-French Mixed Language of the Canadian Métis.* Oxford: OUP.
Bakker, P. 2000. Convergence intertwining: An alternative way towards the genesis of mixed languages. In *Languages in Contact* [Studies in Slavic and General Linguistics 28], eds. D. G. Gilbers, J. Nerbonne and J. Schaeken, 29–35. Amsterdam: Rodopi.
Bakker, P. 2009. Phonological complexity in pidgins. In *Simplicity and Complexity in Pidgins and Creoles*, eds. N. Faraclas and T. B. Klein, 7–27. London: Battlebridge.
Bakker, P., and M. Mous, eds. 1994. *Mixed Languages: 15 case studies in language intertwining.* Amsterdam: IFOTT.
Baxter, A. N. 1983. Creole universals and Kristang (Malacca Creole Portuguese). In *Papers in Pidgin and Creole Linguistics* 3, 143–160. Canberra: Pacific Linguistics.
Baxter, A. N. 1988. *A Grammar of Kristang (Malacca Creole Portuguese)* [Pacific Linguistics. Series B; no. 95]. Canberra: Pacific Linguistics.
Baxter, A. N. 2005. Kristang (Malacca Creole Portuguese) – a long-time survivor seriously endangered. *Estudos de Sociolingüística* 6 (1): 1–37.
Baxter, A. N., and P. de Silva. 2004. *A Dictionary of Kristang (Malacca Creole Portuguese), with an English-Kristang Finderlist.* Canberra: Pacific Linguistics, Australian National University.
Bouquiaux, L., J.-M. Kobozo, and M. Diki-Kidiri. 1978. *Dictionnaire Sango-Français et Lexique Français-Sango.* Paris: SELAF.
Callaway, J. 1820. *A Vocabulary in the Ceylon Portuguese and English Languages, with a Series of Familiar Phrases.* Colombo: Wesleyan Mission Press.
Cardoso, H. C. 2009. The Indo-Portuguese Language of Diu. PhD dissertation, University of Amsterdam.
Chung, S.-F. 2005. *Kena* as a third type of Malay passive. *Oceanic Linguistics* 44: 194–214.

Clements, J. C. 1996. *The Genesis of a Language: The Formation and Development of Korlai Portuguese* [Creole Language Library 16]. Amsterdam: John Benjamins.
Clements, J. C. 2007. Korlai (Creole Portuguese) or Nɔ Liŋ. In *Comparative Creole Syntax* [Westminster Creolistics Series 7], eds. J. Holm and P. Patrick, 153–173. London: Battlebridge.
de Granda, G. 1984. El vocabolario fundamental del criollo afro-portugues de Annobón: Rasgos característicos. *Verba* 11: 25–37.
Fontes, C. S. F. 2007. Estudo do Léxico São-tomense com Dicionário. MA dissertation, Universidade de Coimbra.
Forman, M. L. 1972. Zamboangueño Texts with Grammatical Analysis: A Study of Philippine Creole Spanish. PhD dissertation, Cornell University.
Forman, M. L. 1993. Verb serialization, word order typology, and Zamboangueño: A comparative approach. *Oceanic Linguistics* 32: 163–82
Frake, C. O. 1971. Lexical origins and semantic structures in Philippine Creole Spanish. In *Pidginization and Creolization of Language*, ed. D. Hymes, 223–242. Cambridge: CUP.
Golovko, E. V., and N. B. Vakhtin. 1990. Aleut in contact: The CIA enigma. *Acta Linguistica Hafniensia* 72: 97–125.
Gómez Rendón, J. 2008. *Mestizaje Lingüístico en los Andes: Génesis y Estructura de una Lengua Mixta*. Quito: Abya-Yala.
Good, J. 2009. Loanwords in Saramaccan. In *Loanwords in the World's Languages: A Comparative Handbook*, eds. M. Haspelmath and U. Tadmor, 918–943. Berlin: Mouton de Gruyter.
Grant, A. P. 1999. *Mixed Languages: A Conspectus. April 1999.* Ms.
Grant, A. P. 2001. Language intertwining: Its depiction in recent literature and its implications for theories of creolisation. In *Creolization and contact* [Creole Language Library 23], eds. N. Smith and T. Veenstra, 91–111. Amsterdam: John Benjamins.
Grant, A. P. 2002. Fabric, pattern, shift and diffusion: What change in Oregon Penutian Languages can tell historical linguists. *Proceedings of the Meeting of the Hokan-Penutian Workshop*, ed. L. J. Buszard-Welcher, 33–56. Berkeley CA: University of California.
Grant, A. P. 2008a. The Portuguese elements in Papiamentu. In *Linguistic Studies on Papiamentu*, eds. N. Faraclas, R. Severing and C. Weijer, 47–72. Willemstad: Fundashon pa Planifikashon di Idioma.
Grant, A. P. 2008b. A constructivist approach to the history of Papiamentu. In *Linguistic Studies on Papiamentu*, eds. N. Faraclas, R. Severing and C. Weijer, 73–112. Willemstad: Fundashon pa Planifikashon di Idioma.
Grant, A. P. 2009. Admixture, structural transmission, simplicity, and creolisation. In *Simplicity and Complexity in Creoles and Pidgins*, eds. N. Faraclas and T. B. Klein, 125–152. London: Battlebridge.
Hagemeijer, T., and O. Ogie. 2011. Èdò influence on Santome: Evidence from verb serialisation. In *Creoles, Their Substrates and Language Typology* [Typological Studies in Language 95], ed. C. Lefebvre, 37–60. Amsterdam: John Benjamins.
Hancock, I. F. 1970. Some Dutch-derived items in Papia Kristang. *Bijdragen tot de Taal-, Land- en Volkenkunde* 126: 352–56.
Hancock, I. F. 1973. Malacca Creole Portuguese: A brief transformational outline. *Te Reo* 16: 23–44.
Hancock, I. F. 1975. Malacca Creole Portuguese: Asian, African or European? *Anthropological Linguistics* 17: 211–36.
Holm, J. A., and P. L. Patrick. eds. 2007. *Comparative Creole Syntax*. London: Battlebridge.
Ing, R. O. 1967. A brief outline of Chabacano phonology. *Le Maitre Phonétique* 128: 26–33.

Jacobs, B. 2009. The Upper Guinea origins of Papiamentu: Linguistic and historical evidence. *Diachronica* 26 (3): 319–79.

Klein, T. B. 2011. Typology of creole phonology: Phoneme inventories and syllable templates. *Journal of Pidgin and Creole Languages* 26: 155–93.

Kouwenberg, S. 1994. *A Grammar of Berbice Dutch Creole*. Berlin: Mouton de Gruyter.

Kouwenberg, S. 2000. Loss in Berbice Dutch Creole negative constructions. *Linguistics* 38: 889–923.

Lorenzino, G. A. 1998. *The Angolar Creole Portuguese of São Tomé: Its Grammar and Sociolinguistic History*. Munich: Lincom.

Marbeck, J. M. 1995. *Ungua Adanza – An Inheritance*. Malacca: Loh Printing Press.

Marbeck, J. M. 2004. *Linggu Mai: Mother Tongue, a Kristang Keepsake*. Lisbon: Calouste Gulbenkian Foundation.

Matras, Y. 1998. Utterance modifiers and universals of grammatical borrowing. *Linguistics* 36: 281–331.

Matras, Y. 2003. Mixed languages: Re-examining the structural prototype. In *The Mixed Language Debate: Theoretical and Empirical Advances*, eds. Y. Matras and P. Bakker, 151–176. Berlin: Mouton de Gruyter.

Maurer, P. 1995. *L'Angolar: Un Créole Portugais Parlé à São Tomé*. Hamburg: Buske.

Maurer, P. 2009. *Principense*. London: Battlebridge.

McWhorter, J. H. 2003. *Defining Creole*. Oxford: OUP.

Mous, M. 2003. *The Making of a Mixed Language: The Case of Ma'a/Mbugu* [Creole Language Library 26]. Amsterdam: John Benjamins.

Muysken, P. 1997. Media Lengua. In *Contact Languages: A Wider Perspective* [Creole Language Library 17], ed. S. G. Thomason, 365–426. Amsterdam: John Benjamins.

Muysken, P. 2003. The grammatical elements in Negerhollands: Loss, retention, reconstitution. In *Germania et Alia: A Webschrift for Hans den Besten*, eds. J. Koster and H. van Riemsdijk. www.let.rug.nl/koster/DenBesten/Muysken.pdf (accessed February 27, 2011).

Nolasco, R. M. 2005. The Chabacano challenge to Philippine ergativity. In *Linguistics and Language Education in the Philippines and Beyond: A Festschrift in Honor of Ma. Lourdes S. Bautista*, eds. D. T. Dayag and J. S. Quakenbush, 401–433. Manila: De La Salle University Press.

Parkvall, M. 2001. Reassessing the role of demographics in language restructuring. In *Degrees of Restructuring in Creole Languages* [Creole Language Library 22], eds. I. Neumann-Holzschuh and E. W. Schneider, 185–213. Amsterdam: John Benjamins.

Riego de Dios, M. I. O. 1989. *A Composite Dictionary of Philippine Creole Spanish (PCS)*. Manila: Linguistic Society of the Philippines and Summer Institute of Linguistics.

Romaine, S. 1994. Germanic creoles. In *The Germanic Languages*, eds. E. König and J. van der Auwera, 566–603. London: Routledge.

Ross, M. D. 1996. Contact-induced change and the comparative method. In *The Comparative Method Reviewed*, eds. M. Durie and M. D. Ross, 180–217. Oxford: OUP.

Scantamburlo, L. 1999. *Dicionário do Guineense*. Lisbon: Colibri.

Scully, V., and C. Zuzarte. 2004. *The Most Comprehensive Eurasian Heritage Dictionary. Kristang-English/English-Kristang*. Singapore: SNP International.

Senna Fernandes, M., and A. N. Baxter. 2004. *Maquista Chapado: Vocabulary and Expressions in Macau's Portuguese Creole*. Macau: Macau International Institute.

Smith, I. R. 1977. Sri Lanka Creole Portuguese Phonology. PhD dissertation, Cornell University.

Smith, I. R. 1979a. Convergence in South Asia: A creole example. *Lingua* 48: 193–220.

Smith, I. R. 1979b. Substrata vs. universals in the formation of Sri Lanka Portuguese. In *Papers in Pidgin and Creole linguistics* 2, ed. P. Mühlhäusler, 183–200. Canberra: Pacific Linguistics.
Smith, I. R., H. C. Cardoso, and J. C. Clements. In preparation. Swadesh list for English, mediaeval Portuguese, Korlai, Daman, Diu and Sri Lanka Creole Portuguese. Ms.
Smith, N. S. H. 1987. The Genesis of the Creole Languages of Surinam. PhD dissertation, Universiteit van Amsterdam.
Smith, N. S. H. 1999. Younger languages: Genetically modified? Paper presented at the *Second International Workshop on Mixed Languages*, University of Aarhus, May.
Smith, N. S. H., and H. Cardoso. 2004. A new look at the Portuguese element in Saramaccan. *Journal of Portuguese Linguistics* 3 (2): 115–47.
Smith, N. S. H., and V. Haabo. 2007. The Saramaccan implosives: Tools for linguistic archaeology. *Journal of Pidgin and Creole Languages* 22: 101–22.
Tirona, T. 1923. An account of the Ternate dialect of Cavite. Tagalog Paper 487, H. Otley Beyer Collection, Philippine National Library, Manila.
van Gijn, R. 2009. The phonology of mixed languages. *Journal of Pidgin and Creole Languages* 24: 100–21.
Zenk, H. B., T. Johnson, and S. B. Hamilton. 2010. Chinook Jargon (Chinuk Wawa) etymologies. *University of British Columbia Working Papers in Linguistics* 27: 270–348.

Appendix
Borrowed forms on the Swadesh lists of the profiled mixed creoles

Angolar (forms are from Kimbundu unless otherwise indicated)

ane/ene	'they'	málá	'guts'
bètà	'to beat'	mbézi	'moon'
fèngè-fèngè	'thin' < ?	mbosi	'fog, cloud'
fùmà	'to swell' < ?	mèmà	'the back'
íkwé	'seed' < Bini	mínhóngà	'sea'
ílígõ`	'smoke' < Bini	monobja	'road'
ìnkìlò	'tail'	mpúnà	'knee'
írú	'louse' < Bini	nake	'eight'
kíkíe	'fish'	ndatxi	'root'
kíóngó	'snake' < ?	ndaru	'standing up' < ?
kokola	'to scratch' < ?	ndjô	'a lot, many' < ?
kokwa	'bark, skin' < ?	nètà	'thick'
kondogaru	'round' < ?	ntê`	'head'
kota	'new'	nθúkù	'night'
kúànà	'four'	ôgô	'forest, woods' < Bini
kwin	'ten'	rièdharu	'to think of' < ?
lùkwà	'to throw'	sìngò	'neck'
makêrí	'twenty'	situ	'animal, meat'
mànhà	'to tie' < ?	sisika	'to cut'

tano	'five'	θámáno	'six'
tátà	'father'	θambári	'seven'
têtèmbù	'star'	úvwà	'nine'
êθê	'you plural' < ?	vina	'to dig' < Bailundu
tubuka	'to dig'	vakana	'to hear' < Kikongo
txórórò	'small' < ?	zìárú	'white'

Berbice Dutch (forms are Ịjọid unless otherwise indicated)

aka	'tooth'	kiri	'earth, ground'
akalu	'moon'	kori	'to work'
an	'and' < Guyanese Creole English	koro	'to fall, drop'
		kunu	'to smell'
angga	'at'	kurheli	'fog, smoke' < Arawak/Lokono
apara	'bark of tree, skin'		
ba	'to kill'	kurkuru	'black'
bara	'hand, arm'	mɛnɛ/mina	'meat, flesh'
beri	'ear'	minggi	'lake, water'
bia	'to cook'	mono	'sleep'
bibi	'mouth'	muni	'black, said of skin'
biɛbiɛ	'red, yellow'	musu	'much, many' < prob. Portuguese
bifi/bi	'to say'		
bionto	'to think'	nama	'animal, meat'
bita	'clothes'	nanggwa	'long, tall'
bolo	'belly'	nimi	'to know'
bolo	'to lie down'	nini	'nose'
bu	'to drink, to suck'	nunu	'to pull'
buma	'to throw away'	ori/o/a	's/he'
bwa	'foot, leg, claw'	pamba	'wing'
dangga	'there'	pi	'to give'
deki	'to take'	poko	'neck'
dondo	'to suck, breast'	potɛ	'old'
eni/ini	'they'	pu	'to split'
ɛnɛ	'rain'	poši	'to squeeze'
feni	'bird'	pundi	'to squeeze'
fini	'fire'	purikida	'rotten' < Arawak/Lokono
furi	'not to be'	soko	'to dig'
gjofu/gefu	'to hit'	tembi	'to stab'
jefi	'to eat, food'	tibi	'head'
jɛrma	'woman, wife'	toko	'child'
juku	'louse'	toro	'eye'
kali	'small'	tuku	'root'
kanɛ/ka	'not'	wangga	'where'
kɛnɛ	'person'	wenggi	'to walk'
kiba	'short'		

Korlai Portuguese (forms are from Marathi unless otherwise indicated; bracketed forms are light verbs of Portuguese origin)

ani	'and'	loTu	'push'
bərəf (hika)	'to freeze'; bərəf 'ice, snow'	pənkhə	'wing'
bəsku	'to stab, pierce'	reti	'sand'
bhoTal	'dull, blunt'	rhen	'dust' < ?
čūč	'narrow' < ?	suskar- (tuma)	'to breathe'
dabu	'to squeeze'	šiŋg	'horn'
dawri	'left side'	tarta (hika)	'to float'
dhopa	'knee'	təla	'lake'
dhag	'cloud'	wahun (anda)	'to flow'
ful	'flower'	wičar (hedze)	'to think'
gol	'round'	ye	'this'
karən	'because'		

Saramaccan (these forms follow the semantic domain order for forms of various origins in the listing in Good 2009; <ë> and <ö> are [ɛ] and [ɔ])

1. Loans from Dutch:

dáka	'ay'	baláki	'to vomit'
ɛ́isi	'ice'	tánda	'tooth'
jáa	'year'	nêgi	'nine'
kɔtö	'cold'	tánda	'tooth'

2. Loans from Gbe:

zín	'to press, to squeeze'	andí	'what?'
logoo	'round'	ambɛ	'who?'
bë	'red'		

3. Loans from Igbo:

un	'you (PL)'

4. Loans from Loango Bantu:

bundji	'fog'	tutú	'horn, throat'
taatá	'father, father's brother'	djukú	'to vomit'

5. Loans from Sranan:

wɔlúku	'cloud'	féki	'to wipe'
nái	'to sew'	híi	'all'
kándi	'to pour, to lie down'	kaábu	'to scratch'
guúun	'green'		

6. Loans from Suriname Portuguese:

téla	'land'	teéja	'star'
lío	'river or stream'	vɛntu	'wind'
matú	'woods or forest'	tjúba	'rain'
páu	'wood, tree'	síndja	'ash'
líba	'moon, month, above'	tjumá	'to burn'

wómi	'man'	panjá	'to hold'
mujeë	'woman'	dá	'to give'
mií	'child'	déndu	'inside'
bítju	'worm'	töɔtö	'left, crooked'
kákisa	'skin or hide, bark'	zúntu	'near'
puúma	'body hair, feather'	lóngi	'far'
lábu	'tail'	gaán	'big'
wójo	'eye'	pikí	'small'
búka	'mouth, edge'	fitjá	'narrow'
gangáa	'neck'	fínu	'thin'
máun	'arm, hand, branch'	túu	'all'
húnjan	'fingernail, claw'	gaándi	'old'
hánza	'wing'	didía	'day'
tiípa	'intestines or guts'	línzo	'smooth'
gumbitá	'to vomit'	munján	'wet'
duumí	'to sleep'	kéndi	'hot, warm'
vívo	'to be alive'	búnu	'good'
póndi	'rotten'	sábi	'to know'
bebé	'to drink'	kandá	'to sing, the song'
tjupá	'to suck'	kondá	'to count, to tell'
fuúta	'fruit'	lánza	'a spear'
óbo	'egg'	bajá	'to dance'
foló	'flower'	akí	'here'
latjá	'to split'	alá	'there'
feegá	'to rub'	óto	'other'
peetá	'to squeeze'	ku	'with'
kaí	'to fall'	mángu	'thin'
buwá	'to fly'	súndju	'dust'
kulé	'to flow, to run'		

7. From Wolof:

nján   'to bite, to eat'

Zamboangueño (borrowed forms are from Hiligaynon unless otherwise indicated)

'anak, bata'	'child'	kalíwa	'left side'
'anut	'to float'	kamó	'you (PL)'
buling	'dirty'	kay	'because'
buluk	'rotten'	kilaya	'how?' < Portuguese
daàn	'old' (of things)	kitá (including hearer);	
dyutay	'small'	kami (excluding hearer)	'we'
gamit	'root'	kusu	'to rub'
gulud	'mountain'	kutu	'louse'
gumita'	'to vomit' < Portuguese	lagit	'thin'
hende'	'not' (used with present and future tense verbs)	mapurul	'dull, blunt'
		maskín	'if' (also *si*) < Portuguese
man-'ipit	'to squeeze'	na	'at, in' < Portuguese

nana	'mother'	*sapa'*	'river'
pandak	'short'	*silá*	'they'
pati	'and' (also Spanish *i*)	*tata*	'father'
punó	'tree'	*tuhud*	'knee'
saksak	'to stab'	*'ulan*	'rain'
sangkil	'spear'		

Language index

A
Aeta 197
African American Vernacular English 338
Afrikaans 353
Agta 200
Agutaynen 197
Aklanon 197, 242
Aleut 344–348, 350, 356
Angolar 47–49, 53, 63, 74, 298–299, 327–330, 334–336, 338–341, 347–350, 354–357
Arabic 197–198
Aragonese 220
Arawak 331, 335–336, 341, 347, 361
Asian Creole Portuguese [see also *Luso-Asian Creoles*] 47–51, 53, 58, 63–65, 73–76, 298–299
Aymara 198

B
Baba Malay 52, 62–63, 147
Bahasa Ternate 335
Bailundu 331, 361
Baluga 197
Bantuanon 241
Barbadian Creole 338
Batak 197, 200
Batavia Creole Portuguese 1, 53, 56–59, 73–74, 77, 101, 104–105, 108–112, 114, 116, 132–133, 135–141, 143–144, 164
Batticaloa Creole Portuguese 100, 108–113, 117, 154, 293, 321
Bazaar Malay 101–102, 119–120, 129, 131–133, 136, 140, 143–145, 272, 284, 353
Berbice Dutch 289, 327–331, 335–341, 347–349, 351, 354–355, 361

Betawi 132, 143
Bidau Creole Portuguese 52–53, 118, 225
Bikol 187, 191, 194, 197, 200
Bini 329, 331, 340, 360

C
Cannanore Creole Portuguese 15, 24–35, 37–46, 53, 94–97, 108–114, 117, 119
Cantonese 52, 63, 79, 105–106, 108, 114, 117, 132, 135, 137, 143, 154, 156, 241, 259, 266–268, 272–276, 280–284, 316, 319, 323, 352
Cape Dutch Pidgin 182, 197–198
Cape Verdean Creole 278, 338–340
Catalan 220
Cebuano 4, 132, 145, 154, 156, 176, 183, 187, 194, 197, 200, 213, 227, 229, 332, 337, 347
Chabacano/Chavacano [see also *Philippine Creole Spanish*] 4–5, 8–9, 132–141, 149–150, 154–156, 164–176, 182–183, 186–187, 191–196, 205, 213–218, 227–231, 233–234, 239–240, 245–258, 327, 338, 347–348, 356
Chamorro 200
China Coast Pidgin [see also *Chinese Pidgin English*] 245, 281
Chinese 6–9, 18, 63–64, 77, 156, 164, 182, 187, 197–198, 245, 263–274, 279–284, 319, 352
Chinese Pidgin English [see also *China Coast Pidgin*] 6–9, 182, 187, 197–198, 245, 263–265, 267–276, 278–282, 280–284

Chinuk Wawa [see also *Grand Ronde Chinook Jargon*] 328, 340
Cocama 198
Cochin Creole Portuguese 53, 63, 73, 94, 97
Cotabato Creole Spanish/ Cotabateño [see also *Chabacano/Chavacano*] 327, 329, 332, 335, 354
Cree 344–345, 347–348, 356
Creolese [see also *Guyanais/ Guyanese Creole English*] 329, 331, 335–336
Cushitic 344–345, 347–348

D
Daman Creole Portuguese 15, 24–35, 37–46, 88, 91, 108–114, 119, 132–133, 135–141, 144, 289–291, 293, 308–312, 318–319, 351–352
Davao Creole Spanish/ Davaueño [see also *Chabacano/Chavacano*] 5, 329
Diu Creole Portuguese 1, 4, 15, 19, 21–35, 37–46, 83, 88–91, 94, 108, 111, 113–116, 125–126, 132–141, 144, 149–150, 154–158, 169–173, 178, 289–294, 308–313, 318–319, 328, 351–352
Dravidian languages 15, 25, 30–33, 35, 94, 98, 137–138, 155, 352
Dutch 24, 28, 30, 37, 43, 46, 120, 131, 144, 197–198, 328–329, 331, 335–337, 347–348, 351–353, 356, 362

E
Èdó/ Èdóid 336, 354

English 9, 19–20, 24, 28, 30–31,
    37–46, 74, 83–84, 119–120, 125,
    142, 159, 184, 195–196, 200,
    210, 212, 225, 229, 232–233,
    240, 242, 257, 259, 263–276,
    278–284, 294, 318, 320,
    328, 331–332, 336, 338–342,
    344–352

F
Fa d'Ambu 328
Fon 340
Forro [see also *Sãotomense*] 328
French 179, 184, 223, 328, 338,
    344–348

G
Gbe 329, 336, 347–348, 350, 354,
    356, 362
German 197–198
Grand Ronde Chinook Jargon
    [see also *Chinuk Wawa*] 328
Guadeloupean 338
Guaraní 198, 200
Gujarati 19, 30, 32–35, 88–89, 91,
    108, 113, 115, 132, 144, 154–155,
    176, 293, 352
Gullah 338
Guyanais/Guyanese Creole
    English [see also *Creolese*]
    329, 331, 335, 338–341, 347,
    351, 361

H
Haitian 338–339
Hakka 63, 352
Hawaii Creole English
    IX, 278–280, 339
Hiligaynon 132, 145, 154, 156,
    176, 197, 200, 214, 227,
    229–230, 233, 239–248, 254,
    259, 332–333, 336–337, 340,
    347–349, 353–354, 363
Hindi 19, 31, 35, 37, 229–230, 333
Hokkien 52, 63, 77, 132, 154–156,
    241, 319, 352–353

I
Ibanag 187, 197
Ibero-Romance languages
    154–155, 223, 231, 327–328

Ijo/ Ijoid languages 329, 331, 335,
    337, 340–341, 347–348, 351,
    354–355, 361
Indo-Aryan/Indic languages
    15, 20, 25, 31–33, 35, 51, 77, 88,
    91, 99, 137, 147, 153, 155
Indo-Portuguese Creoles 5–9,
    15–25, 28–30, 32–35, 37,
    47–48, 53–55, 62, 64, 73–75,
    77, 94–96, 113, 117, 133–134,
    155, 159, 171, 173–174, 185, 205,
    232, 234, 270, 272, 289–294,
    308–311, 314–315
Inga 198, 200

J
Jamaican Creole 338–339
Japanese 332
Javanese 101, 145, 270

K
Kannada 31–32
Kapampangan 187, 194, 197, 200
Kari'na 331, 347
Kikongo 329, 331, 335–336, 340,
    361
Kimbundu 329, 331, 336, 347–
    348, 354, 360
Kinaray-a 176, 197, 214, 229–230,
    233
Kittitian 338
Konkani 31–32, 352
Korlai Creole Portuguese
    1, 15, 19–20, 22, 24–35, 37–46,
    47–48, 51, 53–55, 58, 60–64,
    75–77, 91, 93–94, 108–117,
    119, 125, 132–133, 135–141, 144,
    149–150, 154–155, 158–159,
    170–173, 289–291, 293, 308–
    312, 318–319, 327–329, 331, 334,
    336–341, 347–349, 351–352,
    354–355, 362
Krio 339

L
Leonese 220
Loango Bantu 329, 347, 354, 362
Lokono 335, 361
Louisianais 338–340
Luso-Asian Creoles [see also
    Asian Creole Portuguese]

4, 6, 81–82, 85, 87, 98, 114, 116–
    119, 314–315, 318, 351–352, 356

M
Ma'á 344–348, 350
Maasai 344–345
Macanese/Macau Creole
    Portuguese [see also
    Maquista/Makista] 1, 6–9,
    46, 49, 52–53, 56–57, 59,
    73–74, 105–112, 114–115, 117,
    125–126, 134, 149–150, 154–
    156, 163–164, 170–172, 174, 177,
    182–187, 198–199, 225, 241,
    259, 265–267, 270, 277–278,
    280, 282–283, 289–291,
    294–296, 298–301, 303–313,
    315–316, 318–323, 357
Macau Pidgin Portuguese
    267–269, 283
Malabar Coast Pidgin/Malabar
    Pidgin Portuguese 47, 75, 320
Malacca Creole Portuguese [see
    also *Papia Kristang*] 1, 5, 8–9,
    47–48, 52–53, 56–67, 69–72,
    75–77, 100–105, 108–112, 114,
    116–117, 131–141, 143–145,
    149–150, 155, 161–165, 169–175,
    182–183, 186–187, 205–207,
    209, 213, 223–226, 231, 289–
    291, 294, 308–313, 315–316,
    318–319, 322, 328, 351–353
Malay [see also *Vehicular
    Malay*] 37, 62–64, 72, 75–76,
    100–102, 104, 108, 113–114,
    116–117, 119–120, 129, 131–133,
    135–137, 140, 143–145, 154–156,
    161–162, 181–182, 186, 197–199,
    205–206, 224–228, 231,
    234, 241, 259, 270, 272, 284,
    314–316, 319, 323, 332, 335, 339,
    352–353
Malayalam 19, 24, 28, 30–35, 37,
    49–50, 62, 64, 77, 94–95, 99,
    108, 114, 132, 352
Malayo-Portuguese Creoles 5, 8,
    101–102, 113, 270
Mandaya 187, 197
Mangalore Creole Portuguese
    53–55, 58, 63, 73–75, 118
Mangyan 197

Mansaka 200
Maquista/Makista [see also *Macanese/Macau Creole Portuguese*; *Patuá*] 105, 132–141, 143–144, 266, 289, 294, 299, 301–303, 306–307, 313, 323
Maranaw 332
Marathi 19–20, 22, 24–25, 27–28, 30, 32–35, 51, 60, 64, 75, 77, 91–93, 108, 113, 132, 137–138, 154–155, 158, 293, 328, 331, 334, 336, 340, 347–348, 351–352, 354, 362
Martiniquais 338
Mauritian 337–338, 349
Media Lengua 344–348, 350
Mednyj Aleut 344–348, 350, 356
Michif 344–348, 350, 357
Mindanao Creole Spanish/Mindanao Chabacano [see also *Chabacano/Chavacano*] 215, 230, 327–340, 342–343, 347–350, 353–355

N
Nagamese 339
Nagapattinam Creole Portuguese 53, 75, 98, 118
Nahuatl 198, 332
Ndyuka 339, 354
Negerhollands 197, 338–340
Negrito 200
Norteiro Creole Portuguese 76, 113–115, 117, 223
Nubi 339

O
Odionganon 241

P
Palawano 197
Palenquero 339
Papia Kristang [see also *Malacca Creole Portuguese*] 100, 102, 131, 182, 186, 205–206, 215, 223–224, 226, 232–233, 241, 270, 277–278, 289–290, 328, 338–339, 351–353

Papiamentu 182, 197, 281, 328, 338–340, 349, 356
Patuá [see also *Macanese/Macau Creole Portuguese*; *Maquista/Makista*] 105
Philippine Creole Spanish [see also *Chabacano/Chavacano*] 186, 191, 230, 354
Pitcairnese 339
Portuguese 3, 7–10, 15–35, 37–62, 72–77, 81, 84–87, 90–97, 100–108, 111–117, 119–120, 132–135, 137, 140–144, 150, 152–158, 162, 164, 171, 174–177, 181–187, 189, 196–199, 205–213, 215, 218–221, 223–226, 231–234, 263–272, 274, 276–284, 290–300, 303–307, 311, 315–316, 318–323, 328–329, 331–332, 334–342, 347–349, 351–355, 360–363
Provençal 223

Q
Quechua/Quichua 198, 200, 344–345, 347–348, 356

R
Rabaul Creole German 197
Ramoaaina 197–198
Réunionnais 339, 341
Romblomanon 251
Russian 344–348, 356

S
Sambal 197, 200
Sango 328, 340
Sãotomense [see also *Forro*] 328–329, 335–336, 338–339, 347–348, 350, 354–355, 357
Saramaccan 327–331, 334, 336, 338–342, 347–350, 354–357, 362
Seselwa 339
Shambala 346
Sibalenhon 241
Sinama 332, 347
Sinhala 19, 24, 28, 30, 32–34, 52, 77, 98–100, 108, 112–113, 117, 129, 131–132, 137, 139, 144, 154–155, 293, 321, 351–352

Skepi Dutch 341
Spanish 3–6, 8–10, 18, 20, 132–133, 135–136, 140–142, 150–152, 154–155, 162, 164, 168–169, 174–177, 181–183, 186–191, 194–197, 199, 205–206, 210, 213–216, 218–223, 226–234, 239–240, 254–255, 258–259, 281, 327–340, 342–350, 353–355, 364
Sranan 328–329, 331, 334, 336, 338–339, 342, 347, 350, 354, 357, 362
Sri Lanka Creole Portuguese 1, 15, 19, 23–24, 26–35, 37–46, 52–54, 58, 62–63, 74, 77, 98, 125–126, 132–133, 135, 137–139, 142–144, 149–150, 155, 159–160, 170–174, 176, 182, 184–185, 208–210, 213, 223–225, 231–232, 328, 338–339, 351–353
Sri Lanka Malay 339, 353
Swahili 344, 346

T
Tagalog 4, 9, 132, 145, 154–156, 165–166, 173, 177, 182–183, 187, 194–195, 197, 200, 216–217, 227–230, 240–241, 255, 329, 332, 335–337, 340, 347, 354
Tagbanwa 197, 200
Tamil 19, 24, 28, 30, 32–34, 37, 52, 98–100, 108, 112–113, 117, 120, 131–132, 134–136, 139–140, 143, 145, 154–155, 321, 351–353
Tayo 339
Ternate Chabacano/Ternateño [see also *Chabacano/Chavacano*] 5, 8, 125, 129, 132, 144, 150, 165–169, 205–206, 213, 216–218, 226–227, 230–231, 233, 245, 255, 335
Tetum 52, 118
Tok Pisin 34, 182, 197–198, 270, 320, 339
Tugu Creole Portuguese 1, 9, 53, 56, 59, 63, 73–74, 100–101, 104–105, 108–112, 114–116, 125–126, 141–142, 164, 182–183, 186, 205, 224–225, 310–311
Tuscan 223

V

Vehicular Malay [see also *Malay*] 52, 62–64, 72, 76, 132, 135, 143–144, 315

Visayan 4, 9, 187, 191, 194, 197, 213–214, 216, 239–242, 245, 251, 259

W

Waray 197, 214

Wayana 347

Y

Yakan 332, 347

Yogad 197

Z

Zamboanga Chabacano/Zamboangueño [see also *Chabacano/Chavacano*; *Mindanao Creole Spanish*] 5–6, 9, 129, 132, 135–136, 144, 150, 154–155, 168–170, 183, 192–196, 198–199, 205–206, 213–216, 226–227, 229–231, 239–241, 245–259, 327, 335, 339–340, 354, 363

Location index

A
Algarve 212
Amazon 198
Ambón 184
Andalusia 189
Annobon 328
Argentina 219
Ayutthaya 3
Azores 276

B
Basilan 184, 213, 239
Bassein/Vasai 3, 91
Batavia 1, 7, 12, 53, 56–59, 73–74, 77, 100–101, 104–105, 108, 111, 114–116, 131–133, 135–141, 143–144, 164, 315
Batticaloa 4, 23, 98–100, 108, 111–113, 117, 131, 154, 223, 293, 352–353
Benin 356
Bidau 52–53, 118, 225
Bolivia 198
Bombay/Mumbai 16, 91–93, 113, 119
Brazil 210–211, 278

C
Calicut/Kozhikode 15–16, 22, 30, 35, 48
Canary Islands 221
Cannanore/Kannur 4, 15–16, 19–23, 29–30, 33–35, 37, 48, 53, 77, 94–97, 108, 111, 113–115, 117, 119–120, 155
Canton/Guangzhou 8–9, 263–265, 267–270, 280, 282–284, 313
Caribbean 125–127, 144, 339
Cavite 5, 149, 155, 165–168, 174, 176–177, 183
Central African Republic 328

Ceylon [see also *Sri Lanka*] 4, 51, 74, 132, 184, 187, 223
Chaul 16, 22, 24, 51, 329
Chile 189, 195, 219
China 4, 22, 105, 154, 189, 199, 245, 264–271, 280–283, 315, 319, 323
Cochin/Kochi 3, 16, 25, 30, 35, 48–49, 53, 63, 73, 76–77, 94, 97, 115, 176
Colombo 52
Copper Island 345
Costa Rica 189, 195, 234
Cotabato 4–5, 184, 215, 233, 239, 245, 327, 329, 332, 354
Cuba 219
Cuzco 198

D
Daman 4, 15–16, 19, 21–23, 25, 27, 29, 33–35, 37, 83, 88, 91, 108, 111, 113–114, 119, 126, 132–133, 135–141, 144, 155, 289–290, 292–294, 310, 351–352
Davao 5, 184, 187, 239
Diu 1, 4, 15–16, 19, 21–24, 29, 33–35, 78, 83, 88–91, 94, 108, 111, 113–116, 125–126, 132–141, 144, 149–150, 154–158, 169–173, 289–294, 308–313, 318–319, 328, 351–352

E
East Timor [see *Timor*]
Ecuador 189, 195, 345

G
Gândara 211
Ghana 356
Goa 3, 22, 76, 292, 313, 316
Guam 4, 10

Guangzhou [see *Canton*]
Guyana 329

H
Hong Kong 82, 86, 120, 155, 182–183, 263–264, 269–270, 280, 283, 291, 294, 318, 321

I
India 1, 3–4, 15–16, 19, 22, 25, 31, 35, 49, 72, 75–76, 88, 91, 98, 113, 132, 154–155, 174, 189, 199, 314, 352
Indonesia 22, 101, 164

J
Japan 1, 3, 353
Java 4–5, 100

K
Kannur [see *Cannanore*]
Kochi [see *Cochin*]
Korlai 1, 4, 15–16, 19–24, 29, 33–35, 47–49, 53–55, 58, 60–64, 75–77, 91, 93–94, 108, 111, 113–117, 119, 125–126, 132–133, 135–141, 144, 149–150, 154–155, 158–159, 170–172, 289–290, 292–294, 310, 327–329, 334, 336–341, 347–349, 351–352, 354–355, 362
Kozhikode [see *Calicut*]

L
Luzon 183, 197, 213–214, 255

M
Macau 1, 4–10, 47, 49, 52–53, 56–57, 59, 73–74, 82, 91, 105–108, 110–111, 114–115, 117, 125–126, 132, 134, 140, 149–150, 154–156, 163–164, 171–172,

174, 177, 182–187, 198, 225, 263–266, 268–270, 277–278, 280, 282–283, 289, 291, 294, 306, 313–321, 323, 356
Madrid 220
Mahé 53, 94–96
Malabar 47–48, 51–52, 75, 77, 320
Malacca 1, 4–5, 7–9, 47–49, 52–53, 56–67, 69–72, 75–77, 100–105, 108, 111, 114–117, 131–141, 143–144, 149–150, 154–155, 161–165, 169–175, 182–183, 186–187, 205–207, 223–226, 231, 289–290, 313–315, 319, 328, 351–353
Malaysia 4, 22, 101, 131, 144, 155, 239
Mangalore 48, 53–55, 58, 63, 73, 75, 118
Manila 4, 183, 233, 250
Manila Bay 5, 150, 154–156, 164–173, 176–177, 213, 329, 332, 335, 347
Manitoba 345
Mato Grosso 210
Mexico 188–189, 195, 199, 219
Minas Gerais 210
Mindanao 4–5, 155, 176, 183–184, 187, 197, 213, 215, 218, 229–230, 239, 254, 327–330, 332–340, 342–343, 347–350, 353–355
Mindoro 197
Moluccas 3–5, 181, 226
Mozambique 211
Mumbai [see *Bombay*]
Murcia 189

N
Nagapattinam 4, 53, 75, 98
Negros 240
North Dakota 345

O
Oregon 328, 358

P
Palawan 197
Panay 233, 240, 242
Papua New Guinea 182, 197–198
Paraguay 218–219
Philippines 4–5, 8, 127, 138, 149, 154–155, 173–174, 181–183, 186–187, 189–190, 195–197, 199, 206, 213, 226–227, 229–231, 239, 244, 281, 323, 332, 335
Pollok 184
Portugal 4, 17, 19, 22–23, 115, 211–212, 276
Puno 198

Q
Quilon 4, 48

R
Recife 210

S
Sabah 239, 253
São Paulo 210
Semporna 239
Sergipe 210
Seville 221
Shanghai 291, 318
Siberia 345
Singapore 4, 59–60, 82, 102, 119–120, 155, 351–352

Spain 4, 22–23, 189, 195, 200, 220–222
Sri Lanka [see also *Ceylon*] 1, 4, 9, 15, 19–23, 29, 33–35, 37, 51–55, 62–63, 74–77, 98–99, 113, 115, 125–127, 131–144, 149–150, 154–155, 159–160, 170, 172, 174, 176, 182–185, 205–210, 213, 223–225, 231–232, 293, 328, 338–339, 351–353

T
Tarragona 196
Tayabas 183
Ternate [Moluccas] 4–5, 226, 335
Ternate [Philippines] 5, 149–150, 155, 165–169, 174, 176, 183, 205, 213, 216–218, 226–227
Timor 4, 52–53, 118
Trincomalee 4, 131
Tugu 1, 7, 53, 56, 59, 63, 73–74, 100–101, 104–105, 108, 111, 114–116, 164, 182–183, 186, 205, 224–225, 310

U
Uruguay 221, 234

V
Vasai [see *Bassein*]
Visayas 197
Vypeen 97

Z
Zamboanga 149–150, 154–156, 167–174, 176–177, 183, 192–196, 200, 205, 215–216, 229, 239, 246–257, 327, 329, 354

General index

A

Ablative 88–89, 91–92, 96, 99, 102, 104, 107, 118–119
Accusative 69, 71–73, 95, 98, 100, 233, 247–248, 254, 257, 354
Acrolect [see *Lect*]
Adjective 60, 64, 77, 82, 118, 130, 135–140, 142–143, 145, 151, 190, 217, 244, 335, 340, 344, 352, 355
Adposition 92, 118, 126, 129–130, 137, 294, 340, 342–344, 347, 349
    Postposition 20, 61–62, 91–92, 94–95, 128, 137, 143, 228
    Preposition 61–62, 65, 76, 85, 89, 95, 102–104, 107, 119, 129, 133, 137, 142, 188, 207–208, 278–280, 312, 342, 352
Adstrate 8–9, 19, 21, 23–25, 28–29, 81–82, 85, 87–88, 91, 94, 98, 100–102, 105, 108–117, 120, 125–128, 131–132, 142–143, 149–150, 154–156, 158, 171, 174–176, 227, 330–332, 346–347, 350, 355
Adverb(ial) 60, 63–64, 84, 88, 98–99, 106, 129–130, 151, 155, 162, 174, 184, 186, 188, 190–191, 195, 199, 206, 209–210, 225, 228, 230, 245, 297, 306, 322, 342–343, 347
    Adversative 199
    Degree 106
    Deictic 347
    Locative/Place 60, 63, 342–343, 347
    Negative [see *Negation*]
    Phasal 347
    Temporal/Time 84, 342, 347

Adversative adverb [see *Adverb*]
Affricates [see *Consonants*]
Agreement 134, 142, 211, 302–304, 306, 342–343
Allomorphy 293, 303, 311, 330, 346
Allophony 24–26, 28, 35, 336
Animacy 239, 241, 245, 249, 251
    Animate 70–71, 156–158, 168–169, 242–243, 245, 257
    Inanimate 159, 169, 243, 245, 249, 257, 259
Animate [see *Animacy*]
Anterior 269, 310, 312, 317, 322, 340
Article 86, 97, 118, 129–130, 152, 246, 248, 250–253, 256–258, 276, 333, 340, 342–343, 347
Aspect [see also *TAM/Tense-Aspect-Mood marker*] 77, 106, 129–130, 193, 206–207, 213–216, 225, 230–233, 272, 274, 290, 293, 295–299, 302–307, 309, 311–313, 319, 321–322, 330, 342
Atelic [see *Telicity*]
Auxiliary 157, 213, 216, 233, 274, 282, 303, 307, 309–310, 312, 321–322, 342–343, 353

B

Basic lexicon [see also *Core lexicon*; *Swadesh list*] 6, 327–328, 336–337, 343, 351–352, 355
Basic variety [see *Second-language acquisition*]
Basilect [see *Lect*]
Bilingualism [see also *Multilingualism*] 10, 18, 20, 62, 314, 316, 320, 352, 354

Borrowing [see also *Loans/Loanwords*] 6, 8, 15–16, 18–20, 27–30, 33, 116, 186–188, 197, 211, 228, 239, 254, 257, 259, 333–336, 340, 343, 346, 351–353, 355–356, 360, 363

C

Calque 175, 269, 283
Canton trade [see also *Trade*] 8–9, 263–265, 269, 282
Casados 3, 314–315
Case 49, 75, 83–85, 88–89, 91–95, 98, 100, 102, 106, 108–109, 111, 115–119, 333, 340, 342–344, 349, 352, 356
Catholicism [see also *Christianity*] 19, 22, 190, 292
Christianity [see also *Catholicism*] 3, 5, 21–22, 76, 131, 190, 199, 205, 313–318, 323–324
Coda [see *Syllable*]
Comitative 102
Comparative construction [see *Comparison*]
Comparative particle [see *Comparison*]
Comparee [see *Comparison*]
Comparison 82–120, 188, 340, 352
    Comparative construction 6, 81–89, 91–96, 98–101, 104–106, 108–110, 112, 114, 116–120
    Comparative particle 84–87, 89–93, 95–98, 100–107, 119
    Comparee 82, 84–85, 89–93, 95–97, 99–100, 102, 104–105, 107, 120
    Comparison of inferiority 83, 89, 96

Comparison of superiority 83, 89, 102
Index of comparison 83, 89, 91–93, 95–96, 99–102, 104–108, 110, 113
Parameter of comparison 82, 85, 89–93, 95–96, 99–102, 104–108, 120
Standard of comparison 82–85, 88–109, 112, 117–118, 120
Complementation 64, 278, 280, 284
Complement 137, 279
Complement clause 157, 278, 281
Complementizer 60, 89, 157, 263–264, 272, 278–282, 284, 342–343, 349
Complement clause [see *Complementation*]
Complementizer [see *Complementation*]
Completive 310, 312
Concessive 6, 8, 159–160, 165, 167, 169, 172–174, 181–199, 230
Conditional 151, 159–160, 172–174, 192
Congruence 9, 81, 112, 117
Conjugation 233, 290, 293, 303–305, 307, 311, 321, 341, 356
Conjunction 37, 84, 96, 102, 187–189, 191, 194, 210, 214, 223–224, 227–228, 270, 278
Coordinating conjunction [see *Coordinator*]
Subordinating conjunction [see *Subordination*]
Consonant clusters 206, 232
Consonants 20, 24–28, 30–33, 126, 240, 289, 294, 350
Affricates 25, 28, 34
Liquids 25, 249
Plosives 232, 351
Sibilants 25, 336
Contemplated aspect 213–215, 217
Coordination 84, 206, 208, 210–212, 214–215, 223–224, 227–229, 231, 296, 343, 346

Coordinator [see also *Conjunction*] 94, 216, 229, 232, 346, 348
Copula 25, 82, 85–86, 88–96, 98–100, 102, 104–105, 107–108, 110, 113, 119, 263–264, 272–280, 282, 306, 309, 311, 313, 323, 340, 342–344
Core lexicon [see also *Basic lexicon*; *Swadesh list*] 15, 18, 20–21, 23–24, 28–29, 33, 330, 340
Corpora 7, 50, 65, 67–70, 72, 81, 89, 91–93, 95–96, 98, 103–104, 107, 118, 144, 191, 210, 212, 239, 246–259, 267, 272, 289–291, 294, 296, 298–307, 309–312, 319–322
Correlative 137–138, 228
Creole continuum 266, 294–295, 318

D

Dative 72, 77, 85, 95, 99, 139, 157, 160, 347
Decreolization 9, 53, 74, 258–259, 289, 291–293, 295, 307, 320
Degree adverb [see *Adverb*]
Deictic adverb [see *Adverb*]
Demonstrative 47, 61–62, 88–89, 104, 129–130, 259, 276, 301
Distal 89, 94, 98–99, 102, 254, 256–257
Proximal/Proximate 88–89, 93–94, 98–99, 102, 106
Deontic modality 296, 310
Derivation 60, 64, 330, 333, 335–336, 342–343, 346, 351
Dialect [see *Lect*]
Dictionaries 7, 164, 175, 184, 190, 194, 222, 228–229, 242, 244–245, 251, 259, 352
Diglossia 76
Direct object 294, 333–334
Discourse particle 342–343
Disjunction 84, 190, 209, 217, 224
Distal [see *Demonstrative*]
Disyllabic 205–206, 232
Double-negative [see *Negation*]

E

Early stage of acquisition [see *Second-language acquisition*]
Education [see also *Schooling*] 9, 19, 35, 106, 240, 294, 318
Emigration [see *Migration*]
Emphasis 62, 69, 71–72, 145, 153, 161, 167, 170, 173, 208, 210–211, 215, 217–218, 227–228, 232, 246, 248–249, 251–252, 255, 333
Etymology 6, 58, 61, 72, 116, 182, 186, 198, 209, 213, 229, 240, 270, 328, 331–332, 334, 346
Existential 61, 63, 71, 73, 150, 152, 156, 161–162, 164–173, 177, 213–216, 218, 250, 253, 255, 272, 274–278, 284, 309, 311–312, 333

F

Feitoria [see also *Trade*] 48, 51
Focus 100, 152, 159, 191, 193–194, 210–212, 215, 217, 219–221, 229, 347, 349, 354
Fossilization 168, 221, 311, 322
Founder Principle 34–35
Free-choice indefinite [see *Indefinites*]
Frequency 9, 20, 25, 32, 34, 50, 60, 62, 70, 74, 107, 144, 162, 185, 210–211, 228, 232, 246, 253, 258, 290, 293–295, 300, 303–304, 308, 311, 319, 322–323, 335, 351
Function words 6, 8, 101, 282, 336, 341, 346, 349, 355
Future 47, 60, 139, 160–161, 164, 206, 209, 298, 301–303, 312, 363

G

Gender 342–343
Generic pronoun [see *Pronoun*]
Generic noun 149–150, 152–153, 156, 158, 160–161, 163–166, 169–171, 175
Genitive 20, 35, 47–65, 67, 69–77, 92, 94, 133–135, 137–139, 145, 228, 243–244, 246–247, 250–256
Glide 25, 54, 311

General index

Grammaticalization 6, 8, 47, 53, 58–60, 63, 75, 118, 149, 153, 161, 169, 174, 225, 233, 322

H
Habitual 272, 296–297, 301–302, 310, 312–313, 316, 321–322
Hinduism 21, 97, 292

I
Immigration [see *Migration*]
Imperative 70, 206, 214, 233, 333
Imperfective 96, 163, 165–166, 213–217, 229–230, 247, 250–251, 253–254, 256, 258, 289–290, 295, 297–300, 302, 305–308, 311–313, 319, 321–322
Inanimate [see *Animacy*]
Indefinite quantifier [see *Indefinites*]
Indefinites 6, 129–130, 149–177, 191, 194–195, 259, 333, 347, 351, 353
    Free-choice indefinite 158, 166, 172–173, 177
    Indefinite pronoun [see *Pronoun*]
    Indefinite quantifier 191, 194
    Negative indefinite 159–160, 167, 169–170, 173
    Realis indefinite 161, 172, 175
Index of comparison [see *Comparison*]
Index of Reliance on Lexifier [see *Typological tug-of-war*]
Indicative 289–291, 294–300, 304, 308–309, 313, 320
Indirect object 85
Infinitive 32, 34, 157, 280, 289–290, 299–300, 303, 305, 308, 310, 319, 321
Inflection [see also *Verb morphology*] 12, 97, 289–292, 294, 296–300, 302–308, 310–313, 319–322, 330, 335–336, 341, 343, 346, 348, 351, 355–356
Innovation 9, 24–25, 87, 112, 117, 134, 258, 310, 334, 351
Instrumental 34–35, 60, 64, 88, 102, 134, 347

Intensification 191, 193–194, 210, 215–216, 218, 227, 231
Interlanguage [see *Second-language acquisition*]
Interrogative [see also *Question word*] 47, 130, 139, 142–143, 149, 152–153, 157–166, 168–173, 175–176, 195, 243, 247, 333, 342, 344, 347, 349, 353–354
Interrogative pronoun [see *Pronoun*]
Irrealis 47, 157, 161, 206, 209, 213–214, 302, 312, 335, 340, 342
Isogloss 197–198

K
Kinship 66, 68, 76, 250

L
Lançados 3
Language shift 8–9, 15–16, 18–20, 32–33, 320
Late stage of acquisition [see *Second-language acquisition*]
Lect [see also *Register*] 64, 150, 169, 312
    Acrolect 25–26, 28, 37, 53, 96, 103, 114–115, 118–119, 293–294, 310, 313
    Basilect 53, 114, 290–291, 320
    Dialect 6, 10, 181, 183–187, 190, 194, 197–198, 205, 208, 212, 223, 229, 232–233, 241, 266, 271, 294
Lexicalisation 177, 255, 309, 311
Lexicon 6, 10, 15, 18, 20–21, 24–25, 28–29, 33, 126, 128, 149, 232, 240, 245, 255, 266, 268–270, 272, 274, 281, 293, 315, 327–330, 332–336, 340, 342–344, 346, 350–352, 354–356
Lexifier 6, 8–10, 81–82, 84–85, 94, 103, 108–117, 120, 125–145, 152, 154–156, 160, 169–170, 274, 281, 283, 290–291, 294–299, 303, 307, 310, 319–320, 327–328, 331, 334, 336–338, 340–343, 346–347, 349–350, 353–357

Lingua franca 4, 131, 143–144, 186–187, 196, 264–265, 268, 281, 283
Liquids [see *Consonants*]
Loans/Loanwords [see also *Borrowing*] 3–4, 10, 101, 177, 227–228, 255, 257, 259, 327, 331–332, 334, 340, 344, 350–352, 357, 362
Locative 37, 60–64, 66, 75, 77, 94, 99, 102, 104, 118–119, 133, 138, 150, 161–163, 166–167, 244, 252–256, 258, 263, 273, 275–277, 301, 306–307, 340, 342
Locative/Place adverb [see *Adverb*]

M
Mestiços 3, 314–315
Metatypy 8, 115, 332, 334, 351–354
Migration 17–19, 182, 200, 209, 220, 234, 240, 315, 318, 345
Missionaries 3–4, 49, 53–54, 58, 74, 76, 126, 134, 141, 184, 190–191, 196
Mixed language 6, 335, 343–347, 350, 355–356
Mixed-lexifier creole 327–328, 349–351, 355
Modality [see also *TAM/Tense-Aspect-Mood marker*] 129–130, 151, 187, 190–191, 197–198, 213–214, 289, 296, 302, 310, 342
Modal verb 207, 214–216, 230, 233, 343, 347
Monogenesis 281–282
Monosyllable 206
Multilingualism [see also *Bilingualism*] 4, 64, 127

N
Nasal vowels [see *Vowels*]
Naturalistic language acquisition [see *Second-language acquisition*]
Negation 6, 10, 47, 61–62, 69–71, 97, 100, 125, 149, 151, 153, 156–160, 162–170, 173, 175, 177,

194, 205–220, 222–233, 243, 246–247, 252–253, 255, 273, 290, 300–301, 307, 333, 335, 338, 347
  Double-negative 206, 212, 215, 217, 229, 231
  Negative concord 157, 177, 232
  Negative particle 6, 205, 209–210, 213–214, 216, 229, 233, 347
  Negator 158, 160, 162, 205–206, 213–216, 218, 224–225, 228–230, 232–233, 333, 340, 342–344, 349
  Predicate negation 159–160, 162–163, 167, 344
Negative adverb [see *Negation*]
Negative concord [see *Negation*]
Negative indefinites [see *Indefinites*]
Negative particle [see *Negation*]
Negator [see *Negation*]
Nominalization 60–61, 63–64, 77
Nominative 37, 50, 52, 100, 243, 255, 258, 354
Noun phrase 47–48, 50, 54–57, 68, 70, 82–84, 90, 102, 126, 130, 137, 142–143, 151–152, 158, 193, 210, 221, 229, 234, 256, 340, 343, 347
Numeral classifiers 6, 239, 241–253, 255, 257, 259, 354
Numerals 129–130, 142, 152, 241–243, 333, 335, 342–344, 347

O

Oblique 85, 88–90, 103, 157, 215, 217, 229, 233, 279–280, 340, 342–343
Onset [see *Syllable*]
Oral vowels [see *Vowels*]
Orthography [see also *Spelling*] 55, 119, 240, 246, 309

P

Parameter of comparison [see *Comparison*]
Participle 32, 34, 137–138, 159–160, 322

Passive 70, 105, 118, 144, 233, 254, 353, 357
Past 32, 34, 73, 86, 95–96, 101, 133–134, 138–139, 156–158, 160, 163, 196, 276, 280, 289–290, 295–302, 304–313, 319, 321–323, 333
Perfective 134, 159–160, 165–168, 206–207, 213–215, 217, 224–226, 246–254, 256–258, 272–273, 289–290, 295–313, 319, 321–322
Personal pronoun [see *Pronoun*]
Phasal adverb [see *Adverb*]
Phoneme 16, 24–28, 240, 246, 336, 351
Phonological inventory 8, 15, 20–21, 23–24, 29–30, 33, 35
Phrasebooks 7, 267–273, 281, 283–284
Plosives [see *Consonants*]
Possession 4, 20, 47–60, 63–66, 71–77, 89–90, 92–94, 101, 104, 107, 119, 134, 213, 216, 233, 272–278, 306–307, 309, 311–312, 330, 340, 342, 344, 347, 349, 353–354
  Possessee [see also *Possessum*] 48–50, 52, 60–61, 65, 71, 74
  Possessive determiner 20, 49–51, 54, 56, 58–59, 71–75
  Possessive marker 51, 53, 75–76, 340–342
  Possessive pronoun [see *Pronoun*]
  Possessor 20, 35, 47–53, 55, 57–59, 61, 65, 68–76, 130, 134–135, 142, 343, 349
  Possessum [see also *Possessee*] 20, 35, 130, 134–135, 142, 145, 343, 349
Post-basic variety [see *Second-language acquisition*]
Post-nominal genitive 6, 47–53, 55, 57–61, 63–64, 69–70, 73–77
Postposition [see *Adposition*]
Post-tonic syllable [see *Syllable*]
Predicate negation [see *Negation*]
Preposition [see *Adposition*]

Present 25, 85–86, 88–89, 91, 93–95, 97, 138–139, 159–160, 206, 276, 289–290, 294–296, 298–304, 306, 308–310, 313, 319–323, 363
Preterit 20, 32, 34, 294, 296–297
Pro-adjective 151
Pro-adverb 151, 155
Progressive 69, 71–72, 225, 232, 295, 301–303, 306, 310, 312–313, 319–322
Pronoun 49–59, 68–72, 76–77, 84–85, 88, 94, 125–126, 129, 134, 145, 149, 151–156, 158, 160–164, 168, 170–177, 195, 228, 232–233, 251, 258, 293, 296, 333, 335, 340–344, 347, 349
  Generic pronoun 152
  Indefinite pronoun [see also *Indefinites*] 149, 151–155, 161–164, 171, 173–175, 347
  Interrogative pronoun 152, 158, 164, 168, 171, 173, 342, 344, 347
  Personal pronoun 52, 84–85, 88, 233, 296, 333, 340, 342–344, 347, 349
  Possessive pronoun 51, 53–59, 134, 347
  Relative pronoun 125, 176, 347
  Subject pronoun 49–51
Pro-verb 151
Proximal/Proximate [see *Demonstrative*]
Purposive marker 342–343

Q

Quantifier 118, 152, 156, 164, 177, 191, 193–194, 198, 210, 241, 243–245, 253– 254, 342–343, 347
Question word [see also *Interrogatives*] 126, 170–171, 227, 240, 247, 293, 343, 347

R

Realis 149, 151, 158–159, 161, 163, 172–173, 175, 214
Realis indefinite [see *Indefinites*]

General index 375

Reciprocal 75, 247, 251, 333, 342–343, 347
Reduplication 152, 162–164, 166, 170–173, 175–177, 352–353
Reflexive 340, 342–344, 347
Register [see also *Lect*] 7, 53–54, 58, 103, 125, 155, 169, 174–175, 214, 224
Reinóis 3, 314
Relative clause 62–63, 130, 137–138, 142–143, 166, 168–169, 173
Relative pronoun [see *Pronoun*]
Relativizer 63, 76, 84, 89, 101, 119, 138, 166, 177, 342–343
Relexification 5, 8, 214, 226, 230–231, 234, 269, 272, 281–282, 293, 329, 356

S
Salience 50, 293, 319
Schooling [see also *Education*] 19, 23, 235, 240, 260, 318–320
Second-language acquisition 17, 19–20, 33, 50–51, 142, 290–293, 295, 304–305, 310, 313, 316, 319–320
  Basic variety 18, 289, 291–294, 315, 320
  Early stage of acquisition 49, 289
  Interlanguage 292
  Late stage of acquisition 291
  Naturalistic acquisition 19, 290–295, 305, 319–320
  Post-basic variety 289, 291–292
  Target language 18–21, 32–33, 142, 291–295, 316, 319–320
Sibilants [see *Consonants*]
Similative 82
Social stratification 7, 293, 319
Spelling [see also *Orthography*] 177, 199, 200, 208–209, 229, 233–234, 240, 246, 254, 259, 357

Standard of comparison [see *Comparison*]
Stative 207, 215, 335, 344
Stress 24, 26, 32, 34, 47, 50, 55, 64, 75, 119, 205, 289, 291
Subject pronoun [see *Pronoun*]
Subordinator/Subordinating conjunction [see also *Conjunction*] 5, 65, 84, 112, 118, 142–143, 182, 250, 253–254, 267, 314
Substrate 9, 15, 29, 47, 51–52, 60, 62, 64, 73, 75, 81, 112, 125–144, 154–155, 164, 176, 197, 227, 230, 239, 240–241, 246, 255, 258–259, 272, 282, 291–293, 315–316, 321, 328, 330–332, 340, 342–343, 346–347, 349–352, 354–355
Substrate Influence Score [see *Typological tug-of-war*]
Superlative 103, 118–119, 193, 343
Superstrate 21, 23, 125, 127, 131, 143, 149, 169, 174–175, 177, 197, 289–295, 298–299, 301–313, 319–322, 330–331, 346–347, 355
Swadesh list [see also *Basic lexicon*; *Core lexicon*] 327–328, 331, 334–336, 344, 351–352, 355–357
Syllable 15–16, 26, 29–35, 50, 75, 187, 205, 213, 284, 289, 311, 344, 350
  Coda 27, 30–33, 351
  Onset 30, 350–351
  Post-tonic syllable 15, 29–34
  Syllable structure 15–16, 30–33, 35
Syllable structure [see *Syllable*]
Syncretism 118–119

T
TAM/Tense-Aspect-Mood marker 126, 129–130, 293, 295, 306–307, 315, 321, 336, 343
Target language [see *Second-language acquisition*]

Telic [see *Telicity*]
Telicity 297, 305, 321
Temporal/Time adverb [see *Adverb*]
Tense [see also *TAM/Tense-Aspect-Mood marker*] 24–26, 77, 129–130, 207, 290, 293–299, 301–313, 319–321, 330, 333, 342, 363
Tone 330, 336, 350–351
Trade 3, 8–10, 22, 48–49, 53, 76, 131, 240, 263–271, 280–283, 313
Transfer 8, 33, 49, 142, 308, 319, 327, 332–333, 340, 345, 351, 353, 355–356
Typological distance 15, 127, 155, 174, 309
Typological tug-of-war 111, 115–116, 125–126, 141–142
  Index of Reliance on Lexifier 110–112, 114–115, 120
  Substrate Influence Score 130–131, 134, 140–141, 143–145

V
Verb morphology [see also *Inflection*] 6, 8, 20, 290–291, 293, 295–296, 305, 313, 319–320, 342–344
Voicing 25, 119, 205
Volitive 310, 312
Vowels 24–28, 30, 36, 55, 205, 259, 284, 293, 296–298, 304, 307, 311, 313, 336, 350
  Nasal vowels 24–26, 28, 350
  Oral vowels 26

W
Word-final stress [see also *Stress*] 32, 34
Word order 6, 20, 85, 89, 90–95, 99–100, 102, 104–105, 107–109, 112–113, 117, 120, 125–130, 132–140, 142–145, 228, 294, 327, 334, 336–337, 352